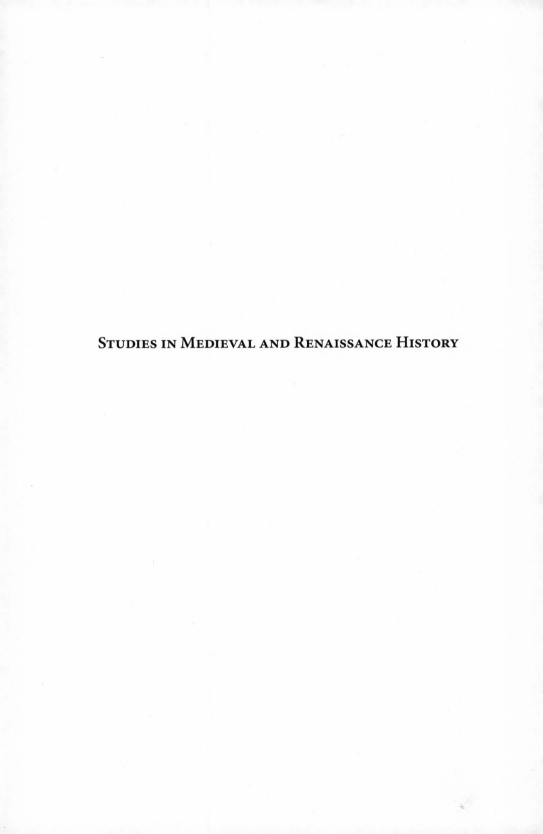

STUDIES IN MEDIEVAL AND RENAISSANCE HISTORY

Studies in Medieval and Renaissance History

Edited by Cynthia Kosso and Anne Marie Scott

Third Series, Volume XII
(Old Series Volume XXXVII, New Series Volume XXVII)

AMS Press, Inc.

New York

Studies in Medieval and Renaissance History
ISSN 0081-8224

Studies in Medieval and Renaissance History is published under the auspices of the Arizona Center for Medieval and Renaissance Studies

International Standard Book Numbers
ISBN-10: 0-404-64550-X (Set)
ISBN-13: 978-0-404-64550-2 (Set)

ISBN-13: 978-0-404- 64562-5 (Series III.12)

Library of Congress Card Number 63-22098

All AMS books are printed on acid-free paper that meets the guidelines for performance and durability of the Committee on Production Guidelines for Book Longevity of the Council on Library Resources.

AMS PRESS, INC.
Brooklyn Navy Yard, 63 Flushing Avenue-Unit #221
Brooklyn, NY 11205-1073, USA
www.amspressinc.com

Manufactured in the United States of America

TABLE OF CONTENTS

ABSTRACTS

Charlemagne's Expeditionary Levy: Observations Regarding
liberi homines
Bernard S. Bachrach

CAROLINGIAN MILITARY ORGANIZATION was tripartite in nature. At the basic level, the later Roman requirement that all able-bodied males, regardless of wealth or legal status and including slaves, were required to participate in the defense of the local area in which they lived. The second element included those who were identified by the government for participation in expeditionary service beyond their home territory and was based, in essence, upon their wealth. The third element was composed of the military households of the kings and of their magnates, both lay and ecclesiastical. These men were paid professional soldiers having regular employment. Since the end of the Second World War, there has been little scholarly controversy regarding the first and third groups identified above. With regard to expeditionary levies, now often referred to as Select Levies, however, some old arguments have been revived that claim these men, particularly those described as *liberi homines*, ceased to be of military value during the imperial period of Charlemagne's reign. As a result, according to those making the claim, the Carolingians altered their traditional expansionist strategy. This study demonstrates that the *liberi homines*, even the poorest of them, remained an important part Charlemagne's expansionist imperial military strategy. In addition, it is clear that most of these men were of Gallo-Roman origins.

Studies in Medieval and Renaissance History, 3rd Series, Vol. 12 (2016)

Disorder and Lawlessness in Fifteenth Century England: A Cornish Case Study
David M. Yorath

JOHN BEAUMONT OF Tregonan (1451–ca. 1487), bastard and rebel, played a minor but instructive role in the histories of Devon and Cornwall in the later medieval period. Like his father, Henry Bodrugan of Gorran (ca. 1426–ca. 1503), he was a prominent landowner in the two counties and served frequently on royal commissions in the reigns of Edward IV and Richard III. He was unswervingly loyal to his father and to the wider Yorkist cause, and this intractability, ultimately, proved his undoing, for, although he did not join Richard III and his supporters at Bosworth Field, on August 22nd, 1485, he did subsequently share in their fate. What follows is a short, source-based examination of Beaumont's life, with some accompanying notes and observations on wider developments pertinent to the history of the southwest at this time.

Medicine for a Great Household (ca. 1500): Berkeley Castle Muniments Select Book 89
Linda Ehrsam Voigts and Ann Payne

SELECT BOOK 89 in the Muniments of Berkeley Castle is a previously unstudied decorated manuscript from the end of the fifteenth century or early years of the sixteenth. It is a rare and important example of an English language medical compendium written for a great household, and largely for use by women.

The codex consists of two closely related parts, both introduced by detailed contents lists. Part I contains thirty-two texts on medical therapy, including treatises on distillation and treatment of wounds, copies of the Antidotarium Nicholai and Circa instans, and two lengthy receptaria. Part II consists of recipes, some specified for members of royal or noble families. Recipes in both parts are characterized by polypharmacy and call for an extensive use of exotic spices and precious metals and jewels.

This study addresses SB 89 as a household book for noble women and provides a detailed discussion of the date, decoration, and original ownership of the codex. The coat of arms with which the manuscript begins makes clear that the book was produced for the Scropes of Bolton, a family with close ties both to the court and household of Henry VII and to the household of the monarch's mother, Lady Margaret Beaufort. The study includes a discussion of plague and sweating sickness during the reign of Henry VII (1485–1509), epidemic diseases that figure in both parts of SB 89. Appendices provide a physical description of SB 89 with later provenance, a list of recipes occurring in both parts of the codex, identification of the thirty-two texts in Part I, and a transcription of the seventy-one surviving recipes in Part II. Three genealogy charts, two tables, eight color plates, and eleven black-and-white figures are also supplied.

"It's good to talk: conversations between gods, men and beasts in Early Modern English versions of Lucian's 'Dialogues'"
Paul Hartle

THIS ESSAY TRACES the reception and transmission of Lucian's works to English readers in the sixteenth and seventeenth centuries. It assesses the Humanist response to Lucian and his influence on the work of More and Erasmus, before examining his literary and moral reputation in Elizabethan and Stuart writing. It focusses on the texts in which Lucian is introduced to English readers without either Greek or Latin, especially the versions of Francis Hickes (1634), Thomas Heywood (1637), Jasper Mayne (1663), and Ferrand Spence (1684–85). It analyzes the ways in which those versions engage with the social, religious and political contexts into which they were published, and draws attention to other texts which claim paternity from Lucian (and sometimes parody the arch-parodist). Finally, it speculates on the contributory impact of Lucian to the topsy-turvy experience of civil war and interregnum and subsequently to the growing intellectual climate of rationalism and atheism after the Restoration.

Charlemagne's Expeditionary Levy: Observations Regarding *Liberi Homines*

Bernard S. Bachrach
University of Minnesota

CHARLEMAGNE'S FATHER KING Pippin (d. 768), his grandfather Charles Martel (d. 742), Mayor of the Palace, and his great grandfather, Pippin II (d. 714), also Mayor of the Palace, all pursued a vigorous, long-term, and consistent offensive military strategy focused on reuniting under Carolingian control the then politically fragmented *regnum Francorum*.[1] The success of these efforts by the early Carolingians and subsequent territorial expansion by Charlemagne, which doubled the size of the lands under Frankish rule, was made possible by a well-organized complex of military institutions. These institutions can be traced back to the Merovingian era and include elements that had been developed during the later Roman Empire.[2] Campaigns by Charlemagne's "military

---

[1] Bernard S. Bachrach, *Early Carolingian Warfare: Prelude to Empire* (Philadeplhia: University of Pennslyvania Press, 2001), 1-50. For a detailed examination of Charlemagne's early military operations, see idem, *Charlemagne's Early Campaigns (769-777): A Diplomatic and Military Analysis* (Leiden: Brill, 2013).

[2] Bachrach, *Early Carolinglian Warfare*, 51-83.

Studies in Medieval and Renaissance History, 3rd Series, Vol. 12 (2016)
Copyright © 2016 AMS Press, Inc. All rights reserved.

machine"[3] were based on meticulous planning by his "general staff," the *Magistratus*.[4]

Early Carolingian military organization was tripartite in nature.[5] At the basic level, the Carolingians maintained the later Roman requirement that all able-bodied males, regardless of wealth or legal status and including slaves, were required to participate in the defense of the local area in which they lived.[6] The second element of this military organization included those

---

[3] Regarding the "military machine" model, see Alessandro Barbero, *Charlemagne, Father of a Continent*, trans. Allan Cameron (Berkeley: University of California Press, 2004), 149; Roger Collins, *Charlemagne* (Toronto: University of Toronto Press, 1998), 18, prefers "military machinery"; and Janet Nelson, "Literacy in Carolingian Government," *The Uses of Literacy in Early Medieval Europe*, ed. Rosamond McKitterick (Cambridge: Cambridge University Press, 1990), 258-96, at 278, prefers "war machine." The state of the question is well-stated by Stefan Weiss, "La Fer et l'Acier," *Francia*, 35 (2008): 33-47, who observes, "L'Advantage technique des Franc était encastré dans une organisation du pouvoir incomparable, qui avait su développer de manière créative dans un organisation de 'l'Antiquité" (46).

[4] Rosamond McKitterick, *Charlemagne: The Formation of a European Identity* (Cambridge: Cambridge University Press , 2008), 271, observes, in the context of the *Magistratus*, that Charlemagne's "Campaigns were subjected to meticulous strategic planning." For more detail regarding the *Magistratus*, see Bernard S. Bachrach, "Charlemagne and the Carolingian General Staff," *The Journal of Military History*, 66 (2002): 313-57.

[5] For a summary, see Bernard S. Bachrach and Charles R. Bowlus, "Heerwesen," in *Reallexikon der Germanischen Altertumskunde*, ed. Heinrich Beck, et al. (Berlin-New York, 2000), 14, 122-36, with the substantial corpus of scholarly works cited there.

[6] Janet L. Nelson, "Charlemagne and the Paradoxes of Power," in *Challenging the Boundaries of Medieval History: The Legacy of Timothy Reuter*, ed. Patricia Skinner (Turnhout: Brepols, 2009), 29-50, at 45, summarized the situation, there was a "universal obligation to do military service" and as the *Codex Theodosianus* makes clear, this obligation was in force insofar as military service was to be undertaken "'to protect our provinces and their fortunes.'" See also Bachrach, *Early Carolingian Warfare*, 52-53. Regarding the participation of slaves in the local defense, see Timothy Reuter,"Plunder and tribute in the Carolingian Empire," in *Transactions of the Royal Historical Society*, 5th ser. 35 (1985): 75-94. There is no doubt that slavery was widespread throughout Charlemagne's *regnum*, and for a sense of the order of magnitude of this institution it may be noted that Alcuin, as lay abbot of Marmoutier and St. Martin of Tours, took note of the fact that these two monasteries possessed some 20,000 slaves (*servi*). See the discussion by Bachrach, *Charlemagne's Early Campaigns*, 52-53.

This legislation in no way harkens back to a putative aspect of Germanic society as Tacitus described early in the second century A.D., a description by which too many scholars have been misled. With special attention to the elimination of Tacitus' vision of early Germanic military institutions for the treatment of early medieval

who were identified by the government for participation in expeditionary service beyond their home territory, a service based, in essence, upon their wealth.[7] The third element was composed of military households, *obsequia*, of the kings and of their magnates. These fighting men were paid professional soldiers having regular employment. They might be recruited from any stratum of society, including *servi*.[8] These men may be contrasted to mercenaries to whom time-limited contracts were offered and, thus, could be considered temporary members of the royal *obsequium* or the military household of one or another magnate who hired them.[9]

---

military organization, see Steven C. Fanning, "Tacitus, Beowulf and the *Comitatus*," *The Haskins Society Journal*, 9 (2001): 17-38; and Walter Goffart, "Frankish Military Duty and the Fate of Roman Taxation," *Early Medieval Europe*, 16 (2008): 166-90, 178-79, and n. 39. Also see Franz Staab, "A Reconsideration of the Ancestry of Modern Political Liberty: The Problem of the So-called 'King's Freemen' (*Königsfreie*)," *Viator*, 11 (1980): 51-69, at 51-54, 61-64. Cf. Reuter, "Plunder and Tribute," 239, who embraces the terminology of the Tacitean *comitatus*, without taking note of its exaggerated use by some, as playing an important part in various unsavory aspects of the development of German nationalism or in support of an unrealistic romantic view of the German past. The intention of invoking Tacitus' ideas, as relevant to the early Middle Ages in an effort to defend a primitivist view of the military organization of the Frankish *regna*, is made clear by Reuter's avoidance of what the contemporary neutral usage "military household" as developed by J. O. Prestwich, "The Military Household of the Norman Kings," *The English Historical Review*, 96 (1981): 1-35.

[7] Regarding the wealth requirement, see Goffart, "Frankish Military Duty," 166-90; and Bachrach, *Charlemagne's Early Campaigns*, 5-6. A useful analogue is the select *fyrd* that was developed in later Anglo-Saxon England along the lines similar to those that had been employed by the Franks. See C. Warren Hollister, *Anglo-Saxon Military Institutions on the Eve of the Norman Conquest* (Oxford: Oxford University Press, 1962); and idem, *The Military Organization of Norman England* (Oxford: Oxford University Press, 1965). For later Anglo-Saxon England as a Carolingian-type state in military terms as in other ways, see James Campbell, *Essays in Anglo-Saxon History* (London: Hambledon Press, 1986). Cf. Richard Abels, *Lordship and Military Obligation in Anglo-Saxon England* (Berkeley: University of California Press, 1988).

[8] Bachrach, *Early Carolingian Warfare*, 65-76. Regarding "unfree" men serving in these *obsequia*, see *Legum sectio II. Capitularia regum Francorum*, I, ed. Alfred Boretius, *Monumenta Germaniae Historica* (Hannover: Hahn, 1883) *CRF*, no. 25, ch. 4. Cf. Étienne Renaud, "La politique militaire de Charlemagne et la paysannerie franque," *Francia*, 36 (2009): 1-33, at 6, n. 33, who ignores this well-known and important text. Rather, he claims "Ces cavaliers étaient sans doute des hommes libres."

[9] For background, see Bernard S. Bachrach, "Merovingian Mercenaries and Paid Soldiers in Imperial Perspective," in *Mercenaries and Paid Men in the Middle Ages: Proceedings of a Conference held at University of Wales, Swansea, 7th-9th July*

Since the end of the Second World War, there has been little scholarly controversy regarding the view that all able-bodied males in the *regnum Francorum* were required to play a role in the defense of the locality in which they lived.[10] Similarly, it is generally agreed that the military households of the kings and of the magnates constituted the paid core of the professional armed forces of the Frankish kingdom and later of the Carolingian empire under Charlemagne's rule.[11] With regard to expeditionary

---

2005, ed. John France (Leiden: Brill, 2008), 167-92. The king's military household constituted the core of the regular standing army under the early Carolingians. These men included both *presentales,* who were assigned to serve at the court and in its environs, that is, in close proximity to the ruler, and those established on military lands, *beneficia,* throughout the kingdom and in garrisons. See Bernard S. Bachrach, "Military Lands in Historical Perspective," *Journal of the Haskins Society,* 9 (1997): 95-122; and idem, "On Roman Ramparts, 300-1300," in *The Cambridge Illustrated History of Warfare: The Triumph of the West,* ed. Geoffrey Parker (Cambridge: Cambridge University Press, 1995), 64-91. Cf. Timothy Reuter, "The recruitment of armies in the early Middle Ages: What Can We Know?" in *Military Aspects of Scandinavian Society in a European Perspective, AD. 1-1300,* ed. Anne Norgard Jorgensen and Birthe L. Clausen (Copenhagen: National Museum, 1997), 32-37, who considers mercenaries to be a fourth element of Frankish military organization rather than adjuncts recruited to augment already existing *obsequia* (35).

[10] Timothy Reuter, "Plunder and tribute in the Carolingian Empire," *Transactions of the Royal Historical Society,* 5th ser. 35 (1985): 75-94; and reprinted in idem, *Medieval Polities and Modern Mentalities,* ed. Janet L. Nelson (Cambridge: Cambridge University Press, 2006), 231-50, at 246, recognizes the universal obligation for participation in *"defensio patriae";* and Goffart, "Frankish Military Duty," 178-79, and n. 38-39, discusses various of the failed theories involved in arguments regarding the so-called Germanic obligation.

[11] J.-F. Verbruggen, "L'Armée et la Stratégie de Charlemagne," in *Karl der Grosse: Lebenswerk und Nachleben,* 5 vols. ed. W. Braunfels and Helmut Beumann (Düsseldorf: L. Schwann, l965), I, 420-34, at 421, claims that Charlemagne's royal vassals, who served as heavily armed mounted troops, were the elite of the Carolingian army. This position is taken as well by Bachrach, *Early Carolingian Warfare,* 65-76; and Josef Fleckenstein, "Adel und Kriegertum und ihre Wandlung im Karolingereich," *Settimane di Studio del Centro Italiano di Studi sull'alto Medioevo,* 27 (1987): 2 vols., I, 67-94, at 90, who, however, fails to appreciate the complex composition of Charlemagne's military forces in terms of the campaigns in which they operated. The tactical importance of these heavily armed mounted troops remains a question specifically for the types of offensive military operations that required very large numbers of men to fight on foot. Of importance are tasks such a besieging fortress cities of later Roman origin or of even lesser fortifications in circumstances that required the operation of machines, the digging of mines, and the storming of the walls with very long ladders. For the centrality of siege warfare during the early

levies, now often referred to as Select Levies, there has been considerable debate. In both the nineteenth century and more recently, some scholars have argued that these men and particularly those described as *liberi homines* ceased to be of military value during the imperial period of Charlemagne's reign (800-814) and, as a result, the Carolingians altered their traditional expansionist strategy.[12] The aim of this study is to demonstrate that the *liberi homines*, even the poorest among them, not only were an important part Charlemagne's expeditionary forces, but remained so during the imperial period. Indeed, the costs of undertaking offensive military service had no adverse impact on their economic position.

Middle Ages, see Peter Purton, *A History of the Early Medieval Siege, c. 450-1220* (Woodbridge,UK: Boydell & Brewer, 2009) and with a focus on the Carolingian era, see the discussion by Bachrach, *Charlemagne's Early Campaigns*, 310-73.

Cf. Renaud, "La politique militaire de Charlemagne," 6, who follows Reuter, "The recruitment of armies," 32-37, and others, such as Guy Halsall, *Warfare and Society in the Barbarian West, 450-900* (New York: Routledge, 2003), 215-27, who do not recognize the fundamental importance of sieges, including those of Charlemagne's reign that were focused on the conquest and ruling of territory throughout the lands of the erstwhile Roman Empire. They also do not give due consideration to the large numbers of men required to lay siege to a fortress city or even to a lesser stronghold. Regarding the demand for large numbers of troops to execute sieges, see Bernard S. Bachrach and Rutherford Aris, "Military Technology and Garrison Organization: Some Observations on Anglo-Saxon Military Thinking in Light of the Burghal Hidage," *Technology and Culture*, 31 (1990): 1-17.

[12] During the past few decades several scholars have become involved in this discussion and many of their works are cited by Timothy Reuter. See Reuter, "Plunder and Tribute," 231-50; idem, "The End of Carolingian Military Expansion," in *Charlemagne's Heir: New Perspectives on the Reign of Louis the Pious (814-840)*, ed. Peter Godman and Roger Collins (Oxford: Oxford University Press, 1990), 391-405; and reprinted in idem, *Medieval Polities and Modern Mentalities*, ed. Janet L. Nelson (Cambridge: Cambridge University Press, 2006), 251-67; idem, "The Recruitment of Armies," 32-37; and idem, "Carolingian and Ottonian Warfare," in *Medieval Warfare: A History*, ed. Maurice Keen (Oxford: Oxford University Press, 1999), 13-35. Since Reuter's much lamented premature death, the subject has come to the attention of Etienne Renaud, "Un Élite paysanne en crise? Le poids des charges militaries pour les petits alleutiers entre Loire et Rhin au IXe siècle," *Élites au haut moyen âge, crises et renouvellements*, ed. Francois Bougard, Laurent Feller, and Régine Le Jan (Turnhout: Brepols, 2006), 315-36; and idem, "La politique militaire de Charlemagne," 8-27. For these *liberi homines* being required by the central government to serve as Select Levies in Charlemagne's expeditionary forces, see *CRF*, no. 48, ch. 2. As emphasized by Goffart, "Frankish Military Duty," 175, at least some of these men also were slave owners.

Who were the liberi homines?

In regard to Charlemagne's reign, some scholars are inclined to characterize the *liberi homines* as "peasants," despite the fact that these men are referred to in Charlemagne's military capitularies as free men, that is, not as the dependents of one or another lay or ecclesiastical *senior*. These *liberi homines* not only owned, in governmentally assessed value, at least one *mansus* as an allod (*proprietas*), but they also owned slaves (*mancipia*).[13] Our understanding of the *liberi homines* is further complicated because scholarly theories regarding Carolingian social structure have long encumbered the term "free" and the term "peasant" with a great deal of socio-economic and legal baggage that has dubious value and causes considerable confusion.[14]

Traditionally, the two most frequently encountered distractions concerning those *liberi homines* who are treated in Charlemagne's

---

[13] Cf. Goffart, "Frankish Military Duty," 173, would seem to claim that all of these small slave owning landowners (175) were, in fact, "dependent peasants" who held tributary *mansi*. Goffart identifies the properties, concerning which he is generalizing as *mansi ingenuiles* or *mansi serviles*. Such a manse holder, who, according to Goffart, likely would be described in a polyptch as an *ingenuus* or a *servus,* was a dependent or, as Goffart claims, a "dependent peasant." However, Goffart does not show that *ingenuus* and *liber homo* have the same meaning in the context of Charlemagne's military capitularies, or, in fact, that the latter's allod (*proprietas*) was, in fact, a tributary manse. In addition, he does not identify *ingenui* in Charlemagne's military capitularies as slave owning allodialists who were mobilized individually to serve as members of the Select Levy. I would further suggest that Goffart's "dependent peasants" are not relevant to the present discussion of *liberi homines*. The capitulary to which Goffart refers (*CRF,* no. 50, ch. 1) does not deal with dependents holding tributary manses, but with *liberi homines* and with *mansi* that are classified as allodial property (*proprietates*). Concerning the process of mobilization, see F. L. Ganshof, "Charlemagne's Army," *Frankish Institutions under Charlemagne,* trans. Bryce and Mary Lyon (Providence, R.I.: Brown University Press, 1968), 62-64. Regarding the need that "free peasants" not have lords, see Renaud, "Un Élite paysanne en crise?" 316. Regarding other of Charlemagne's military capitularies dealing with these *liberi homines*, possessing allods, who were to serve in expeditionary levies, see *CRF*, I, no. 34, chs. 12, 13b; no. 44, ch. 15; no. 48, ch. 2; no. 50, ch. 1; and no. 99, ch. 7.

[14] The debate concerning the meaning of "free" within the context of theories regarding so-called *Gemeinfreiheit* and so-called *Königsfreiheit* with their confusions and special pleading is clearly set out by Johannes Schmitt, *Untersuchungen aus den Liberi Homines der Karolingerzeit* (Frankfort-am-Main: Peter Lang, 1977), 1-41.

military capitularies have been the highly controversial and theoretically driven categories of the *Gemeinfreie* and the *Königsfreie*. The construction of the former, based in large part on information provided by Tacitus' *Germania*, written late in the first century A.D., held that all free men or *Gemeinfreie* were arms worthy, that is, *Waffenfähig*. Therefore, it was assumed for the purpose of this theory that they owed offensive as well as defensive military service, wherever and whenever the king or his representative issued orders for their mobilization and muster.[15]

The theory of the *Königsfreie*, and the coining of the term itself, postulated that a special category of free men was created by the royal government from among the *Gemeinfreie*. These men, it is thought, were provided with economic support by the king in order to undertake expeditionary military service.[16] Undergirding the development of the *Königsfreie* theory was the understanding that the *Gemeinfreie*, in general, lacked the means to support themselves for the undertaking of expeditionary military operations. The obligation to undertake expeditionary service was viewed by scholars, but not proven, to have been a very heavy economic burden.[17] This burden will be shown to be not particularly onerous from an economic perspective.

After about a century of vigorous controversy, in the wake of World War II, scholars finally disposed of the theory of the *Gemeinfreie*.[18] However,

---

[15] The importance of the *Gemeinfreie* was highlighted by Georg Waitz, *Deutsche Verfassungsgeschichte*, 8 vols. Kiel: Homann, 1844-78), I, and numerous scholars followed his views well into the twentieth century. See the very useful discussion by Staab, "A Reconsideration," 54-55, regarding the impact of Waitz's theory.

[16] For a sample of studies by the creators of the *Königsfreie* theory see Theodor Meyer, "Die Entstehung des 'modernen' Staates im Mittelalter und die freien Bauern," *Zeitschrift für Rechtsgeschichte, germanistische Abteilung*, 57 (1937): 210-88; idem, "König und Gemeinfreiheit im frühen Mittelalter," *Deutsches Archiv für Erforschung des Mittelalters* 6 (1943): 329-62; and Heinrich Dannenbauer, "Die Freien im karolingischen Heer," in *Aus Verfgassungs und Landesgeschichte: Festschrift zum Geburtstag von Theodor Mayer*, 2 vols. (Lindau: J. Thorbecke, 1954), I, 49-64.

[17] For example, it is asserted without supporting evidence by Reuter, "Plunder and Tribute," 244, that "warfare of the kind waged by the Franks in the eighth century . . . was extremely expensive for the participants, however they fought."

[18] See Staab, "A Reconsideration," 54-55; and Anne K.G. Kristensen, "Free Peasants in the Early Middle Ages: Freeholders, Freedmen or What?" *Mediaeval Scandinavia*, 12 (1988): 76-106, at 104.

aspects of this theory can be identified as being implicit in some recent works.[19] By comparison with the theory of the *Gemeinfreie*, the theory of the *Königsfreie* had a much shorter life span, less than a half-century. The *coup de grâce* was finally administered by the trenchant critiques of H. K. Schulze and Johannes Schmitt; these have been strengthened by others.[20] Finally, scholars now can agree with Kristensen's unambiguous observation, "let us bury the *Königfreie* alongside the *Gemeinfreie* for ever."[21] As a result, we can discuss the *liberi homines*, treated in Charlemagne's military capitularies, without the distraction of having to deal with Germanist theories concerning either the *Gemeinfreie* or the *Königsfreie*.

Liberi homines *and Later Roman Law*

The *Gemeinfreie* and the *Königsfreie* theories were indebted to a series of lengthy developments in German scholarship, which were based on

---

[19] Reuter, "The end of Carolingian military expansion," 256, calls attention to its occasional use.

[20] H.K. Schulze, "Rodungsfreiheit und Königsfreiheit. Zu Genesis und Kritik neuerer verfassungsgeschichtlicher Theorien," *Historische Zeitschrift*, 219 (1974): 529-50; and Schmitt, *Untersuchungen*, 1-41. See the observations by Werner Rösener, *Peasants in the Middle Ages*, trans. Alexander Stützer (Urbana, IL: University of Illinois Press, 1992), 227, who gives the major credit for dismantling the *Königsfreie* theory to Schulze, while Kristensen, "Free Peasants in the Early Middle Ages," 76-106, focuses on Schmidt's more lengthy contribution.

[21] Kristensen, "Free Peasants in the Early Middle Ages," 76-106, who, following up on Schmitt's work, see n. 19 above, has played an important part in helping to end this fruitless debate. See also 104. For further discussion of the rejection of the *Königsfreien* theory, see Reuter, "Plunder and Tribute," 243. Neither Kristensen nor Reuter seem to be aware of the earlier and effective criticism of these theories by Staab, "A Reconsideration," 51-69.

Rejection of the *Königsfreien* theory, however, should not obscure the fact that the Frankish kings like the Roman Empire maintained military colonies. A useful discussion of the historiography is provided by Anne K.G. Kristensen, "Danelaw Institutions and Danish Society in the Viking Age," *Mediaeval Scandinavia*, 8 (1975): 27-85, at 37-41; and for a more recent treatment of the matter, see Thomas Anderson, "Roman Military Colonies in Gaul, *Salian Ethnogensis* and the Forgotten Meaning of *Pactus Legis Saliae* 59.5," *Early Medieval Europe*, 4 (1995): 129-44. For both the Merovingians and the Carolingians, and also for both the later Roman Empire and the middle Byzantine empire, see Bachrach, "Military Lands," 95-122. The fighting men established in military colonies under Charlemagne constituted the part of the *obsequium regalis that* was not billeted in and around the royal court, that is, they were not *presentales*.

the assumption that the *liberi homines* were to be understood in terms of the so-called early medieval German "constitution" (*Verfassung*).[22] It is somewhat ironic, therefore, that the two sources upon which scholars relied to play key roles in the development of these ideas, Tacitus' *Germania* and *Lex Salica*, which was reissued frequently between ca. 500 and ca. 800 both by Frankish rulers and men of lesser authority, did not employ the term *liberi homines*. Rather, both texts use the term *ingenui*, which is not used in Charlemagne's military capitularies to designate those members of his expeditionary levies under discussion here.[23]

The elimination of a role for the *Gemeinfreie* and *Königsfreie* in Charlemagne's military organization allows a critical examination of "free" and "peasant" status in regard to the treatment of the *liberi homines* as it functioned throughout the *regnum Francorum*.[24] In this context, it is clear that terms such as *liber homo* and allod (*proprietas*) as used in Charlemagne's military capitularies can be seen to have much the same meaning as they had during the later Roman Empire and in the Merovingian era, that is, "free men" and "property possessed in full ownership," respectively.[25]

---

[22] Staab, "A Reconsideration," 52-61.

[23] Ibid., 52; and regarding the usage in Charlemagne's military capitularies, see *CRF*, no. 34, chs. 12, 13b; no. 44, ch. 15; no. 48, ch. 2; no. 50, ch. 1; and no. 99, ch. 7.

[24] For introductory purposes, see Alexander C. Murray, *Germanic Kinship Structure; Studies in Law and Society in Antiquity and the Early Middle Ages* (Toronto: University of Toronto Press, 1983).

[25] See Adolf Berger, *Encyclopedic Dictionary of Roman Law* (Philadelphia: American Philosophical Society, 1953), 562, in regard to liber homo and also 441 and 658 in regard to *proprietas* in the context of *dominium*. It is useful also to examine Ernst Levy, *West Roman Vulgar Law: The Law of Property* (Philadelphia: American Philosophical Society, 1951) 19, who points to the continuity of *dominium* (*proprietas*), and 156-76. Theodore Rivers, "The Meaning of *alodis* in the Merovingian Age," *Studies in Medieval and Renaissance History*, XI (1989): 3-35, provides an excellent examination of various aspects of allodial land tenure, which enables the reader interested in Roman law, to see that *alodis* (Lat. for Frankish *alod*) is basically a Frankish synonym for *proprietas*. For the Carolingian period, see Schmitt, *Untersuchungen aus den Liberi Homines*, 78-96, with specific regard to Charlemagne's military capitularies for the equation *proprietas = alodis*; and Élisabeth Magnou-Nortier, "Recherches sur l'alleu dans ses rapports aved le pouvoir (Ve-XIII)," *in Aux sources de la gestion publique*, III, *Hommes de Pouvoir, Ressources et lieux du Pouvoir* (Ve-XIIIe siècles) ed. Élisabeth Magnou-Nortier (Lille: Presses universitaires de Lille, 1997), 143-205, at 160-72; and Hartwig Ebner, *Das freie Eigen* (Kalgenfurt:

Additional support for this view of Roman influence on Carolingian terminology and conceptualization in these matters is provided by the fact that advisers at Charlemagne's court were studying the *Codex Theodosianus* and the *Codex Justinianus*.[26] Perhaps even more importantly, they were engaged also with the work of the famed third-century jurist Iulius Paulus.[27] Obviously, these royal advisers were in a position to inform Charlemagne regarding the proper meaning of terms such as *liber homo* and *proprietas* in later Roman law. Therefore, it is noteworthy that Iulius Paulus had made clear that there are only two legal classes, "the free and the unfree,"[28] or as Charlemagne manifested this dichotomy in a capitulary issued during the imperial period, "non est amplius nisi liber aut servus."[29] It is obvious that the *liberi homines* possessed the status of the former, that is, *liber* and not *servus*. The *liberi homines* and their *proprietates* in terms of later Roman legal categories also fit very well in a milieu that saw the long-term reliance by the central government of the *regnum Francorum* on the *mansus* for assessment purposes, and especially for the assessment of unpaid military service.[30]

Verlag des Geschichtsvereines für Kärnten, 1969), 230-35; For the use of Roman law in Charlemagne's capitularies, see F. L. Ganshof, *Droit Romain dans les Capitulaires* (Milan: Giuffrè`, 1969); and J. Gaudemet, "Survivances romaines dans le droit de la monarchie franque, du Ve au Xe siècle," *Tijdschrift voor rechtsgeschiedenis*, 23 (1955): 149-206.

[26] Janet Nelson, "Translating Images of Authority: The Christian Roman Emperors in the Carolingian World," in *Images of Authority: Papers Presented to Joyce Reynolds on the Occasion of her 70th Birthday*, ed. M.M. Mackenzie and Charlotte Roueché (Cambridge: Cambridge University Press, 1989), 194-202; also Janet Nelson, "Charlemagne and the Paradoxes of Power," 45. With regard to the *Codex Justianus*, see Gerhard Ladner, "Justinian's Theory of Law and the Renewal of Ideology of the *"Leges barbarorum,"* *Proceedings of the American Philosophical Society*, 119 (1975): 191-200, at 199; and Carine van Rhijn, "Charlemagne and the Government of the Frankish Countryside," in *Law and Empire: Ideas, Practices, Actors*, ed. Jeroen Duindam, Jill Harries, Caroline Humfress, and Nimrod Hurvitz (Leiden/Boston: Brill, 2013), 157-76, at 159.

[27] Nelson, "Charlemagne and the Paradoxes of Power," 45.

[28] Ibid.

[29] *CRF*, no. 58, ch. 1. But, cf. Reuter, "The End of Carolingian Military Expansion," 262, who does not recognize that this capitulary represents a Roman legal principle nor that it had general currency during Charlemagne's reign.

[30] Goffart, "Frankish military duty," 166-90.

Peasants

By contrast with the term "free," the term "peasant" and perhaps even more so the notion of a "free peasant" remains highly problematic.[31] This is the case, at least in part, because scholars have not been able to provide an epistemologically valid definition for either of these formulations.[32] It is worthy noting that A. K. G. Kristensen affirms, "we lack any clear definition of what is meant by free peasants."[33] Etienne Renaud is fully in accord with Kristensen's assessment of the situation admitting that providing a valid definition of "peasant" has been futile. Nevertheless, he observes that "la quête des paysans alleutiers du monde franc s'apparente à celle du monstre du Loch Ness."[34] On the whole it is prudent to follow Werner Rösener's observation that "a peasant as a member of a legally defined social estate is recognizable from the beginning of the High Middle Ages" and "appears . . . on the European stage only from the eleventh century onward."[35]

Charlemagne's military capitularies, under discussion here, treat those who are eligible for expeditionary service in the Select Levy exclusively as *liberi homines*.[36] Terms such as *rustici*, *plebei*, *agristes*, and

---

[31] Kristensen, "Free Peasants," 76, sees the matter of *liberi* and "peasants" or "free peasants" as "probably the most crucial of all in early social and legal history." As shown by Chris J. Wickham, "Problems of Comparing Rural Societies in Early Medieval Western Europe," *Transactions of the Royal Historical Society*, 6th ser. 2 (1992): 221-46, scholarly views regarding the importance of so-called "Free Peasants" in early medieval society has been determined by the traditions of national historiographies. Thus German scholars and those who write Anglo-Saxon history see the matter as exceptionally important, while Italian and French scholars are not highly exercised in regard to "free peasants." As made clear by Kristensen (*loc. cit.*), it is also regarded to be of great importance by at least some Scandinavian scholars.

[32] In regard to the struggle by scholars to treat the term "peasant" and its modifiers, see Schmitt, *Untersuchungen*, 1-41; and Kristensen, "Free Peasants," 76-106. Neither scholar provides an epistemologically valid definition. A useful tour of the horizon is provided by Werner Rösener, *Peasants in the Middle Ages*, trans. Alexander Stützer (Cambridge: Cambridge University Press, 1992), 18-22.

[33] Kristensen, "Danelaw Institutions," 33.

[34] Renaud, "Un Élite paysanne en crise?" 315.

[35] Rösener, *Peasants in the Middle Ages*, 18, 22.

[36] Regarding the relevant texts where the term *liberi homines* is used to identify expeditionary levies, see CRF, no. 34, chs. 12, 13b; no. 44, ch. 15; no. 48, ch. 2; no. 50, ch. 1; and no. 99, ch. 7.

pagani, which, despite the lack of a valid definition, often are understood by many modern scholars to mean "peasants," are not used in these documents by Charlemagne for military purposes.[37] Therefore, it seems prudent to avoid the term "peasant" in any guise, even for heuristic purposes, when discussing the *liberi homines* who were eligible to be mobilized for service in the Select Levy and, therefore, to think of them as "free men" who owned allodial lands and slaves, and consequently were obligated to serve in the Select Levy.[38]

Liberi homines as Militia Men

As made clear above, the Germanic models of *Gemeinfreiheit* and the *Königsfreien* regarding early medieval social organization no longer command scholarly support. However, the animating principles for the adoption of one or another of these models of social history on occasion still influence discussion of Carolingian military organization in the reign

---

[37] Renaud, "Un Élite paysanne en crise?" 315-36, ignores these terms, which traditionally are translated into English as "peasant" or into French as *paysan*. See in addition, idem, "Les *mancipia* carolingiens étaiet-ils des esclaves? Les données du polyptyque de Montier-en-Der dans le contexte documentaire du IXe siècle," in *Les moines du Der: 763-1790*, ed. Patrick Corbet with Jackie Lusse and Georges Viard (Langres: D.Guéniot, 2000), 179-209. It would seem that in Renaud's calculus, it is unclear where the Latin terms traditionally translated as "peasant" are to be located. By contrast, Hans-Werner Goetz, "Social and Military Institutions," in *The New Cambridge History, 2: C.700-c. 900*, II, ed. Rosamond McKitterick (Cambridge: Cambridge University Press, 1995), 451-80, at 455, prefers *rusticus* as the basic Latin word for peasant.

[38] A major methodological problem is evident among those scholars who deal with the so-called "peasant" question in the context of Charlemagne's military capitularies. There is a tendency to conflate evidence from a variety of sources on the basis, for example, of the untested assumption that some words, for example, *liber* and *ingenuus*, have the same meaning regardless of context. It is common among some scholars to apply to Charlemagne's reign information that is found in later Carolingian texts or from texts that are post-Carolingian without providing proof that the meaning carried in these later texts is the same as that found in Charlemagne's military capitularies. Finally, those scholars in search of so-called "free peasants" deploy sources from beyond the borders of Francia. Among many such efforts, see Schmitt, *Untersuchungen aus den Liberi Homines der Karolingerzeit, passim*; Kristensen, "Free Peasants," 76-106; and Renaud, "Un Élite paysanne en crise?" 315-36.

of Charlemagne.[39] Many scholars, particularly in the German tradition, espouse the idea that Charlemagne's subjects were warlike Germans who highly valued their role in military affairs.[40] For example, Timothy Reuter asserts that we would learn more about the Carolingians, or even about Charlemagne himself, "if we had more in the way of Beowulf or Icelandic sagas: but the *Hildebrandslied* and (perhaps) Waltharius point the way." He goes on to suggest that "more of such things [that is, an exposé of a Germanic value system] may have been found in the *antiquissima et barbarissima carmina* which Charlemagne tried to collect."[41] In support of these radical views, Reuter embraced an exaggerated interpretation of the importance of tribute and plunder to the Carolingian economy during Charlemagne's reign.[42]

---

[39] See the literature discussed by Eckhard Müller-Mertens, *Karl der Grosse, Ludwig der Fromme und die Freien. Wer waren die liberi homines der karolingischen Kapitularien (742/43-832* (Berlin: Akademie Verlag, 1963), 120-33, 140-41; Schmidt, *Untersuchungen*, 211-24; Fleckenstein, "Adel und Kriegertum," 82; Ganshof, "Charlemagne's army," 59; and Goetz, "Social and military institutions," 479, where he observes "Military service was obligatory for all freemen within the realm."

[40] Regarding the supposed Germanic warlike mentalité, see Hans Delbrück, *History of the Art of War within the Framework of Political History*, trans. Walter J. Renfroe, Jr. (Westport, CT: Greenwood Press, 1982), III, 17-18, 30-42, and 65, where he writes: "the strength of the early Germanic tribes was based on absolute barbarism, in which the man is only a warrior and only the warrior is a man." See also the useful, though romantic, discussion of a matrix of these primitive values by Michael J. Enright, *Lady with a Mead Cup: Ritual, Prophecy and Lordship in the European Warband from La Téne to the Viking Age* (Portland,OR: Blackrock Co., 1996). Nelson, "Charlemagne and the Paradoxes of Power," 41, seems to agree with Reuter's view (see n. 42) below, that "men engaged in warfare because it was an honourable, noble activity and way of life."

[41] Reuter, "Plunder and Tribute," 247.

[42] The emphasis on plunder and tribute as key aspects of the Carolingian economy by Reuter, "Plunder and Tribute," 231-50, is regarded as misleading by Janet Nelson, "The Henry Loyn Memorial Lecture for 2006: Henry Loyn and the Context of Anglo-Saxon England," *The Haskins Society Journal*, 19 (2007): 155-75, at 160, who chides those who have become too enamored of Reuter's formula. She observes, "Plunder and tribute may be all the rage, but what sense can be made of the reign of Charlemagne if you have not read your capitularies and in particular De Villis and their management by carefully supervised and accountable stewards?" For a discussion of the place of plunder and tribute in the Carolingian economy during Charlemagne's reign, see Bachrach, *Charlemagne's Early Campaigns*, 45-58, in general, and 56-58, for the minor role of "plunder and tribute." Neither plunder nor tribute

On the whole, the answer to the question (Who were the *liberi homines*?) rests upon the obvious fact that they were something other than heirs to a supposed heroic Germanic past, with all of the misleading baggage attached to that construct by the frequent scholarly misuse of Tacitus' *Germania* and of early medieval fantasy literature such as *Beowulf*.[43] If, in fact, the putative Germanic value of glory hunting were thought to be normal behavior in practical situations with regard to military operations in the *regnum Francorum*, more recent research has made clear that such behavior is absent from accounts of military operations during the Merovingian era in the sixth and seventh centuries.[44]

The great majority of Charlemagne's subjects in the *regnum Francorum*, including the *liberi homines*, lived west of the Rhine. As Nelson has observed, the emperor "certainly felt a lot more at home west of the Rhine than east of it."[45] The people living west of the Rhine, by and large, were the descendants of those Gallo-Roman and a smattering of Germano-Roman small farmers who had dwelled throughout the hexagon and in its environs when various so-called "barbarian" rulers replaced the imperial authorities in Gaul during the later fifth century.[46]

---

is seen as playing a noteworthy role in the Carolingian economy by Verhulst, *The Carolingian Economy*; regarding the economics illustrated by Capitulary de Villis, see Bernard S. Bachrach, "Are They Not Like Us? Charlemagne's Fisc in Military Perspective," in *Paradigms and Methods in Early Medieval Studies (The New Middle Ages)*, ed. Celia Chazelle and Felice Lifshitz (New York: Macmillan, 2007), 319-43.

[43] For a thoroughgoing critique of this approach to military values in early medieval society, see Fanning, "Tacitus, Beowulf and the *Comitatus*," 17-38; also Roberta Frank, "The Ideal of Men Dying with their Lord in the Battle of Maldon: Anachronism or Nouvelle Vague," in *People and Place in Northern Europe, 500-1600: Essays in Honour of Peter Hays Sawyer* (Woodbridge,UK: Boydell & Brewer, 1991), 95-106; and eadem, "Germanic legend in Old English literature," in *The Cambridge Companion to Old English Literature*, ed. M. Godden and M. Lapidge (Cambridge: Cambridge University Press, 1991), 88-106.

[44] See Walter Goffart, "Conspicuous by Their Absence: Heroism in the early Frankish Era (6th-7th cent.)," in *La funzione della'eroe germanico. Storicità, metafora, paradigma*, ed. Teresa. Pároli (Rome: Calamo, 1995), 41-56; and Delbrück, *History of the Art*, III, 65, who get emphasizes that this "condition [among the Germans of being a warrior] had already disappeared by the eighth century."

[45] Nelson, "Charlemagne and the Paradoxes of Power," 46.

[46] For the broad picture, see Walter Goffart, *Barbarian Tides: The Migration Age and the Later Roman Empire* (Philadelphia: University of Pennsylvantia Press, 2006).

It is unlikely that even two percent of men, women, and children living west of the Rhine ca. 800 could be considered "Germans."[47]

This population spoke late Latin.[48] The people of Gaul, including the Franks, who had settled within the borders of the hexagon, had been Nicene Christians for some three centuries when Charlemagne came to power.[49] The population operated in a society that was dominated by later Roman institutions. These included highly functional governmental structures at both the central and local levels as well as ubiquitous church institutions. All of these legal structures were based on the "written word" in Latin.[50] Even the so-called "barbarian" laws were written in Latin and

---

[47] The population of Charlemagne's empire ca. 800 is estimated to have been in the twenty million range: Reinhard Schneider, *Das Frankenreich* (Munich: Oldenbourg, 1982), 124. Patrick Geary, *Before France & Germany: The Creation & Transformation of the Merovingian World* (New York: Oxford University Press, 1988), 115, estimates the Frankish settlement west of the Rhine ca. 500 at a maximum of between 150,000 and 200,000 men, women, and children. In the three centuries between the reign of Clovis d. 511 and Charlemagne d. 814, there is no reason to believe that either the number or the percentage of native Frankish speakers dwelling west of the Rhine increased. This view is supported from a military perspective, that is, in terms of the men who were called up for military service, by the Oath of Strasburg in 842 according to which it is made clear that those serving in the armies of Charles the Bald's West Frankish kingdom did not understand German.

[48] Michael Banniard, *Viva voce: Communication écrit et communication orale du IVe au IX siècle en occident latin* (Paris: Institut des e'tudes augustiniennes, 1992); Roger Wright, *Late Latin and Early Romance in Spain and Carolingian France* (Liverpool: F. Cairnes, 1982); idem, "REVIEW ARTICLE: Michael Banniard, *Viva voce: Communication écrit et communication orale du IVe au IX siècle en occident latin* (Paris: Institutes études augustiniennes, 1992)," *Journal of Medieval Latin*, 3 (1993): 78-94; and for background, see Edgar C. Polomé, "The Linguistic Situation in the Western Provinces of the Roman Empire," *Aufstieg und Niedergang der römischen Welt*, II, 29, 2 (1983): 509-53, 527-32.

[49] Yitzhak Hen, *Culture and religion in Merovingian Gaul, A.D. 481-751* (Leiden: Brill, 1995).

[50] See Alexander C. Murray, *Germanic Kinship Structure; Studies in Law and Society in Antiquity and the Early Middle Ages* (Toronto: University of Toronto Press, 1983); idem, "From Roman to Frankish Gaul: 'Centenarii' and 'Centenae' in the Administration of the Merovingian Kingdom," *Traditio*, 44 (1988): 60-100; idem, "The position of the grafio in the constitutional history of Merovingian Gaul," *Speculum*, 64 (1986): 787-805; "Merovingian Immunity Revisited," *History Compass*, 8 (2010): 913-28; and idem, "So called Fictitious Trial in the Merovingian *Placita*," in *Gallien in Spätantike und Frühmittelalter: Kulturgeschichte einer Region*, ed. Steffen Diefenbach and Gernot Michael Müller (Berlin: Walter de Gruyter, 2013), 298-326.

demonstrate the profound influence of Roman legal thinking.[51] Much of the population, moreover, lived under what we call "vulgar" Roman law.[52]

As a consequence of deep Latinization, Charlemagne's *liberi homines* are to be seen as the posterity of Gallo-Roman and a smattering of Germano-Roman small farmers of the later empire, who, like their progenitors, in general, were not eager to go off to war.[53] It should not be surprising, therefore, that some of Charlemagne's *liberi homines*, not unlike their Roman predecessors, made efforts to avoid military service.[54] Charlemagne vigorously enforced the military obligations, whether paid or unpaid, of the *liberi homines* (and his other subjects) on the basis of the assessment of their property, by the imposition of large fines.[55] Charlemagne enforced the royal will through the close scrutiny of affairs at the local level with the help of his *missi dominici*, who were sent by the central government to oversee the administration of the provinces by

---

See the basic work by Rosamund Mckitterick, *The Carolingians and the Written Word* (Cambridge: Cambridge University Press, 1989).

[51] See Alexander Murray, "So Called Fictitious Trial in the Merovingian Placita," 298-326; Peter Hoppenbrouwere, "*Leges Nationum* and Ethnic Personality of Law in Charlemagne's Empire," in *Law and Empire: Ideas, Practices, Actors*, ed. Jeroen Duindam, Jill Harries, Caroline Humfress, and Nimrod Hurvitz (Leiden: Brill, 2013), 251-74; and in more general terms, Janet L. Nelson, in "Kingship and Empire," in *The Cambridge History of Medieval Political Thought, c. 330-c.1450*, ed. J. H. Burns (Cambridge: Cambridge University Press, 1988), 211-51, at 214-15.

[52] Janet Nelson, "Translating Images of Authority: The Christian Roman Emperors in the Carolingian World," in *Images of Authority: Papers Presented to Joyce Reynolds on the Occasion of her 70th Birthday*, ed. M. M. Mackenzie and Charlotte Rouché (Cambridge: Cambridge University Press, 1989), 194-205; and reprinted in eadem, *The Frankish World, 750-900* (London: , 1996), 89-98, at 90. See Ernst Levy, *West Roman Vulgar Law: The Law of Property* (Philadelphia: American Philosophical Society, 1951).

[53] Concerning a wide variety of corruption in the Roman army, see Ramsey MacMullen, *Corruption and the Decline of Rome* (New Haven,CT: Yale University Press, 1988), 39-41, 53-55, 121-70, 173-77, 185-89, 191-93, 196, 223-24, 231, 244, 260, 268-69, and 272-74, who unfortunately exaggerates somewhat.

[54] See *CRF*, no. 34, ch. 13; no. 44, ch. 15; no. 50, chs. 2, 3; and no. 74, ch. 1, which do not specifically refer to *liberi homines*. These few examples do not seem sufficient to support Cam, *Local Government*, 135, who claims there were "frequent illegal attempts . . . to avoid the burdon of service."

[55] Regarding punishment with large fines, see *CRF*, no. 27, ch, 1; no. 33, ch. 7, 8; no. 34, ch. 13b; no. 44, ch. 19; no. 49, ch. 1; no. 50, ch. 2, 3, 5, 6, 7; no. 73, chs. 1-9; no. 74, ch. 2; no. 77, ch. 9; and no. 85, ch. 3,4,5.

local officials.[56] In light of the government's effective enforcement mechanisms, it seems likely that relatively few of the tens of thousands of *liberi homines*, living in the *regnum Francorum*, succeeded in efforts to avoid expeditionary military service in the Select Levy.[57]

The "Demise" of the Select Levy

Recent scholarship regarding the supposed demise of the Select Levy focuses, in large part, on the *liberi homines*. Some scholars hypothesize that these men were exhausted economically because of the frequent military campaigns that they were required to undertake during the course of more than a century of offensive military operations orchestrated by Charlemagne and his predecessors.[58] In the tradition that helped to

---

[56] Regarding the *missi dominici*, the basic work remains, Victor Krause, "Geschichte des Instituts der *missi dominici*," *MIÖG*, 2 (1890): 193-300; and concerning enforcement mechanisms see the recent study by Rosamond Mckitterick, "Charlemagne's *Missi* and Their Books," in *Early Medieval Studies in Memory of Patrick Wormold*, ed. Stephen Baxter, Catherine Karkov, Janet L. Nelson, and David Pelteret (Farnham, UK: Ashgate, 2009), 253-67. Regarding punishment with large fines, see *CRF*, no. 27, ch, 1; no. 33, ch. 7, 8; no. 34, ch. 13b; no. 44, ch. 19; no. 49, ch. 1; no. 50, ch. 2, 3, 5, 6, 7; no. 73, chs. 1-9; no. 74, ch. 2; no. 77, ch. 9; and no. 85, ch. 3,4,5.

[57] Regarding the effectiveness of Charlemagne's orders at the local level, see Carine van Rhijn, "Charlemagne and the Government of the Frankish Countryside," in *Law and Empire: Ideas, Practices, Actors*, Jeroen Duindam, Jill Harries, Caroline Humfress, and Nimrod Hurvitz (Leiden: Brill, 2013), 157-76. The demonstration by Nelson, "Charlemagne and the Paradoxes of Power," 38, that even high profile scholars, such as Fichtenau and Ganshof, found it necessary to manipulate the information found in the capitularies to support arguments for Charlemagne's supposed ineffective military administration during the imperial period provides *prima facie* evidence that their scholarly position was so weak that it could not stand on its own without chicanery. Renaud, "Un Élite paysanne en crise?" 326-28, worked diligently to identify men whom he believes to have been *liberi homini* and who escaped expeditionary military service. He would appear to have found two examples; one occurred in 856 and the second in the tenth century.

[58] See Reuter, "Plunder and Tribute," 245, who rejects the hypothesis that these men were worn down by excessive military service. Reuter observes that it "is difficult to see, however, why such service should have become problematic only after nearly a hundred years of almost continuous warfare." Reuter's subsequent remarks encourage the reader to wonder whether the above-cited quotation was meant to be understood as a tongue-in-cheek comment as he hypothesizes that over the long

support the creation of the *Königsfreien*, but not necessarily linked to this now discredited theory, it is often asserted without proof that offensive military service was an expensive burden under which Select Levies suffered and ultimately one that they could not sustain.[59] Scholars taking a Marxist approach have argued that the deleterious economic impact of frequent offensive military service was worsened by lay and episcopal aristocrats operating at the local level, who, for all intents and purposes, robbed the *liberi homines* of their lands and thus made it impossible for them to afford costly offensive military service as expeditionary levies.[60]

Most recently, Etienne Renaud has crafted an imaginative and well-rounded model in support of his theory for the demise of the *liberi homines*: "Ici, de petits propriétaires affaiblis par de lourdes obligations militaires, par plusieurs années consécutives de mauvaise récoltes ou par une accumulation de dettes, donnent lieurs biens à une église et les reprennent en précaire, moyennant un cens modique, pour eux-mêmes et leurs descendants."[61] In this context, Renaud wants his readers to focus

---

term, "small freeman would have lost rather than gained from Carolingian warfare" (244). By contrast, Reuter argues that the mobilization of these *liberi homines* was an institutional innovation. These men, according to Reuter, were to be used for defensive purposes. He fails, however, to give due attention to those capitularies, for example, *CRF*, no. 34, chs. 12, 13b; no. 44, ch. 15; no. 48, ch. 2; no. 50, ch. 1; and no. 99, ch. 7, that *inter alia* order the mobilization and muster of these men for offensive military operations beyond the frontiers of the empire.

[59] See Reuter, "Plunder and Tribute," 244.

[60] With regard to a Marxist problematic, see Müller-Mertens, *Karl der Grosse*, 93-110, who titles this section "Die Oppressiones Der Armen und Mindermächtigen." *Loc. cit.* 83, he asserts that those *liberi homines* who owned as many as three or four *mans*i can only be considered *Bauern*, by which he means "peasants." However, he provides no justification to support this quantitative view and does not provide an argument to support his conclusion that *liberi homines* owning five *mansi* as allods, who are discussed in the same military capitulary (*CRF*, no. 48, ch. 2) that provides Müller-Mertens with information concerning those who hold three or four manses, are not to be considered peasants. Schmitt, *Untersuchungen*, 95-99, also wants to classify *liberi homines* with either three or four manses as "peasants" as does Renaud, "Une Élite paysanne en crise?" 321, who also prefers a model of three or four manses as a "peasant" holding. He takes this position without evidence, reference to a Marxist problematic, or mention of Müller-Mertens. Kristensen, "Free Peasants in the Early Middle Ages," 84-85, stresses that a dividing line between those *liberi homines*, who own either three or four *mansi*, and the *liber homo*, who has an allod of five *mansi*, is arbitrary.

[61] Renaud, "Un Élite paysanne en crise?" 325.

on what he believes are the very numerous "plus pauvres des paysans alleutiers." He claims that these "peasants" held only a "lopin de terre" as "tenanciers d'un grand propriétaire foncier." In this context, he seems to confound very poor "peasants," who possess small dependent holdings, with the *liberi homines* who owned *mansi* in allodial tenure and slaves and who were dependent only on Charlemagne as king and emperor rather than local secular or ecclesiastical magnates who possessed vast estates.[62]

Renaud, in addition, is hard put to find any evidence for the impoverishment of the very poor allod-holding "peasants," who supposedly were dependent on great landowners during Charlemagne's reign or for that matter during the ninth century as a whole. As a result, he finds it necessary to admit, "les données font défaut pour les IXe siècle."[63] In the face of this admitted lack of evidence, Renaud claims on the basis of weak information from the twelfth century, that is, more than four hundred years after Charlemagne's death, that large numbers of such free peasant landowners became impoverished.[64] Yet, he recognizes that "Les historiens ont depuis longtemps l'impression" that the "phénomène est impossible à mesurer." Nevertheless, he asserts with great confidence, but without

---

[62] Ibid.

[63] See Renaud, "La politique militaire de Charlemagne," 11, for this formulation and n. 52, for his admission that there is no evidence for the ninth century. Yet he asserts that large numbers of such supposedly impoverished free peasant landowners, whom he believes became dependents of great landowners, was a "general phenomenon." However, because of a lack of ninth-century evidence, as noted above, Renaud found it necessary to cite information, which, in itself, is hardly statistically robust, from the Mâcon region that was generated during the twelfth century, that is, more than three hundred years after Charlemagne's death. Without making a counter argument, Renaud, "Une élite paysanne en crise?" 318, observes that "Les historiens ont depuis longtemps l'impression" that "the phénomène est impossible à mesurer" by which "des petits alleutiers se réduit considérablement entre le VIIe et le XIIIe siècle." By contrast, Goetz, "Social and military institutions," 456, asserts without caveat or evidence that the distinction between "'warriors' and 'peasants' (*milites* and *rustici*)... sheds light ... on the fact that 'peasants' (who formerly were soldiers) began to be excluded from military service from the end of the eighth century."

[64] Renaud, "La politique militaire de Charlemagne," 11, regarding his use of "evidence" from the Mâcon region that was generated during the twelfth century. The point seems to have been missed by Renaud that if the impoverishment of these "peasants" took place in the twelfth century, they had been in place without becoming impoverished during the previous three centuries.

documentary or any other type of evidence, that the "des petits alleutiers se réduit considérablement entre le VIIe et le XIIIe siècle."[65]

The Capitularies

The lack of documentary evidence encouraged Renaud, as others before him, to turn to Charlemagne's military capitularies. He observes, for example, "elle doivent s'appuyer sur une analyse rigoureuse des sources, au premier chef les dispositions des capituaires."[66] It is to be emphasized, however, that none of Charlemagne's military capitularies provide any statistical data, much less robust figures upon which firm conclusions of a quantifiable nature may be drawn. Even Renaud, as one of those who continues to play a leading role in the argument that Charlemagne's military capitularies provide evidence for the supposed decline in the importance of the Select Levies, recognizes that one must confront "l'absence de données chiffrées fiables" in regard to these documents.[67] Thus, like others who follow this line of reasoning, Renaud recognizes that evidence for the expiration of Charlemagne's Select Levy cannot be found in a straight forward reading of the texts of the emperor's military capitularies. Rather, he observes, it is necessary, to rely on "l'evolution du vocabulaire et du contexte sociopolitique."[68]

First, with regard to supposed vocabulary changes in regard to Charlemagne's military capitularies, terms such as *rustici, plebei, agristes,* and *pagani,* which often are translated as "peasant" by modern scholars, are

---

[65] Renaud, "Une élite paysanne en crise?" 318.

[66] See Renaud, "La politique militaire de Charlemagne," 19-26, 28-33, and 2, where he observes "elle doivent s'appuyer sur une analyse rigoureuse des sources, au premier chef les dispositions des capituaires." As will be seen below, Renaud's analysis of Charlemagne's capitularies is less than rigorous as he fails to heed the long-established warnings that "generalizations on the subject [based on the capitularies] are thus attended with danger, and alterations must be followed from year to year," For this warning, see Helen Maude Cam, *Local Government in Francia and England: A Comparison of the Local Administration and Jurisdiction of the Carolingian Empire with that of the West Saxons* (London, University of London Press,1912), 132.

[67] Renaud, "La politique militaire de Charlemagne," 19.

[68] See ibid.

not used.[69] Rather, Charlemagne's military capitularies use only the term *liberi homines*, who, with one minor exception, are all seen to own allods and slaves.[70] As made clear above, scholars have failed to develop, much less deploy, an epistemologically valid definition for "peasant" or "free peasant" in regard to Charlemagne's reign within the context of treating those of his capitularies that dealt with expeditionary military service. Therefore, it seems prudent to avoid the term "peasant" completely when discussing the *liberi homines*, who were eligible to be mobilized for service in the Select Levy during Charlemagne's imperial period.[71]

When examining the evidentiary value of Charlemagne's surviving military capitularies, themselves, in the context of the hypothetical impoverishment of the *liberi homines*, it is of the utmost importance to understand that these documents, by and large, were time-conditioned in nature.[72] There is little or no evidence from most capitularies with

---

[69] Renaud, "Un Élite paysanne en crise?" (315-36) ignores these terms, which traditionally are translated into English as "peasant." See in addition, idem, "Les *mancipia* carolingiens étaiet-ils des esclaves?" 179-209. It would seem that in Renaud's calculus, it is unclear where the Latin terms traditionally translated as "peasant" are to be located. By contrast, Goetz, "Social and Military Institutions," 455, seems to prefer *rusticus* as the basic Latin word for peasant and does not confront the matter of *liberi homines* in this context.

[70] Regarding the relevant texts where the term *liberi homines* is used to identify expeditionary levies, see *CRF*, no. 34, chs. 12, 13b; no. 44, ch. 15; no. 48, ch. 2; no. 50, ch. 1; and no. 99, ch. 7.

[71] A major methodological problem is evident among those scholars who deal with the so-called "peasant" question in the context of Charlemagne's military capitularies.

[72] An illuminating example of the kind of year to year changes that affected the *liberi homines*, can be seen in the context of Charlemagne's orders that were issued between 806 and 808 to deal with food shortages in many places (*loca*), but obviously not throughout the realm as a whole, due to serious crop failures that were identified by the central government as having a potential impact on mobilization. See *CRF*, no. 44, ch. 4, where Charlemagne makes clear, by and large, that each situation was to be handled on an *ad hoc* basis; *CRF*, no. 46, ch. 18; *CRF*, no. 48, ch. 2, where Charlemagne makes clear that the word "omnes" was to be modified geographically as the region between Seine and the Loire, as made clear by Ganshof, *Charlemagne's Army*, 61; and Renaud, "La politque militaire de Charlemagne," 10. It is illuminating to compare *CRF*, no. 74, ch. 8, with *CRF*, no. 48, ch. 2, *CRF*, no. 50, ch. 1, where the particulars are much altered and also *Annales regni Francorum*, ed. F. Kurze, *Scriptores Rerum Germanicarum:Monumenta Germaniae Historica* (Hannover: Hahn, 1895) ARF, an. 808.

which scholars can construct models for military institutions or any type of long-term strategy during Charlemagne's reign.[73] As F. L. Ganshof, the leading twentieth century expert in regard to these documents observed after a review of Charlemagne's military capitularies, "they contain, in relation to military institutions, few dispositions general and normative but numerous dispositions more concrete in respect to a given situation as, for example, a specific campaign."[74]

---

[73] Alfred Boretius, *Beitrage zur Capitularienkritik* (Leipzig: Duncker & Humblot, 1874), 71-92, the editor of the capitularies, was mostly on the mark when he saw Charlemagne's capitularies as "transitory" with the exception of the "capitula legibus addenda." Cam, *Local Government*, 131, concluded, "it is necessary to remember [Alfred] Boretius's warning of their [the capitularies] fleeting nature." She emphasizes that "generalizations . . . are attended by great danger, and alterations must be followed from year to year." The view was echoed by F.L. Ganshof, *Recherches sur les Capitulaires* (Paris: Sirey, 1958), 89-93, where "La durée de valitité des capitulaires" is examined briefly and, 89-90, where Boretius' views, see supra, are affirmed. For some recent observations, see McKitterick, *Charlemagne*, 233-37.

It is important to make clear that most of Charlemagne's capitularies do not survive and none of those that do survive are originals. Regarding the accepted view concerning large scale capitulary losses for Charlemagne's reign, see Hubert Mordek, "Recently Discovered Capitulary Texts Belonging to the Legislation of Louis the Pious," in *Charlemagne's Heir: New Perspectives on the Reign of Louis the Pious (814-840)*, ed. Peter Godman and Roger Collins (Oxford: Oxford University Press, 1990), 436-53, at 448. With regard to some examples, see *CRF*, no. 24, ch. 1, which calls attention to a lost *edictum* of King Pippin and to several of Charlemagne's no longer extant *edicta*; no. 28, ch. 25; no. 33, ch. 39; no. 43. chs. 22, 30, 37; no. 44, chs. 6, 14, 22; no. 46, chs. 1, 10; no. 46, ch. 10; no. 49, ch. 1,; no. 50, ch. 2; and no. 56, ch. 4. See the useful information summarized by Janet L. Nelson, "The Voice of Charlemagne," in *Belief and Culture in the Middle Ages: Studies Presented to Henry Mayr-Harting*, ed. R. Gameson and H. Leyser (Oxford: Oxford University Press, 2001), 76-81; and reprinted with the same pagination in eadem, *Courts, Elites, and Gendered Power in the Early Middle Ages* (Aldershot: Boydell & Brewer, 2007), 77; and Rosamond McKitterick, "Charlemagne's *missi* and their books," in *Early Medieval Studies in Memory of Patrick Wormold* ed. Stephen Baxter, Catherine Karkov, Janet L. Nelson, and David Pelteret (Farnham, UK: Ashgate, 2009), 253-67, at 253-54.

[74] Ganshof, "Charlemagne's Army," 152, n. 2, for the quotation, which, of course, echoes Cam, *Local Government*, 132, who claims "generalizations on the subject are thus attended with danger, and the alterations must be followed from year to year."

An excellent example of the abuse of the capitularies by modern scholars to create Carolingian "institutions" is the claim by Renaud, "La politique militaire de Charlemagne," 10, that the so-called "clubbing provisions" of "le capitulaire de 808 . . . rendre compte du sysème "normal" de conscription." Renaud's justification for

None of the military capitularies issued by Charlemagne during the imperial period provides evidence that the *liberi homines*, who owned between one-half a *mansus* and five *mansi* as allods along with slaves, were considered poor, much less impoverished.[75] However, in the context of a famine in 806, exceptionally brief and time-limited attention is called to some *liberi homines*, living between the Seine and the Loire, who were so poor, "sic pauper," that they possessed neither allodial lands nor slaves. Yet, even these men are recorded as having an income in cash of at least five *solidi*, which was regarded by Charlemagne's assessors as providing sufficient surplus wealth for them to be able to pay to the government one *solidus*, that is, twelve *denarii*, to aid in the mobilization and muster of a *liber homo* to serve in the expeditionary levy.[76]

---

this conclusion is not based on any of Charlemagne's so-called "clubbing" capitularies (*CRF*, no. 48, ch. 2; no. 49, chs. 2,3; and no. 50, ch. 1), which vary considerable in detail, but on several capitularies (*loc. cit.* note 50) issued by Louis the Pious well after Charlemagne's death. These later capitularies, however, are not consistent with a supposed norm created by Charlemagne in the above mentioned capitulary of 808. Nor, in addition, are they consistent with each other in presenting a norm for the reign of Louis the Pious. For other efforts to assert that the so-called "clubbing" capitularies are to be seen as an established institution, see Halsall, *Warfare and Society*, 93-95; and Reuter, "Plunder and Tribute," 244-45. Fleckenstein, "Adel und Kriegertum," 85-86. Halsall, *Warfare and Society*, 89-95 and Goetz, "Social and Military Institutions," 479-80, are among those who try to construct military institutions from time-conditioned capitulary chapters.

[75] Renaud, "Un Élite paysanne en crise?" 317, who cites several capitularies (n. 10) to support his notion that *liberi homines* were considered *pauperes*. Although some of these documents refer to *pauperes*, they do not provided evidence that the government considered *liberi homines*, who owned allods and slaves, to be *pauperes*. In fact, none of the texts that Renaud cites demonstrates that at any time during this period the government considered the *liberi homines* to be *pauperes*. For the texts at issue see *CRF*, no. 44, chs. 15, 16. In addition to this text, also cited in Renaud, loc. cit. n. 10, are the following: (1) *CRF*, no. 34, ch. 12, which refers to some *liberi homines* who were *pauperes*, and not, as Renaud would seem to believe, that all *liberi homines* were *pauperes*. *Pauperes*, rather than the term *pauper*, is used as a description of the man's assets, not of his status; (2) *CRF*, no. 50, ch. 5, which says nothing of poverty, nor do the other nine chapters, which deal with military matters; (3) *CRF*, no. 73, chs. 2, 3, 5, all of which refer to *pauperes* and to military service, but none of which address concerns regarding *liberi homines* and (4) *CRF*, no. 78, ch. 22, which treats *pauperes* but says nothing of *liberi homines* or of military service.

[76] *CRF*, no. 48, ch. 2. Unfortunately, specialists in Carolingian social and economic history have not provided an epistemologically sound definition for *pauper* or

Scholars, using charters and capitularies as well as narrative sources, have been unable to support the assertion that the *liberi homines*, treated in Charlemagne's military capitularies, were so thoroughly impoverished that they no longer provided the substantial manpower for Carolingian offensive operations between 800 and 814. By contrast, the Marxist approach favored by Müller-Mertens, noted above briefly, produced, in the early 1960s, what then appeared to be a cogent argument for impoverishment that requires some discussion. It is clear that Charlemagne made substantial efforts during the imperial period to protect the *liberi homines* from exploitation by local aristocrats. In fact, the emperor emphasized that he was not going to permit the *liberi homines* to become impoverished as a result of inimical practices by either lay or ecclesiastical magnates.[77] Thus, as emperor, he delegated increased authority to his

---

pauperes as used in Charlemagne's documents, much less in his military capitularies. Therefore, many scholars would seem to be satisfied with the negative formulation offered by Karl Bosl, who argues that a *pauper* is someone who is not a *potens*. Of course, this formulation is of no help in trying to ascertain if the *liberi homines* treated in Charlemage's military capitularies were so impoverished that they could not afford to serve in the Select Levy. Nevertheless, Renaud asserts ("Un Élite paysanne en crise?" 325) that the situation during the early ninth century left the *liberi homines*, "particulièment fragiles sur le plan économique ou social" and, therefore, foreshadowed their elimination from playing an offensive role in the Carolingian military.

    With regard to the unhelpful exclusive dichotomy between *pauper* and *potens*, coined by Karl Bosl, see his "Potens und Pauper: Begriffsgeschichtlich Studien zur gesellschaftliche Differenzierung im frühen Mittelalter un zum "Pauperisimus" des Hochmittelalters," in *Alteuropa aund die moderne Gesellschaft: Festschrift für O. Brunner* (Göttingen: Vandenhoeck & Puprecht, 1963), 60-87, at 63, as generally accepted by Goetz, "Social and military institutions," 455; and Janet Nelson, "Munera," in *Les élites et la richesse au haut moyen âge*, ed. Jean-Pierre Devroey, Lautent Feller, and Régine Le Jan (Turnout: Brepols, 2010), 383-401, at 384. However, cf. O.G. Oexle, "Potens und Pauper im Frümittelalter," in *Bildhafte Rede in Mittelalter und früher Neuzeit. Probleme iher Legitimation und ihrer Funktion*, ed. W. Harms and K. Speckenbach (Tübingen: M. Niemeyer, 1992), 131-49, who vigorously objects to Bosl's formulation. None of these works, moreover, casts light on the matter of Charlemagne's expeditionary levies.

[77] See *CRF*, no. 18, ch. 4, where King Pippin sets the tone for protecting these men and exerts pressure on local officials to refrain from imposing excessive exactions on *pauperes homines*. This phraseology is used, on occasion, to refer to those who serve in the expeditionary levies as, for example, in no. 44, ch. 16, where Charlemagne excoriates local officials for oppressing *liberi homines*, who are classified

missi dominici, who were sent from the court to execute and, when necessary, to enforce the royal will in protecting these *liberi homines*. The *missi* were given the power to oversee the execution of these royal orders, and if necessary, to punish those who were found to have been disobedient.[78]

Scholars, such as Müller-Mertens, believe these orders by Charlemagne were not successful because it is assumed that if the central government found it necessary to issue more than one order on the same subject, the repetition was to be taken as evidence of the orders' failure to have been enforced effectively. Therefore, it was argued that if Charlemagne, in fact, failed to protect his *liberi homines* from the depredations of the local aristocracy, these men were impoverished. It was further claimed that, as a result of impoverishment, the role that these men traditionally had played in offensive military operations was severely curtailed and the offensive capability of Charlemagne's armies were undermined.

This approach to the capitularies issued by Charlemagne to protect the *liberi homines* failed for several reasons. First, it ignored the generally transitory nature of the military capitularies, which were issued to deal with specific situations in different locations and at different times. Secondly, the overall inclination to see royal failure was based upon a

---

as *pauperes*. In no. 34, ch. 12, Charlemagne orders that those at the local level who coerce *liberi homines*, who also are *pauperes*, to do military service when it is not required of them by the central government, are to be punished. In no. 73, chs. 2 and 3, Charlemagne calls attention to efforts by bishops, abbots, and their advocates, that is, lay administrators of church resources, along with *comites* and their *centenarii*, who try to mobilize poor men, *pauperes*, and to force them to attend the muster when it is not their turn to serve. This process, it is made clear in the text, could result in the militia men becoming impoverished, because they either handed over their *proprietates* to their oppressors or found it necessary to sell their lands.

As part of this pattern of oppressing men eligible for expeditionary military service, Charlemagne takes note of those who had handed over or sold their allods to local magnates and, as part of this corrupt practice, were exempted by the local authorities from military service. See also no. 33. ch. 29. All of these nefarious practices Charlemagne strongly condemns and threatens punishments. Thus I agree with Nelson, "Charlemagne and the Paradoxes of Power," 37-38, who discusses this matter in regard to Charlemagne's successful efforts to protect the lower echelons of society so as to preserve their ability to go to war. See also Bachrach, *Early Carolingian Warfare*, 58-59.

[78] See *CRF*, no. 23, ch. 27; no. 24, chs. 2, 3, 6, 7, 35; no. 25, ch. 6; no. 33, chs. 7, 28, 29; no. 34, ch. 12; no. 44, ch. 13; no. 73, chs. 1-9; and no. 85, chs. 1-7. See the discussion by Nelson, "*Munera*," 386.

now-discredited model that saw the aristocracy as over-mighty and the king's power as correspondingly weak.[79] In fact, the view of some scholars that Charlemagne's capitularies were regarded by the aristocracy as mere "suggestions" has been firmly debunked as more information has become available regarding the successful enforcement of the royal will by the *missi dominici* in the use of capitularies.[80] It is now agreed that Charlemagne's efforts in general, and in regard to his military operations in particular, were successfully accomplished by the emperor's *missi*, who thwarted aristocratic attempts to subvert the expeditionary levies.[81] In fact, arguments that Charlemagne failed to maintain effective control of the *liberi homines* have been shown to have been based upon an untenable manipulation of various sources by modern scholars.[82]

---

[79] Regarding these now rejected interpretations, see Christiana Pössel, "Authors and recipients of Carolingian capitularies, 779-829," in *Texts and Identities in the Early Middle Ages*, ed. R. Corradini, R. Meens, C. Pössel, and P. Shaw (Vienna: Verlag der O"sterreichische AKademie der Wissenschaften, 2006), 253-74; McKitterick, *Charlemagne*, 233-37, and Bachrach, *Charlemagne's Early Campaigns*, 23-44.

[80] The basic work remains Victor Krause, "Geschichte des Instituts der *missi dominici*," *Mitteilungen des Instituts für* österreichische *Geschichtsforschung*, 2 (1890): 193-300; but now see the important observations by McKitterick, *Charlemagne*, 213-17, 256-66, regarding their effectiveness.

[81] Nelson, "*Munera*," 386, notes, "Le but de cet article est de monstrer que . . . . pendant le regne de Charlemagne . . . les efforts du souverain pour containdre les élites . . . à se conformer au discours sur la gratuité de la justice." She succeeds very well.

[82] It is important to avoid the tendency to exaggerate corruption, which is a staple for many of those scholars who tend to treat Charlemagne's imperial years as a period of failure. For example, in their efforts to undermine a once very positive view of Charlemagne's last years, Fichtenau, *The Carolingian Empire*, 180-81, at n. 3; and F.L. Ganshof, "La fin du règne de Charlemagne, Une décomposition," *Zeitschrift für Schweizerische Geschichte*, 28 (1948): 133-52; trans. by Janet Sondheimer as "The Last Period of Charlemagne's Reign: a study in decomposition," in idem, *The Carolingians and the Frankish Monarchy* (London: Longman, 1971), 240-55, 248, misused the emperor's military capitularies to this end. It is particularly noteworthy that both scholars call attention to *CRF*, no. 73, chs. 6 and 9, issued in 811, as evidence "for the growth of disobedience among the emperor's subjects," which supposedly undermined the mobilization of forces for expeditionary service. Actually, as pointed out by Nelson, "Charlemagne and the Paradoxes of Power," 29-50, at 38, the text draws attention to complaints made by some *comites* to the effect that in their districts some *pagenses* refused to obey comital orders in regard to military matters. However, according to the capitulary, these *paganses* preferred to await the

The "End" of Charlemagne's Offensive Strategy

It should be clear from the discussion above that there is no corpus of evidence, either qualitative or quantitative in nature, for the impoverishment of the *liberi homines*, who are acknowledged to have served as the rank and file of Charlemagne's expeditionary levies. Nevertheless, Renaud would have his readers believe that these so-called "peasant" levies were impoverished and asserts that the demise of this institution was responsible for what he claims was "la fin de l'expansion militaire carolingienne."[83] Renaud's belief that Charlemagne undertook a radical change of strategy from a traditional Carolingian offensive orientation to a defensive posture supposedly is evidenced by the emperor's frontier policy. Renaud ineffectively argues, "la création du système des 'marches' au tournant des VIIIe et IXe siècles" constitutes evidence for Charlemagne's new defensive strategy as driven by his inability to muster large armies of expeditionary levies needed for offensive operations.[84]

---

direct orders of the emperor's *missi* in regard to mobilization. Halsall, *Warfare and Society*, 94, follows the negative views of Ganshof and Fichtenau with regard to this capitulary, as does Renaud, "Une Élite paysanne en crise?" 323.

Ganshof and Fichtenau, however, cite only the complaints by the counts but ignore the second part of the text regarding the primacy and effectiveness of the emperor's *missi*. Nelson, *loc. cit.* 38, chides both Fichtenau and Ganshof for quoting only that part of the text convenient for their views, that is, the apparent disobedience of some *pagenses*. Nelson goes on to emphasize the unquoted part, which notes, "the people of the counties were increasingly disobeying the counts and running to the *missi*." Nelson makes clear "that was just what Charlemagne had foreseen, planned for, and was surely very happy indeed to hear." The central government established its control of military mobilization at the local level. In support of Nelson's view, see *CRF*, no. 74, ch. 2, regarding the overall dominance of the king's *missi* at the local level. It also is to be noted that Charlemagne issued orders, see *CRF*, no. 26, ch. 26, and no. 33, ch. 30, so that anyone, who believed that local officials had harmed him through corruption or by not following Charlemagne's orders, was to be protected in order to go to the royal court to make his case.

[83] Renaud, "La politique militaire de Charlemagne," 17.

[84] See Renaud, "Une Élite paysanne en crise?" 322; and idem, "La politique militaire de Charlemagne," 17. Here, Renaud seems to be following Reuter, "End of Carolingian Military Expansion," 251-67. Of course, if upon becoming emperor Charlemagne had abandoned offensive military operations, this would have been grist for Einhard's mill, who used Suetonius' *Vita* of the emperor Augustus as his main model for his *Vita Karoli*. However, while Suetonius calls attention to Augustus' calling a halt to Roman expansion, Einhard ignores this very important matter.

The focus on the establishment of marches along the frontiers of the *regnum Francorum*, especially in the region of the Elbe and of the Pyrenees by Charlemagne, demonstrates Renaud's fundamental misunderstanding of early Carolingian frontier strategy along the borders of the realm.[85] The construction of frontier fortifications and the staffing of these strongholds with various types of troops, both regulars, that is, professional soldiers, often drawn from the royal *obsequium* or the military households of various royal *fideles*, and local militia men, had a twofold purpose. From a defensive perspective, the building of numerous strongholds along a frontier that had been created by recent conquests, for example, the Elbe and the Spanish March, was necessary in order to secure this territory against potential enemy efforts to reconquer the land and/or to undertake raids into areas, which would result in the harassment of Charlemagne's newly settled and/or newly liberated Christian subjects.

From an offensive perspective these new strongholds or refurbished erstwhile Roman fortifications, for example, the fortress city of Barcelona, served as bases for the supply of Charlemagne's offensive military forces. These were mustered along the Pyrenean frontier in the south in order to advance into enemy territory in *Hispania* against the Muslims for the purpose of territorial conquest. The fortifications along the Elbe in the east were established to defend the frontier of newly acquired, formerly Roman, territory. However, the offensive capacity of the troops on the Elbe frontier was not oriented toward further conquest. The lands

---

[85] Herwig Wolfram, "The Creation of the Carolingian Frontier-system c. 800," in *The Transformation of frontiers from late Antiquity to the Carolingians*, ed. Ian Wood and Helmut Reimitz (Leiden: Brill, 2000), 23-245, claims that the development of a system of marches "must lie in the end of the military expansion of the Carolingians'" (244). His observation, however, is contradicted by the corpus of information that Wolfram, himself, discusses throughout the article, which suggests the growing sophistication of the planning and implementing various march organizations. In fact, the notion that Carolingian military expansion ended during Charlemagne's reign is an unsupportable myth. Much more representative of contemporary thinking regarding frontier defense is provided by Helmut Reimitz, "Conversion and Control: The Establishment of Liturgical Frontiers in Carolingian Pannonia," in *The Transformation of Frontiers from Late Antiquity to the Carolingians*, ed. Ian Wood and Helmut Reimitz (Leiden: Brill, 2000), 189-207, who observes, "In the last few years our view of this general form [the marches] has evolved, and now we see Carolingian frontiers as dynamic regions rather that static borders" (192).

to the east of the river had never been a part of the Roman Empire and their conquest, therefore, was not part of Charlemagne's long-term strategy. The Elbe frontier, however, was provided with infrastructure such as bridges and defended bridgeheads to undertake military operations largely of a punitive nature east of the river. This, of course, was a well-known Roman imperial strategy for defending those frontiers that they intended to stabilize.[86] A similar strategy was used in regard to the Danish territory, which also had never been a part of the Roman Empire.[87]

This type of dual defensive-offensive strategy along the frontiers of the *regnum Francorum* had been employed frequently by the early Carolingians, well before Charlemagne's elevation to the imperial throne and his putative embrace of a purely defensive military posture. The actual nature and purpose of a fortified frontier is very well-illustrated by the "Germar Mark," which was developed initially by Charlemagne's father Pippin and his uncle Carloman the Elder, before the former was elevated to the Frankish throne in 751. The numerous fortifications constructed in a strategic pattern throughout this *Mark* created a position that modern scholars recognize as a "defense in depth." It was established defensively for the purpose of protecting the newly acquired territory and its Frankish settlers, who could be threatened both by Saxons and by Slavs from the east. Offensively, these fortifications served as bases to project Carolingian forces further to the east against these same Saxons and Slavs with the ultimate strategic goal of acquiring more territory, which, itself, was then protected by additional fortifications.[88]

---

[86] It is clear, for example, from *CRF*, no. 74, ch. 8, that in October of 811, Charlemagne's orders to establish some additional logistic requirements for men undertaking expeditionary service, who were to muster on the Elbe in order to advance across the river against the Slavs were for punitive purposes and so were the orders for those who were to muster in the foothills of the Pyrenees in order to advance against the Muslims in Hispania.

[87] Cf. Neils Lund, "Scandinavia; 700-1066," in MCMH, II, ed. Mckitterick, 202-27, at 206-208.

[88] See Bachrach, *Charlemagne's Early Campaigns*, 584-89, 601-602, with the substantial scholarly literature cited there.

Charlemagne's Imperial Military Strategy

A proper understanding of how post-coronation era strategic planning, which undergirded the establishment of marches by the Carolingians, places in high relief the information provided both by the narrative sources and by the capitularies regarding Charlemagne's imperial military strategy. These sources make clear that Charlemagne maintained a traditional Carolingian offensive strategy and that these efforts were similar to, if not more ambitious than, those that he had undertaken during some of the decades prior to his coronation.[89] There have been, however, frequent recent scholarly pronouncements regarding Charlemagne's supposedly new and radical strategic reorientation from the offense to the defense.[90] Therefore, it is important to emphasize that the chronology of Charlemagne's offensive operations aimed at territorial expansion, which resulted in the final conquest of the Saxon region ca. 804 and of the Avar region at about the same time, took place in both cases about four years after his elevation to the imperial title.[91]

---

[89] Reuter, a supporter of the view that Charlemagne radically altered his strategy from offense to defense, recognizes that the story told by the numerous Carolingian narrative texts concerning the imperial period indicate "no apparent differences [in regard to the earlier period], except for invasions—real and threatened—between the period 802-30." ("End of Carolingian Military Expansion," 251-52.) Reuter, while making clear that he is aware that the narrative sources indicate the dominance of continued Carolingian offensive military operations by Charlemagne's armies during the imperial period, nevertheless misleads his readers in this very same sentence. During the period prior to Charlemagne's coronation, there were both real and threatened invasions of Carolingian-ruled territory. Concerning these see Bachrach, *Charlemagne's Early Campaigns*, passim. Reuter recognizes that the information provided by Böhmer and Mühlbacher, *Regesta Imperii*, vol. I, 158-25, supports my argument that the accounts of Charlemagne's military operations in the imperial period of his reign and compared to campaigns prior to 800 are essentially the same.

[90] For example, it is claimed that Charlemagne's previous offensive strategy saw "The tailing-off of wars of conquest in the 790s, and their cessation in the very early 800s." See Marios Costambeys, Matthew Innis, and Simon Maclean, *The Carolingian World* (Cambridge: Cambridge University Press, 2011), 159.

[91] See Marios Costambeys, Matthew Innes, and Simon McLean, *Carolingian World*, 75, regarding the continuing of these wars of expansion after Charlemagne's coronation. While contrary to the available written evidence, these authors believe that "Charlemagne's previous offensive strategy saw "The tailing-off of wars of conquest in the 790s, and their cessation in the very early 800s" (159).

The successful conclusion of two major offensive military strategies initiated prior to 800 in the Saxon and Avar territories cannot also be claimed to have been defensive efforts. These efforts were not the only offensive military operations undertaken during Charlemagne's imperial years. As indicated throughout the surviving narrative sources, Carolingian armies advanced against the Muslims settled south of the Pyrenees, whose fortified cities and lesser strongholds of later Roman origin were besieged and often captured by Carolingian armies. Carolingian armed forces, operating from bases in Italy and in the southern reaches of the *regnum Francorum*, also saw the initiation of a major offensive military strategy in the western Mediterranean, both on land and at sea, which was largely an offensive innovation of the imperial period.[92] In addition, Charlemagne's armies operated on the east coast of the Adriatic and along the west coast of Italy. Initiatives in the Holy Land with the apparent support of Harun al Rashid, the Muslim Caliph in Baghdad, mark yet another area that was intended for the expansion of Carolingian strategic influence, if not for actual military conquest.[93]

The Enduring Expeditionary Levies

Scholarly speculation that has focused on the demise of Frankish expeditionary levies, while being used as "evidence" for Charlemagne's imagined need to employ a defensive military strategy during the imperial period, has been stimulated over time by an even broader purpose. This purpose is connected to the scholarly aim of characterizing the *liberi homines* as peasants, which was partly intended to set the stage for their disappearance as an important offensive element in the military organization of the *regnum Francorum* and/or its successor states. In this context, the demise of the Select Levy is thought to have been a prerequisite for the

---

[92] Böhmer and Mühlbacher, *Regesta Imperii*, vol. I, 158-225; and in greater detail, Bernard S. Bachrach, "Charlemagne's Mediterranean Empire," in *Mediterranean Identities in the Premodern Era: Entrepôts, Islands and Empires*, ed. John Wadkins and Kathryn Reyerson (Burlington, VT: Ashgate, 2014), 155-72.

[93] See the important documentation discussed in detail by Michael McCormick, *Charlemagne's Survey of the Holy Land: Wealth, Personnel, and Buildings of a Mediterranean Church between Antiquity and the Middle Ages* (Washington DC: Dumbarton Oaks, 2011); and see also, Bachrach, "Charlemagne's Mediterranean Empire," 154-72.

establishment of "feudalism." This theoretical construct, which now has been abandoned as a result of Susan Reynold's magisterial critique in *Fiefs and Vassals*, was based on the hypothesis that the large numbers of foot soldiers, for example, men such as the *liberi homines*, were replaced by relatively small numbers of heavily armed mounted vassals. The latter are assumed to have served in the personal armed followings of the Frankish nobility and often received "fiefs" to support their service.[94]

These so-called "feudal" vassals of the early Middle Ages are seen by many scholars to have evolved over time into "knights," who are believed to have spurred the development of chivalry, which often is viewed as an essential characteristic of the upper levels of medieval society in a socio-military context.[95] Although Reynolds' views have been widely accepted regarding the misleading use of the feudal construct, many scholars, such as Renaud, focus on the demise of Charlemagne's expeditionary levies in order to argue for a rapid change in military institutions that brought about the emergence of a knightly class of mounted troops.[96] In this context, it is important to emphasize that for more than two centuries, it has remained uncontroversial among scholars that during the Merovingian period, the offensive military forces of the *regnum Francorum* were numerically dominated by armies composed of militia troops comprised of so-called "free peasants" who were foot soldiers.[97] These men who

---

[94] Regarding the demise of "feudalism" as a no longer viable construct for the discussion of early medieval military organization, see the magisterial work by Susan Reynolds, *Fiefs and Vassals: The Medieval Evidence Reinterpreted* (New York: Oxford University Press,1994).

[95] See Janet Nelson, "Ninth Century Knighthood" The Evidence of Nithard," in *Studies in Medieval History presented to R. Allen Brown*, ed. Christopher Harper-Bill, J. Holdsworth, and Janet Nelson (Woodbridge, UK: Boydell & Brewer, 1988), 255-66; and reprinted in eadem, *The Frankish World* (London: Hambledon Press, 1996), 75-87. For a fully developed but flawed treatment of this historical process, see Dominique Barthélemy, *The Serf, the Knight, and the Historian*, trans. Graham Robert Edwards (Ithaca,NY: Cornell Unversity Press, 2009). For a critique of Barthélemy's treatment of the subject, see the "Review Article" by Bernard S. Bachrach, *The Journal of Military History*, 73 (2009): 1307-10.

[96] See as discussed above, Renaud, "Un Élite paysanne en crise?" 315-36; and more precisely idem, "La politique militaire de Charlemagne," 27, who sees the process as taking place much more rapidly that does Kristensen.

[97] See Bernard S. Bachrach, *Merovingian Military Organization: 481-751* (Minneapolis,MN: University of Minnesota Press, 1972), which should be read along with a series of studies by the same author, and which develop and/or modify various

constituted the greater part of the *regnum Francorum,* both geographically and demographically making up the population of Gaul, are to be
understood as the Gallo-Roman ancestors of the *liberi homines,* my focus
here.

As a result of this consensus regarding Merovingian armies, scholars
searching for the beginnings of "feudalism" found that it was necessary
to identify the processes of institutional change from large numbers of
foot soldiers to small numbers of heavily armed cavalry as having taken
place no earlier than among the Carolingians. The *locus classicus* for an
early and rapid process of such institutional change was established during the late nineteenth century by Heinrich Brunner.[98] He believed that
feudalism (*Lehnwesen*) developed during the middle third of the eighth
century. He argued that Charles Martel, the Mayor of the Palace (718-
742), in the wake of his victory with an army of foot soldiers over the
forces of Abd-al-Rachman III, the Muslim governor of Spain, at Poitiers
in 732, converted the Frankish military into a force of heavily armed
mounted vassals.[99] In order to support these mounted troops, Charles

---

aspects of the earlier study: "Was the Marchfield Part of the Frankish Constitution?"
Mediaeval Studies, 36 (1974): 78-85; "The Imperial Roots of Merovingian Military
Organization," *Military Aspects of Scandinavian Society in a European Perspective, AD.
1-1300,* ed. Anne Norgard Jorgensen and Birthe L. Clausen (Copenhagen: National
Museum, 1997), 25-31 (in quarto); "Gregory of Tours as a Military Historian," in *The
World of Gregory of Tours,* ed. Kathleen Mitchell and Ian Wood (Leiden: Brill, 2002),
351-63; "Quelques observations sur la composition et les caractéristiques des armées
de Clovis," in *Clovis: Histoire et Mémoire,* 2 vols. ed. Michel Rouche (Paris: Presses de
l'Université de Paris-Sorbonne, 1997), 689-703 (which volume cited here?); "Merovingian Mercenaries and Paid Soldiers in Imperial Perspective," in *Mercenaries and Paid
Men in the Middle Ages: Proceedings of a Conference held at University of Wales, Swansea, 7th-9th July 2005,* ed. John France (Leiden: Brill, 2008), 167-92; and "Vouillé in the
Context of the Decisive Battle Phenomenon," in *The Battle of Vouillé 507 CE: Where
France Began,* ed. Denuta Shanzer and Ralph W. Mathisen (Berlin: Walter de Gruyter,
2012), 11-42. Cf. the interesting perspective of Laury Sarti, *Perceiving War and the Military in Early Christian Gaul (CA. 400-700 A.D.* (Leiden: Brill, 2013).

   [98] See Carl Stephenson, "The Origins and Significance of Feudalism," *Mediaeval Institutions, Selected Essays,* ed. Bryce D. Lyon (Ithaca, NY: Cornell University
Press, 1954), 205-33.

   [99] "Der Reiterdienst und die Anfänge des Lehnwesens," *Zeitschrift de Savigny-
Stiftung für Rechtsgeschichte, Germanistische Abtheilung,* VIII (1887), 1-38; and
reprinted in idem, *Forschungen zur Geschichte des deutschen und frannzösischen
Rechts* (Stuttgart, 1894), 39-74.

supposedly borrowed large quantities of church lands and lent these to his vassals so that they could afford to fight as heavily armed cavalrymen. It was this process, according to Brunner and his supporters, that created what amounted to a "feudal revolution."[100]

Many scholars, however, rejected Brunner's notion of a military revolution that focused on a hypothetical change in Frankish military organization from large armies based on militia levies of foot soldiers to small forces of heavily armed cavalry in a very rapid mid-eighth-century time frame.[101] Broad opposition to Brunner's hypothesized revolution was based on the argument that the process of institutional change in regard to military organization and the demise of expeditionary levies of foot soldiers developed slowly and in some areas of Western Europe extended into the twelfth century.[102] For example, Kristensen summarizes these views when she observes, "The development of the use in warfare of heavily armed feudal cavalry . . . gradually brought it about that the personal military service of the peasant-soldiers became of less real moment in many places."[103]

Various chronologies have been embraced by those scholars who reject Brunner's theory of a "feudal" revolution. Therefore, the dating of

---

[100] Concerning this argument, see J.-F. Verbruggen, "L'Armée et la Stratégie de Charlemagne," *Karl der Grosse: Lebenswerk und Nachleben*, 5 vols., ed. W. Braunfels and Helmut Beumann (Düsseldorf: L. Schwann, 1965), I, 20-34, at 421; and Leopold Auer, "Zum Kriegswesen unter den frühen Babenbergen," *Jahrbuch für Landeskunde von Niederösterreich*, 42 (1976): 9-25, at 16, who identifies the central question as the relation between "Kriegswesen und Sozialstruktur."

[101] For a lengthy list of scholars who rejected Brunner's thesis of revolutionary change, see Lynn T. White Jr. *Medieval Technology and Social Change* (Oxford: Oxford University Press, 1962), 137-38. White, 1-38, tried to resuscitate Brunner's thesis by arguing that the introduction of the stirrup was the invention that brought about this supposed "feudal revolution." However, not only has Brunner's thesis been decisively undermined, but White's efforts to save the "revolution" from the dust bin of history has also been shown to be without merit. For the state of the question on these points, see the survey of the literature by Kelly DeVries and Robert Douglas Smith, *Medieval Military Technology*, 2nd ed. (Toronto: Toronto University Press, 2012), 99-114.

[102] Kristensen, "Danelaw institutions," 41, represents the views identified regarding the rejection of Brunner's thesis as cited in detail by White in the previous note.

[103] Kristensen, "Danelaw institutions," 41, sees this process as taking place very slowly, well into the high Middle Ages. Cf. "Renaud, "Un Élite paysanne en crise?" 315-36; and more precisely idem, "La politique militaire de Charlemagne," 27, who sees the process as taking place much more rapidly than does Kristensen.

the supposed demise of so-called peasant levies who were deployed for offensive purposes remains controversial. Josef Fleckenstein claims, for example, "Das Fussvolk tritt jedenfalls völlig in den Hintergrund" by the later Carolingian era.[104] By contrast, Carl Ferdinand Werner rejected the Carolingian period as one of radical changes in military organization and argues that the date for the diminution in the importance of levies of foot soldiers should be put in the late tenth century.[105] Hans Fehr also rejected Brunner's model and suggested that the late ninth century was the likely period of change. However, he recognized that "free peasants" were permitted to carry honorable weapons in the later eleventh century. Therefore, clearly they could participate in offensive military operations, which is made clear during the Saxon wars of Henry IV (d. 1106).[106]

The lengthy continuity of "peasant" levies used for offensive purposes throughout the history of the Carolingian empire and various successor states is not controversial.[107] Thus Renaud, who at the outset of his study asserted that great change took place during Charlemagne's imperial

---

[104] See Fleckenstein, "Adel und Kriegertum," 86.

[105] Karl Ferdinand Werner, "Heeresorganization und Kriegsführung im deutschen Königsreich des 10. und 11. Jahrhunderts," *Settimane di Studio de Centro Italiano sull'alto Medioevo*, 15 (1968): 791-843, at 842-43. For a detailed examination of the evidence regarding the German kingdom and the myth of a military revolution, see two studies by Bernard S. Bachrach and David S. Bachrach, "Saxon Military Revolution, 912-73: Myth and Reality," *Early Medieval Europe*, 15 (2007): 186-222; and "Early Saxon Frontier Warfare: Henry I, Otto I, and Carolingian Military Institutions," *Journal of Medieval Military History*, X (2012): 17-60.

[106] Hans Fehr, "Das Waffenrecht der Bauern im Mittlelater," *Zeitschrift der Savigny-stiftung für Rechtsgeschichte. Germanistische Abteilung*, 35 (1914): 111-211, makes clear (at 158-61) the continued right of "peasants" to bear so-called noble arms, e.g. swords.

[107] For continuity in the western parts of the *regnum Francorum* in the post-Carolingian era, see Bernard S. Bachrach, "Dudo of Saint Quentin as a Military Historian," *The Haskins Society Journal: Studies in Medieval History*, 12 (2002): 155-85; and idem, "Ademar of Chabannes as a Military Historian," in *Where Heaven and Earth Meet: Essays on Medieval Europe in Honor of Daniel F. Callahan*, ed. Michael Frasseto, Matthew Gabriele and John D. Hosler (Leiden: Brill, 2014), 42-62. This institution was imported into later Anglo-Saxon England, as is made clear by Hollister, *Anglo-Saxon Military Institutions*; and idem, *The Military Organization of Norman England*; and into Moravia on the Carolingian frontier as discussed by Alexander Ruttkay, "The Organization of Troops. Warfare and Arms in the Period of the Great Moravian State," *Slovenska Archeologia*, 30 (1982): 165-98.

period, found it necessary to postpone the demise of the expeditionary levy and tentatively concluded that it was only at "la fin du IXe siècle" that warfare came "favoriser les monopole des armes par les nobles, les chevaliers et leurs auxiliaires."[108] However, Renaud came to realize that Werner was right in seeing expeditionary levies of foot soldiers playing an important offensive role in the armies of Otto I (d. 973).[109] Of course, Renaud's need to recognize the continued importance of the offensive role of "peasant" levies into the later tenth century completely undermined his assertion that the demise of the Select Levy took place during Charlemagne's imperial years. In concert with the failure to prove the demise of the Select Levy, his assertion that Charlemagne's need to pursue a defensive military strategy falls of its own weight.[110]

Selection Mechanisms for Expeditionary Service

Because Charlemagne's military capitularies were time- and mission-conditioned, numerous methodological limitations come to the fore when efforts are made to try to use sections of capitularies issued during the imperial era for drawing conclusions regarding early (pre 800) Carolingian military institutions. Nevertheless, some recent scholars have claimed that none of the capitularies or, for that matter, any other source that survives from prior to 800 provide evidence for the Frankish government having established "selection mechanisms" of any kind regarding those who were to undertake expeditionary military service.[111] These scholars argue on the basis of the selective use of a few particular post-coronation military capitularies. These capitularies employ time

---

[108] See Renaud, "La politique militaire de Charlemagne," 27.

[109] Renaud, "Un Élite paysanne en crise?" 333, regarding his acceptance of Werner's views.

[110] Renaud, "La politique militaire de Charlemagne," 17. However, cf. Reuter, "End of Carolingian Military Expansion," 260-61, who sees the increasing importance of the *liberi homines*, during the imperial period, as an element deployed for the local defense but is contradicted by the emperor's military capitularies.

[111] See Reuter, "End of Carolingian Military Expansion," 259, who claims that "nowhere in the sources for the Merovingian or early Carolingian period is there anything which looks like a possible selection mechanism"; he is followed by Renaud, "La politique militaire de Charlemagne," 9.

conditioned and situationally specific "selection mechanisms," such as on the impact of a famine. Accordingly they argue that it was only after Charlemagne became emperor that he institutionalized criteria for those who were to serve in the Select Levy.[112]

In addition, it is erroneous to argue that Frankish governments did not establish a selection mechanism of any kind for the mobilization of their expeditionary levies until sometime after Charlemagne's elevation to the imperial title. As just one example, Gregory of Tours, writing in the early 590s, takes note of expeditionary levies from the Touraine serving in the Poitou, beyond the borders of their home *pagus*, as part of King Guntram's army. Gregory observes that some men, who were not a part of this levy, had illicitly accompanied the members of the expeditionary levy and went from the Touraine into the Poitou in order to acquire booty in the region.[113] Clearly, some men from the Touraine possessed the means to go on campaign but had not been selected to serve for this particular operation. What was obvious to Gregory of Tours was no less obvious to Charlemagne, who understood that expeditionary service in the Select Levy was governed by an *antiqua consuetudo*, which established an economic base as a selection mechanism.[114] This ancient custom

---

[112] See Renaud, "La politique militaire de Charlemagne," 9; and Reuter, "End of Carolingian Military Expansion," 256-63.

[113] In addition to Gregory of Tours, *Liberi Historiarum X*, ed. Bruno Krusch Willhelm Levison, *Monumenta Germaniae Historica; Scriptores rerum Merovingicarum*, I.1 (Hannover: Hahn, 1951), Gregory, Hist., bk. VII, ch. 28, discussed above, see idem, bk. VII, ch. 24, which indicates that Guntram levied an army "from among all men who owed service from all of the peoples of his realm" for expeditionary service. From this it is obvious that not all men under his rule were obligated to perform expeditionary service. In addition, idem, bk. V, ch. 26; bk. VI, ch. 12; and VII, ch. 24 provide examples of the Frankish government during the Merovingian period imposing a fine, *heribannus,* on those who failed to appear when mustered. Regarding this fine, as Goffert, "Frankish Military Duty," 167, observes, these men "had enough property to pay it or, better, to finance what the property was for, namely, military service." Regarding the Carolingians, see *CRF*, no. 74, ch. 8, which is discussed below.

[114] The term *antiqua consuetudo*, as employed in Charlemagne's capitularies, can be traced to institutional structures that were in use at least during the Merovingian era and often earlier, that is, to material found in the *Codex Theodosianus* or other later Roman texts. Many of these ancient customs, such as keeping bridges and roads in repair, were of signal importance for successful military operations and, in fact, the Anglo-Saxons recognized these *consuetudines* to be of such critical

was a long-established minimum level of resources that had to be available for any man to be mobilized for expeditionary military operations.[115]

With this selection mechanism in place, a base was established regarding who could be mobilized for offensive military service by the count of each *pagus* upon receiving Charlemagne's orders. After receiving orders from the central government, the local officials decided, according to already established criteria, who would be required to serve from among those dwelling in the *pagus*.[116] If, for example, Charlemagne wanted to

---

importance that they copied them when developing the *trinoda necessitas,* regarding which see Richard Abels, *Lordship and Military Obligation in Anglo-Saxon England* (Berkeley-Los Angeles: University of California Press, 1988), 53; and Alan Cooper, "The Rise and Fall of the Law of the Anglo-Saxon Highway," *Haskins Society Journal,* 12 (2002): 39-69, at 44. The importance of the *antiquae consuetudines* to Charlemagne's administration are to be found, for example, in *CRF,* no. 74, ch. 4; no. 98, ch. 3. See Alexander C. Murray, "'*Pax et Disciplina,*' Roman Public Law and the Merovingian State," in *Proceedings of the Tenth Annual International Congress of Medieval Canon Law,* ed. Kenneth Pennington, Stanley Chodorow, and Keith H. Kendall (Vatican City: Biblioteca Apostolica Vaticana, 2001), 269-85, and reprinted in idem, "'*Pax et Disciplina,*' Roman Public Law and the Merovingian State," *From Roman Provinces to Medieval Kingdoms,* ed. Thomas F. X. Noble (New York: Routledge, 2005), 376-88. Eugen von Frauenholz, *Die Heerwesen der germanische Frühzeit, des Fränkenreiches und des rittleliche Zeitalters* (Munich: C.H.Beck, 1935), 15, shows how the Lombards in the seventh century also accommodated themselves to later Roman practices.

[115] Renaud, "La politque militaire de Charlemagne," 4, takes note of these requirements in *CRF,* no. 74, ch. 8, but fails to recognize that this *antiqua consuetudo* established a selection mechanism for a lower limit of the economic means required for service in the Select Levy. To put the matter of *antiquae consuetudines* in historical perspective, it is obvious that such terminology never was applied by Charlemagne in any of his surviving capitularies to an institutionalized behavior that had been established sometime after 800. See *CRF,* no. 24, ch. 8; no. 25, ch. 1; no. 30, ch. 6; no. 43, ch. 24; no. 44, ch. 8; no. 46, ch. 10; no. 90, ch. 8.

[116] It is clear that the count, or one of his subordinates, made the decision at the local level; see *CRF,* no. 73, ch. 3. Reuter, "End of Carolingian Military Expansion," 259, correctly argues that "Even selection on the basis of a property qualification would still have produced very large armies." Thus, as a proponent of small armies, Reuter rejects the notion of a property qualification, claims that all free men must serve, and asserts that this is only possible if a defensive strategy was at issue. Of course, Goffart, "Frankish Military Duty," 166, 177, demonstrates that Reuter's rejection of a property qualification is without merit and notes that the texts are focused on those who "paid taxes" at the "upper level." He also takes note of magnates, some of whom own thousands of manses (169). In this context, see CRF, no. 77, ch. 9, issued

have large numbers of heavily armed mounted troops mustered for a particular campaign, those *liberi homines* who were too poor to provide such
service were not eligible to be called up. In fact, the count was forbidden
by Charlemagne's orders to coerce them to undertake service that the
central government regarded as being beyond their means.[117] For heavily armed mounted troops, the count was required to mobilize men who
owned or possessed at least twelve *mansi*.[118]

In the capitulary that calls attention to the *antiqua consuetudo*, Charlemagne describes the nature of the "ancient custom," that is, the primary
selection mechanism regarding the minimum quantities of supplies and
equipment that were required for a man to have available for his personal
use in order to participate in an offensive military campaign as a member of the Select Levy.[119] This text unambiguously indicates that anyone
whom government officials legitimately could mobilize for *expeditio* was
to have available the minimum economic means to provide for himself
the food that he would need for three months of military operations,
the clothing that he would need for six months in the field, and also the
armaments that he would need for the latter period of time.[120] As late in
Charlemagne's reign as the autumn of 811, the government continued to
follow what clearly was a long-established *consuetudo*, which set a minimum wealth requirement for those who could be selected for participation in offensive military operations.[121] It is perhaps equally important

---

either in 802 or 803 by Charlemagne at Aachen, where the emperor warns ecclesiastical *immunists*, who owned vast numbers of *mansi*, that they are to see to it that the
men whom they are required to send or bring to the muster were appropriately armed.

[117] *CRF*, no. 33, ch. 12 restricts the count from coercing men who owed service to do more than was required by their economic situation to meet these illicitly
imposed responsibilities.

[118] According to already existing criteria, men who owned twelve *mansi* owed
service as heavily armed mounted troops. See *CRF*, no. 44, ch. 6; and also no. 77, ch.
9, regarding heavily armed mounted troops.

[119] See *CRF*, no. 74, ch. 8. Cf. Reuter, "End of Carolingian Military Expansion,"
259.

[120] *CRF*, no. 74, ch. 8.

[121] Ironically, Renaud, "La politque militaire de Charlemagne," 30, reprints the
capitulary in which this *antiqua consuetudo* is discussed, but he ignores its obvious
long-term existence prior to Charlemagne's elevation to the imperial throne. Such
recognition obviously would undermine his view that some sort of great change took
place in 808.

that none of Charlemagne's surviving capitularies are seen to repeal or nullify this or any other *antiqua consuetudo*.[122]

Charlemagne's Large Armies

In addition to the view that the use of Carolingian levies of foot soldiers were replaced by heavy cavalry, many scholars assumed that the forces mobilized for the Select Levy were so numerous that their effective elimination from offensive campaigns resulted in a *volte face* in Charlemagne's traditional offensive military strategy.[123] Although neither Charlemagne's military capitularies nor the narrative sources provide direct information regarding the size of any force mustered to serve in the Select Levy, these same sources do demonstrate continued Carolingian offensive military operations beyond the frontiers of the empire throughout the imperial years of Charlemagne's reign.[124] For example, the lengthy siege

---

[122] See *CRF*, no. 162, ch. 3, which would seem to suggest that the *antiqua consuetudo* was still in force in 825.

[123] Regarding the large numbers of men required for siege operations, see Bernard S. Bachrach and Rutherford Aris, "Military Technology and Garrison Organization: Some Observations on Anglo-Saxon Military Thinking in Light of the Burghal Hidage," *Technology and Culture*, 31 (1990): 1-17. Renaud, "La politque militaire de Charlemagne," 17, not only believes that the Select Levy saw a vast diminution of personnel, but that this situation was of major importance in regard to Charlemagne's supposed change in military strategy from the offensive to the defensive following his imperial coronation. Cf. the curious views of Halsall, *Warfare and Society*, 90, 94-95, who argues that the early Carolingians had abandoned the use of the Select Levy but that after becoming emperor Charlemagne "wanted to raise an army in the old style . . . as had been the case in the sixth century." In support of his interpretation, Halsall (73), asserts, that "in the early eighth century, Frankish armies were made up of nobles, their retainers and adherents," and he claims that Charles Martel's "wars were fought with mounted armies of his family's and their allies' dependents, retainers and adherents" (74). Regarding Charles Martel, see Bernard S. Bachrach, "Charles Martel, Mounted Shock Combat, the Stirrup and Feudalism," *Studies in Medieval and Renaissance History*, 7 (1970): 49-75; reprinted with the same pagination in idem, *Armies and Politics in the Early Medieval West* (London, 1993).

[124] As Reuter, "End of Carolingian military expansion," 351-52, put it, the story told by the numerous Carolingian narrative texts concerning military operations during Charlemagne's reign as emperor indicate "no apparent differences [in regard to the earlier period]." Reuter, of course, was interested in seeing radical change take

of Barcelona's city walls required three armies and a fleet. Such a siege could not be carried out by the deployment of small numbers of heavily armed mounted troops.[125] To reverse Fleckenstein's enthusiasm for the dominance of heavy cavalry, quoted above, it is clear that whatever horsemen that were mustered for the siege of Barcelona were, of necessity, "fully in the *Hintergrund*."[126]

In addition to recognizing the role Select Levies played in siege warfare, Charlemagne understood the importance of mustering large numbers of troops to maintain his fundamental long-term campaign strategy of dealing with the enemy from a position of exceptional numerical strength. This is a strategy that modern scholars characterize as the projection and deployment of "overwhelming force."[127] As numerous

---

place during Charlemagne's imperial years, but he could not find evidence to support this view in the numerous narrative sources.

[125] Regarding the central role played by sieges in early medieval strategy and military operations, see Jim Bradbury, *The Medieval Siege* (Woodbridge, UK: Boydel & Brewer, 1992); Peter Purton, *A History of the Early Medieval Siege, c. 450-1220* (Woodbridge UK: Boydel & Brewer, 2009), *passim*; and Bachrach, *Charlemagne's Early Campaigns*, 310-73. It is to be noted with regard to the post-coronation period, that sieges were especially important against later Roman fortress cities and lesser fortifications in northeastern Spain. For a useful introduction to these operations, see Bernard S. Bachrach, "Military Organization in Aquitaine Under the Early Carolingians," *Speculum*, 49 (1974): 1-33; and reprinted with the same pagination in idem, *Armies and Politics in the Early Medieval West* (London: Ashgate , 1993). For the present state of the question, see Weiss, "La Fer et l'acier," 44, who observes, "Sous les Carolingiens, la grande masse de l'armée était composée de fantassins." Cf. Renaud, "La politique militaire de Charlemagne," 6, who follows Reuter, "The Recruitment of Armies," 32-37, and others, such as Guy Halsall, *Warfare and Society in the Barbarian West, 450-900* (New York: Routledge, 2003), 215-27, do not recognize the crucial importance of sieges, which were the fundamental element of early medieval military operations, including those of Charlemagne's reign.

[126] Translation of Fleckenstein, "Adel und Kriegertum," 86

[127] As noted by J.F. Verbruggen, *The Art of War in Western Europe during the Middle Ages, from the Eighth Century to 1340,* trans. Sumner Willard and S.C.M. Southern (2nd ed. Woodbridge, UK: Boydell & Brewer, 1997), 283, "Charlemagne's armies were bigger than those of his enemies." In this context, Verbruggen gives Charlemagne credit for recognizing "the superiority of numbers as the most important factor in the result of a combat." He goes on to discuss Charlemagne's strategy (313-16) and observes that "Charlemagne used his superior strength to carry out concentric advance into enemy territory" (313). For greater detail, see Bachrach, *Early Carolingian Warfare*, 135-36, 159, 192, 194, 243, 254. Cf. Renaud, "La politique

examples from Charlemagne's reign make clear, the successful tactical implementation of overwhelming force, often by the use of several armies deployed in pincer movements, tended to encourage the enemy's rapid withdrawal from a campaign or their surrender. This success occurred because troops who are greatly outnumbered are less likely to fight than those who believe that they have an opportunity to emerge victorious in battle.[128]

Charlemagne, by deploying overwhelming force, avoided battles in the field. As a result, his own troops rarely suffered noteworthy casualties by engaging in large-scale pitched battles. It is clear that Charlemagne understood that winning bloodless victories provided a positive incentive for his troops to go on campaign and played a key role, along with effective logistical support, in maintaining their high morale. It is evident, as well, that Charlemagne did not undertake military operations for the purpose of winning personal glory at the expense of his soldiers' well-being. Like all good commanders, Charlemagne did not consider his troops to be expendable, an aspect of his generalship that the men who served under his command were well aware and undoubtedly appreciated.[129]

The Cost of Service in the Expeditionary Levy

In 811, Charlemagne called attention to the fundamental selection mechanism that identified the minimum wealth requirement for service *in expeditione*. As noted above, according to this *antiqua consuetudo*, each man who was obligated to undertake offensive military service as a member of the Select Levy was required to possess sufficient surplus wealth so that he could provide at his own expense the food stuffs (*victualia*) that he required for three months of campaigning in the field against the enemy, as well as sufficient weaponry and clothing (*arma* and *vestimenta*) for

militaire de Charlemagne," 2, who believes that Charlemagne had small armies and asserts that he did not adhere to what modern scholars call the doctrine of overwhelming force. In the process, he ignores Verbruggen's discussion and the evidence.

[128] Bachrach, *Early Carolingian Warfare*, 135-36, 159, 192, 194, 243, 254.

[129] See Bachrach, *Early Carolingian Warfare*, 133-36, 159; and Bachrach, *Charlemagne's Early Campaigns*, *passim*.

six months of such military operations.[130] Charlemagne, of course, could increase the quantity of service owed even by those who possessed the basic requirements when he deemed it necessary.[131] However, those men who possessed only the minimum level required by the *antiqua consuetudo* could be helped by a government subsidy to attend the muster or be left at home because they lacked the resources to serve.[132]

---

[130] CRF, no. 74, ch. 8. Nb. those who see a decrease in the number and importance of the poorer members of the Select Levy, either ignore this "ancient custom" as is the case with Reuter, "Plunder and Tribute," 231-50; and idem, "The End of Carolingian Military Expansion," 251-67; or, like Renaud, "La politique militaire de Charlemagne," 4, fail to recognize that it constituted a selection mechanism.

[131] *CRF*, no. 74, ch. 8, was issued to make clear special additional regulations for those expeditionary levies who would be campaigning south of the Pyrenees against the Muslims or east of the Elbe against the Slavs. It is noteworthy that at this time, Charlemagne was not thinking in terms of mobilizing his expeditionary levies for deployment in Italy. Like other capitularies discussed above, this one too is both time-conditioned by Charlemagne's near-term plans and also geographically limited.

[132] *CRF*. no. 74, ch. 8. One can infer that the government would pay whatever expenses for food that were incurred for the additional three months, or perhaps even more, if the levies continued to serve beyond three months. This same capitulary provides evidence for the particularities determining the requirements imposed on the military. On the occasion of issuing this capitulary, Charlemagne temporarily divided a part of the *regnum* north of the Alps into three zones. One zone was the region between Rhine and the Elbe; a second zone was the region between the Loire and the Rhine; and the third zone was the region between the Loire and the Pyrenees. It may be added here (*CRF*, no. 75) that immunists were required to see to it that the troops whom they commanded on campaign also had food for three months and both clothing and weapons for six months, which suggests that these logistic requirements embedded in the *antiqua consuetudo* had a very broad application. The claim by Renaud, "La politique militaire de Charlemagne," 21, that Carolingian expeditionary levies, here referred to as "paysans conscrits," were not used by Pippin in his invasion of Aquitaine (*The Fourth Book of the Chronicle of Fredegar with its Continuations*, trans. J.M. Wallace-Hadrill [London: Nelson, 1960] *Fredegar cont.*, chs. 49-51) because this force was encamped through a part of the winter, is clearly undermined by the *antiqua consuetudo* identified in *CRF*. no. 74, ch. 8. Renaud, in fact, seems to misread Fredegar cont., *loc. cit.*, as Pippin mustered his army late in the autumn of 767 and, at the beginning of winter, called a halt to operations and sent his *totam exercitum* into winter quarters in Burgundy. He then mustered them again in mid-February but sent them home before the winter came to an end. In fact, it seems clear that the entire time during which these particular expeditionary levies were on campaign was a period of fewer than six months. After Pippin sent the *exercitus* home, he operated (*Fredegar cont.*, ch. 52) with local military

Some scholars, ignoring the *antiqua consuetudo*, assert that the "expense of military service . . . was considerable" even though it is not made clear what they mean by "considerable" in regard to expeditionary service in the Select Levy.[133] However, an estimate of the costs entailed for a campaign of three months, at least in terms of the food needed for each man to function in the field, can been calculated by using traditional logistic tables, as human food requirements fall within established norms.[134] A comparison of these costs with the surplus wealth of *liberi homines*, who owned *allods* and slaves, makes clear that their campaigning expenses were not high in relation to their assets. The long-term survival of Select Levies was a key part of early medieval military organization throughout western Europe for offensive purposes and was not negatively impacted by the expenses that these men incurred while on campaign.

For heuristic purposes, the observation can be made that an able-bodied man on military campaign required during the Roman Empire, on average, approximately 3,000 calories per day depending upon the particular soldier's age, height, weight, and assigned duties. The same is still true today in the American army.[135] Therefore, there is no reason to

---

forces mobilized in nearby *pagi* under their *comites* and *presentales* from his military household.

[133] See Reuter, "Plunder and tribute," 244. Reuter could not have been aware of Goffart's demonstration ("Frankish Military Duty," 166-90) that this unpaid service was performed in lieu of paying a land tax; and see Renaud, "Une Élite paysanne en crise?," 322, who also believes that the cost of service was exceptionally burdensome to members of the Select Levy.

[134] See Bernard S. Bachrach, "The Crusader March from Dorylaion to Herakleia," *Shipping, Trade and Crusade in the Medieval Mediterranean: Studies in Honour of John Pryor*, ed. Ruthy Gertwagen and Elizabeth Jeffreys (Farnham,UK: Ashgate, 2012), 231-54, regarding the quantities of food needed for field rations on a daily basis by military personnel while undertaking expeditionary military service.

[135] See the chart provided by Bernard S. Bachrach, "Some Observations on the Role of the Byzantine Navy in the Success of the First Crusade," *Journal of Medieval Military History*, 1 (2002): 83-100, esp. 97-98. Those interested in the matter of the early medieval diet in the West will find the numerous controversies usefully identified by Kathy L. Pearson, "Nutrition and the Early-Medieval Diet," *Speculum*, 72 (1997): 1-32.

It is obvious that neither Charlemagne nor any of his advisers were able to calculate the caloric value of any foods. However, they could ascertain when the soldiers on campaign under their command lacked sufficient energy to perform their

believe that during the Carolingian era soldiers on campaign required field rations significantly in excess of 3,000 calories in order to keep them fit for undertaking military operations both on the march, when encountering the enemy on the battle field, or when undertaking the siege of a fortification. It should be noted that some scholars argue for smaller rations, even as low as 1,750 calories, while other scholars suggest diets in the range of some 2,000 calories. These lesser figures obviously would result in lower costs for Select Levies on campaign.[136]

To simplify our understanding of the logistic requirements, these 3,000 or so calories could be provided on a daily basis by the consumption of approximately 1.5 kilograms of flour baked into biscuits or bread.[137] A three-month or roughly ninety-day grain ration weighs in the neighborhood of 135 kilograms. This load is about three times the weight that an average soldier can be expected to carry in a backpack while on the march.[138] In terms of transportation, this calculation regarding the weight of the food required to meet the fighting man's caloric needs for a period of three months does not take into consideration the weight of the six month allotment of clothing or of the weapons that each man was required to bring on campaign. When the weight of food, clothing, and weapons are added together, it is clear that the total, on average, should be estimated at a minimum of approximately 150 kilograms.[139]

We must recognize that the weight of the load at issue for a man undertaking expeditionary service required that various means had to

---

tasks. In addition, the Carolingian government was not the first to send armies on campaigns, and Charlemagne's advisers were well-positioned to learn from what had been normal field rations in the past. See Jonathan P. Roth, *The Logistics of the Roman Army at War (264 BC–AD 235)* (Leiden: Brill, 1999), 8-67, who discusses various Latin and Greek sources that provide information regarding the feeding of the Roman army.

[136] Ole Benedictow, *The Medieval Demographic System of the Nordic Countries* (Oslo: Middelalderforlaget, 1993), 100.

[137] Roth, *The Logistics of the Roman Army*, 8-67, provides exceptional detail regarding the caloric value of various types of food eaten by soldiers.

[138] See Marcus Junkelmann, *Die Legionen des Augustus: Der römische Soldat in archäologische Experiment* (Mainz: P. von Zabern, 1986), 197-201, which also includes experimental data.

[139] A useful introduction to the archaeological evidence for armaments is Simon Coupland, "Carolingian Arms and Armor in the Ninth Century," *Viator,* 21 (1990): 29-50; and also Weiss, "La Fer et l'acier," 33-47.

be available for transporting the assets of each member of the Select Levy while he was on campaign and assumes that he had these required assets in his possession. Transportation demands could be met in a variety of ways, such as through the use of pack horses, carts, and when applicable, river boats or perhaps even larger sea-worthy craft, or even with a combination of two or more of these methods.[140] Accessing these means of transport might have added something to the expense of going on campaign for each member of the Select Levy, unless the government or some wealthy private entity played a role in paying all or at least some of the transportation costs. In this regard, it is important that men going to and from military campaigns not only were able to transport the assets that they carried tax free, but also were protected by royal edict should they be despoiled while en route to or from their service.[141]

Members of the Select Levy could likely access the food needed by purchase while in the field. It is clear that local markets where food and clothing could be purchased were to be found throughout Charlemagne's lands and that these were supervised by the government.[142] One of the purposes of government policing of markets, in addition to collecting tolls, was to control prices. This meant that when there was an obvious imbalance between supply and demand, for example, a food shortage that threatened price stability, government officials were in a position to intervene in order to stop potentially serious price fluctuations.[143] In addition, there is substantial evidence that the central government maintained a matrix of administrative structures that were used to supervise

---

[140] See Bernard S. Bachrach, "Carolingian Military Operations: An Introduction to Technological Perspectives," *The Art, Science, and Technology of Medieval Travel*, ed. Robert Bork and Andrea Kahn (Aldershot, UK: Ashgate, 2008), 17-29, regarding matters of transportation and comparisons between the costs for hauling loads on land and water. In terms of the transportation of food and equipment, it may be noted that a Roman *contubernium* of eight men employed a mule and a slave for support purposes. See Roth, *The Logistics of the Roman Army*, 77-78.

[141] See *CRF*, no. 44, ch. 13; and no. 24, ch. 8.

[142] Note *CRF*, no. 44, ch. 14, with further discussion by Verhulst, *The Carolingian Economy*, 89-90.

[143] For a discussion of Carolingian edicts and of their Roman legal inspiration regarding the need to assure fair prices as a means of maintaining economic stability and social justice, see Kenneth S. Cahn, "The Roman and Frankish Roots of the Just Price of Medieval Canon Law," *Studies in Medieval and Renaissance History*, 6 (1969) 3-52, esp. 36-43.

the collection of, or to collect, food stuffs from throughout the *regnum Francorum* for military purposes. This supervised collection was done in order to minimize profiteering.[144]

It is clear that effective arrangements were made on a consistent basis for Select Levies, as well as for other elements in Charlemagne's army, to sustain themselves while on campaign, and this especially was the case within the recognized borders of the Frankish kingdom and of the Lombard kingdom after 774.[145] Evidence for the value of Charlemagne's system of military supply can be inferred from several sources. First, there are no complaints concerning the looting of food in regard to Charlemagne's troops on the march, and this is important, especially in regard to stories traditionally told by ecclesiastical authors, who, as scholars are aware, were well known to whine about the damage done to the lands and other resources of the church even by so-called friendly forces.[146] Second,

---

[144] See *CRF*, no. 18, ch. 6; no. 20, ch. 17; no. 77, ch. 10; no. 75; and for detailed localized studies of magazines, see Wilhelm Störmer, "Zur Frage der Funktionen des kirchlichen Fernbesitzes im Gebiet der Ostalpen vom 8. bis zum 10, Jahrhundert," in *Die Transalpinen Verbindungen der Bayern, Alemannen und Franken bis zum 10. Jahrhundert*, ed. Helmut Beumann and Werner Schröder (Sigmaringen: Thorbecke, 1987), 379-403; and Jean Durliat, "La polyptyque d'Irminon pour l'Armée," *Bibliothèque de École des Chartes*, 141 (1983): 183-208.

[145] See Bachrach, *Charlemagne's Early Campaigns*, 65-73; and cf. the hyperbole of Reuter, "Recruitment of Armies," 36, who claims that armies in the 10,000 range moving around the countryside would have left swathes of destruction everywhere more comparable with the downwind ellipse of fallout from a nuclear weapon. Halsall, *Warfare and Society*, 129, takes Reuter's hyperbole seriously and quotes it to support his own view of the situation. However, Reuter, "Plunder and Tribute," 234-36, is unable to produce evidence that Charlemagne's armies destroyed the areas through which they marched within the *regnum Francorum*.

[146] See the discussion by Bachrach, *Charlemagne's Early Campaigns*, 66; cf. Janet Nelson "Violence in the Carolingian World and the Ritualization of Ninth-century Warfare," in *Violence and Society in the Early Medieval West*, ed. Guy Halsall (Woodbridge,UK: Boydell & Brewer, 1998), 90-107, at 93, who asserts that "Legal documents also testify to much illegitimate violence perpetrated by armies against the peasantry of their own kingdom encountered en route." However, the references that she provides do not implicate Charlemagne's armies in such violence while they were operating within the borders of the *regnum Francorum*. Concerning the anti-military bias of early medieval narrative texts, mostly authored by clerics, see Elisabeth Magnou-Nortier, "The Enemies of the Peace: Reflections on a Vocabulary, 500-1100," in *The Peace of God: Social Violence and Religious Response in France around the Year 1000*, ed. Thomas Head and Richard Landes (Ithaca: Cornell University

there are no accounts in the narrative sources concerning Charlemagne's campaigns in regard to the types of food shortages suffered by armies that can be identified, for example, in descriptions of some Merovingian long-range military operations.[147]

On the whole, it seems evident that the advice offered in Vegetius' *De re Militari* book III, chapter 3, whose text was well known by the Carolingians, was taken very seriously by Charlemagne and his advisers, particularly in regard to the warning that a lack of supplies was the worst enemy that any army could face while on campaign.[148] In fact, Charlemagne ordered that when in friendly territory, the logistic practice that was to be followed was that only water and grass might be taken from the countryside without both the permission of the owners and payment.[149] The Franks had adopted these regulations, which were of Roman imperial origin, at least some three centuries earlier, something evidenced by Clovis' military operations in Aquitaine in 507.[150]

The supplies that members of an expeditionary levy were required to provide for themselves while on campaign makes it possible to gain some insight regarding the economic burdens that a poorer member of the Select Levy found it necessary to sustain. However, these costs were incurred only during those campaigning seasons when it was the particular fighting man's turn either to serve personally or to provide a

---

Press, 1992), 58-79; Donald A. Bullough, "Was there a Carolingian Anti-War Movement," *Early Medieval Europe* (12 (2004): 365-76; and Goffart, "Conspicuous by Absence," 41-56. For a useful examination of the clerical bias in favor of "peace," see Paul J. E. Kershaw, *Peaceful Kings, Peace, Power, and the Early Medieval Political Imagination* (Oxford: Oxford University Press, 2011).

[147] Regarding Merovingian logistics in the present context, see Bernard S. Bachrach, *Merovingian Military Organization 481-751* (Minneapolis-Minnesota, 1972), 26-27, 60-61.

[148] See David S. Bachrach, *Warfare in Tenth-Century Germany* (Woodbridge, UK: Boydell & Brewer, 2012), 102-34; and cf. Christopher Allemand, *The De Re Militari of Vegetius: The Reception, Transmission and Legacy of a Roman Text in the Middle Ages* (Cambridge: Cambridge University Press, 2011), 63-69.

[149] Regarding Charlemagne's orders, see *CRF*, no. 18, chs. 6,7; no. 20, ch. 17; no. 24, chs. 7, 8; and no. 25, ch. 6.

[150] With regard to Clovis and the maintenance of Roman logistic traditions while his army was on the march, see Bernard S. Bachrach, "Vouillé in the Context of the Decisive Battle Phenomenon," in *The Battle of Vouillé 507 CE: Where France Began*, ed. Denuta Shanzer and Ralph W. Mathisen (Berlin: Walter de Gruyter, 2012), 11-42.

substitute for whom he was obligated to provide economic support. In this context, it is generally agreed that under normal conditions grain prices were stable throughout Charlemagne's reign and this was the case especially throughout royally supervised markets.[151] As a result of government price fixing aimed at stabilization, a *modius* of oats, of barley, of rye, and of wheat sold for one, two, three, and four *denarii*, respectively.[152] To put the main question simply: what was the likely minimum cost of the food that each man was required to provide for his sustenance during a period of some ninety days while on campaign?

According to well established government regulations, a *modius* of grain baked in a "public oven" was to provide twenty-five loaves of bread with each one weighing a little bit less than one kilogram.[153] For the price of one *denarius*, that is, one twelfth of a *solidus*, an impecunious or frugal soldier could purchase more than the minimum caloric-sufficient ration for twelve to thirteen days on campaign. Ninety to ninety-two days on campaign would cost him about seven *denarii* or a bit more than one-half

---

[151] With regard to abnormal situations in which it was recognized that harvests were not adequate, Charlemagne's government took specific actions to control prices, especially grain prices. See Adrian Verhulst, "Karolingische Agrarpolitik: Das Capitulare de Villis und die Hungernöte von 792/93 und 805/06," *Zeitschrift für Agrargeschichte und Agrarsoziologie*, 13 (1965): 175-89; Cahn, "The Roman and Frankish Roots," 36-43; and also more generally, Jean-Pierre Devroey, "Units of Measurement in the Early Medieval Economy: The Example of Carolingian Food Rations," *French History*, 1 (1987): 68-92; reprinted with the same pagination in idem, *Études sur le grand domaine carolingien* (Aldershot, UK: Ashgate), 1993.

[152] Verhulst, *The Carolingian Economy*, 124. It is clear that Verhulst (118) is using the reformed weights and measurements established by Charlemagne in 793-94, which was done in concert with the monetary reform undertaken at the same time. Regarding the extensive controversy concerning the weight of the *modius* and the effectiveness of Charlemagne's reforms, see the discussion by Devroey, "Units of Measurement," 68-92. Devroey is undoubtedly correct in noting that Charlemagne's reforms in weights and measures were not rapidly assimilated, especially in some out of the way areas where his direct influence might not be felt. However, the topic under discussion here concerns markets and other operations under direct government control. Regarding Charlemagne's efforts in relation to food shortages and grain prices, see *CRF*, no. 28, chs. 4, 25; no. 46, ch. 18; and no. 44, ch.4.

[153] Verhulst, *The Carolingian Economy*, 124. See also the very important study by Devroey, "Units of Measurement," 68-92, regarding the overall complexity faced by modern scholars concerning the problems posed by the study of Carolingian weights and measures.

of a *solidus* for bread. A more well off or less parsimonious soldier, who might choose to eat the most expensive bread, which was baked from wheat, would be required to pay slightly more than two *solidi* to meet more than his caloric needs while serving for three months on expeditionary service.

Several observations are in order regarding the cost of food rations. First, it may be assumed that under normal conditions, a member of the Select Levy would have sufficient food to eat and clothing to wear while remaining at home. Second, if this member of the Select Levy were mobilized and chose to find the means to transport his food from home, he would be eating on campaign, essentially, what he would have been eating had he remained at home. He could transport the resources that he needed for the campaign without paying taxes or tolls.[154] If, however, the levy member chose to purchase his food while on campaign, the food that he normally would have eaten, if he had stayed at home, could be sold or bartered in the local market without having to pay a tax, because this was his "military food." This would help to defray the cost of his basic caloric needs while on campaign.[155] It can be assumed safely that it was not necessary for a member of the levy to purchase new weapons or new clothing each time that he was mobilized.

Government-controlled prices for flour and baked bread could be enforced rigorously on military campaigns where Charlemagne and/or his hand-picked officials from the central government were normally on the scene. Price gauging was unlikely during the course of military operations for the imperial period—there is a distinct lack of complaints regarding such matters registered in Charlemagne's military capitularies. The government was very sensitive to food shortages that could result in stressful conditions both in military and civilian contexts.[156] Thus, on occasion, it was permitted to allow a measured rise in prices to take place in order to reflect market conditions. These actions on prices combined with a threat by the government of severe punishments for price gauging may likely played a role in maintaining price stability and undermined

---

[154] *CRF*, no. 29, ch. 13.

[155] Regarding these local markets, see Verhulst, *The Carolingian Economy*, 97.

[156] See *CRF*, no. 21, ch. 4, no. 24, ch. 44; no. 28, ch. 4; no. 46, chs. 9, 18; no. 48, ch. 18.

efforts at market manipulation by private entrepreneurs.[157] Of course, if merchants concluded that they were not being appropriately remunerated for their grain, they could withhold it from the market. However, in the context of a time-limited military campaign, such a policy likely would result in serious opportunity costs, i.e. economic losses, for such merchants.

Although prices likely were stable, it is unlikely that even the poorest of the expeditionary levies survived on bread and water the entire three months while on campaign. Evidence suggests that the diet of men on campaign was somewhat more varied. For example, government-controlled "war carts" were under orders occasionally to carry flour, wine, and sides of bacon as well as an abundance of other types of food.[158] In addition, it seems likely that for some military operations, cattle on the hoof were incorporated into Carolingian marching columns.[159] Further, the consumption of beer and wine is mentioned in various sources, and some men, while on campaign, and contrary to government regulations regarding behavior while on the march, are known to have violated orders. Such men not only were found to be drunk but also to have gotten some of their fellow soldiers drunk. These men were punished in various ways according to the seriousness of their offenses.[160]

Most men while on campaign purchased "extras" that were available from a wide variety of sources including government stocks, which were hauled in the so-called "war wagons," mentioned above.[161] In order to avoid simply providing a minimum estimate for the cost of the food

[157] Verhulst, *The Carolingian Economy*, 123-25.

[158] *CRF*, no. 77, ch. 10, and, in addition, Charlemagne required that the war carts used on campaign by bishops, counts, abbots, and high royal officials were to carry a similar variety of food stuffs for the troops.

[159] *ARF, an.* 810, provides a contemporary report of a wide-spread outbreak of disease that killed off large numbers of cattle, and the author implies that these losses had a negative impact on military operations.

[160] See *CRF*, no. 50, ch. 6.

[161] Concerning what we have labeled "extras" that are known to have been available on campaign, see *CRF*. no. 48, ch. 3; no. 75; and no. 77, ch. 10. With regard to details concerning the provision of logistic support from the royal fisc, see Bachrach, "Are They Not Like Us?" 319-43; regarding supplies provided for military operations by an important monastic fisc, see Durliat, "La polyptyque d'Irminon pour l'Armée," 183-208. In regard to the early medieval diet, in general, see Pearson, "Nutrition and the Early-Medieval Diet," 1-32.

required by the members of the expeditionary levy, it may be suggested, at least for heuristic purposes, that the cost of these hypothetical "extras" might double the total expenses for the soldier who paid the minimum of approximately seven *denarii* for his bread. It is likely that the most important and perhaps the most expensive "extra" that might be purchased regularly as field rations was some sort of meat.[162]

A preference for beef may be seen not only in terms of its lesser cost per kilogram than other smaller domesticated animals, for example, sheep, goats, and pigs, but also in regard to the eating habits of the population in at least some parts of the *regnum Francorum*.[163] Meat of any kind was the best source of protein available at the time, and it would help to keep the soldier in good physical condition so that he might more

---

[162] Animals on the march are discussed by Bernard S. Bachrach, "The Crusader March" from Dorylaion to Herakleia," in *Shipping, Trade and Crusade in the Medieval Mediterranean: Studies in Honour of John Pryor*, ed. Ruthy Gertwagen and Elizabeth Jeffreys (Ashgate, UK: Farnham, 2012), 231-54.

[163] There was a clear preference for beef in the region that now comprises the Netherlands, as pointed out by Geard F. IJzereef, "The Animal Remains," in *Farm Life in a Carolingian Village: a Model Based on Botenical and Zoological Data from an Excavated Site*, ed. W, Groenman van Waateringe and L.H.van Wingaarden-Bakker (Assen, Netherlands: Van Gorcum, 1987), 39-51, at 48; as well as ibid., and Frits Laarman, "The Animal Remains for Deventer (8th-9th centuries)," *Berichten van de Rijksdienst voor het Oudheidkundig Bodmeonderzoek*, 36, (1986), 405-43, and 406-18, for cattle, in general, and 414, for recognition that small breeds of cattle are at issue. This preference for beef is also noted by J.P. Pals, "Observations on the Economy of the Settlement," in *Farm Life in a Carolingian Village: a Model Based on Botenical and Zoological Data from an Excavated Site]*, ed. W, Groenman van Waateringe and L.H.van Wingaarden-Bakker (Assen , Netherlands: Van Gorcum, 1987), 118-29, at 121-22. As the above studies have shown, of those who ate meat on a regular basis pork likely was more available, but far more research is needed on these matters.

It is surprising that in Italy, where a so-called Mediterranean type diet is often thought to have prevailed, the consumption of meat and especially of beef was very popular and this was especially the case with regard to the army. See Michael MacKinnon, *Production and Consmption of Animals in Roman Italy: Integrating the Zooarchaeological and Textual Evidence* (*JRA Supplementary Series* no. 54, 2004), 189-239. By contrast, according to I. Jzereef and Laarman, *loc. cit.*, 410, the percentage of beef in the diet of this region would seem to have declined into the later Middle Ages and the early modern period.

effectively endure the rigors of campaigning.[164] Of course, Charlemagne and his advisers had no scientific understanding regarding what modern researchers identify as protein, much less how it affected human physical and/or mental performance on military campaign. However, the Carolingian leadership, like their Roman predecessors, likely did have some ideas regarding the kinds and quantities of food that kept their fighting men in sufficiently good condition to carry out their duties as well as the kinds and quantities of field rations needed to sustain both high morale and effective performance.[165]

In trying to estimate the quantity and cost of these posited "extras," one notes that scholars have been able to identify prices for a lengthy list of goods, many of which concerned food, that are relevant to the Frankish kingdom at this time.[166] It is also important to note that there is a scholarly consensus that prices remained relatively stable throughout the

---

[164] In general, regarding diet, see Pearson, "Nutrition and the Early-Medieval Diet," 1-32. As noted above, an inference is to be drawn from *ARF, an.* 810, that a large scale loss of cattle due to an epidemic likely had a negative impact on campaigning.

[165] Regarding the Roman military diet, see R.W. Davies, "The Roman Military Diet," *Britannia*, 2 (1971): 122-42. Roman sources regarding diet and especially the preference for boiled meat were available to the Carolingian court. In this regard, see Apicius, *De re coquinaria* and Celsus, *De medicina*, which provides useful information regarding food for soldiers on campaign as noted by MacCinnon, *Production and Consumption*, 210, 226. Concerning the *mss.* see L. D. Reynolds, "Apicius," and M.D. Reeve, "Celsus," both in *Texts and Transmission; A Survey of the Latin Classics*, ed. L. D. Reynolds (Oxford: Oxford University Press, 1983), xxviii, 1-14, 251, and xxviii, xxx, 46-47, 353, respectively. Bernhard Bischoff, *Manuscripts and Libraries in the Age of Charlemagne*, trans. and edited Michael Gorman (Cambridge: Cambridge University Press, 1994), 143, 150 for Apicius, and cf. 151, regarding Celsus, who Bischoff believes never reached Charlemagne's court. In the context of Roman advice regarding diet it is noteworthy that boiled meat was favored for soldiers (MacCinnon, *loc. cit.*, 210) as Einhard (Éginhard, *Vie de Charlemagne*, ed. and trans. Louis Halphen [Paris: Socie'te' d'E'dition—Les Belles Lettres, 1947], ch. 22), points out, the doctors at Charlemagne's court prescribed boiled beef for the emperor's diet.

[166] See Benjamin Guérard (*Polyptyque de l'abbé Irminon: our Dénobrement des manses, des serfs et des reveue de l'abbayed de Saint-Germain-des-Prés sou le régne de Charlemagne, publié d'après le manuscrit de la Bibliothéque du roi, avec des prolégoménes pour servir à l'histoire de la condition des personnes et des terres depuis les invasions des barbares jusqu'à l'institution des communes* (Paris: Imprimerie royale, 1844), vol. I *Prolégoménes, commentaires et* éclaircissements, vol. II, *Polyptyque*), I, 140-55, for the list.

period.[167] Of course, the focus here is on prices that were in place during normal conditions rather than during food shortages and famines.[168] In addition, Charlemagne's kingdom-wide monetary reforms, which saw a rise in the weight of the silver *denarius* in 794, also had an effect on the denomination of prices established for goods and services. However, it is not difficult for modern scholars to make the necessary conversions when the situation is relevant in regard to pre- and post-reform prices.[169] Nevertheless, one may aver that under normal conditions a cow was valued at one *solidus*, that is, twelve *denarii*, as made clear in the late redactions of the Ripuarian law during this period.[170]

On the basis of archaeological evidence, a cow weighing about 265 kilograms could provide in the neighborhood of 120 kilograms of meat and meat products, including animal fat, for human consumption.[171]

---

[167] Regarding price stability in the *regnum Francorum*, see Renée Doehaerd, *The Early Middle Ages in the West: Economy and Society*, trans. W.G. Deakin (Amsterdam: Elsevier, 1978), 240-41. It is worthy of note, as well, that in the Byzantine empire from the sixth to the eleventh century, commodity prices remained stable under normal conditions. See Cécile Morrisson and Jean-Claude Cheynet, "Prices and Wages in the Byzantine World," in *The Economic History of Byzantium from the Seventh through the Fifteenth Century*, 3 vols., ed. Angeliki E. Laiou (Washington, DC: Dumbarton Oaks, 2002), I, 815-78, at 858.

[168] In regard to additional capitularies that concern food shortages, see *CRF*, no. 44, ch. 4, where the nature of Charlemagne's orders makes clear, by and large, that each situation was to be handled on an ad hoc basis and in a manner that obviously did not create institutionalized or long-term norms.

[169] See Phillip Grierson and M.A.S. Balckburn, *Medieval European Coinage, vol. I The Early Middle Ages (Fifth through Tenth Centuries)* (Cambridge: Cmabridge University Press, 1986); and Simon Coupland, "Charlemagne's Coinage: Ideology and Economy," in *Charlemagne Empire and Society*, ed. Johanna Story (Manchester: Manchester University Press, 2005), 211-39.

[170] *Lex Rip.*, ch. 40 (36), 11, sets the value of a "horned cow that is healthy and able to see" at one *solidus*. It is also noteworthy that in the Saxon region, which seems to have been poorer than the rest of the *regnum Francorum*, an ox that was about eighteen months old also was valued at one *solidus*, something made clear in *CRF*, no. 27, ch. 11. For additional information on prices, see Guérard (*Polyptyque de l'abbé Irminon*, I, 141-42, regarding cows and 145, 147, regarding pigs, and 147, for sheep.

[171] For the weight of cows, in general, and regarding the weight of its edible parts after slaughter in the northern region of the Carolingian *regnum*, see Pals, "Observations on the Economy," 120; and Pearson, "Nutrition and the Early Medieval Diet," 16, who follows Pals. Cf. Roth, *The Logistics of the Roman Army*, 29, who suggests that the edible parts of a bovine is at about 50% to 60% of its total weight

These estimates seem to include bone marrow and the use of the animal's bones as well as muscles and tendons in various types of stew.[172] In order not to seem to exaggerate the size of bovines in the Carolingian *regnum*, we are using the 120 kilogram figure for the edible substance of an "average" cow.[173] Average weights for many bovines raised in the *regnum Francorum*, as a whole, likely were greater.[174]

From a logistic perspective, it should be emphasized that after slaughter, meat from cattle as well as from sheep, goats, and pigs did not have to be eaten immediately but could be preserved by processes such as salting, drying, and smoking. As a result, preserved meat could be taken on the

or somewhat greater than that calculated for cattle in the Carolingian Netherlands, as above.

[172] Concerning the cooking of bone, see John Pearce and Rosemary Luff, "The Taphonomy of Cooked Bone," in *Whither Environmental Archaeology*, ed. Rosemary Luff and Peter Rowley-Conway (Oxford: Oxford University Press, 1994), 51-56; and more broadly, Raymond Edwin Chaplin, *The Study of Animal Bones from Archaeological Sites* (London: Seminar Press, 1971). Useful background is provided by Nanna Noe-Nygaard, "Butchering and Marrow Fracturing as a Taphonomic Factor in Archaeological Deposits," *Paleobiology*, 3 (1977): 218-37; and also Pals, "Observations on the Economy of the Settlement," 121-22.

[173] It should be noted that this information has been developed on the basis of evidence excavated at the Carolingian village of Kootwijk north of the Rhine, which the excavators have recognized was a rather poor environment for the raising of large and fat cattle. See W. Groenman van Waateringe and L.H.van Wingaarden-Bakker, "Introduction: Reflections of a Farmer in the Early Tenth Century," in *Farm Life in a Carolingian Village: a Model Based on Botanical and Zoological Data from an Excavated Site*, ed. W. Groenman van Waateringe and L.H.van Wingaarden-Bakker (Assen: Van Gorcum, 1987), 1-5, at 2, discuss the poor environment at Kootwijk for raising cattle.

[174] For comparative information concerning Anglo-Saxon Britain, see Peter Arundel Jewell, "Changes in Size and Type of Cattle from Prehistoric to Medieval Times in Britain *Zeitschrift für Tierzüchtung und Züchtungsbiologie*, 77 (1962): 159-67; and the more broadly based study of Barbara A. Noddle, "Determination of the body weight of cattle from bone measurements," in *Domestikations-forschung und Geschichte der Haustiere*, ed. J. Matolcsi (Budapest: Akade'miai Kiado', 1973), 377-89. See also for comparison, MacKinnon, *Production and Consumption*, 189-90, and 227 for Appendix 12, which provides data for the early empire in Italy. MacKinnon puts the average weight of a cow at about 400 kilograms and the edible parts at approximately 200 kilograms. This latter figure is more than 60% greater than the Carolingian average as estimated in regard to cows raised in the Netherlands. However, during the later Roman Empire (*loc. cit.* 215) the weight of cattle seems to decline, while the weight of pigs is seen to increase.

march for a rather lengthy period of time and distributed during a campaign in small allotments.[175] When one of these processes of preserving meat was employed, the difficulty of maintaining the weight and health of herded animals was avoided.[176] Fish, of course, also could be preserved for use as field rations.[177]

It is evident that some ten kilograms of beef product could thus be purchased for a single *denarius*. For an expenditure of four *denarii*, a soldier could purchase forty kilograms of beef. Such a purchase meant that for each day while on campaign, even the least well-off member of an expeditionary levy could obtain approximately 440 grams of beef or about one pound per day for a period of ninety days, which was approximately the period for which he was required to provide for his own field rations.

Adding meat to his diet, a soldier could reduce his bread ration, discussed above, by perhaps as much as thirty or thirty-five percent. As a result, he would have available additional funds with which to purchase other extras, such as beer and wine.[178] For comparative purposes, it is worth mentioning that poorer members of Charlemagne's Select Levy, that is, *liberi homines* who possessed only a single *mansus* were in a position to enjoy field rations, especially in regard to the quantity of meat that they could afford, superior to those available to the forces of Tsar Nicholas II of Russia in around 1900.[179]

---

[175] Regarding techniques for preserving of meat, see Pearson, "Nutrition and the Early-Medieval Diet," 8, with the scholarly works cited there; as well as MacCinnon, *Production and Consumption*, 172.

[176] It is well established that under normal conditions during military campaigns, cattle on the hoof lose weight. At a rate of approximately thirty kilometers per day, the normal pace for a marching column and about ten kilometers per day longer than is necessary to give the cattle sufficient time to graze, there is no doubt that there will be weight loss. See J. Frank Dobie, *Up From Texas* (New York: Random House, 1955), 62 and 64.

[177] Regarding techniques for preserving fish, see Pearson, "Nutrition and the Early-Medieval Diet," 9; and MacCinnon, *Production and Consumption*, 172.

[178] For other "extras" see the prices noted by Guérard, *Polyptyque de l'abbé Irminon*, I, 146.

[179] See Peter Sauer, "Shchi and Borscht, 1900," in *The Joy of Field Rations*, (June 12th, 2012): http://joyoffieldrations.blogspot.com/2012/07/shchi-and-borscht-1900. html. The information documented here by Sauer regarding the field rations of

The "Assessment Manse" and the Wealth of the *Liberi Homines*

The *mansus* was the established unit of assessment through which the wealth of those who owned land was calculated by officials of the central government for the purpose of determining the type of military service that was owed. This process of assessment may have been inaugurated as early as the later Roman Empire when the bipartite form of estate organization, which was composed of a *mansus indominicatum* and dependent *mansi*, began gradually to replace the traditional *latafundium* in Gaul.[180] The system of assessment on the basis of the *mansus* was adopted gradually by the Merovingians. During this same period, traditional taxes on land paid in money, which had dominated during the later Roman Empire, were phased out slowly and replaced by various types of service to the government and most especially military service owed by land-owners. This manse-based system of assessment was continued by the Carolingians.[181] It may have been the case that this system of agricultural organization and taxation for military purposes served as a stimulus for Charlemagne's government to impose the bipartite model of estate organization in order to make more uniform the assessment process throughout Carolingian lands.[182]

It is important to recognize that the term *mansus*, as used in various parts of the *regnum Francorum*, is widely recognized by scholars to have had a great many meanings.[183] However, the type of *mansus* under

---

Nicholas II's army is consistent with stories told by my grandfather, Nathan Greenblatt, who served in the Tsar's infantry forces at this time.

[180] Regarding the development of the bipartite estate and its introduction into Gaul, see Peter Saris, "The Origins of the Manorial Economy: New Insights from Late Antiquity," *English Historical Review*, 119 (2004): 280-311.

[181] Goffart, *Frankish Military Duty*, 166-90.

[182] Concerning Charlemagne's efforts to impose the bipartite system in Bavaria and parts of Provence, see Christoph Sonnlechner, "The Establishment of New Units of Production in Carolingian Times: Making Early Medieval Sources Relevant for Environmental History," *Viator*, 35 (2004): 21-48.

[183] Regarding the wide semantic field involved in studying the manse, see F.L. Ganshof, *Feudalism*, trans. Philip Grierson 3rd English. ed., (New York: Harper , 1964), 37; Jean Durliat, "Le manse dans le polyptyque d'Irminon. Nouvel essai d'histoire quantitative," *La Neustria: Les pays au nord de la Loire de 650 à 850*, 2 vols., ed. Hartmut Atsma (Sigmaringen: Thorbecke, 1989) I, 467-504; and more briefly in idem, *Les finances publiques de Diocletien aux Carolingiens (284-889)* (Sigmaringen:

consideration here may perhaps have differed from many if not most *mansi* in regard to how they were understood by contemporaries and most importantly by Charlemagne and his officials.[184] Therefore, it will be useful here to differentiate this particular type of manse from other *mansi* by using the label "assessment *mansus*." Perhaps it goes without saying that each "assessment *mansus*" throughout the *regnum Francorum* had to be of approximately the same generally agreed upon value as all other *mansi* placed in this same category. This would enable those Carolingian administrators, who were charged with making assessments in regard to how much military service was owed, to determine his assessment on the basis of the same criteria.[185]

It is clear that the central government, and likely most others who dealt with *mansi*, recognized that throughout the Frankish kingdom all land of the same surface area was not of the same value or quality. Therefore, the term *mansus*, as used for assessment purposes, had to have been applied to lands of varying size.[186] Some *mansi* are known to have been as small as twelve *banuaria* or about fifteen hectares, while other *mansi* were as large as thirty-six *banuaria* or about forty-five hectares.[187] An "assessment *mansus*" was regarded as being capable of supporting a family from which a sufficient surplus was available so that one member of the family could serve personally when it was his turn for undertake

---

Thorebecke, 1990), 196-203. See as well, the perceptive observations of Walter Goffart, "From Roman Taxation to Medieval Seigneurie: Three Notes: 1. The Iugum in Ostrogothic Italy; 2. The Ambulatory Hide; 3. Flodoard and the Frankish Polyptych," *Speculum*, 47 (1972): 165-87, 373-94; reprinted in idem, *Rome's Fall and After* (London: Hambledon Press, 1989), 167-211; and Adriaan Verhulst, "Economic Organisation," *The New Cambridge Medieval History: c. 700-c. 900*, II, ed. Rosamond McKitterick (Cambridge: Cambridge University Press, 1995) 481-509, 978-84.

[184] Goffart, "Frankish Military Duty," 167-90.

[185] Goffart, "Frankish Military Duty," 170-72.

[186] Ibid.

[187] There is a controversial scholarly literature regarding the surface area of a *banuarium* and, therefore, of *mansi* measured in *banuaria*. For the sake of simplifying matters, I have used some of the measures provided by the polyptch of the monastery of Saint Bertin as discussed by Renaud, "La politique militaire de Charlemagne," 25, who seems to follow F. L. Ganshof, "Manorial Organization in the Low Countries in the Seventh, Eighth, and Ninth Centuries," *Transactions of the Royal Historical Society*, 4th ser., 31 (1949): 29-59, at 40. For a brief review of the literature concerning the size of a *banuarium*, see Pearson, "Nutrition and the Early-Medieval Diet," 20, n. 175.

expeditionary service or was able to provide support for a replacement.

I suggest that this characterization of an "assessment *mansus*" was used by the Carolingians and by the Merovingians, in part, because this approach has an analogue with regard to the Anglo-Saxon hide. In the early eighth century, Bede (d. 735) described the hide as "*terra unius famil-iae*," which he qualifies with the phrase "according to the way in which the Angles estimate" ("*iuxta aestimationem Anglorum*").[188] The way in which the "Angles" made their assessments of a hide is not explained by Bede. However, it is clear that the hide in Anglo-Saxon England early in the eighth century, as understood by Bede, did have a common value with other property designated as a hide.[189] This approach appears similar to the Carolingian "assessment *mansus*," which did not have a fixed size, but, like the hide, had a fixed value for assessment purposes. Through the late Roman period, all lands were subject to a land tax among other exactions and these payments were taken from the surpluses, that is, resources that were above what was necessary to feed, clothe, and oth-erwise maintain the landowner, his family, his slaves, and his animals. The elimination of this land tax meant that the surplus production of these lands, by and large, remained in the hands of the landowner.[190] The

---

[188] *Bede's Ecclesiastical History of the English People*, ed. Bertram Colgrave and R. A. B, Mynors (Oxford: Oxford University Press, 1967), bk. ii. ch. 9, bk. iii. chs. 4, 24, bk. and bk. iv, ch. 21, provides the main references. Frederic William Maitland, *Domesday Book and Beyond* (Cambridge: Cambridge University Press, 1897), 357-520, provides an excellent introduction to the problems involved in studying the hide, and for further references to Bede and the hide see 508-15. See also, Goffart, "From Roman Taxation to Medieval Seigneurie," 168. In mid-nineteenth century United States, a farm of forty acres along with a mule was thought satisfactory for the support of a family. This is about the same size as a manse of twelve *banuaria*.

Numerous scholars have elaborated hypotheses regarding the meaning of the term *manse* as the farm or homestead of a single family. See Marc Bloch, *Les carac-teres originaux de l'histoire rural français*, 2nd ed., 2 vols., by R. Dauvergne (Lon-don and Paris: Routledge, 1961-1962), I, 155-66; and Georges Duby, *Rural Economy and Country Life in the Medieval West*, trans. C. Postan (Philadelphia: University of Pennsylvania Press, 1962), 28-33. None, however, as pointed out by Goffart, "Frank-ish Military Duty," 171, n. 15, has done so as a "unit of valuation" aimed at assessing military service.

[189] See J.M. Wallace-Hadrill, *Bede's Ecclesiastical History of the English People: A Historical Commentary* (Oxford: Oxford University Press, 1988), 33.

[190] The fate of the Roman tax system in the Frankish Empire is a highly contro-versial topic. Regarding the argument for extensive continuity, see Jean Durliat, *Les*

governments of the Carolingians and the Merovingians accessed these surpluses by requiring military service in place of the land tax. In economic terms, the Frankish system had a positive result for the landowner because he was not usually required to do expeditionary military service every year, whereas under the Roman system land taxes accrued on an annual basis. In addition, the marginal cost of military service was less than paying land taxes, because all of the taxes went to someone else. The only "loss" that was suffered by the landowner in this post-Roman system was his time, as it was still necessary for him to eat and clothe himself whether or not he was on campaign.

Carolingian Government Bureaucracy

The considerable administrative effort undertaken by the Carolingian government that was entailed in the process of identifying and registering "assessment *mansi*" can be better understood if seen within the framework of the highly sophisticated and complex bureaucratic assets commanded by Charlemagne. These bureaucratic assets were firmly based on the "written word," both at the level of the central government and at the local level.[191] The vast apparatus of Carolingian governmental administration is evidenced in many sources. These include inventories of the royal fisc, inventories of *beneficia* held from the king both in terms of lands of the royal fisc and in regard to *precariae pro verbo regis*, and inventories of all lands in the possession of churches and monasteries as well as of the possessions of laymen. These governmental efforts were supported by the administrative capacity of the great ecclesiastical

----

finances publiques de Dioclétien aux Carolingiens (284-889) [with a preface by K.F. Werner] (Sigmaringen: Thorbecke, 1990); and Elisabeth Magnou-Nortier, *Aux origines de la fiscalité moderne: La système fiscal et sa gestion dans la royaume des Francs à l'épreuve des sources (Ve-XI siècles* (Geneva: Droz, 2012). Although somewhat tendentious, several good critical points are made by Chris Wickham, "La chute de Rome n'aura pas lieu," *Le moyen âge*, 99 (1993): 107-26. However, I find that Goffart, as illustrated in "Frankish Military Duty," 166-90, strikes a more helpful balance.

[191] See Rosamund McKitterick, *The Carolingians and the Written Word* (Cambridge: Cambridge University Press, 1989); and Janet Nelson, "Literacy in Carolingian Government," *The Uses of Literacy in Early Medieval Europe*, ed. Rosamond McKitterick (Cambridge: Cambridge University Press, 1990), 258-96.

landowners and also by lay land-owners, who produced polyptychs that were available to the royal government.[192]

A good example of the broadly based and detailed nature of Charlemagne's government records, both those maintained locally and those available both indirectly and directly to the central government, is provided by the apparatus that was employed to maintain information regarding those who were required to take the oath of faithfulness to Charlemagne. From a variety of documents, it is evident that every male twelve years of age and older of the entire population of the *regnum Francorum*, the *"cunctas generalis populi,"* which also included both *coloni* and *servi* as well as free men, were required by an *antiqua consuetudo* to be listed in local records. These lists of potential oath-takers had to have resulted from some type of "census" that each count was required to compile and to keep current for the *pagus* that he administered. Each registered male was required to take an oath of faithfulness to Charlemagne. After the oath was taken, it was listed on a register of some sort along with whatever particulars that were needed to assure the ability of the government to know his identity. Copies of the lists of those who took the oath were provided to Charlemagne's *missi dominici* for transmission to, and use by, the royal court.[193]

---

[192] Of the numerous items noted here, see Bachrach, "Are They Not Like Us?" 319-43, regarding information concerning the lands of the royal fisc, as the administration of these assets generated vast quantities of "paper work" at the local level, which, in turn, was made available to the central administration on a regular basis. In addition, the government also possessed masses of data concerning both the holdings of ecclesiastical institutions and of laymen. These data were a *sine qua non* for the *divisiones* of the Frankish kingdom perhaps as early as 742, but surely by 768 and 806. See F.L. Ganshof, "Zur Entstehungsgeschichte und Bedeutung des Vertrages von Verdun (843)," *Deutsches Archiv für Erforschung des Mittelalters*, 12 (1956): 313-30, and translated as "The genesis and significance of the Treaty of Verdun (843)," by Janet Sondheimer in *The Carolingians and the Frankish Monarchy: Studies in Carolingian History* (London: Longman, 1971), 289-302.

[193] Despite the lacunose nature of Charlemagne's surviving capitularies, these documents, among others, provide substantial information regarding the vast quantities of information available at the local level to the count of the *pagus* and both directly and indirectly to the central government. For the relevant administrative "paper work," see *CRF*, no. 23, ch. 18; no. 25, chs. 1, 2, 6; no. 33, ch. 2; no. 34, ch. 19; no. 46, ch. 2; and no. 80, ch. 13.

Interpretation of the historical significance of the oaths of faithfulness ordered by Charlemagne, as contrasted to the obvious administrative structures and

Surplus Income and Preliminary Conclusions

Although few of the time-conditioned administrative records have survived, there is some evidence that casts light on what may be the surplus production that enabled *liberi homines* to undertake expeditionary
military service. In a capitulary issued by Charlemagne at Aachen in 807,
the relevant royal officials took the position that a *liber homo* dwelling
between the Seine and the Loire who owned both slaves and an allodial
property identified as an assessment *mansus* was to be understood to
have had surplus income from his allod of at least two *solidi*. The *liber
homo* could be required to pay these two *solidi* as a tax to support a man
who was identified as capable of serving in an expeditionary levy.[194]
These assessments, however, were made only in the wake of a serious
famine (*"Memoratorium qualiter ordinavimus propter famis inopiam"*)
and cannot be considered to have been either normal surpluses or normal assessments.[195]

What may be considered the minimum surplus income—identified above, for the *liber homo* who owned slaves and a single *mansus* in
allodial tenure under the very stressful economic conditions caused by
a famine—was put at twenty-four *denarii*. Therefore, a man who was
mobilized for service in an expeditionary levy and owned a single *mansus* easily could support himself on campaign for three months if he ate
the cheapest bread at a cost of about seven *denarii* for three months and
significantly increased his expenses by spending another four *denarii*
on "extras," for example, a daily ration of beef. Indeed, with at least two

---

"paperwork" that had to be in place in order to execute the royal orders to have
the oaths taken and registered, is an exceptionally controversial matter. On this,
see F. L. Ganshof, "Charlemagne et le serment," in *Mélanges d'histoire du Moyen
Age dédiés à la mémoire de Louis Halphen* (Paris: Presses UIniversitaires de France,
1951), 259-70, and reprinted as "Charlemagne's Use of the Oath," in *The Carolingians
and the Frankish Monarchy: Studies in Carolingian History*, trans. Janet Sondheimer
(London: Longman, 1971), 111-24; and Matthias Becher, *Eid und Herrschaft: Untersuchungen zum Herrscherethos Karls des Grossen* (Sigmaringen: Thorebecke, 1993).

[194] *CRF*, no. 48, ch. 2. Reference also is made in this capitulary to a "half-manse"
(*dimidium mansus*) owned as an allod by a *liber homo*, who also owned slaves. This
man was judged by the government to have available surplus income of at least one
solidus, i.e. twelve *denarii*. The matter of a part of a *mansus* owned by a *liber homo*
raises several complicated questions, which I hope to address in the future.

[195] *CRF*, no. 48. ch. 2.

solidi or twenty-four *denarii* in surplus income dedicated to his military service, one of these *liberi homines* could spend considerably more than a *solidus* for his field rations while on campaign.

It is obvious from the capitulary, which was issued regarding a mobilization in the wake of the famine of 806, that the counts of the *pagi* possessed a detailed record of the allods owned by *liberi homines* who dwelled in the region between the Seine and the Loire. In addition, this same capitulary makes clear that these counts also had records regarding *liberi homines* who were regarded as being "poor" because they owned neither allods nor slaves. Nevertheless, according to these same records, it is evident that at least some of these relatively "poor" men were known to have had available a sufficient surplus in moveable wealth that amounted to at least five *solidi*. As a result, under difficult conditions, the government ordered six such men to be grouped together, necessarily under the direction of a local official, so that each man could contribute a *solidus* and make it possible for one of their number to go on campaign.[196] While the capitulary does not specify the sources of wealth possessed by these men, one likely possibility is payment for service as craftsmen of which there were a large and growing number in Charlemagne's empire.[197]

The surpluses available to *liberi homines*, who owned an allod and possessed slaves, as estimated on the basis of the tax imposed in 807, is very likely to be an underestimate of the average total surplus income that they actually earned on a yearly basis under normal conditions. This observation would seem to be confirmed by a comparison with the surpluses available from tributary *mansi*, as contrasted to those manses possessed in allodial tenure by the *liberi homines*. An examination of the polyptych of Saint Germain des Prés, which was drawn up about a decade or so after Charlemagne's death but provides no reason to believe that the monastery's agricultural organization had been altered in this brief period, indicates that the dependents living on its lands performed

---

[196] *CRF*, no. 48, ch. 2. The matter of *liberi homines* who have neither allodial lands nor slaves is a subject that I hope to discuss in a future study. In the present context, it seems that the man who went on campaign as the representative of this group of landless *liberi homines* had the opportunity to earn a profit of perhaps as many as five *solidi* from this service. This profit included four of the five *solidi* contributed by his partners and a fifth *solidus* of his own that he did not have to contribute to sustain himself on campaign.

[197] Verhulst, *The Carolingian Economy*, 72-84.

labor services for Saint Germain and that they also paid dues or rents both in kind and in cash to the monastery. Under normal conditions, these payments, on average, amounted to more than two *solidi* per *mansus*. In light of these "rents," it is noteworthy that more than half of the moveable resources collected by the monastery from these dependents was paid to the central government to support its military operations.[198]

Of particular interest, in the present context, is the fact that those dependents of the monastery of St. Germain, who held *mansi ingenui*, were required to pay, on average, approximately one and one-half *solidi* each year for support of military operations, i.e. *ad hostem*. The exaction of payment was done through a well-established process that was called *hostilitium*.[199] Moreover, in addition to paying cash for the support of the army, Saint Germain's dependents also paid as *hostilitium* various numbers of horses, oxen, cows, sheep, and pigs. These, in turn, like the cash payments, were provided for the support of military forces on campaign.[200] In short, the dependent manse holders of Saint Germain, who were of lower status and less affluent than the *liberi homines*, who have been the subject of this study, paid various rents and dues that exceeded the cost for expeditionary military service incurred by a *liber homo* owning a single *mansus* and slaves.

Various of the specific mobilization arrangements that the *Magistratus* recommended to Charlemagne for a particular campaign subsequently are known to have found their way into capitularies that have survived. It is clear that few of Charlemagne's military capitularies were intended to create institutional structures or long-term requirements and this was especially the case in regard to the *liberi homines*. By contrast, there is every reason to believe that the *antiqua consuetudo*, which established

---

[198] The basic study here is Durliat, "La polyptyque d'Irminon pour l'Armée," 183-208.

[199] See *Das Polyptychon von Saint-Germain-des-Prés*, ed. Dieter Hägermann (Köln: Bohlau, 1993), 269; and for further discussion, see Durliat, "La polyptyque d'Irminon pour l'Armée," 183-208.

[200] Ibid. It is noteworthy. as an examination of the polyptych of Saint Germain incicates (*Das Polyptychon von Saint-Germain-des-Prés*, ed. Dieter Hägermann, see 270-71) that only some possessors of *mansi ingenui* belonging to the monastery were themselves *ingenui*. For example, *coloni* also are seen to possess such manses. From a negative perspective, it is important that no *liberi homines* possessing *mansi liberi* are to be found among the dependents of Saint Germain in this polyptych.

the quantity of field rations that each member of a levy was required to have available for service *in expeditione*, set the base or minimum as a selection mechanism. This ancient custom remained the selection mechanism for expeditionary forces of limited means, who obviously served as foot soldiers, and it remained constant from Merovingian times through Charlemagne's imperial years. In addition, there is no evidence to suggest that the absolute number of *liberi homines* owning allods and slaves, who were able to pay for their field rations without suffering economic privation, had declined during the early Carolingian period through the end of Charlemagne's reign. Expeditionary levies were maintained well into the tenth century and beyond. It is clear that when Charlemagne received intelligence that abuses were taking place that might threaten to impoverish some small landowners who owed expeditionary military service, as seen above, he cracked down vigorously on the malefactors and saw to it that those men who had been abused had their resources restored.

Further, the analysis here has shown definitively that there is no basis for asserting that some sort of monumental though undocumented crisis forced Charlemagne, after becoming emperor, to alter Carolingian military organization or, for that matter, to change radically his traditional long-term offensive strategy, which is chronicled in the narrative sources and supported by the surviving capitularies of the post-800 period. It is methodologically unsound to retroject information from the greatly troubled reigns of Louis the Pious and of his sons or from even later periods as evidence for what occurred during Charlemagne's imperial years. Charlemagne continued to pursue an offensive military strategy aimed at expanding both the territorial extent and the influence of the empire after becoming emperor in 800. It is clear from my analysis that the humbler members of the *liberi homines* of the Select Levy remained an integral element in the Carolingian army throughout Charlemagne's reign. From a purely military perspective, this was the case, in part, to sustain Charlemagne's adherence to the doctrine of overwhelming force when facing enemies in the field and also, in part, because he saw that it was necessary to sustain effective siege operations with large numbers of foot soldiers.

DISORDER AND LAWLESSNESS IN FIFTEENTH-CENTURY ENGLAND: A CORNISH CASE STUDY[*]

David M. Yorath
University of Bristol

THE LINK BETWEEN the armigerous class and the disordered state of law enforcement in the provinces has long been a theme in the historiography of late medieval England. Although qualified by Christine Carpenter and K. B. McFarlane in the middle of the twentieth century, and, more recently, by scholars such as Jonathan Mackman and Phillipa Maddern, the perception of the fifteenth century as being endemically lawless remains a commonplace.[1] One reason for this perceived state of

[*] I am indebted to Ms. Angela Broome for her assistance in identifying relevant material.

[1] K. B. McFarlane: "Bastard Feudalism," *Bulletin of the Institute of Historical Research*, 20 (1945): 161-80; idem, "The English Nobility in the Later Middle Ages," *12 Congres Internationale des Sciences Historiques, 1: Rapports: Grand Themes,* (1965), 337-45; idem, *The English Nobility of Later Medieval England,* (Oxford: Oxford University Press, 1973); Christine Carpenter, "Political Society in Warwickshire, c. 1401-72" (PhD Thesis, University of Cambridge, 1976), 25-32; idem, *Locality and Polity: A Study of Warwickshire Landed Society 1401-1499.* (Cambridge: Cambridge University Press, 1992). For those that perpetuate the commonplace, see E. Acheson, *A Gentry Community: Leicestershire in the Fifteenth Century, ca. 1422-ca. 1485* (Cambridge: Cambridge University Press, 1992); John Chynoweth, "The Gentry of

affairs has been sought from the failure of central government to enforce law and order and address the burgeoning politicization of the realm's greater subjects—a line of thought, first pronounced, by the contemporary political theorist, Sir John Fortescue, in his "A Learned Commendation of the Politique Lawes of Englande."[2] Other scholars, meanwhile, have pointed to the failings of "under-mighty kings," such as Henry VI, as a primary cause for the decline in royal authority. They argue that the failings of successive monarchs stimulated "the development of partial government. . . and [consequently] set the scene for civil strife."[3]

Whatever the truth, this debate on the circumstances of rebellion and disorder has been liberating, and it has freed the period from an aridity that arose from overemphasis on institutions. It has also refocused attention where it belongs: on the interplay of the small number of people in whose hands political power and authority lay. Consequently, the study of the magnate classes and their position in the mechanics of local government has increased in recent years. Frequent themes in these new works include the nature of political interest and the extent of unity within the county community. They also address what are now common questions such as: How much control did the aristocracy and

---

Tudor Cornwall" (PhD Thesis, University of Exeter, 1994), 113-41; M. Cherry, "The Struggle for Power in Mid-Fifteenth Century Devonshire," in *Patronage, the Crown and the Provinces in Later Medieval England*, ed. R. A. Griffiths (Gloucester: Sutton, 1981); C. W. Collins, *The Wars of the Roses* (Oxford: John and Henry Parker, 1864); C. Given-Wilson, *The English Nobility in the Middle Ages* (London: Routledge, 1987); H. Kleineke, "Poachers and Gamekeepers: Four Fifteenth Century West Country Criminals," in *Outlaws in Medieval and Early Modern England: Crime, Government and Society, ca. 1066-ca. 1600*, ed. J. C. Appleby and P. Dalton (Farnham: Ashgate, 2009), 129-48; P. Maddern, *Violence & Social Order: East Anglia 1422-1442* (Oxford: Clarendon Press, 1992); R. H. Tawney, "The Rise of the Gentry," *Economic History Review*, 11 (1941): 1-13; and C. J. Tyldesley, "The Crown and the Local Communities in Devon and Cornwall from 1377 to 1422" (PhD Thesis, University of Exeter, 1978), 14-32.

[2]   S. Lockwood, ed., *Sir John Fortescue: On the Laws and Governance of England* (Oxford, 1997). Works that emerged shortly after McFarlane include L. Stone, "The English Aristocracy – A Restatement," *Economic History Review* 4 (1954): 91-97; J. H. Hexter, *Reappraisals in History* (London: Longmans, 1961), 117-52; and J. R. Lander, *Crown and Nobility, 1450-1509* (London: Edward Arnold, 1976).

[3]   R. Stansfield, *Political Elites in South West England, 1450-1500* (New York: Edwin Mellen Press, 2009), 189.

gentry actually have? How did the situation change during the century? And could these persons be characterised as "great rulers"?[4]

It is clear, and fair to say, that standards of government varied from area to area and depended, largely, on the authority and integrity of local officials—especially in regions where the central law courts were not the preferred medium of redress—and it was therefore not uncommon, in areas where capable officers were not numerous, for noble and gentry landowners to fill this vacuum. Cases where this was the norm, rather than the exception, at this time were in areas far removed from the seat of royal authority, and in areas where the enforcement of law was absolutely dependent on the power of local men. One such place was Cornwall, a shire at the south western most tip of the kingdom, where an absence of resident magnates had forced successive monarchs to devolve law making and enforcement powers to individuals who were sometimes the biggest criminals of the area.[5]

An exemplar, in this case, is Sir Henry Bodrugan of Gorran (ca. 1426–ca. 1503). He is an individual frequently cited by historians of the period. And, indeed, his career is curious, for, although he was heir-general to one of the largest estates in the county, the lengthy list of offences he is said to have committed, together with the high-handed methods in which he executed his will, have seen him become a byword for disorder and the peculiarly disturbed nature of the period.[6] A. L. Rowse,

---

[4]   J. Chynoweth, *Tudor Cornwall* (Stroud: Tempus Publishing, 2002); Stansfield, *Political Elites in South West England, 1450-1500* and M. Stoyle, "The Dissidence of Despair: Rebellion and Identity in Early Modern Cornwall," *The Journal of British Studies*, 38 (1999): 423-44. For gentry studies, see Alison James, "'To Knowe a Gentilman': Men and Gentry Culture in Fifteenth Century Yorkshire" (PhD Thesis, University of York, 2009), 77-121; P. Fleming, "Politics," in *Gentry Culture in Late Medieval England* (Manchester: Manchester University Press, 2005), ed. R. Radulescu and A. Truelove, 50-51; Robert Charles Kinsey, "Legal Service, Careerism and Social Advancement in Late Medieval England: The Thorpes of Northamptonshire, c.1200-1391" (PhD Thesis, University of York, 2009), 137-51.

[5]   John Colshull and John Herle, who held main offices in the county in the late fourteenth century, both used their positions to prosecute rivalries and secure advantages. C[ornwall] R[ecord] O[ffice] ME/716; T[he] N[ational] A[rchives] C 1/7/323. For Borlase's notes, see W. Borlase, *The Antiquities of Cornwall* (London: W. Bowyer and J. Nichols, 1769).

[6]   I. Arthurson, "A Question of Loyalty," *The Ricardian*, 7 (1987): 401-10; *The Parochial History of Cornwall*, vol. II, ed. D. Gilbert, (London: Nichols and Son,

in his excellent biography, suggests that this instability, and Bodrugan's frequent descent into petty lawlessness, stemmed from a long, frustrated minority and his exposure, as a teenager, to the wider, national struggles for supremacy.[7] He was a charge of Thomas Courtenay, Earl of Devon, between 1441 and 1447, and he would therefore have been conscious of the long-running feud between his master and William, Lord Bonville.[8] He also sat regularly on commissions in the south west,[9] and it was probably through this work that he established liaisons with Joan Beaumont, the estranged wife of William Beaumont of Shirwell.[10] In 1450, the two appear to have struck up a relationship, and a year later, Joan gave birth to a son, "John," at her manor of Youlston, in north Devon.[11] Although Bodrugan was known locally as the child's father —since William did not return to the area before his death, in 1453[12] —the boy took the name "Beaumont" to avoid scandal. And it is with the career of this particular individual, and the role that he played in local government, that this article is interested.

John Beaumont, sometimes referred to as John Bodrugan or John Beamond, was the only surviving child of Henry and Joan. Born in 1451, details of his youth are disappointingly scant, save that he spent the first

---

1838), 106-107; Kleineke, "Poachers and Gamekeepers," 129-48; P. Maddern, "Bodrugan [Trenowith], Sir Henry (c.1426-1487/1503)," in *Oxford Dictionary of National Biography*, vol. VI, 415-16.

[7]   Julian Cornwall, too, writes that the region's remoteness inhibited the emergence of independent, freethinking landholders. See J. Cornwall, *Revolt of the Peasantry 1549* (London: Routledge, 1977). A. L. Rowse, "The Turbulent Career of Sir Henry de Bodrugan," *History*, 29 (1944): 17-26; J. Whetter, *A Study of a Cornish Medieval Knightly Family* (Gorran: Lyfrow Trelyspen, 1995), 135-37. For details of the complaints lodged against Bodrugan, see TNA KB 27/852, m. 35; TNA C 1/37/47; TNA C 4/5/106; and TNA C 4/3/37.

[8]   For details of the Bonville-Courtenay dispute, see R. L. Storey, *The End of the House of Lancaster* (Gloucester: Sutton, 1986), 84-92.

[9]   C[alendar of]P[atent]R[olls], 1452-1461, 609; CPR, 1461-1467, 28.

[10]   Joan was the daughter of William Courtenay, a cousin of Philip Courtenay of Powderham. *Visitation Devon 1564*, ed. F. C. Colby (Exeter: W. Pollard, 1881), 16.

[11]   W. Hals, *The Complete History of Cornwall* (Truro, 1750), 151.

[12]   J. Maclean, *The Parochial and Family History of the Deanery of Trigg Minor, in the County of Cornwall* (London: Nichols and Son, 1873), 532.

three years of his life at his mother's residence before relocating to Bodrugan, near Gorran Haven in Cornwall, upon his parent's marriage, in February 1454.[13] As a bastard, it is unlikely he received a formal education;
he, instead, probably spent much of his youth participating in various
country pursuits, such as hawking and hunting, entertaining guests, and
accompanying his father on errands around the county.[14] A change in
his circumstances would have occurred, however, when his mother died
of 'sweating sickness."[15] This would have constituted an enormous blow,
not just emotionally, for, although he had the support of his father, he
was not his legal heir—a fact that doubtless colored their relationship.
Not long after, perhaps in an attempt to remedy this legal problem for
John and to alleviate his own debts,[16] Henry Bodrugan attempted to have
John accepted as heir to his "father," William Beaumont's, inheritance.
The Cornish chronicler, William Hals of Merther, remarked that John
was "encouraged to speak openly" and "make known his true parent-
age and descent[,] . . . claiming the lands and inheritance of his father,
William Beaumont, as his legitimate heir."[17] These efforts commenced
around 1468–69. However, it appears that John and Henry had set the
wheel in motion before this time, for we find a record in Chancery, dated
1467, noting "John Beamond[t]'s" attempts to obtain possession of lands
at Pilton in north Devon, late of his "father."[18] These efforts, ultimately,
proved unsuccessful, as did a further claim upon Beaumont lands near
Barnstaple. As an apparent consequence, therefore, efforts were made by
other legal heirs to ward off challenges to the patrimony – efforts which
included securing a writ of bastardry against John:

---

[13] Borlase, in his MS collections, describes Bodrugan manor as "very extensive" and states that there was "nothing in Cornwall equal to its magnificence." There
remains a building on the site, but the original house was pulled down in 1786.

[14] An interest in archery is perhaps indicated by a purchase order of arrows
in 1474 and 1475 – although this may have been placed at the instruction, or in
the absence, of his father, who was a keen huntsman. (Henderson MS XII, no. 18;
Henderson's manuscript includes copies and notes of documents held at Cornwall
Record Office.)

[15] C[alendar of] I[nquisitions] P[ost] M[ortem], vol. II, 50.

[16] TNA C 131/73/1/12/2.

[17] Hals, *The Complete History of Cornwall,* 151.

[18] CPR, 1467-1477, 204.

> Whereas it was understood that Joan, wife of Henry Bodrugan, late
> wife of William Beaumont, had issue one John, the lawful son of the
> said William, it has been proved that the said John is a bastard, and
> that Philip Beaumont is brother and next heir to the said William.[19]

How this was legally binding, when the married couple (Joan and William) were living in the same country, if not the same county, remains
unclear. However, as the present study will show, it did not bring an end
to the matter.

Still John and Henry did not relent, and following the death of the
Beaumont heir-general, Philip Beaumont, in 1473, they made considerable progress on the matter, with the subsequent heir, Thomas Beaumont,
who, ostensibly, was more receptive to their ambitions. This may have
stemmed from his own Yorkist sympathies, but, whatever the truth, relations between the men were good, and, in June 1475, John was given the
manors of Lanteglos, Faweston, Wotton, and Trevelys, in the borough
of Polruan, Cornwall; pasture and moorland near Sandelane, Wiltshire;
and in Devon, lands at Gittisham, Lampford, Bilston, Tottescome and
Wampford, late of William Beaumont.[20] These were supplemented, as
well, not long after, with deeds — which were likely intended as a gift, to
celebrate John's marriage to Isabella Calwodleigh —to the "meadow of
Rowyndemede, adjoining the water running near Stonar and "fishing in
the water from Barnstaple to Pylbrygge."[21] Land, and the wealth derived
from it, was, as any medievalist will know, a measuring stick of one's
influence in their local environs, and these awards confirmed both the

---

[19] "Bastard" is defined by the *Oxford English Dictionary* as "one begotten and
born out of wedlock; an illegitimate or natural child." The word comes from the Old
French "bastard," which is believed to have originated from a combination of "bast,"
a pack-saddle used as a bed by muleteers at inns, with the generally pejorative suffix
"-ard," to imply a "pack-saddle child" as opposed to a legitimate child of the marriage bed. The same word appears in Provencal, Italian, Portuguese and Spanish, and
was also Latinised as "bastardus" – a term which tends to be used in English medieval Latin wills with rather more frequency than "illegitimus." For details of John's
writ, see CPR, 1461-1467, 539-40. There is also a brief note on the claim in H. Nicolas,
A Treatise on the Law of Adulterine Bastardy (London: W. Pickering, 1836), 57-58.

[20] N[orth] D[evon] R[ecord] O[ffice] 48/25/9/5; NDRO 3704M/EF1; W[iltshire]
& S[windon]_A[rchives] SE 9/6/674; R. W. Dunning, *A History of the County of Somerset*, vol. V. (Bridgwater: Victoria County History, 1985), 69-71.

[21] TNA C 146/3243.

extent of John's new sphere of influence and, remarkably, the new found legitimacy of his claim to the Beaumont patrimony.

Curiously, despite now having considerable interests in Devon, John settled at the manor of Tregonan, near St Ewe, Cornwall. Here, he and Isabella produced and raised four children – Henry, Joanne, Mary, and Phillipa[22] – and we may assume that the estate's proximity to Goran, as well as John's engagement, at this time, in a dispute with Piers Bevyll, over deeds to the manor of Penelewey, near Philleigh, ten miles away, on the Roseland Peninsula, influenced his decision to remain in the county. It may also have been influenced by his growing interest in local government from 1471. For example, we find that he served as a witness in a dispute between Sir Thomas Arundell of Lanherne and Sir John Fortescue, the MP for Tavistock, in this year, and a year later, with his father, and other local Yorkists, Thomas Lucombe, Thomas Trefry, and John Pensouns, worked on a commission to investigate the despoilment of a Breton vessel at Fowey.[23] In 1473, he also served, independently, to reinstate the prior, Thomas Oliver, at Buckland Abbey,[24] and he must have impressed, for in January 1474, his name appears at the top of an order from Edward IV to summon all able-bodied men in south Cornwall for an assault on St Michael's Mount, which had been seized by John de Vere, Earl of Oxford, the previous September.[25] This rapid ascent was confirmed soon after, by his attendance on commissions in Devon and Cornwall as well as frequent appearances, as a witness, at Truro and Launceston assizes.[26]

John's career was now set on upward trajectory, and would develop markedly during Edward IV's second reign. Swathes of lands came his

---

[22] Hals, *History of Cornwall*, 151.

[23] CPR, 1467-1477, 354.

[24] This was a drawn-out affair. In 1469, Henry Bodrugan, John Fortescue, Richard Edgcumbe, et al. were appointed to arrest William Breton, who had taken the Abbey by force. They were ordered, presumably by mistake, to expel Thomas Oliver who, it was said, was "pretending to be its abbot." The said commission of 1473—which included Beaumont—contained orders to forcibly expel Breton and reinstate Oliver. CPR, 1467-1477, 171, 403-404.

[25] C. Scofield, "The Early Life of John de Vere, Earl of Oxford," *English Historical Review*, 29 (1914): 239-40; Stansfield, *Politic Elites in South West England, 1450-1500*, 327; Whetter, *Medieval Knightly Family*, 165.

[26] CRO BLIS/80; CRO ME/2656; and CPR, 1476-1485, 23.

and his father's way, as did local office—although senior posts, such as the Shrievalty, continued to elude them. This is not altogether surprising, for Bodrugan, himself, and John to a lesser extent, showed few signs of abandoning their high-handed approach to law enforcement. This kind of law enforcement was evident during the autumn of 1473 and spring of 1474, when the royal law courts, the king's council, and the Parliamentary Commons all heard accusations from persons who had fallen victim to them. One complainant, Thomas Neville, remarked that it was impossible to obtain a remedy via common law, "for if any person would sue the said Henry Bodrugan, John Beamond[t] and Richard Bonython or any of their servants, they would be murdered and slain, and utterly despoiled of their goods."[27] Perhaps the most forceful charge levelled against them, though, came from four rivals of the county. Their petition, directed to the king, explained in colorful terms the "robberies, dispoyleries of marchauntes, straungers, . . . murthers, robberyes aswell [sic] by water as by lond, entres with force and wrongfull enprisonementes" of both men, and it went on to relate an act of piracy against a Breton vessel by two of Bodrugan's ships.[28] It was also claimed that, on September 20th, 1473, the two men had raided houses at Truro and Helston and taken household goods, corn, and livestock worth more than £18; had later set fire to Otis Philip's manor at Polwhele, in St Clement and made off with weaponry and silver, as a well as a substantial quantity of tin; and, on May 10th, 1474, plundered household goods worth over £30 from Arundell's house at Tolverne.[29]

The prosecutor's evidence must have been damning, for, in June 1474, Parliament approved measures to bring them to justice. A writ of charges was published and disseminated countywide, summoning John and his father appeared before the King's Bench on July 11th, and when they failed to attend the summons, they were formally attainted of felony and their lands seized by crown officials.[30] Bodrugan's influence, though, would prove telling. For he was still a member of the Commons, and an important one at that, and, in January 1475, he and his attorney, John Trenowith, appealed the attainder. They claimed that, in seizing Neville's

---

27   Rot[uli] Parl[iamentorum], VI, 133.

28   CPR, 1461-1467, 488; Rot. Parl., VI, 138-40.

29   Kleineke, "Poachers and Gamekeepers," 140-41.

30   TNA C 66/534/20; TNA SC 8/30/1458; and CCR, 1468-1476, 434.

tin mine, and a neighbouring mine owned by Nicolas Roche,[31] Henry and his son had been affecting their duties as justices of the peace, by upholding the rights of tinners reportedly forced from the area. They also remarked that Henry's wife, and John's stepmother, Margaret Lisle, had, in consequence of the initial ruling, lost her lands and had nothing to live on, and had brought the entire family to the point of "extremitye."[32] The statement was plausible enough, and evidently swung the case their way, for, a month later, we find that both Henry and John's attainders were nullified and their lands and offices restored in full.

It is not clear whether this, and other legal disputes, had an impression. A. L. Rowse suggested that events of this period had a "chastening effect" on Bodrugan, and he forswore his use of a "strong hand."[33] Yet, we find, on more than one occasion in the period thereafter that law courts hearing complaints against the family – actions that eventually persuaded John and his father to sue for a pardon for all prior offences.[34] These subsequent transgressions, dated 1479-1484, were, for the most part, petty crimes and individual cases connected to Henry Bodrugan's prodigality.[35] However, John, too, appears very much to have laboured under some financial difficulty. His share of the Beaumont inheritance was, as we have seen, only partial, and according to various chancery records and the inquisitions following his attainder, he leased out a number of manors in south Cornwall and north Devon to alleviate the pressure, with his manor of Faweton, for instance, being taken on by Stephen Harris in 1484, at a yearly rent of 1d.[36]

They were not alone in this regard. Disputes over debts, property, and office were commonplace, especially in areas where the king's will was

---

[31]   CRO ME/422; CRO ME/2656.

[32]   CPR, 1467-1477, 491; CPR, 1476-1485, 48.

[33]   Rowse, "Sir Henry de Bodrugan," 22-24; Whetter, *Medieval Knightly Family*, 157.

[34]   TNA SC 1/50/142; CPR, 1476-1485, 180, 576.

[35]   Certainly the latter was becoming a growing problem, a fact exemplified by the many Chancery records recording his debts at this time, and by his manorial accounts, which noted lavish expenditure on guests. The single largest debt with which Bodrugan contended at this time was for £200. For details, see C[alendar] C[lose]R[olls], 1468-1476, 371; CCR, 1476-1485, 16, 111; CPR, 1467-1477, 576; and CPR, 1476-1485, 80, 268.

[36]   Buildings near John's base of Tregonan were also leased out to Alan Blakeney at a rate of 80s *per annum*. TNA C 142/23/86.

not directly carried. The Courtenay-Bonville discord, for instance, filled Devon with disquiet for years. Civil war also multiplied opportunities for private feuds. One such clash close to John's sphere of influence, between Thomas Trethewy of Reskymer and John Vyvyan of Trelowarren, arose over the latter's right to the manor of Trelowarren.[37] Another, longer-winded, and more violent example was the feud between Thomas Clemens and John Glyn of Morval over the deputy-stewardship of the Duchy.[38] Glyn had replaced Clemens, a former custodian of the office, in November 1468.[39] Accordingly, on January 8th, 1469, when Glyn was holding the court of the manor within the castle at Liskeard, he was attacked by a band brought together by Clemens, his servants beaten, and himself wounded and imprisoned for five hours "so that none of his friends might come." They also tore up court rolls, cut off the purse hanging from Glyn's girdle containing money and bills, and forced him to sign a bond of £200, promising not to take action against them.[40] These offences, and others against Glyn, appear to have been ignored, despite obvious petitioning,[41] until a commission, comprising John and his father, was appointed to arrest Clemens and his accomplices in 1475. This is the last we hear of Clemens. As for Glyn, it appears that he became disenchanted with the state of the local law courts, and between 1477 and 1483, he was arrested on numerous occasions for violently pursuing those he believed to have done him wrong.[42]

By the latter date, John and Henry Bodrugan's political standing in the region had peaked. They did continue to prosper, financially, in the form of land grants and awards, during the short reigns of Edward V and Richard III, and notably played an important role in the suppression of local disturbances following the Buckingham plot of November 1483—hunting Lancastrian rebels, Robert Willoughby, Thomas

---

[37] CRO V/T/1/31.

[38] For details of Glyn's career, see: D. M. Yorath, 'John Glyn of Morval, c.1420-1472', *Cornish Studies* (Forthcoming, 2016).

[39] Rot. Parl. VI, 35; *Magna Britannia*, vol. III, ed. S. Lysons, (London: T. Cadell and W. Davies, 1814), 240; A. L. Rowse, *Tudor Cornwall* (London: Jonathan Cape, 1947), 107.

[40] Ibid.

[41] TNA SC 8/29/1439.

[42] TNA C 1/53/24; TNA SC 8/345/E1345; and CPR, 1467-1477, 552.

Arundell, John and William Treffry, and Richard Edgcumbe[43]—but the frequency, and their length in office, had slipped. For example, we find that the last recorded grants they received under the Yorkist regime were dated December 1483 and January 1484 and concerned estates at Brendon, West Ashford, Ilfracombe, Clyst Champernon, Tywardreath, and Woodbury.[44] The high profile offices and awards continued to elude them, and were seemingly reserved for those of the king's inner circle: Sir James Tyrell, the person widely believed to have fulfilled Richard's order to eliminate Edward IV's two sons, for instance, was given the lands late of John Arundell for his loyal service and subsequently made sheriff of Cornwall;[45] John, Lord Dynham, acquired the post of master forester of Dartmoor, the stewardship of the borough and manor of Bradnigh, and parts of the Courtenay estate in south Devon;[46] and Halnether Mauleverer, the post of Justice of the Peace (JP) with the manor of Boconnoc, late of Edward, Earl of Devon.[47]

Things were to take a turn, anyway. The national picture was blackening, with conspiracy and rumor abounding throughout the winter of 1484-85 of a further challenge to Richard III's rule. For John, this was initially of no consequence, and it was very much business as usual. In May 1484, for example, we find that he represented Cornwall at Parliament, perhaps in *lieu* of his father, and during the following September, he was appointed to investigate yet another case of piracy at Fowey.[48] Early

---

[43] On Edgcumbe, Richard Carew recounts the story of how "[he] was driven to hide himself in those his thicke woods [at Cotehele], which overlook the river [Tamar], what time being suspected of favouring the Earl of Richmond's party against King Richard the Third, hee was hotely pursued, and narrowly searched for [by Henry Bodrugan, John Beaumont, John Trenowith and others]; which extremity taught him a sudden policy, to put a stone in his cap, and tumble the same into the water, while these rangers were close at his heels, who, looking down after the noyse, and seeing his cap swimming thereon, gave over their farther hunting, and left him liberty to shift away, and ship over into Brittaine." *Richard Carew of Antony*, ed. F. E. Halliday, (London: Melrose, 1953), 16.

[44] TNA E 175/5; Harl. 433, II, 58, 124-25.

[45] CRO AR/23/3; R[oyal] I[nstitute of] C[ornwall] Z/13/16; Harl[eian M[anuscript] 433, II, 34; M. Mercer, *The Medieval Gentry: Power, Leadership and Choice during the Wars of the Roses* (London: Continuum, 2010), 104.

[46] Harl. 433, I, 161.

[47] RIC TAM/1/1/18; CPR, 1476-1485, 502.

[48] CPR, 1476-1485, 355.

in 1485, he featured on a commission of array in Devon, and between February and May, he appeared twice as a witness at Truro assizes. The threat to Richard III by now, though, was gaining momentum, via a little known Lancastrian claimant, in Brittany, and on August 22nd, 1485, after landing at Milford Haven, in south Wales, this twenty-eight year-old, Henry Tudor, Earl of Richmond, with a force of about three thousand men, defeated and slew Richard near the town of Market Bosworth. Richard, despite claims to the contrary, had the support of dozens of allies and their retinues here. But, for lack of evidence, we cannot say whether John and Henry Bodrugan were present, although it does look unlikely.[49] Contemporary sources note that Bodrugan and his second wife, Margaret Lisle, were in Gloucester between August 3rd and 14th, 1485, while John was busy at the law courts at Launceston and Truro, in Cornwall.[50] Their omission from Michael Drayton and William Hutton's accounts of the event, too, suggest that they chose, or were perhaps ordered, to stay in the West Country, perhaps to apprehend Tudor and his fleeing army.[51] We simply cannot say.

Whatever the reason, the outcome of the battle spelled disaster for John and his father. England's new king, Henry VII, having been assisted by a large body of westerners, was inclined to reward them with office and land, a move that saw some of Henry Bodrugan's old rivals encroach on, and gradually undermine, his and John's sphere of influence in south Cornwall. In September 1485, for instance, one of the king's most trusted allies, Sir Robert Willoughby, was made appointed receiver of the Duchy of Cornwall, custodian of Launceston Goal, and high steward of the king's household;[52] Bodrugan's longstanding rival, Sir Richard Edgcumbe, became comptroller of the household, chamberlain of the exchequer, and keeper of Launceston castle;[53] Sir John Treffry, who had been knighted shortly after Tudor's landing at Milford Haven, received the estates of Langham and Launden, late of Lord Zouche; and his brother,

---

[49]   MacLean, *Trigg Manor*, 552.

[50]   W[estminster] A[bbey] M[uniments] 6034 (cited in Whetter, *Medieval Knightly Family*, 189).

[51]   M. Drayton, *Poly-Olbion* (London, 1612); W. Hutton, *The Battle of Bosworth Field* (Birmingham, 1788).

[52]   RIC TAM/2/6/5.

[53]   CPR, 1485-1494, 7, 17; W. Campbell, ed., *Materials for a History of the Reign of Henry VII*, vol. I (London, 1873), 18, 19.

William, was made usher of King's Chamber, surveyor of customs in London, keeper of the stannary jail at Lostwithiel, and controller of the coinage of tin in Devon and Cornwall.[54] Curiously, there was no immediate major shift in power, as one might expect. For, indeed, some thirty percent of officials who had held office in the region between 1480 and 1485 continued to do so under Henry VII. Sir James Tyrell retained his role as JP in Cornwall[55] and featured in local politics through to his execution in 1502; John Trenowith continued to serve at Truro assizes;[56] and even John and his father, Henry Bodrugan, despite now being politically marginalized, made efforts to cultivate the new regime, and appeared on three commissions between November 1485 and August 1486.[57]

The new order, though, eventually proved too much. Lancastrian will was gaining traction, and without the aid of former Yorkists, John Dynham, and Hugh and Philip Courtenay, John and Henry appear to have had difficulty executing office and orders in their local environs. It also seems, too, that they were subject to a campaign of harassment from some their neighbors. For example, there survive two cases, heard before the Bishop of Worcester between Michaelmas 1485 and Hilary 1486, which comment upon the unauthorized occupation of their estates at Pendrym and Fenton by supporters of Sir Richard Edgcumbe.[58] And, although they ultimately secured legal favor in their disputes, the problem was such that both men were compelled to make overtures to the Royal Household and, specifically, to Robert Willoughby and Reginald Bray for redress. This yielded some success, and in October 1486 an indenture was signed between the parties, promising the annexation of part of their estate in exchange for protection and the return of lands seized by Walter Enderby and others at Losburgh, Markewyll, and Trethewe.[59] The practicalities of this "deal" and its detail, though, were not lasting. And, by the close of 1486, it was clear that John and Henry Bodrugan had grown tired of the now near-constant legal challenges, and seeing no other option or peaceful

---

[54] A. F. Pollard ed., *The Reign of Henry VII from Contemporary Sources,* vol. I (London: Longmans, 1914), 88, 90.

[55] Rowse, *Tudor Cornwall,* 119.

[56] RIC HC/1/8; RIC TTY/1/2; RIC Z/13/16; and CCR, 1485-1500, 263.

[57] CRO ME 821/24.

[58] Beaumont and Bodrugan were plaintiffs against William Richards, Richard Boteller, John Menwynnek, and Lawrence Penkivel. TNA C 1/34/47.

[59] TNA C 142/1/20; CCR, 1485-1500, no. 83; Rowse, 'Sir Henry de Bodrugan," 26.

method of redress available to them, they decided to fight fire with fire, with physical force. This resulted in a series of summons for "unlawful behaviour," and, on February 8th, 1487, orders were given to Richard Edgcumbe, John Trevanion, and others to apprehend "John Beaumont, his father, Henry Bodrugan, and others who have withdrawn to private places in Devon and Cornwall."[60] Bodrugan, it seems, was apprised of this by his tenants and withdrew to a place called "woeful moor," where, after a short and bloodied skirmish, he slipped away to a nearby cliff and "leapt down into the see . . . onto a grassy island, where, instantly, a boat attended him . . . and transported him to France."[61] Whether John, too, escaped at this remarkable juncture is not known, but it does seem likely. That he left the country is certain, for, on March 12th 1487, he was tried *in absentia* of "certain high treasons" against the king at Launceston, before William Collowe, Richard Edgcumbe, Thomas Wode, and others.[62] The process was continued at Lostwithiel in the weeks thereafter, and it was also there, sometime later, that he was formally attainted, together with his father, on the evidence of John Trelawney, Peter Tregose, and his old rival, Piers Bevyll.

Henry VII and his council noted that John had escaped, first to Brittany and then Ireland, and that, with his father, had been in secret correspondence with other displaced Yorkists. This is possible, for we know, at about this time, that John de la Pole, Earl of Lincoln, and Francis, Lord Lovell had begun to formulate a plot to overthrow the English king and restore Yorkist rule. This challenge was eventually launched from Ireland —a country sympathetic to the Yorkist cause and one with strong ancestral ties to the Bodrugan household. With these circumstances, it seems probable that John Henry Bodrugan communicated or perhaps met with the Yorkist faction in Dublin. Certainly, Henry VII considered there to be a link between the two parties, for, on November 15th, 1487,

---

[60]   Campbell, *Materials*, II, 118; Pollard, *The Reign of Henry VII*, I, 46.

[61]   The story of John's flight is not recorded, but it seems likely that he escaped at the same time, although perhaps via a different method to cliff-jumping, for, on March 10th, 1487, he was tried *in absentia* of "certain high treasons" against the king at Launceston. This process was continued at Lostwithiel before John Trelawney, Peter Tregose, Peter Bevyll, and John Langforth, coroner of Cornwall, until the attainder was completed. For the tale of Bodrugan's escape, see *Richard Carew of Antony*, 15-16; Hals, *History of Cornwall*, 151; and MacLean, *Trigg Manor*, 551.

[62]   CIP M, III, 372.

he charged both of "imagining and compassing the death of the king, in the company of the earl of Lincoln" and of being present at "Edward Plantagenet's" (the Pretender, Lambert Simnel's) coronation in Dublin.[63] Some contemporaries believed that John and Henry later joined the rebels on their passage to, or on their landing at, Furness Fells in Lancashire. However, their relatives, Richard Antron and John Reskymer, in a Star Chamber case of 1511, rejected this charge and stated: "the said Sir Henry and his son were never in the company of the said earl, nor never spoke with him nor never sent him message nor none otherwise, nor never committed any treasons."[64] In the case of Bodrugan, this seems plausible enough. Perhaps he had had enough. After all, he was, by now, an elderly widower. For John, though, it is an altogether different matter. He was a man in his prime, thirty-seven years old in 1487, who had lost all and who had everything to gain from unseating Henry VII.[65] However, again, the evidence is scant. For example, neither man is named in contemporary accounts of the resulting battle, at Stoke Field, on June 16th, 1487, but they do appear in the November Act of Attainder:

> be it enacted by our sovereygne lorde the kyng, by the advyse of all the lordes s"puall and temporall, and the comons in this present parliament assembled, and by the auctorite of the same, that the said John, late Earl of Lincolne, Sir Henry Bodrugan, Thomas Broughton, knyghts, John Beaumond &c. to be reputed, jugged and taken as traytours, and convicte and attaynte of high treason &c.[66]

The truth may never be known; nor does the mystery end there, for the next, and, as it would prove, final stage of John's life is equally cloudy. J. C. Wedgwood, in his error-strewn *Biographies of the Members of the Commons House, 1439-1509*, suggests that John fought with the rebels at Stoke and was subsequently "captured, attainted and beheaded." This

---

[63] TNA C 142/23/86; Rot. Parl., VI, 397-400, 412; "The Voyage of Sir Richard Edgcumbe sent by K. Henry VII, into Ireland in 1488 to take new oaths of allegiance from the Nobility and others who had declared for Lambert Simnel," in *Hibernica*, ed. W. Harris, (1757).

[64] TNA STAC 2/23/305; Rowse, 'Sir Henry de Bodrugan," 24-25.

[65] He had left his wife and children behind and had made no arrangements – as his ancestor Otto had done – for the continuation of the family line.

[66] CRO ME/632.

course of events is possible, but it is cast into doubt by Wedgwood's failing to name his source. We can, with reasonable confidence, however, assume that John died or was presumed dead by the autumn of 1487, for there survives notice of *inquisitions post mortem* being carried on his estates in May and June of 1488.[67]

For John and Henry Bodrugan's tenants, in Devon and Cornwall, their masters' rapid fall from grace in 1485-86, subsequent flight to Ireland, and presumed deaths in 1487 (or 1488) and 1503 aroused waves of hostility towards the Tudor regime. Henry VII's and his allies' treatment of their masters had offended one of the strongest sentiments of the day: "the sanctity of the family inheritance, the hereditary 'lifelod' – that god-made right that nothing could, or should, obliterate."[68] The appropriation and subsequent division of their lands to comparative "outsiders," too, drove some to violence, and this may explain why inquisitions in 1488 were not conducted near their center, as was custom, but forty miles away, on the Devon-Cornwall border, at Callington.[69] Here, on the testimony of John Bukeden, an individual who had no obvious connection with the area, it was decided that the Bodrugan and Beaumont estates should be divided among the King's Lancastrian supporters. Payments were made to Hugh Eldon, Walter Smert, and to others to whom John owed debts, and in April 1488, further grants were made to the king's councillor and knight of the body: Sir Thomas Lovell was granted a large portion of Henry's estate; William Trevanion, who had fought in the king's vanguard at Stoke, the family's manors at Restronguet and Newham;[70] Lancastrian

---

[67]   To further complicate matters, we know that Thomas Beaumont, on November 28th, 1487, promised to bequeath to John the manor of Gittisham, which he had partially acquired in 1478, and other lands in Cornwall, Dorset, and Gloucestershire. This suggests that, if John had died at Stoke Field, news was slow in reaching his relatives. The strongest evidence there is to support a claim that John died in the fall of 1487 or early 1488 is that his name drops from all court records and writs in the latter year. TNA C 142/23/318; J. C. Wedgwood, *History of Parliament: Biographies of the Members of the Commons House, 1439-1509* (London, 1936), 58.

[68]   Lander, "Attainder and Forfeiture," 268.

[69]   It seems that there was trouble at the time of John's arrest. An inquisition, dated January 1488, records that the manor of Polruan, in which John had an interest, was of "no value on account of the devastation and desolation caused by men of the area." CIP M, III, 189.

[70]   RIC HC/1/8; Gilbert, *History of Cornwall*, IV, 275.

favorite, Richard Nanfan, lands at Lanteglos, Faweton, and Trevelys;[71] Sir Robert Willoughby, the manor of Trethew;[72] and to their pursuer, Sir Richard Edgcumbe, lands around Bodrugan, near Chapel Point, where, two years earlier, John and his father had made their dramatic escape.[73] The rest of John's estate and the wardship of his son, Henry, were purchased by Richard, Bishop of Exeter, and Sir William Hody, Baron of the Exchequer, for 800 marks.

Interestingly, there is no mention of John's wife, Isabella, in any of the grants – even though she was alive at the time. Nor is there reference to his daughters, Joanne, Mary, and Phillipa, who may have reached majority, married, or remained in their mother's charge.[74] It should also be noted, on the particular point of acquisition, that if Hody and the Bishop of Exeter were willing to pay the king 800 marks for the wardship, then the issues and profits made from the lands and from the sale of the boy's marriage must have had the potential to net them a handsome return on their investment. In 1489, a formal appeal was made on behalf of Henry Beaumont to reverse his father's attainder. The reversal was granted in January 1490, but on the condition that Bishop Hody retained the wardship "with profits and revenues and licence to enter all castles, lands, manors, from the death of John Beaumont . . . during the nonage of the said Henry."[75] If Henry died during this time, the estate would devolve upon John's daughters, Joanne, Mary, and Philippa, and their heirs. If he refused to marry, the property would stay with Hody and the Bishop of Exeter, thereby alienating any inheritance the family might have enjoyed.[76] Furthermore, the restitution did not extend to those properties held by the Beaumont family in Treganowe, Cornwall, where grants

---

[71] CRO AR/23/4; RIC HC/1/8; RIC TAM/1/1/19; and CPR, 1485-1494, 232, 253, 378.

[72] Henderson MS, XII, no.8; CPR, 1485-1494, 7, 17, 27.

[73] CRO ME/486; CRO ME/622; RIC HB/7/38; and TNA PROB 11/27, fols. 242-43; *Magna Britannia*, III, 115; *The Survey of Cornwall by Richard Carew*, ed. J. Chynoweth, N. Orme, and A. Walsham, vol. 47 (Exeter: Cornwall Record Society, 2004), 141.

[74] Hals, *History of Cornwall*, 151.

[75] TNA C 65/126, f. 3; Rot. Parl., VI, 246, 273, 360, 406, 412-13; J. Hutchins, *The History and Antiquities of the county of Dorset*, vol. I (Wakefield: EP Publishing, 1973), 317.

[76] Powell MSS/36/979; Wedgwood, 58.

made to Sir Richard Nanfan were to stand. Nor did it make reference to Henry Beaumont's sisters. Savings were made for Isabella, granting her title and interest "in any of the premises," meaning that she retained the rights associated with her jointure, personal inheritance, and possibly her dower portion as well. Tenants and others who had held lands of John Beaumont at the time of his attainder were also safeguarded.[77]

In 1502, Henry Beaumont finally received license from the king to enter "all the possessions of the said John, who was attainted of high treason." This would suggest that he attained full legal age, although there is no mention of his marital status.[78] He did eventually recover some of his father's estates, but it was not a complete restitution; he received about a third of his family's former lands and subsequently took it upon himself to challenge some of the earlier rulings, in particular those pertaining to his father's former estate at Tregonan.[79] The Beaumont inheritance was still in play, too, and, in March 1507, shortly after the death of Hugh Beaumont, the brother of Thomas, Henry attempted to assert his rights over the patrimony, a move that was countered by Hugh's daughter, Margaret, the wife of Devon JP, John Chichester, and Joan, the sister of William Beaumont and spouse of John Bassett:

> Whereupon, according to the form of the statutes, he [Henry Beaumont] made his entry upon the same, and delivered ejectments to Chichester and Basset, and their tenants, then in possession thereof; and accordingly brought down a veneer façade, and tried upon the same at common law at the next assizes held at Exon upon the demise of Sir Thomas Beaumont, and other trustees for the heirs of William Beaumont, esquire, aforesaid.[80]

At the assizes, Chichester and Bassett jointly reaffirmed their belief —seemingly without evidence—that John Beaumont had been formally bastardised, in 1468, and that his supposed father, William Beaumont,

---

[77] Rot. Parl., VI, 360, 406, 412-13; J. Maclean, "Notes," *Transactions of Bristol and Gloucestershire Archaeological Society*, 10 (1885): 200.

[78] CPR, 1494-1509, 301; Rot. Parl., VI, 413.

[79] In January 1507, he tried to recover some of the lands late of Sir Richard Nanfan, including his father's former residence of Tregonan. Maclean, "Notes," 200.

[80] Hals, *History of Cornwall*, 151-52.

"never saw nor cohabited with his said wife [Joan]." However, it seems that this could not be gainsaid because of Joan's legal marriage to William. The court therefore passed verdict in favour of "John Beaumond[t]', as William's "legitimate son and heir." The dispute rumbled on, though, and in 1509 commissions were, again, issued to interview witnesses in Devon and Cornwall, and the case was eventually heard the following year, before John Morton, Bishop of Ely, "who . . . hearing fully . . . and giving full consideration to the proof and allegations on both parts, reaffirmed John's legitimacy, and gave judgment to the defendant, [Henry] Beaumont."[81] Bassett and Chichester maintained their position, though, and upon the presentation of new evidence, they subsequently gained the favor of Parliament and persuaded the King to rule that John Beaumont and his heirs should "no longer be called by that name" but "rather John, the son of Henry Bodrugan, second husband of Joan, his mother."[82] It was an anticlimactic conclusion. John's son, Henry, was granted Gittisham manor, near Honiton, in 1513, as part of ruling, and the rest of the patrimony, including many of his father's land gains, was divided among Thomas's true heirs.[83] Henry later married Elizabeth, the daughter of Robert Howell of Cothelstone, and their son, Humphrey, who, like his father and grandfather, served the Crown in the counties of Devon and Cornwall, subsequently died childless in 1547.

While, to some, John Beaumont's career may typify local abuse of office, it is, perhaps, best understood in light of the political and administrative realities of the period. The Crown's lack of magnate support in the far south west, together with the prominent standing of his father, probably created a greater tolerance to his unlawful behavior than might otherwise have been the case. Equally, in some instances, high-handed conduct may have been required to execute the Crown's will: it was, in

---

[81]   Ibid., 152.

[82]   RIC HB/2/50; RIC HB/5/73.

[83]   Henry subsequently married Elizabeth, daughter of Robert Howll of Cothelstone. They had one son, Humphrey, who married Joan, daughter of John West, Lord de la Ware, but they were childless, so the line died out. Henry Beaumont, himself, son and heir of John Beaumont of Tregonan, died in 1547, aged sixty-six. Hals, *History of Cornwall,* 152; W. Pole, *Collections Towards a Description of the County of Devon* (London: J. Nichols, 1791), 163; Prince, *The Worthies of Devon,* 31; *T. Westcote's View of Devonshire,* ed. T. Oliver and P. Jones (Exeter : William Roberts, 1845), 307.

the words of one authority, "very characteristic" of this time.[84] This is no defence but ought to be taken into consideration. There were other factors, too, such as the remoteness of the region, which posed consistent problems, irrespective of the reigning monarch or dynasty. In such a culture, men turned for support to those with physical power who were not reluctant to use it (albeit, most commonly in pursuit of their own interests),[85] and this fact probably explains why the Bodrugans, despite their transgressions, were so greatly revered: the "love the tenants of south Cornwall bore the family," recounted Thomas Tonkin, was "in such veneration . . . that the elder sort of people cannot mention their ruin without much regret to this day."[86] In this we may include John, for it is clear that he was a dependable JP and commissioner, and a good lord to his tenants. This praise is something that stands greatly to his credit, and his reputation should not be denied him.

---

[84]   Rowse, *Tudor Cornwall*, 102-107.

[85]   Indeed, after Bosworth there is evidence that the Edgcumbes, Willoughbys, Nanfans, and other prominent county families behaved in a not too dissimilar manner. TNA STAC 2/21/117; TNA STAC 2/25/199; and CRO ME/3080.

[86]   Gilbert, *History of Cornwall*, II, 107.

MEDICINE FOR A GREAT HOUSEHOLD (CA. 1500): BERKELEY CASTLE MUNIMENTS SELECT BOOK 89

Linda Ehrsam Voigts and Ann Payne

CONTENTS

Studies in Medieval and Renaissance History, 3rd Series, Vol. 12 (2016)

Illustrations

Color Plates

1. BCM SB 89, Part I, f. [i], first leaf, containing arms, scrollwork letter "h," prologue, and beginning of contents list for Part I
2.a. BCM SB 89, Part I, f. [i], detail of scrollwork letter "h," arms, and prologue
2.b. BCM SB 89, Part I, f. 1, detail of oak leaf initial letter "T"
3. BCM SB 89, Part I, f. 1, recipes for three distilled waters
4.a. Oxford, Bodleian Library, MS Ashmole 1504, f. 48v, shield of arms of John de Vere, thirteenth Earl of Oxford, impaling the arms of his second wife, Lady Elizabeth Scrope (d.1537)
4.b. Garter stall plate for John, fifth Lord Scrope of Bolton, from William H. St John Hope, *The Stall Plates of the Order of the Garter*, plate 70
5. BCM SB 89, Part I, f. 86v, and Part II, f. [ii], showing end of Part I, beginning of Part II.
6. BCM SB 89, Part II, f. 7v, recipes, nos. 39 (end), 40, 41, and 42 (beginning); "Thomas Griggs" (later hand) noted in margins
7. BCM SB 89, Part II, f. 9, recipes, nos. 47 (end), 48, 49, 50, and 51 (rubric only)
8. BCM SB 89, Part II, f. 12v, recipes, nos. 64, 65, and 66 (rubric only); "manus christi" (later hand) in upper margin; see also fig. 7 for the first of two rubrics for no. 64.

Black/White Figures

1. BCM SB 89, Part I, f. 14v, five ointments text (conclusion, in red) and beginning of wounds text
2. BCM SB 89, Part I, f. 41v, recipes for "powder imperyall"
3. BCM SB 89, Part I, f. 43v, prologue and incipit, *Antidotarium Nicolai* [two lines at bottom begin text]

4. BCM SB 89, Part I, f. 77v, last two recipes in *receptarium* A, text on humoral complexions, signs of the Zodiac, and planets; scraped legal jottings, *temp.* Eliz.I, in left hand margin
5. BCM SB 89, Part I, f. 83, *De conferentibus* including section on the eyes
6. BCM SB 89, Part II, f. 3, recipes, nos. 12 (end), 13, 14, 15, 16, and 17 (rubric only)
7. BCM SB 89, Part II, f. 12, recipes, nos. 62 (end), 63, and 64 (rubric only; see also plate 8 for second rubric and recipe text on f. 12v)
8. BCM SB 89, Part I, f. 78v, Planetenkinder for "Saturnus," "Jubiter," "Mars," and "Sol"
9. Brass of Lady Elizabeth Scrope, Countess of Oxford, 1537, in Wivenhoe Church, Essex
10. Beaufort-Beauchamp Hours, London, British Library, Royal MS 2 A.xviii, f. 2, detail of medical recipe in script similar to BCM SB 89
11. London, British Library, Arundel MS 130, f. 1, shield of arms of the fifth Earl of Northumberland, after 1489

ALL IMAGES FROM Berkeley Castle Muniments Select Book 89 are reproduced by permission of Mr. R. J. G. Berkeley and the Trustees of the Berkeley Will Trust (plates 1, 2.a, 2.b, 3, 6–8, figs. 4–6 with Digital Imaging by DIAMM). Bodleian Library, MS Ashmole 1504, f. 48v, reproduced by permission of the Bodleian Libraries, University of Oxford. William H. St John Hope, *The Stall Plates of the Order of the Garter: 1348–1485* (London, 1901), plate 70, reproduced by courtesy of the Society of Antiquaries of London. Brass of Lady Elizabeth Scrope, Countess of Oxford, 1537, in Wivenhoe Church, Essex, reproduced by permission of H. Martin Stuchfield (© *The Monumental Brasses of Essex*, by William Lack, H. Martin Stuchfield, and Philip Whittemore [London, 2003]). Beaufort-Beauchamp Hours, British Library, Royal MS 2 A. xviii, f. 2 (flyleaf), and British Library, Arundel MS 130, f. 1, ©The British Library Board.

List of Abbreviations

AN	*Antidotarium Nicolai*
BCM SB 89	Berkeley Castle Muniments, Select Book 89
BL	London, British Library
Bodl.	Oxford, Bodleian Library
CI	*Circa instans*
Complete Peerage	[G. E. C.] G. E. Cokayne et al., eds., *Complete Peerage of England, Scotland, Ireland*, new ed., 14 vols. (London, 1910–98)
EETS	Early English Text Society
eTK	Database of 33,000 records from Lynn Thorndike and Pearl Kibre, *A Catalogue of Incipits of Mediaeval Scientific Writings in Latin* (1963), searchable under Digital Tools at the website of the Medieval Academy of America or under IndexCat at the History of Medicine website of the U.S. National Library of Medicine
eVK2	database of 10,000 records created by Linda Ehrsam Voigts and Patricia Deery Kurtz, *Scientific and Medical Writings in Old and Middle English: an Electronic Reference*, 2nd edition, searchable under Digital Tools at the website of the Medieval Academy of America or under IndexCat at the History of Medicine website of the U.S. National Library of Medicine
MED	*Middle English Dictionary* in Middle English Compendium at http://quod.lib.umich.edu/m/med/
ODNB	*Oxford Dictionary of National Biography*
OED	*Oxford English Dictionary*
SB	Select Book
STC	A. W. Pollard, G. R. Redgrave et al., eds., *A Short-Title Catalogue of Books Printed in England*, 2nd ed., rev. (London, 1976, 1986, 1991)
S	"Synonomy"
Test. Ebor.	*Testamenta Eboracensia*
TNA	London, The National Archives

1. Introduction: Medicine for a Great Household

Here ffolowythe the table off this boke in the whiche is
contaynyd many Sundry medicynys bothe off phisik
and Surgery greatly profytable to the helth off
man And woman Also this table Shall lede you directly
to euery mydycyne And in what leffe you Shall ffynd it The
Chapter Superscrybyd Aboue on euery leffe

THIS PASSAGE ON the first leaf introduces the unbound manuscript
designated Select Book 89 in the Muniments of Berkeley Castle, a manuscript that was purchased at a Sotheby's sale in 1924 by the eighth Earl
of Berkeley (plate 1). See section 2 (**Date, Decoration, and Original
Ownership of BCM SB 89**) and **Appendix A** for the physical description
and provenance of this codex, henceforth cited as SB 89. This previously
unstudied manuscript from the end of the fifteenth century or the early
years of the sixteenth is a rare and important example of an English medical compendium written at that time for a great household, and probably for the women of that household. The language of the texts is mostly
English,[1] written in a single clear late-medieval hand, with generous use

---

[1] We are deeply grateful to Mr. R. J. G. Berkeley and the Trustees of the Berkeley Will Trust for the opportunity to work with SB 89 in the Berkeley Castle Muniments, and to David J. H. Smith, Hon. Archivist, who kindly let us know about the
contents of this important manuscript and was most generous with his expertise
as we studied it. We thank them for the opportunity to reproduce images from
the Berkeley Castle manuscript. We also owe much gratitude to the Digital Image
Archive of Medieval Music (DIAMM) for supplying us with high-resolution digital
images of SB 89, and to Linda Brownrigg of Anderson-Lovelace Publishers for her

of parchment. The codex contains arms, decoration, and careful rubrication, with detailed tables of contents for each of its two parts. The tables of contents for the two parts do indeed "lede" the reader "to euery mydycyne And in what leffe you Shall ffynd it," as stated in the rubric above, which begins the manuscript (plates 1, 2.a).

The first of two discrete but related sections of SB 89 comprises Part I, folios 1–86, following the contents list on folios [i–xi recto]. It is made up of texts on medical therapy, some lengthy, beginning with distillation recipes. See plates 2.b and 3. See also **Appendix C** for a survey of texts in Part I, citing editions and other manuscripts when known. The contents of SB 89 are not typical of large medical compendia in that both Part I and Part II focus on therapeutic medicine to the exclusion of other types of medical writing. The contents are primarily remedies, some of which derive from the academic medical tradition. Other therapeutic texts, such as the treatise on the treatment of wounds,[2] do not appear to survive elsewhere. Part I concludes with two remedy books of the popular sort containing a considerable number of shorter recipes as well as brief embedded texts. *Receptarium* A in Part I (no. 27) is organized in the traditional head-to-heel order, while the contents of B (no. 31) are more random.

Part II, following an acephalous contents list on folio [ii], begins with new foliation 1–13. This second section is identical to Part I in hand, format, and contents list, but it wants leaves at both beginning and

---

encouragement and support. This study would not have been possible without advice and assistance from countless librarians and archivists and from the following individuals: Richard Aspin, Maredudd Ap Huw, Caroline Barron, Richard Beadle, Martha Carlin, Ann Carmichael, Wendy Childs, Elizabeth Danbury, Maria D'Aronco, Roger Dahood, Diana Greenway, Christopher de Hamel, Luke Demaitre, A. I. Doyle, Ben Elliott, Virginia Ertelt, Edurne Garrido Añes, Monica Green, Angela Hendrickson, Daniel Huws, Caroline Jewers, Peter Jones, Sarah Peters Kernan, David Lepine, Maria José Linares, Michael McVaugh, Jake Walsh Morrissey, Laura Nuvoloni, Lea Olsan, Nicholas Orme, Stella Panayotova, James Payne, Matthew Payne, Nicholas Pickwoad, Susan Powell, Pamela Robinson, Jane Sayers, Kathleen Scott, Jeremy Smith, Jenny Stratford, Thomas Sullivan, OSB, Jennifer Ward, Chris Woolgar, and Kelley Young. Of course, the support of our families was indispensable to our efforts. Responsibility for any errors is ours alone.

We are grateful for the comments of Jeremy Smith that the late-medieval English of SB 89 is an unremarkable London dialect.

   [2] See **Appendix C**, no. 8.

end (plate 5). See **Appendix D** for a diplomatic transcription of Part II where numbers have been supplied with recipes for convenience of reference. This second section of the book is also therapeutic, but it contains elaborate examples of polypharmacy, along with medical-culinary recipes, neither of which characterize Part I. Seventy-one recipes survive in Part II, and rubrics from the acephalous contents list indicate that an additional thirteen recipes are wanting at the end. A significant percentage of the recipes in Part II address epidemic illnesses and the stone. **Appendix B** lists recipes in Part II that also occur in Part I.

Some of the recipes in Part II are specified for members of royal or noble families: no. 14, for my lord; no. 32, the queen's powder; no. 44, as I sent to your ladyship; no. 49, medicine that the king used every day (plate 7); and no. 64, devised for my lady the king's grandmother (plate 8). A number of accoutrements found in a noble household are mentioned: silk bags, silver pots, and clothing and fabrics such as *callet* and *sarcynet*.[3] These Part II recipes require many imported items, often in large quantities: oranges; pomegranates (plate 6); sugar; treacle of Jene/Genoa; and various wines—claret, Angoy/Anjou, and malvesie/malmsey, the sweet wine originally obtained from Napoli di Malvasia in Greece. Not surprisingly, much attention is paid to exotic spices, precious metals (gold and silver), jewels, coral, and ambergris. Distillation is also required in twelve individual recipes in Part II: nos. 1–9, nos. 13–14, and no. 18, but Part II differs from Part I where distillation is concentrated in the initial treatises.

It should be acknowledged from the outset that SB 89 appears to be a copy, perhaps from two unrelated sources. See **Appendix A** for a physical description and **Appendix B** on recipes occurring in both Part I and Part II. Furthermore, there are sections in Parts I and II where text and contents list do not correspond. In some cases, the text contains recipes not listed among contents, and in others, the contents tables cite recipes not to be found in the texts.[4] Perhaps the most telling evidence of copying is the text in Part I called in the Latin tradition *De conferentibus et nocentibus*, although in this manuscript, the common English rubric occurs: "This diatory folowyng was sent to dame Isabell quene of ynglond by the

---

[3] *Callet* and *sarsenet* occur in Part II in recipe no. 34.

[4] Rubrics for recipes 37–40 are not provided in the contents list for Part II. These and other examples of variation between rubrics in contents list and in the text of SB 89 are discussed in **Appendices C** and **D.**

kyng of ffraunce her brother" (no. 32; see **Appendix C**)."[5] In this relatively common listing of things good or bad for various body parts beginning with the brain, the first leaf occurs on Part I, folio 82v, and continues on the facing folio, folio 83. Then, however, the text is interrupted on the next opening (ff. 83v–84) when the scribe returns to the *receptarium* that preceded the treatise. On the following opening (ff. 84v–85), apparently having realized that the *De conferentibus* text has been interrupted with recipes, the scribe provides the conclusion to it on folio 84v before resuming the remedy book.

SB 89: Practical Medicine for a Wealthy Household

This medical codex is not the sort of manuscript that physicians or other professional medical practitioners owned.[6] It is a household book that can be associated with women, and it is unified by a therapeutic focus. It is also exceptional for several reasons. It lacks the language and scholastic

---

[5] This text (eVK2 7251) is also relevant to the subsequent discussion of the date of the manuscript. On eVK2 and eTK, see below n. 7.

[6] See, e.g., the nearly fifty surviving manuscripts owned by a royal physician during the reigns of Henry VI and Edward IV in Linda Ehrsam Voigts, "A Doctor and His Books: The Manuscripts of Roger Marchall (d. 1477)," *New Science out of Old Books: Studies in Manuscripts and Early Printed Book in Honour of A. I. Doyle*, ed. Richard Beadle and A. J. Piper (Aldershot: Scolar Press, 1995), 249–314. Empirics and less-professionally trained leeches also owned books where a range of diagnostic and prognostic texts accompanied *receptaria*. A lengthy medical compilation in Cambridge, Gonville and Caius College MS 176/97, was translated from Latin for an early fifteenth-century barber surgeon, Thomas Plawdon (d. 1413) (eVK2 1143, prologue; 1547, text). See also the discussion of the writings associated with an anonymous leech in Voigts, "Fifteenth-Century English Banns Advertising the Services of an Itinerant Doctor," *Between Text and Patient: The Medical Enterprise in Medieval and Early Modern Europe*, ed. Florence Eliza Glaze and Brian Nance, Micrologus' Library 39 (Florence: SISMEL, Edizioni del Galluzzo, 2011), 245–77. For an empiric's texts, see L. Ayoub, "John Crophill's Books: An Edition of British Library MS Harley 1735," PhD Thesis, University of Toronto, 1994. An itinerant physician with some acquaintance with university medical treatises was the early fifteenth-century Thomas Fayreford; see Peter Jones, "Thomas Fayreford: An English Fifteenth-Century Medical Practitioner," *Medicine from the Black Death to the French Disease*, ed. R. French, Jon Arrizabalaga, Andrew Cunningham, and Luis García-Ballester (Aldershot: Ashgate, 1998), 156–83.

medical theories associated with trained physicians, and even those texts in Part I, like the *Antidotarium Nicolai* on compound medicines and *Circa instans* on simples, that circulated in a university milieu, are intensely therapeutic and practical. Indeed, the focus is so single-mindedly therapeutic that the book lacks the short texts on diagnosis and prognosis common in other Middle English medical compendia—on uroscopy, phlebotomy, humoral diagnosis and prognostication, signs of death—or texts that predict the outcome of illness by lunary calculation or Pythagorean diagrams.[7] This is a book of cures, but a highly specialized one in that the polypharmacy in Berkeley Castle Muniments SB 89 requires an extraordinarily well-stocked armamentarium and a panoply of distillation equipment.

Such an expensive decorated manuscript would be of value only to a noble household, as the royal recipes in Part II suggest. The definition by Julia Boffey of a household book is apposite here: it is "a repository of practical information of more or less domestic kinds."[8] SB 89 is, however, exceptional among medieval household books that survive, not only in its focus on medical therapy, but also because this medical manuscript was produced for a family of the peerage. The arms used by that extended family on the opening leaf (f. [i]; plate 2.a) are discussed in section 2 (**Decoration, Date**, **and Original Ownership of BCM SB 89**), but here it is important to observe that there is much valuable scholarship on the households of noble families at the end of the fifteenth century and beginning of the sixteenth.[9] Kim M. Phillips summarizes another

---

[7]   For the range of topics in Middle English medical writings, see the tkvk-subjectlist accompanying eVK2, Linda Voigts and Patricia Deery Kurtz, eds., *Scientific and Medical Writings on Old and Middle English*, containing ca. 10,000 records. eTK is a similar electronic version of Lynn Thorndike and Pearl Kibre, *A Catalogue of Incipits of Mediaeval Scientific Writings in Latin* (Cambridge, MA, 1963), containing ca. 30,000 records. Both are accessible through two websites with different search engines: (1) the Medieval Academy of America (link in "Resources/Digital Tools"); or (2) the webpage for History of Medicine on the U.S. National Library of Medicine website (link IndexCat, link to databases with tab for eTK and eVK2).

[8]   There is a considerable body of scholarship on medieval household books. The definition by Julia Boffey is found in "Bodleian Library, MS Arch. Selden. B. 24 and Definitions of the 'Household book,'" *The English Medieval Book: Studies in Memory of Jeremy Griffiths*, ed. A. S. G. Edwards, Vincent Gillespie, and Ralph Hanna (London: BL, 2000), 125–34, at 125.

[9]   Regarding noble households of the sort associated with SB 89, the following studies are of great value: C. M. Woolgar, *Household Accounts from Medieval*

significant body of scholarship on the wealth and power of these families and observes that "the upper nobility or peerage had by the end of the fifteenth century actually increased their ascendancy, with clearly defined (though not closed) membership and greater wealth than ever."[10]

There are obvious displays of wealth in SB 89. A surprisingly high proportion of recipes call for expensive exotica, often considerable numbers and large quantities. The recipe for "water of lyffe" (*Aqua vitae*) in Part I (ff. 1r–v) requires the distillation of clear red wine with powder of canel (cinnamon), gillyflower (cloves), ginger, pellitory of Spain, nutmegs, galingale, spikenard, maces, cubebs, grains of paradise, long pepper, black pepper, caraway, tormentil, cumin, fennel seed, smallage, parsley, sage, mint, calamint, and horehound (plate 3).

Both expensive spices and animal products such as ambergris or musk were associated with a display of wealth, power, and prestige. Paul Freedman classifies exotica in ascending order of expense, beginning at the lower end with common but costly spices such as pepper and ginger; ascending to costlier spices such as cinnamon, long pepper, and galingale; going more upmarket to spices from the Moluccas such as cloves and nutmegs; and a final category he calls "extravagantly priced," including ambergris camphor, musk, and saffron.[11] These exotica, along with

England (Oxford: Oxford University Press for the British Academy, 1992–93); Woolgar, *The Great Household in Late Medieval England* (New Haven: Yale University Press, 1999); Woolgar, T. Waldron, and D. Serjeantson, *Food in Medieval England: Diet and Nutrition* (Oxford: Oxford University Press, 2006); and Woolgar, *The Senses in Late Medieval England* (New Haven: Yale University Press, 2006). In the last, see especially chapter 11, "The Great Household at the End of the Middle Ages" (248–59), where Woolgar describes household regulations of 1460–1510.

   [10] Kim M. Phillips, "The Invisible Man: Body and Ritual in a Fifteenth-century Noble Household," *Journal of Medieval History* 31 (2005): 143–62, at 144. Phillips examines the "Harleian Ordinances" for an unidentified noble house (in BL Harley MS 6815, sixteenth-century copy of a late fifteenth-century manuscript), as well as the "Second Northumberland Household Book" (Oxford, Bodleian MS Eng. hist. b. 208, 1500–1519).

   [11] Paul Freedman, *Out of the East: Spices and the Medieval Imagination* (New Haven: Yale University Press, 2008), 128; Freedman also describes saffron as "breathtakingly expensive," 10. See, too, the volumes by Woolgar, cited in n. 9. Ambergris and musk are both called for in SB 89, Part II, nos. 37–39. On the scarcity and expense of ambergris, see the introductory discussion in **Appendix D**.

mummy,[12] are called for in SB 89. Interestingly, in SB 89, "ynglysch saf-feroun" is specified for this crocus pollen (Part II, no. 58; see **Appendix D**). It should be noted that the post mortem inventory of John de Vere, thirteenth Earl of Oxford, who died in 1513, lists nine pounds of saffron at 10 shillings per pound, perhaps from his own estates.[13]

A wealthy household is also necessary for medicines that must be distilled. In Part I, nos. 1–4 deal with distillation, some of which resem-ble recipes in John of Mirfield's *Breviarium Bartholomei* of a century earlier and some of which are similar to recipes in the contemporary Syon Abbey medical compendium. [14] These SB 89 recipes often provide instructions on the distillation process and information on the virtues of distilled waters. For example, the recipe for water of damask that begins the book (f. 1v; plate 3) gives instructions for luting the alembic. In the first of several aqua vitae recipes (ff. 1r–v), discussed above as containing many ingredients, is the comment that high-proof alcohol is lighter than rose water, which is then followed by a series of conventional claims for high-proof alcohol, including its preservative as well as curative quali-ties. These claims are also to be found in treatises on the *ars distillandi*.[15] Distillation recipes are also to be found in Part II, nos. 1–9, 13–14, and 18.

In fifteenth-century England, distillation was an expensive process and was produced on something like an industrial scale. It required fur-naces, purpose-made glass, and specialized knowledge.[16] Skilled distill-ers such as Robert Broke, "master of the king's stillatories" for Henry VI, were well rewarded for their services.[17] Great houses outside of London also had distillation operations. Both Sandal and Pontefract Castles in West Yorkshire maintained substantial distillation equipment in the

---

[12]   Two mummy references in Part I occur in the wounds treatise, folio 16, and folio 18v. See the discussion of *Mumia* or *mummy* in **Appendix C**, no. 8.

[13]   William H. St. John Hope, "The Last Testament and Inventory of John de Veer, Thirteenth Earl of Oxford," *Archaeologia* 66 (1915): 275–348, at 324.

[14]   See comments on texts 1–4 in **Appendix C.**

[15]   Voigts, "The Master of the King's Stillatories," *The Lancastrian Court: Pro-ceedings of the 13ᵗʰ Harlaxton Symposium*, ed. Jenny Stratford (Donington: Shaun Tyas, 2003), 233–52 and plates 59–65; a typical short Middle English distillation treatise is edited from BL Royal 17.A.iii is p. 251.

[16]   S. Moorhouse, "Medieval Distilling-Apparatus of Glass and Pottery," *Medi-eval Archaeology* 16 (1972), 79-121, at 109–13.

[17]   Robert Broke is the subject of Voigts, "The Master of the King's Stillatories."

fifteenth century.[18] Documented association of women with medical distillation on the Continent, also relevant, is discussed in the following subsection

The conspicuous wealth suggested by SB 89 is one element that marks a contrast between the Berkeley Castle manuscript, written for an elite household, and another well-known household book, Lincoln Cathedral MS 91, from earlier in the fifteenth century. This earlier household book is one of two private anthologies compiled and written by Robert Thornton (fl. 1418–56), a member of the Yorkshire gentry. Lincoln Cathedral MS 91 is a more modestly produced book than BCM SB 89 and is made up largely of English and Latin literary and devotional texts. It also contains a medical *receptarium* as a relatively short component, Text 99, folios 280–314v in a 321-folio manuscript. This remedy book, usually referred to as the *Liber de diversis medicinis*, is known from several other manuscripts and has been extensively studied.[19]

SB 89 and Women's Medical Roles in Elite Households

The attention paid to women in the medical texts of SB 89 is particularly significant to this manuscript as a household book, and women's medicine has been a subject of much interest in recent scholarship.[20] Often

---

[18]   Rachel Tyson, *Medieval Glass Vessels Found in England c. AD 1200–1500*, Council for British Archaeology Research Report 121 (York: Council for British Archaeology, 2000), 1–7, 35–40; Philip Mayes and L. A. S. Butler, *Sandal Castle Excavations, 1964-1973: A Detailed Archaeological Report*, ed. Shirley Johnson (Wakefield: Wakefield Historical Publications, 1983), 191–206; and Moorhouse, "Medieval Distilling-Apparatus," 79–121.

[19]   Margaret S. Ogden, ed. *The Liber de Diversis Medicinis*, EETS OS (London: Oxford University Press, 1938; rev. ed. 1969), 207. This compendium and the *receptarium* have been studied at length by George Keiser. See ten citations to his studies in the "Bibliography" of *Robert Thornton and His Books: Essays on the Lincoln and London Thornton Manuscripts*, ed. Susanna Fein and Michael Johnston (York: Medieval Press, 2014), 287–88. See also in that volume Keiser's "Robert Thornton: Gentleman, Reader and Scribe," 67–108; Susanna Fein, "The Contents of Robert Thornton's Manuscripts," 13–65; and Julie Orlemanski, "Thornton's Remedies and the Practices of Medical Reading," 235–55.

[20]   In the considerable body of scholarship on medieval women's medicine in the past two decades, those of Monica Green are indispensable. See especially the

cited in regard to the medical knowledge of late fifteenth-century English women is the letter to Margery Paston written between 1487 and 1495 by John Paston III in which he asks her to send to him in London her *flose vngwentorum* for the knee pains of the King's attorney James Hobart. Included in the letter is his request that she also send him written instructions for administering the plaster.[21]

A recent study by Alisha Rankin with the subtitle "Noblewomen as Healers in Early Modern Germany" includes two valuable case studies of women from the mid-sixteenth century: Dorothea of Mansfeld (ca. 1492–1578) and Anna of Saxony (1532–85). Rankin makes the case that, in "the medieval aristocratic tradition, ladies of the manor, whose 'households' encompassed large estates, were responsible for the basic medical care of their charges." Women in this small demographic had "an unusually high rate of literacy," and they "were given practical training in the basic medicine needed to run their households or estates. Medical recipes thus represented the focus of their practice, and if women owned any medical books at all, they tended to be recipe collections."[22]

Rankin's conclusions are relevant to an understanding of those English women for whom SB 89 was intended, and her emphasis on noblewomen as distillers is also important when one considers that the texts with pride of place in SB 89, Part I, involve distilled medicines, in some instances with precise instructions for the distillation process. See **Appendix C**, nos. 1–5 (Part I, ff. 1–10v). Both Dorothea of Mansfeld and Anna of Saxony possessed distilling houses, and Rankin observes that "the fact that distilling houses were often included in the inventory of a noblewoman's estate after her death indicated the extent to which they

---

collection of her studies in *Women's Healthcare in the Medieval West: Texts and Contexts* (Aldershot: Ashgate, 2000), and *Making Women's Medicine Masculine: The Rise of Male Authority in Pre-Modern Gynaecology* (Oxford: Oxford University Press, 2008). Also valuable is Claire Jones, "An Assortment of Doctors: The Readers of Medical Books in Late Medieval England," *Journal of the Early Book Society* 3 (2000): 136–51.

[21] *Paston Letters and Papers of the Fifteenth Century*, ed. Norman Davis, Richard Beadle, and Colin Richmond, EETS SS 20–22 (Oxford: Oxford University Press, 2004–5) 1:628.

[22] Alisha Rankin, *Panaceia's Daughters: Noblewomen as Healers in Early Modern Germany* (Chicago: University of Chicago Press, 2013), 3, 7, 70. It bears mention that, even though the focus of SB 89 is therapeutic, the text on treatment of wounds (Part I, ff. 14v–22v, no. 8) is uncommon in a recipe collection.

were seen as part of her household."[23] Distilling houses were operated by Anna of Saxony at two of the Elector's palaces, Dresden and Annaburg. They were staffed by many servants, and the distilled therapeutic waters Anna produced were much in demand. At Anna's death, "her stores at Annaburg alone contained 181 different types of distilled waters."[24]

SB 89 is replete with evidence displaying a strong association with the women in noble households. It begins with the rubric claiming that the book is "greatly profytable to the helth off man and woman" (Part I, no. 29). The short text on humoral complexions applies each complexion to women as well as men (Part I, no. 8), and the wound text includes several references to women patients. More than twenty-five recipes in Part I specify uses by women. For example, in Part I, no. 2, in the text on distillation called "Water of Doctor Giles," we find Aqua [vitae] preciosa that "ys precious to gentyll ladys" (f. 3v), and on folio 4v, the conclusion of "Water of Swalows" warns that it will slay a child in a woman's body and concludes that one should "beware of the gyvyng." The subsequent recipe *aqua quinta* or *aqua lacida* also functions as an abortifacient, so "gyve it to no woman with child." Five recipes for compound medicines in the *Antidotarium Nicolai* in Part I are specifically gynecological and are discussed in **Appendix C**, no. 25.

Part II is likewise rich in references to women, and their social status is sometimes indicated: no. 8, "good for all cold sykenesse of the mother [*uterus*] of women it helpyth them gretly to conceive"; no. 32, "The quenys powder"; no. 44, "as I sent to your ladysheppe"; and no. 64, "diuysyd for my lady the Kyngis gramother" (plate 8). Recipe no. 34 in Part II calls for a powder to be basted in what was certainly a noblewoman's cap, called "callet" with "sarcynet" on the inside[25] (**Appendix D**).

The medical-culinary recipes in Part II, many of which make extensive use of sugar,[26] can also be identified with the roles of Tudor ladies. In

[23]   Rankin, *Panaceia's Daughters*, 29.

[24]   Ibid. 129.

[25]   *Callet* does not appear in the *MED*, but *calle* n.1 can mean a kind of headdress, and the word is related to *calotte* or skullcap; see *OED* for much later attestations. *Sarsenet* was a fine light woven silk fabric; see *OED*. For numerous citations, see The Lexis of Cloth and Clothing Project, http://lexisproject.arts.manchester.ac.uk.

[26]   "Candied foods and confections represented the area of greatest overlap between culinary and medical recipes." Rankin, *Panaceia's Daughters*, 73.

addition to the recipes calling for oranges and pomegranates discussed below, three recipes are for quinces (nos. 33, 43, 68), one for rowan tree berries (no. 44), an aspic or jelly made from veal and oxtail (no. 66), and a recipe for salad oil of walnuts (no. 67). These recipes appear to be intended as therapeutic, but one of them may suggest some relationship to a contemporary cookery book.[27]

There is, however, some external evidence linking three other culinary recipes in Part II with pregnancy: two for oranges (no. 60, for oranges baked in sugar caskets, and no. 63, for "oreniette," a syrup made from orange peel (fig. 7),[28] and the recipe for Ipocras of pomegranates (no. 41 and plate 6).[29] Two references in the Paston letters of the late fifteenth-century make a connection between pregnancy and oranges. In a 1470 letter from John Paston III to John Paston II, we find that "Dame Elyzabet Calthorp is a fayir lady and longyth for orangys, thow she be not wyth chyld," suggesting that pregnant women were known to crave oranges.[30] Another letter from John Paston III to John Paston II (1473) contains the following request: "I prey yow and ye haue eny more orangys then ye ocupye, that poore men may haue parte for a gret-belyed [great bellied] lady."[31]

That oranges, as implied in the two Paston letters, and similarly pomegranates, may have been desired in pregnancy also seems to be suggested by the household records of Elizabeth of York (1466–1503, queen

---

[27] *A noble boke of festes ryall and cookery,* printed in 1500 in London by Richard Pynson (STC 3297), lists baked quinces three times among menus for royal feasts. The recipes provided in this book, which are mostly for meats and fishes, include one "ffor to make a gelly of flesshe" similar to SB 89, Part II, no. 66: "To make A good gely."

[28] Both recipes call for copious amounts of sugar and/or honey, necessary for making hard, bitter Seville oranges palatable. Similar recipes can be found in chapter 17 of the Spanish treatise of Juan Vallés (ca. 1496–1563), *Regalo de la vida humana,* transcribed and ed. Fernando Serrano Larráyoz (Pamplona: Gobierno de Navarra-Österreichische Nationalbibliothek, 2008), vol. 1, facsimile. We are most grateful for the assistance of Kelley Young in regard to this text.

[29] The lively discussion on the MedMed listserve, curated by Monica Green, on medieval views relating to oranges or pomegranates and pregnancy was most helpful in exploring this question.

[30] *Paston Letters,* 1:554.

[31] *Paston Letters,* 1:589.

consort to Henry VII from 1486).[32] In 1502 or early 1503, she received from the "prothonotarye of Spayn" a gift of oranges. This gift probably arrived during her last pregnancy (she died February 11, 1503, a few days after giving birth); she also received on August 29, 1502, while at Berkeley Castle, a present of oranges and sukcades (*socade*, a sweetmeat), and on November 30, 1502, payment was issued to her fool, "Pache," for bringing pomegranates and apples to her. Similarly, on February 10 or 11, 1503, Pache was again paid for a present of pomegranates and other fruits given to the Queen.[33]

Further evidence for the use of recipes in SB 89 by women occurs in another codex, BL Harley MS 1706, and one of those recipes that were added to the original manuscript also requires pomegranates. In Part II of SB 89 (plate 6), the following unusual recipe occurs:[34]

(41) f. 7v [rubric]: ❡ **ffor to make Ipocras of pomegarnettis ffor them that be in An hote cawse**
Take the wyne of A good pomegarnet And medle it with asmoch water of Rosys and put therto A good quantyte of manus {Christi}[35] with

---

[32] For a recent biography, see Alison Weir, *Elizabeth of York: A Tudor Queen and Her World* (New York: Ballantine Books, 2013).

[33] *Privy Purse Expenses of Elizabeth of York: Wardrobe Accounts of Edward the Fourth, With a Memoir of Elizabeth of York, and Notes*, ed. Nicholas Harris Nicolas (London, 1830), 4, 43, 74, 93.

[34] We are grateful to Sarah Peters Kernan for her search among medieval culinary recipes for this recipe.

[35] SB 89, Part II, contains two recipes for *manus Christi*. The fuller one is no. 65 on folio 12v {Rubric}: To make manus cristi in A fluxe [eVK2 5676.25; symbols, as for the *nomen sacrum* here or for apothecaries' weights and measures, are given as words in curly brackets {}]
Take of fyne Red corall the wayte of vj pennys of good cynamon
The wayte of on grote of perle the wayte of ij {dram} powder these ech
on be them Selfe As sotelly As canne be And take of the levys off
gowld i {dram} of whyte suger on quart dyssolve the gynger with Rose water
wherin you haue Infusyd be the space of A day of Red saunders And of
Lapides emathytes [hematite; *MED*, ematites] of iche grossly powderyd ij peny
     wayght And
then the water straynyd dyssolue your suger And cast your manus {Christi}
/be craft\
SB 89, Part II, contains a second shorter recipe for manus Christi, without rubric, no. 40, following no. 39 for Diamargariton, which also uses powdered pearls. The *Antidotarium Nicolai,* in SB 89, Part I (ff. 46v–47), also includes a recipe for

A few macis And A lytyll galyngale grossly broke then put therto
Asmoch clarett wyne As you haue of wyne of pomegarnettis And of
Rose water and let them stand to gyther iij owers Afterward lett it rynne
throwe A Ipocras bagg.

This recipe for Ipocras of pomegranates in SB 89 is identical with a flyleaf
recipe in BL MS Harley 1706, folio 215v, which may have been copied
from SB 89. Harley 1706 is the much-studied volume of devotional texts
belonging to Elizabeth Scrope Beaumont de Vere, Countess of Oxford
(probably born ca. 1468, d. 1537). As the daughter and one of the coheirs
of Sir Richard Scrope and Eleanor Washbourne, she was the niece of
John, fifth Lord Scrope of Bolton.[36] See section 2, **Date, Decoration and
Original Ownership of BCM SB 89**, and genealogy charts I–III.

Elizabeth was married twice, first in 1486 to William, Viscount
Beaumont. But at some point, apparently in the late 1480s, she and her
husband, who was by then mentally ill, entered the household of the
man who later, in 1508–9, became Elizabeth's second husband (and she
his second wife), John de Vere, thirteenth Earl of Oxford.[37] As Earl of
Oxford, de Vere, with his wife Elizabeth, continued to live at Wivenhoe
and Castle Hedingham in Essex. The earl enlarged the latter to maintain
a household of more than one hundred people, and the castle included a
tennis court. Among his other properties, de Vere owned a great London
house. His decisive role in the Battle of Bosworth earned the confidence
of Henry VII, who made him Lord Chamberlain and Lord Admiral. De

---

Diamargariton calling for "margery perlys thyrlyd and vnthyrlyd." There is exten-
sive literature on diamargariton, which dates back at least to Nicholas Myrepsos, a
C13 Byzantine physician. By the late Middle Ages, both diamargariton and manus
Christi were produced on an industrial scale by friars in Italy. See Angela Montford,
Health, Sickness, Medicine and the Friars in the Thirteenth and Fourteenth Centuries
(Aldershot: Ashgate, 2004), especially 202–3. Chapter 8 in the Spanish treatise by
Juan Vallés (see above, n. 28) also addresses the virtues of *manus Christi* and pro-
vides recipes.

[36] Jennifer Ward, "Elizabeth Beaumont, Countess of Oxford (d. 1537): Her Life
and Connections," *Transactions of the Monumental Brass Society* 17 (2003): 1–13.
See also H. W. Lewer, "The Testament and Last Will of Elizabeth, Widow of John de
Veer, Thirteenth Earl of Oxford," *Transactions of the Essex Archaeology Society* 20
(1933): 7–16. For an example of the exchange of medical recipes in correspondence
among aristocratic women, see Rankin, *Panaceia's Daughters*, 139.

[37] S. J. Gunn, "Vere, John de, thirteenth earl of Oxford (1442–1513)," *ODNB*.

Vere was godfather to Prince Arthur, and he entertained Henry VII at Castle Hedingham at least three times.[38] The lavish scale of his household is demonstrated in two surviving accounts and the extensive inventory of his goods taken on his death in 1513, to be discussed subsequently in this study.[39] The Earl of Oxford was a powerful magnate, exceptionally wealthy, and his wife Elizabeth was a Scrope.

Elizabeth, from 1508 Countess of Oxford, has long been known for the books she owned, in particular two famous miscellanies of Middle English devotional writing.[40] One, Harley MS 1706, was acquired by her between 1486 and 1509 and was repeatedly signed by her as both Elizabeth Beaumont and Elizabeth Oxenford. Of particular importance in this codex is a second medico-culinary recipe relevant to SB 89.[41] In addition to the recipe for Ipocras of pomegranate (identical with Part II of SB 89, Appendix D, no. 41 and plate 6) discussed above, the added medical recipe in Harley 1706, folio 215v, "To make gyngeate(?)," a syrup made from orange peel, appears to be the same recipe as SB 89, Part II, Appendix D,

---

[38]   James Ross, *John de Vere, Thirteenth Earl of Oxford, 1442–1513* (Woodbridge: Boydell Press, 2011), bears as its subtitle the phrase used by a Flemish ambassador to describe de Vere during the reign of Henry VII, "The foremost man of the Kingdom," 98, 215–18.

[39]   At his death in 1513, de Vere owned 116 landed estates with an annual revenue of 2,300 pounds. He left Elizabeth life income from twenty-seven manors and dower income from thirty-two manors (Ross, *John de Vere*, 210, 225). See nn. 37–38 and section 2 (**Date, Decoration, and Original Ownership of BCM SB 89**), which includes further discussion of de Vere's wealth and London property. It should, however, be mentioned here in connection with the recipes for Ipocras of pomegranates in SB 89 and Harley 1706, that among de Vere's accounts is payment for pomegranates (Longleat MS misc. ix, f. 91).

[40]   On BL, Harley 1706, completed "between 1400 and 1500 or a little later," and Bodleian MS Rawlinson. Lit. f. 37, see the important study by A. I. Doyle, "Books Connected with the Vere Family and Barking Abbey," *Transactions of the Essex Archaeological Society* 25, part 2 (1958): 222–43, at 231 for dating. A full description and digital images of Harley 1706 are available online through the British Library Digitised Manuscripts website, http://www.bl./manuscripts.

[41]   Two studies dealing with Harley 1706 are of value here: Andrew Taylor, "Into His Secret Chamber: Reading and Privacy in Late Medieval England," *The Practice and Representation of Reading in England*, ed. James Raven, Helen Small, and Naomi Tadmor (Cambridge: Cambridge University Press, 1996), 41–61, and Dirk Schultze, "Hippocras Bag, Oil of Exeter and Manus Christi: Recipes in BL Harley 1706," *Anglia* 126 (2008): 429–60. Our transcriptions of recipes added to Harley 1706 differ from those of Schultze.

no. 63, "To make oreniette" and fig. 7. The parallels between the recipes for Ipocras of pomegranates and oreniette in SB 89 and Harley 1706 suggest the close relationships of women readers discussed in section 2. That medical and culinary recipes from SB 89 appear in Harley 1706, a book of the Countess of Oxford, underscores the value of SB 89 for women.[42] The link between SB 89 and Harley 1706—as the discussion in section 2 will show—is also significant because the long-lived Countess of Oxford was a member of the family for which SB 89 was written.[43]

---

[42]   Elizabeth Scrope Beaumont De Vere herself also copied out on folio 214v of Harley 1706 the opening words of the medical recipe for oil of Exeter from the facing folio (f. 215), where it is given in full. As Rankin points out, recipes were "potent items of patronage" (*Panaceia's Daughters*, 82).

[43]   More problematic than the connection between SB 89 and Harley 1706 is the relationship between the Berkeley Castle MS and the later composite manuscript at the Bodleian Library, Ashmole MS 1444. On Ashmole 1444, see William Henry Black, *Descriptive, Analytical and Critical Catalogue of the Manuscripts Bequeathed unto the University of Oxford by Elias Ashmole* (Oxford, 1845), cols. 1205–10. See also L. M. Eldredge, *The Index of Middle English Prose, Handlist IX . . . the Ashmole Collection* (Cambridge: Brewer, 1992), 74–78. As Black explains, this volume contains "five old MSS on paper, worn and defaced in many places; they are paged throughout by Ashmole" (col. 1205). At least four recipes from SB 89—usually with significant variants from SB 89—occur in the fourth "manuscript" or booklet, 193–304, from the sixteenth century. A fifth recipe from SB 89 occurs in the fifth "manuscript," 305–90, from "about the time of Queen Elizabeth." We have identified the following texts that occur in both Ashmole 1444 and the Berkeley Castle manuscript:
From booklet IV (C16):
§ p. 234 "Damaske water" corresponds to SB 89, Part I, f. 1, and Part II, no.9, ff. 2r–v; see **Appendix B**;
§ p. 274 "Red manus Christi" is similar to SB 89, Part II, nos. 40 and 65, but much briefer;
§ p. 275 "Ipocras of pomgarnades" corresponds to SB, Part II, no. 41; and
§ p. 281 "Braket . . . devysed by ye Kynges grandom" corresponds to SB 89, Part II, no. 64.
From booklet V (Elizabethan):
§ p. 332 "A medisone for the plage wch the Kinges grace sent my lord Mayer of London" gives as a single recipe what in Part II of SB 89 are nos. 51 (prophylactic) and 52 (when the patient is already infected with the plague). This treatment, whether as two recipes or one, can be found in another manuscript as well. See the discussion of royal plague recipes in section 3 (**Epidemic Disease during the Reign of Henry VII (1485-1509)**), below, and table 1.

2. Date, Decoration, and Original Ownership of BCM SB 89

SELECT BOOK 89 was purchased in 1924 by the eighth Earl of Berkeley (d. 1942), a physical chemist and landowner with a strong interest in medicine. There is no indication that its acquisition was occasioned by any suggestion of a family connection.[1] There is, however, telling evidence for early ownership of the manuscript and the household to which it relates on the damaged first page, where pen and ink decoration includes a shield of arms in the top margin (plates 1, 2.a [detail]).[2]

In 1931, the manuscript was temporarily deposited in the British Museum where Eric Millar (later Keeper of Manuscripts) made a brief report of its contents, describing the coat of arms on the shield at the head of this first page as "Quarterly, 1 and 4 a bend, 2 and 3 a saltire

---

[1] Bought at Sotheby's sale, July 29–30, 1924, lot 157. A further sale of mainly printed books on the following day (Sotheby's, July 31, 1924) included a section of material titled "Jenner Portraits and Relics" (lots 311–40) relating to Edward Jenner (1749–1823), the pioneer of smallpox vaccination who was born and lived in the village of Berkeley in Gloucestershire. It seems likely that it was this Jenner material that attracted the attention of the eighth earl and his agent to the salerooms at this date. On Lord Berkeley, see the entry by John Shorter, "Berkeley, Randal Thomas Mowbray Rawdon, eighth earl of Berkeley (1865–1942)," *ODNB*. For further comments on provenance, see **Appendix A**.

[2] Because the manuscript in its present state is unbound, this first page is the most rubbed and damaged. The volume was cropped for binding (in the late sixteenth century or afterward), so part of the top of the shield has been lost. See further **Appendix A**.

engrailed."[3] The armorial shield may well have been clearer when Millar saw it, since he makes reference to the application, at the request of the owner, of a reagent. Millar adds that he has been unable to find any quartered coat of the kind, and as there was no indication of the tinctures, it was impossible to identify either of the coats separately.

Millar also commented on the shaded pen and ink drawing beside the scrollwork letter "h" that begins the rubric to the content tables: "The initial has a King's head, as you say, but I doubt very much whether this is intended for any king in particular." Again, more may have been visible with the reagent, although it is still possible to confirm that the head and shoulders of the figure appear to show traces of a crown or coronet and plate armor. The drawing also includes a quatrefoil flower and, below the scroll initial, an oak-leaved branch bearing acorns (with slight traces of gold or color), and an oak apple or oak gall in a cluster at the foot. At the top of this spray, a lily or aroid formed like a fleur-de-lis branches toward the right. There may have been another fleur-de-lis to balance, branching left, but this area is now too damaged to allow anything to be discerned. Traces of color, possibly gold, are also visible under ultraviolet light on one edge of the shield, giving an impression of slight depth.[4]

Although it was common for scribes to leave spaces for illustrated initials to be inserted after the writing, the variation in the length of the text lines to accommodate the scrollwork initial letter "h" suggests that, in this case, the drawing was more likely to have been done first (plates 1, 2.a).[5] The only other pen and ink drawing in the manuscript is the oak-leaf initial letter "T" on the first text page, where the lines also adjust slightly, if less obviously (Part I, f. 1; plate 2.b [detail]). This initial looks to be in the same hand—very possibly that of the scribe himself—as the pen decoration on the first page. Since the sharply angled and shaded blank scroll beneath the shield on the first page is so similar to the scrollwork of

---

[3] Letter of Eric G. Millar to G. O. Flynn, agent to Lord Berkeley; dated British Museum, October 15, 1931. The letter is kept with the manuscript.

[4] We are grateful to Professor Jane Sayers for the kind loan of her ultraviolet lamp, and to David Smith, Hon. Archivist at Berkeley Castle, for his assistance in its use and in detecting the traces of gold or color on the shield.

[5] The lines of the opening rubric are staggered so that the fifth line beginning "to" extends to the edge of the scroll initial, the next line contracts, and the last returns again to follow the line of the scroll. We thank Kathleen Scott for this observation and for her valuable advice on the pen and ink decoration in both discussion and correspondence.

the initial letter "h"—and the drawing all of a piece—the arms should be acknowledged as those of the person for whom it was made or intended, an integral part of the manuscript, not added later.

The arms on the shield can be identified as those of Scrope, *azure a bend or* (probably the best known of all English medieval arms), quartered with *argent a saltire engrailed gules*, the arms of the Tiptoft family.[6] The Scropes, one of the leading baronial families in the north of England, acquired the Tiptoft arms in the late fourteenth century when Sir Richard Scrope, later first Lord Scrope of Bolton (d. 1403), married two of his sons to two of the three daughters and coheiresses of Robert, Lord Tiptoft—these Tiptoft heiresses being Sir Richard's wards at the time.[7] The two sons, Roger, later second Lord Scrope of Bolton, and Stephen, deputy lieutenant in Ireland under Henry IV, could then impale their arms with those of Tiptoft; and the next generation could quarter them, as they appear in the Berkeley Castle manuscript.[8] It was these quartered arms that Stephen Scrope (d. 1472), the well-known literary figure in the household of Sir John Fastolf, used on his seal after his mother's death.[9]

Date of BCM SB 89

Stephen Scrope, known for his shared interest in medicine with William Worcester, might seem a promising candidate for ownership of the book, which would make it in effect a Fastolf household book, Stephen himself being kept dependent and notoriously poverty-stricken by his stepfather Fastolf.[10] Certainly both Caister Castle in Norfolk and Fastolf Place in

---

[6] D. H. B. Chesshyre and T. Woodcock, eds., *Dictionary of British Arms: Medieval Ordinary*, vol. 1 (London: Society of Antiquaries of London, 1992), 320, 324.

[7] *Complete Peerage*, 11:539–42; Brigitte Vale, "Scrope, Richard, first Baron Scrope of Bolton (c.1327–1403)," *ODNB*.

[8] Two branches of the Scrope family, Bolton and Masham, emerged in the fourteenth century; the introduction of the Tiptoft arms identifies the shield of arms with the former, the Scropes of Bolton. Their main estates were based around Bolton Castle, in Wensleydale, North Yorkshire.

[9] London, BL, Additional Charter 18,299, dated 1448. Stephen Scrope, author and translator, was the eldest son of Sir Stephen Scrope by Millicent Tiptoft (d. 1446), the second daughter and Tiptoft coheiress, whose second marriage was to Sir John Fastolf.

[10] See Jonathan Hughes, "Scrope, Stephen (1397–1472)," *ODNB*.

Southwark could claim to be of a scale and grandeur that would fit such a book. But the quartered coat of arms remained in use by the Scropes of Bolton—no doubt in recognition of the importance of the Tiptoft inheritance—until well into the sixteenth century, and evidence supporting a later date for the manuscript effectively rules out Stephen's generation as owners.

One intriguing piece of this evidence comes in Part I of the manuscript. In the short text known from its Latin title as *De conferentibus et nocentibus* (no. 32 in Part I, ff.82v–83, 84v), the scribe has inserted his own cri de coeur against new technology; he lists among things harmful or evil for the eyes, "to study moche on whyte bokis And namely pryntyd boke" (SB 89, Part I, f. 83, fig. 5).[11] The term "white books," as identified by Nicholas Pickwood, was the name for unbound sheets, sold in preference to bound books, and the form in which they could be more cheaply transported.[12] In this context, however, it may simply be the brightness of the white paper used in printing that concerns the scribe.[13] We have not found reference to printed books in the many other manuscripts

---

[11] For further discussion of the *De conferentibus* text, see **Appendix C**, no. 32, and section 1 (**Introduction**), 95–96. Not surprisingly, *De conferentibus* is one of a number of medieval texts that address factors causing vision problems. For example, a lengthy *receptarium*, London Medical Society MS 136, now held in the Wellcome Library and edited by Warren Dawson, *A Leechbook or Collection of Medical Recipes of the Fifteenth Century* (London, 1934), attributes to Peter Bonant a list of thirty-three such harmful elements, including "to rede moch on small letters" (160–62). A discussion of this tradition can be found in Joy Hawkins, "Sight for Sore Eyes: Vision and Health in Medieval England," *On Light*, Medium Ævum Monographs, ed. K. P. Clarke and Sarah Baccianti (Oxford: Society for the Study of Medieval Languages and Literature, 2014), 137–56. Hawkins's survey addresses neither *De conferentibus* nor printed books as a hazard to vision, and her comment that the "belief that reading or writing on white paper damaged the eyes apparently dates back to Galen" (147, n. 51) is surely anachronistic.

[12] N. Pickwood, "Onward and Downward: How Binders Coped with the Printing Press Before 1800," *A Millennium of the Book: Production, Design and Illustration in Manuscript and Print 900–1900*, ed. Robin Myers and Michael Harris (Winchester: St Paul's Bibliographies, 1994), 61–106, at 63.

[13] The scribe's concern with the harmful effects of the white paper of printed books mirrors Caxton's complaint about the white paper of manuscripts; in the epilogue to his *Recuyell of the Historyes of Troye* (STC 15375 [1473]), Caxton states that one of his reasons for learning to print was to avoid the need for making manuscript copies of his work, when "myen eyen dimmed with overmuche lokyng on the whit paper."

containing *De conferentibus* that we have consulted, although there are instances where "new books," apparently referring to handwritten codices, are cited.[14] The scribe's complaint could imply he was of a conservative nature, even perhaps fearful for the effect of printing on his livelihood. It recalls, for example, the much-quoted case in which a London stationer, Philip Wrenne, in the course of petitioning against his imprisonment for a debt, sometime before 1500, lamented that he, his wife, and his children would be utterly undone by the demands of the claimant, "in somoche as the Occupation ys almost destroyed by Prynters of Bokes."[15]

Equally likely, however, is that the scribe of SB 89 may simply have had a surfeit of copying printed books. Caxton introduced the printing trade into England in 1476, and books were being imported from the Continent in sizeable if fluctuating numbers from the late 1470s,[16] but the new technology was slow to overtake established methods, and the shift from manuscript to printed text took place over many decades. Scribal copying of printed works was common in this period of overlap.[17]

---

[14] See, e.g., London, Wellcome Library, MSS 397, ff. 68–69; 5262, ff. 54–57v (eVK2 7420, 7418); Willy L. Braekman, *Studies on Alchemy, Diet, Medecine [sic] and Prognostication in Middle English*. Scripta: Mediaeval and Renaissance Texts and Studies 22 (Brussels: Omirel, URSAL,1988 for 1986), 43–82. Andrew Borde in his *Breuiary of Helthe* (1547) prints a version of the text listing among things harmful for the eyes "reydynge in smal printed bokes, specially greke bokes."

[15] TNA, Early Chancery Proceedings, C1/74/50. See C. Paul Christianson, "An Early Tudor Stationer and the 'Prynters of Bokes,'" *The Library*, 6th ser., 9 (1987): 259–62, at 260; Christianson, "The Rise of London's Book Trade," *The Cambridge History of the Book in Britain: Volume III 1400–1557*, ed. Lotte Hellinga and J. B. Trapp (Cambridge: Cambridge University Press, 1999), 128–47, at 131, 139. See also Peter W. M. Blayney, *The Stationers' Company and the Printers of London, 1501–1507*, vol. 1 (Cambridge: Cambridge University Press, 2013), 29 and n. 13. Blayney comments that, even though Wrenne's complaint was premature, "as the volume and variety of printed material increased some textwriters may have felt threatened as they read the printing on the wall." For a later example, "Pryntynge hathe almooste vndone scriueners crafte," from a collection of practice sentences for schoolboys (William Horman, *Vulgaria* [printed by Richard Pynson, 1519]), see Julia Boffey, *Manuscript and Print in London 1475–1530* (London: BL, 2012), 3–4, fig. 2.

[16] Yvonne Rode, "Importing Books to London in the Late Fifteenth and Early Sixteenth Centuries: Evidence from the London Overseas Customs Accounts," *Journal of the Early Book Society* 15 (2012): 41–84.

[17] For instances of manuscripts copied from printed texts, see, most recently, Julia Boffey, "From Manuscript to Print: Continuity and Change," *A Companion to*

Some evidence of date is also provided by manuscripts associated with SB 89. A manuscript in the Huntington Library (MS HM 144, f. 151v) contains, on a flyleaf, a closely related version of the royal recipe for the plague in SB 89 (Part II, f. 9, no. 49; for further discussion and transcription, see table 1). Copies of printed texts included in this manuscript show that it cannot date from earlier than 1482. Another codex, Peniarth MS 369B in the National Library of Wales, with a related but earlier version of the *Circa instans* text found in SB 89 (see **Appendix C**, nos. 10 and 12), can be securely dated from the inclusion in the manuscript of dated deeds copied by the same hand. These deeds (at fols. 14v, 18, and 53v) relate to parishes in Oxfordshire (Cornwell, Salford, and Over Norton) and provide dates of 1482 to 1484–85 (2 Ric. III: no month given).[18] Five recipes are also found copied in the later composite codex, MS Ashmole 1444 in the Bodleian Library in Oxford, from the sixteenth century.[19] Together these related manuscripts make it likely that SB 89 dates from at least the last quarter of the fifteenth century—almost certainly after 1485—and may be of an early sixteenth-century origin. This is consistent with the mixed hand of the scribe, which exhibits both secretary and Anglicana features.[20]

The shape of the shield on the first page (plates 1, 2.a) also has significance for dating the manuscript. Although the top is lost through cropping, there is enough remaining of the shield to reveal that it is waisted at the center; then, after broadening out, the shield curves to a point at the base. This style of Renaissance shield shape seems to have been unknown in England before the last years of the fifteenth century.[21] Early

---

the Early Printed Book in Britain 1476–1558, ed. Vincent Gillespie and Susan Powell (Cambridge: D. S. Brewer, 2014), 13–26, at 20–22.

[18]   We are indebted to Daniel Huws for supplying these references: he has pointed out that some of the documents may have been copied for the sake of their form as precedents (as suggested by the appearance of incomplete names such as "Richard de D."); if so, the Peniarth manuscript could be later in date. The inclusion of William Catesby's name (Peniarth 369B, f. 14v) among signatories in the copy of a letter of presentation to the rectory at Salford, addressed to John Russell, Bishop of Lincoln, April 10, 1482, offers a tenuous link with the Scropes of Bolton to whom Catesby was related; it may be an indication that texts in the Peniarth manuscript circulating in this region were available to the Scrope family (see below, n. 93).

[19]   See section 1 (**Introduction**), 107, n. 43.

[20]   See further **Appendix A**. We thank Pamela Robinson for her judgment from the beginning of our work that the hand was late fifteenth or early sixteenth century.

[21]   Waisted shields without the ogee-shaped base are found earlier, as are others that broaden below a waist to wide, angled corners. From the mid-fifteenth century,

occurrences are uncommon and appear always to point to some association with the fashionable circles of the court. Its use did not become widespread before the second decade of the sixteenth century.

Two fragments of an armorial tapestry now in Winchester College that can be dated to the turn of the century display such a shield.[22] Woven in the Southern Netherlands, the tapestry has arms and heraldic devices that link it to the court of King Henry VII and to his eldest son, Prince Arthur (d. 1502). On a red and blue paneled background, a shield clearly in the waisted form appears together with red and white Tudor roses and the sacred monogram "IHS." The arms on the shield, three gold crowns, one above the other on a blue ground, are the attributed arms of Prince Arthur's namesake, the legendary Arthur, King of Britain. The striped background, woven to look like damask, includes the pomegranate badge of Katherine of Aragon in a repeating pattern, suggesting a link to the betrothal or marriage of Arthur and Katherine. Thomas Campbell has proposed that the fragments come from part of a set of tapestries commissioned by Henry VII for Arthur in the late 1490s. Although he finds no such tapestry in Henry VII's inventories, Campbell makes a persuasive case for identifying it in the collection sold on the death of Henry's mother, Margaret Beaufort, shortly after her son's death in 1509, among ten pieces of "verdors with Jhs the redde rose and the white."[23] Heraldic tapestries such as these would have been conspicuously displayed in royal residences, widely visible on a daily basis to members of the royal household and those attending at court.

The work of another artist-craftsman from the Southern Netherlands—or trained there—furnishes an early instance of this waisted shield in a manuscript. The royal arms of England appear on a shield of this shape in the border of a volume of French Chronicles (part of a vast unfinished set of six volumes) made between 1487 and 1494 for Sir

---

shields that curve concavely on one side and curve convexly (or are straight) on the other commonly occur in German woodcut illustration, often in counterbalancing pairs, and became familiar in England. Under ultraviolet light it is possible to confirm that the shield in SB 89 is symmetrically indented on both sides and broadens to curved, not angled, "hips."

[22] The tapestry fragments are at Winchester College, Winchester, in Hampshire. Described and reproduced in color by Thomas P. Campbell, *Henry VIII and the Art of Majesty: Tapestries at the Tudor Court* (New Haven: Yale University Press for the Paul Mellon Centre for Studies in British Art, 2007), 80–81, fig. 4.14.

[23] Ibid., 81.

Thomas Thwaytes, Treasurer of Calais, as a gift for Henry VII.[24] A further datable witness is provided by the velvet chemise bindings on the
indentures or agreements drawn up between Henry VII and Westminster Abbey in 1504.[25] The indentures concern Henry VII's Chapel (the
Lady Chapel), then under construction at the Abbey and in which Henry
intended his own tomb to be housed. A central silver-gilt enameled boss
on the front and back covers of the bindings bears a crowned shield of the
royal arms between supporters of a dragon and greyhound. This shield is
slightly indented and has a pointed base.

It is the Henry VII Chapel that provides the most prominent and public use of this shield shape with its appearance on the tomb monuments
of Henry VII and his mother, Margaret Beaufort. The chapel was incomplete at Henry's death in 1509. It was not until November 1511 that the
Florentine sculptor, Pietro Torrigiano, was contracted to make Margaret
Beaufort's tomb,[26] and then in 1512, that of Henry VII with his queen,
Elizabeth of York.[27] Gilt-bronze shields of arms, slightly waisted (more
so on the latter tomb), are prominent features on the tomb-chests of both
monuments. A delayed payment in December 1511 is recorded in the
accounts of the executors of Margaret Beaufort's will to "Garter the king

---

[24]   BL, Royal MS 20 E i, f. 47. The shield is pointed at the base but only very
slightly indented at the waist. Reproduced by Richard Marks and Paul Williamson,
eds., *Gothic: Art for England, 1400–1547* (exhib. cat., London: V&A Museum, 2003),
no. 46 (with color plate). See also Scot McKendrick, John Lowden, and Kathleen
Doyle, eds., *Royal Manuscripts: The Genius of Illumination* (exhib. cat., London: BL,
2011), 351.

[25]   Both the king's copy of the foundation indentures (TNA, PRO: E 33/1) and
the copy made for Westminster Abbey (BL, Harley MS 1498) have these chemise
covers; the indented shape of the shield is more clearly defined on the king's copy.
For a description of the chemise binding, see the entry by Mirjam Foot in Marks
and Williamson, *Gothic*, no. 30 (with color ill.). For Harley MS 1498, see McKendrick et al., *Royal Manuscripts*, no. 41. The royal arms inside the lavishly illuminated
volumes and on the seal skippets are on standard straight-sided shields; illustrated
(color plate VIII) in a comprehensive study of the indentures by Margaret Condon,
"God Save the King! Piety, Propaganda, and the Perpetual Memorial," *Westminster
Abbey: The Lady Chapel of Henry VII*, ed. Tim Tatton-Brown and Richard Mortimer
(Woodbridge: Boydell Press, 2003), 59–97.

[26]   Marks and Williamson, *Gothic*, no. 29 (color plate 52).

[27]   Ibid., no. 117 (color plate 55). Also reproduced (color plate VI) and discussed
by Philip Lindley, "'The singuler mediacions and praiers of al the holie companie of
Heven': Sculptural Functions and Forms in Henry VII's Chapel," in Tatton-Brown
and Mortimer, *Lady Chapel*, 259–93, at 266–69.

of haroldes for makyng and declaring my ladies armes in viij schochyns [escutcheons] for my ladies tombe and deliuerede to the florentyne."[28] Involvement by the heralds in providing guidance on the arms in such a case was only to be expected, and waisted shields appear in the drawn and painted heraldic records made by Thomas Wriothesley, Garter King of Arms from 1505 to 1534, and by his colleagues.[29]

Other examples closely connected to the court are to be found in stained and painted glass of the early sixteenth century, notably in the fine work of the leading Anglo-Netherlandish glass painters based in Westminster and Southwark. The most extensive decorative schemes of these glaziers survive at King's College Chapel, Cambridge, and at Fairford parish church in Gloucestershire; in both places, shields with arms and badges similar in shape to SB 89, some held by angels, appear in the tracery glazing of the windows.[30] At King's College Chapel, the work was first contracted in 1515—in fulfillment of the terms of Henry VII's will—to Barnard Flower, the king's glazier from 1505 until his death in 1517. At Fairford, the closeness in style to the Henry VII Chapel in Westminster Abbey indicates that the glazing, dated ca. 1500 to 1515, was also likely to have been under Flower's direction.[31]

---

[28] Cited by Robert F. Scott, "On the Contracts for the Tomb of the Lady Margaret Beaufort, Countess of Richmond and Derby, Mother of King Henry VII, and Foundress of the Colleges of Christ and St. John in Cambridge: With Some Illustrative Documents," *Archaeologia* 66 (1915): 365–76, at 370.

[29] See, e.g., London, College of Arms, MS A. 17, ff. 49v, 52v, painted standards and shields, ca. 1513, in "Armes and Standards and Burials in yᵉ Churches of London" by Thomas Benolt, Clarenceux King of Arms (illustrated in Michael P. Siddons, *Heraldic Badges in England and Wales* [Woodbridge: Boydell Press for the Society of Antiquaries of London, 2009], 1: color plates 9, 11); and BL, Additional MS 45131, f. 109v, a pen and ink drawing of the tomb monument of Sir Thomas Parr (d. 1517), by Sir Thomas Wriothesley, Garter. Wriothesley seems to have employed the waisted shield sparingly when, as here, recording or designing monuments; for simple records of coats of arms, he reverted to the more convenient and standard heater shield.

[30] Richard Marks, *Stained Glass in England during the Middle Ages* (London: Routledge, 1993), 209–20, fig. 178; Sarah Brown and Lindsay MacDonald, eds., *Fairford Parish Church: A Medieval Church and Its Stained Glass* (Stroud: Sutton, 2007), 66–69, 97–99.

[31] Richard Marks ("The Glazing of Henry VII's Chapel, Westminster Abbey," *The Reign of Henry VII: Proceedings of the 1993 Harlaxton Symposium*, ed. B. Thompson [Stamford: Paul Watkins, 1995], 157–74, at 164) argues for a date toward the end of the period 1500–1515, on the grounds that such important work of the foreign

As regards the Scropes of Bolton, examples both in stained glass and in manuscripts show that this waisted shield shape, so closely associated with the sophisticated fashion of the court, was employed by the extended family. Work by Anglo-Netherlandish glaziers at Lullingstone Castle in Kent includes the arms of Scrope on a waisted shield. Here it is the result of a particular family connection, the marriage to the courtier Sir John Peche (b. ca. 1473, d. 1522) of Elizabeth Scrope, a daughter of Robert Scrope and Katherine Zouche (see genealogy chart I and further below).[32]

Although the shield form seems to occur only rarely in English manuscripts, two examples show its use in families connected to the Scropes of Bolton. A decorated initial at the beginning of a Sarum Breviary in the British Library (Arundel MS 130, f. 1; fig. 11) encloses an armorial shield of the SB 89 shape. The arms on the shield are those of the wealthy northern magnate, Henry Algernon Percy (1478–1527), fifth Earl of Northumberland, a nephew of Henry, sixth Lord Scrope of Bolton, and his wife Lady Elizabeth Percy (see genealogy chart III).[33] The fifth Earl of Northumberland succeeded to the title as a minor in 1489 on the death of his father and was the first of his family to use these particular quarterings

---

glass-painters carried out in a Gloucestershire parish church is unlikely to have predated work commissioned for the Henry VII chapel by the king.

   [32] The shield of arms, dated early sixteenth century, is in the north chapel of St. Botolph's Church in the grounds of Lullingstone Castle; a reproduction from a watercolor drawing by Charles Winston, 1841 (BL, Additional MS 35211, f. 263) is available at *Corpus Vitrearum Medii Aevi* [Great Britain] website (http://www.cvma. ac.uk), inventory no. 007309. The shield has the arms of Sir John Peche impaled with the arms (quarterly Scrope and Tiptoft, differenced with a crescent) of his wife Elizabeth Scrope. See C. R. Councer, "Painted Glass at Cranbrook and Lullingstone," *Archaeologia Cantiana* 86 (1971): 35–54. Mary C. Erler, "Exchange of Books between Nuns and Laywomen: Three Surviving Examples," *New Science out of Old Books: Studies in Manuscripts and Early Printed Books in Honour of A. I. Doyle*, ed. Richard Beadle and A. J. Piper (Aldershot: Scolar Press, 1995), 360–73 (at 364–67 and plate 60), discusses the Anglo-Flemish stained glass at Lullingstone (in particular, the east window of the chancel showing three female saints carrying books) as part of her account of the communal nature of women's reading in the household of Lady Elizabeth Scrope Peche.

   [33] R. W. Hoyle, "Percy, Henry Algernon, fifth earl of Northumberland (1478–1527), magnate," *ODNB*. See below, 139–40, for the close connection between the Yorkshire households of the fifth earl of Northumberland and the Scropes of Bolton.

of the Percy coat of arms.[34] The same coat of arms, although on a different shape of shield, appears on the earl's Garter stall plate and is added to Oxford, Bodleian Library, MS Arch. Selden. B. 10, in both cases surrounded by the Garter.[35] The fifth earl had obtained the Garter by April 1499.[36] In Arundel MS 130, the shield has no surrounding Garter. This may suggest, although it certainly does not dictate, a date for that manuscript—and its waisted shield—of between 1489 and 1499, a period when the young earl was being brought up as a royal ward at court.

That the Scrope family and their connections might favor the waisted shield for heraldic display is suggested also by its occurrence in Bodleian MS Ashmole 1504, one of two closely related East Anglian picture books of the early sixteenth century. The Ashmole codex, dated about 1520, forms a pair with a manuscript of some two decades earlier that

---

[34] The breviary has been wrongly dated to between 1446 and 1461 by misattribution of the arms on the shield to Henry Percy, third Earl of Northumberland (d. 1461). For correct identification of the arms, see James Fowler, "On Two Heraldic Bench-ends in Great Sandal Church," *Yorkshire Archaeological Journal* 1 (1870): 131–52. Three of the quarterings on the shield (Poynings, Fitzpaine, Brian) represent lands and title obtained through the marriage of the third earl to a Poynings heiress, but settlement of conflicting claims to the Brian estates was not made until 1488 (John M. W. Bean, *The Estates of the Percy Family, 1416–1537* [Oxford: Oxford University Press, 1958], 118); this no doubt accounts for the delay in introducing the Brian coat of arms. The fourth earl (d. 1489) used the Brian arms only on an escutcheon of pretense; see Rosemary Horrox, ed., *Beverley Minster: An Illustrated History* (Beverley: Friends of Beverley Minster, 2000), 39 and color plate 5.

[35] The armorial shield within the Garter was added with motto, supporters and badges to Arch. Selden B. 10 (fol. 198v; reproduced on the Bodleian Library's LUNA website), a manuscript of Hardyng's *Chronicle* enlarged with a copy of Lydgate's *Proverbes* from Wynkyn de Worde's printed edition (?1510 or 1520); see Malcolm B. Parkes, *English Cursive Book Hands 1250–1500* (London: Scolar Press, 1979), plate 15 (ii). The fifth Earl of Northumberland's enlargements of Arch. Selden B. 10 and its companion, BL, Royal MS 18 D ii (both with elaborate calligraphic penwork), have been the subject of a number of studies; especially relevant here is the discussion by Pat Naylor, "Scribes and Secretaries of the Percy Earls of Northumberland, with Special Reference to William Peeris and Royal MS 18 D. II," *Tudor Manuscripts 1485–1603*, ed. A. S. G. Edwards, English Manuscript Studies 1100–1700, vol. 15 (London: BL, 2009), 166–84; see also Edwards, "Books Owned by Medieval Members of the Percy Family," *Tributes to Kathleen L. Scott. English Medieval Manuscripts: Readers, Makers and Illuminators*, ed. Marlene Villalobos Hennessy (London: Harvey Miller Publishers, 2009), 73–82.

[36] Peter J. Begent, Hubert Chesshyre, and Lisa Jefferson, *The Most Noble Order of the Garter: 650 Years* (London: Spink, 1999), 314.

was once housed at Helmingham Hall in Suffolk and now resides in the Paul Mellon collection at the Yale Center for British Art in New Haven, Connecticut.[37] These handsome, large-folio books—defined by Julia Boffey as household books[38]—both contain almost identical sets of colored drawings of plants and trees, birds and animals, arranged alphabetically under their English names.[39] A great variety of supplementary material included in the Ashmole codex (drawings of household objects, landscape vignettes, stylized flower patterns, and ornamental alphabets) culminates in four elaborate full-page painted shields of arms.[40] The last of these shields, the only one of the SB 89 shape, ends the book, although it may not have done so originally (plate 4.a). It has the arms of John de Vere (d. 1513), thirteenth Earl of Oxford, impaling the quartered Scrope and Tiptoft arms (the same quartered arms as given in SB 89), the arms of his second wife, Elizabeth Scrope Beaumont de Vere, who figures largely in these pages (see section 1 [**Introduction**] and further below).

A direct connection between Elizabeth as Countess of Oxford and the Ashmole manuscript might be indicated by the presence of this shield of arms. The appearance of these arms in a manuscript associated with the Tollemache family of Helmingham, likely owners of the earlier "twinned" Mellon book, has hitherto been explained as simply representing the thirteenth Earl of Oxford as the leading figure in East Anglian society and a fittingly grand and powerful man in the land.[41] But since the book is known to date from a number of years after the death of the thirteenth earl, it can at least be argued that the arms may be those of Elizabeth, as dowager Countess of Oxford. Inclusion of the Waldegrave arms on one of the four heraldic shields lends some support to this. The strong connection between the Waldegraves, a prosperous Suffolk gentry family, and the great house of de Vere has been well documented and appears to have

---

[37]   Nicolas Barker, *Two East Anglian Picture Books: A Facsimile of the Helmingham Herbal and Bestiary and Bodleian MS. Ashmole 1504* (London: Printed for presentation to the members of the Roxburghe Club, 1988).

[38]   Boffey, "Definitions of the 'Household Book'," 126 (see section 1 [**Introduction**], n. 8).

[39]   No connection with SB 89 has been discerned by a comparison of the plants depicted (listed by Barker, "Table," *Two East Anglian Picture Books*, 83–86) and those listed in Part I of SB 89 (*Circa instans* and Synonomy; see **Appendix C**, nos. 10, 12).

[40]   Bodl., MS Ashmole 1504, ff. 46r–v, 48r–v. The two leaves with shields of arms are separated by a leaf containing large foliate designs for letters.

[41]   Barker, *Two East Anglian Picture Books*, 40–41.

continued in Elizabeth's widowhood.[42] On the reverse of the two leaves displaying the arms of Waldegrave and de Vere/Scrope are the arms of the Emperor and of the King of England.[43] This proximity suggests that the shields of these two families are of key importance in the book.[44] It seems entirely possible that the Ashmole version of the East Anglian pattern book could have been commissioned for either of these households.

Decoration of BCM SB 89

Much of the subsidiary material in Ashmole 1504 can be shown to derive from earlier models. In particular, this is true of the ornamental alphabets at folios 42–45v, a matter of relevance for the light these models can throw upon the pen and ink decoration of SB 89. Two alphabets of lowercase scrollwork letters—of the kind termed "banderole" alphabets—in Ashmole 1504 (ff. 42–44) are also present in the Mellon manuscript (f. 1r–v).[45] The first of these banderole alphabets closely resembles one of the sets of sample or pattern scripts in an alphabet book from the Macclesfield collection now in the British Library.[46] This manuscript, dated about

---

[42]　Sir William Waldegrave of Bures (d. 1527), a leading Suffolk landowner, was in the affinity of John de Vere, Earl of Oxford, and an annuitant and executor of his will: Ross, *John de Vere*, 237–38 (section 1 [**Introduction**], n. 13). For Elizabeth's association in retirement with the Waldegraves see below, 148 and n. 157.

[43]　The Waldegrave shield (f. 46) has on the verso, labeled "Empereur," a crowned shield with the double headed eagle, collar of the Toison d'Or and motto for Charles V as emperor (i.e., after 1519); folio 48, labeled "Kkyng," has the royal arms of England surrounded by the Garter with the arms of John de Vere (de Vere quartering Howard) impaling arms of Elizabeth (Scrope quartering Tiptoft) on the verso.

[44]　This remains true whether or not the book is now misordered or lacks, at the end, leaves containing a further series of shields.

[45]　Barker, *Two East Anglian Picture Books*, 39. Banderole alphabets are discussed in a general survey of pattern books by Robert W. Scheller, *Exemplum: Model-Book Drawings and the Practice of Artistic Transmission in the Middle Ages*, trans. Michael Hoyle (Amsterdam: Amsterdam University Press, 1995), especially 293 (fig. 167), 296, 357–58. The designs employ ribbons or strips of parchment in Gothic minuscule letter forms. See also Jonathan J. G. Alexander, *Medieval Illuminators and Their Methods of Work* (New Haven: Yale University Press, 1992), 175, n. 33.

[46]　BL, Additional MS 88,887, ff. 24r–v. See Christopher de Hamel and Patricia Lovett, *The Macclesfield Alphabet Book: BL Additional MS 88887* (London: BL, 2010) [facsimile ed.].

1500, has also been associated with East Anglia.[47] In the Macclesfield volume, the scrollwork letters occur in a mixed alphabet of lowercase and uppercase letters: the lowercase in banderole scrollwork, the capitals formed mostly by what Christopher de Hamel has termed "rustic branch designs."[48] The "h" that begins the prologue on the first page of SB 89 (plate 2.a), although composed of scrolls more sharply angular in appearance, is formed essentially as in the banderole alphabet; careful cross-hatching in pen and ink takes the place of color shading in the model books.[49] The decorated letter "T" at the opening of the first recipe in Part I of SB 89 (plate 2.b) is made up of rustic branches wrapped with scrolls similar to the design of capital letters in the Macclesfield mixed alphabet. This detail suggests that the scribe or artist of SB 89 was familiar with comparable patterns or models.

The models had long been available. At the top end of the range, scrollwork or banderole letters had been used in the calligraphic penwork headings of royal grants and charters from at least the fourteenth century in France, and from the early fifteenth century in England.[50] The 1446 charters for Henry VI's twin foundations, Eton College and King's College, Cambridge, for example, written by John Broke, a chancery clerk, and illuminated by the noted London artist William Abell, are decorated with strapwork and interlace letter forms in the top line.[51] The pen and

---

[47]   De Hamel and Lovett, *Macclesfield Alphabet Book*,15–16.

[48]   Ibid.,14.

[49]   Cf. Bodl., MS Ashmole 1504, f. 42; Yale Center for British Art, Paul Mellon Collection, Helmingham Herbal and Bestiary, f. 1 (reproduced in Barker, *Two East Anglian Picture Books* [facsimile]).

[50]   Many royal documents of Charles V and Charles VI of France from the late fourteenth and early fifteenth century included the scrolled banderole letters in the calligraphic opening title: for examples with color plates, see Ghislain Brunel, *Image du Pouvoir Royal: Les Chartes Décorées des Archives Nationales XIIIe-XVe siècle* (Paris: Centre historique des Archives nationales, 2005), 51, 53–54, 170–74, 206–7. For the most comprehensive discussion of English royal charters, see Elizabeth Danbury, "The Decoration and Illumination of Royal Charters in England, 1250–1509: An Introduction," *England and Her Neighbours, 1066–1453: Essays in Honour of Pierre Chaplais*, ed. Michael Jones and Malcolm Vale (London: Hambledon Press, 1989) 157–79, and her recent survey "Décoration et Enluminure des Chartes Royales Anglaises au Moyen Âge," *Bibliothèque de l'École des Chartes* 169 (2011): 79–108.

[51]   See Danbury, "Décoration," 94–95; Danbury, "Royal Charters,"166–67. The illumination and top line decoration of the 1446 Eton charter is reproduced in William J. Connor, "The Esholt Priory Charter of 1485 and Its Decoration," *Yorkshire*

ink calligraphy includes scrollwork letters from the second of the two banderole alphabets discussed above to complete the king's name after an elaborate initial letter "h" for *Henricus*. An earlier royal charter for Eton College, dated 1442, also attributed to William Abell, employs banderole letters from the first of these two alphabets for the king's name.[52]

Penwork decoration not only was applied to royal grants and charters, and to manuscript codices, but also was featured in the production of the vast numbers of administrative and legal documents, charters, and rolls that were such an important part of the everyday work of medieval English scribes.[53] Some of the closest parallels to SB 89 are to be found in such documents.

The great series of plea rolls for the courts of Common Pleas and the King's Bench affords one of the richest examples of scribal activity of this kind.[54] Decoration was mostly confined to the initial letter "P" for "Placita" beginning the text. This "P" is perhaps best known for enclosing the royal arms or an image of the sovereign, although a much wider range of subject was introduced.[55] The opening lines of the text and the name of the chief

---

Archaeological Journal 80 (2008): 121–52, fig. 4 (detail) at 127; the King's charter is illustrated in *The Cambridge Illuminations: Ten Centuries of Book Production in the Medieval West*, ed. Paul Binski and Stella Panayatova (Cambridge exhib. cat., London: Harvey Miller Publishers, 2005), no. 181, color plate (detail) at 380.

[52] Eton College, ECR 39/8, reproduced in Danbury, "Décoration," 99 (ill. 7), 100.

[53] For a perceptive discussion of the way in which scribes could be involved in documentary as well as literary work, see Andrew Prescott, "Administrative Records and the Scribal Achievement of Medieval England," *English Manuscripts before 1400*, ed. A. S. G. Edwards and Orietta Da Rold, English Manuscript Studies 1100–1700, vol. 17 (London: BL, 2012), 173–99.

[54] The vast cache of medieval pen and ink drawing yielded by the unbroken sequence of decorated plea rolls for the courts of Common Pleas and the King's Bench has been made freely available online under the auspices of the *Anglo-American Legal Tradition* [*AALT*] at the O'Quinn Law Library, University of Houston Law Center: http://aalt.law.uh.edu/. We are indebted to Elizabeth Danbury for introducing us to this site. We also owe thanks to her and to Kathleen Scott for valuable advice concerning comparative material for the pen drawing in SB 89.

[55] Erna Auerbach, *Tudor Artists: A Study of Painters in the Royal Service and of Portraiture on Illuminated Documents from the Accession of Henry VIII to the Death of Elizabeth I* (London: University of London, Athlone Press, 1954), remains the best introduction to the plea roll series of initial letters. For wide-ranging discussion and illustrations of decoration in plea rolls, charters, and other documents, two recent studies are particularly valuable: Connor, "The Esholt Priory Charter of 1485"; and Anne F. Sutton, "An Unfinished Celebration of the Yorkist Accession by a Clerk of

justice who witnessed the roll, or the clerk who engrossed the document, could also be embellished with flourishes and calligraphic initials (some resembling those used in rubrics by the scribe of SB 89), and strapwork or interlace and small drawings could be added. The penwork drawing of the rolls is uneven in quality, ranging from weak to the highly accomplished. It is clear that the court clerks would normally be responsible for both decoration and script, even if the most sophisticated artwork might on occasion involve the services of limners brought in to assist. The plea roll scribes can also be shown to have used patterns. Most strikingly, at least three of the "Placita" initial letters are designs whose original source was a "Figure" alphabet (i.e., with letters formed from carefully arranged human and animal figures) in a woodcut series with the date 1464.[56] Letters from this alphabet occur also in both MS Ashmole 1504[57] and in the Macclesfield Alphabet Book.[58] In another instance, the King's Bench plea

---

the Merchant Staplers of Calais," *The Fifteenth Century, 8: Rule, Redemption and Representations in Late Medieval England and France*, ed. Linda Clark (Woodbridge: Boydell Press, 2008), 135–61.

[56] TNA: CP40/822 [Hilary 1467]; KB27/963 [Easter 1502] and 997 [Michaelmas 1509]. The alphabet is reproduced in facsimile from the 1464 woodcut series in the British Museum in Campbell Dodgson, *Grotesque Alphabet of 1464* (London, 1899). See also [Robert] Massin, *Letter and Image*, trans. C. Hillier and V. Menkes (London: Studio Vista, 1970), figs. 154–57. For a discussion of the plea roll versions of the figure letter "P" (which show that copies of the woodcut letters were available in England from as early as 1467), see Elizabeth Danbury and Kathleen Scott, "The Plea Rolls of the Court of Common Pleas: An Unused Source for the Art and History of Later Medieval England, 1422-1509," *The Antiquaries Journal* 95 (London: Society of Antiquaries of London, 2015), 157–210, at 185–190.

[57] See Barker, *Two East Anglian Picture Books*, 40, and f. 45v [reproduced in facsimile]. Shown as colored drawings are the first four letters of the figure alphabet copied from engravings of the woodcuts made in the late fifteenth century by the south German "Master of the Banderolles." Further copies from this engraved set are in the Victoria and Albert Museum (MSL/1937/ 2090, ff. 3–6v); see Rowan Watson, *Western Illuminated Manuscripts: A Catalogue of Works in the National Art Library from the Eleventh to the Early Twentieth Century*, 3 vols. (London: V&A Publishing, 2011), 2:783, 788 (fig.), 789. For a different figure alphabet in a mid-fifteenth-century English model book (BL, Sloane MS 1448A), see Janet Backhouse, "An Illuminator's Sketchbook," *The British Library Journal* 1 (1975), 3–14, at 9–13, plates 5 and 6; Kathleen L. Scott, *Later Gothic Manuscripts, 1390–1490*, 2 vols., Survey of Manuscripts Illuminated in the British Isles 6 (London: H. Miller, 1996), 1: figs. 347–50; 2: no. 90 (253–56). See also Alexander, *Medieval Illuminators*, 126–28 and n. 33 (175).

[58] De Hamel and Lovett, *Macclesfield Alphabet Book*, 12–13, and reproductions of ff. 15–20v. This full set of the letters is closer to the woodcut series than to the engravings.

roll for Michaelmas term 1494 has in the opening lines the scrolled "h" of the second banderole alphabet in the two East Anglian books (Ashmole, ff. 43–44; Mellon, f. 1v).[59] In the same roll are further calligraphic initials and a profile head of a king alongside the word "Regis." Small pendrawn profile heads (occurring as part of the penwork flourishing of letters known as cadels) were common in the plea rolls—as in manuscript book decoration—and appear also in the Macclesfield alphabets.[60] They are more often grotesque or comic than realistic, and done in simple line, unlike the larger shaded drawing of the head and shoulders in SB 89.

Figurative drawing with shading in pen and ink was less frequently used to embellish initials in archival manuscripts and documents than the calligraphic strapwork and interlace that were more naturally the province of the scribe. Enough exceptions survive from the late fifteenth century, however, to show that this style of shaded pictorial initial, often combined with calligraphic ornament, also had its occasional place.

Decorative penwork in the records held by London's Bridge House Estates provides examples in the manner of the plea roll scribes, and sometimes uses identical motifs.[61] As in the plea rolls, the decoration seems in most cases to have been undertaken by writers of the text.[62] The scribes clearly had recourse to patterns or model sheets. C. Paul Christianson cites as examples three drawings from the Bridgemasters' Accounts for 1484–1509: a delicately drawn heron or crane forming the figure letter "S" of *Summa* beginning the top line of a page of accounts dated 1490 and, in the lower margin of the same page, a heraldic-looking

---

[59] TNA: KB27/933; see *AALT*, http://aalt.law.uh.edu/. The letters in this alphabet are composed of scrolls twisting around a central stem.

[60] De Hamel and Lovett, *Macclesfield Alphabet Book*, 9–10, and reproductions of ff. 3–6v. The Macclesfield ornamented letters are unusual in that, although mostly grotesques, many of the heads are three-quarter or even full face and modeled with extensive shading.

[61] C. Paul Christianson, *Memorials of the Book Trade in Medieval London: The Archives of Old London Bridge* (Cambridge: D. S. Brewer, 1987), especially the section on "Penwork," 41–47 and plates; methods of transfer in outline for the replicated motifs from the plea rolls are discussed at 43–44.

[62] Ibid., 47. Christianson concludes that evidence "suggests circumstantially scribes writing record texts also had proficiency in decorative drawing as well as in the execution of cadels."

griffin and a bear holding a lily. [63] He shows that both the upright bear and the bird almost certainly had their origin in engraved playing cards of ca. 1451–53 designed by the so-called Master of the Playing Cards.[64] Beside the griffin (probably derived from a heraldic exemplar), a scroll records that Normavyle "had me made" (*fieri me fecit*), and gives the year 1490, a reference to its commission by John Normavyle, Clerk of the Bridge House Works at that date.[65]

Similar penwork can be found in a variety of formal accounts, registers, charters, and administrative records, and with patrons not only in London. A collection of materials made in the late 1450s and early 1460s by Thomas Beckington, Bishop of Bath and Wells (1443–65), justifying the English claim to the throne of France, was embellished with both strapwork initials and a number of large figure letters, outlined in pen and carefully shaded to add three-dimensional depth.[66] Part of the decoration in the register of Robert Stillington, Beckington's successor as Bishop of Bath and Wells (1466–91), has been attributed to the same accomplished hand. [67] The first and most elaborate initial letter in

---

[63] London Metropolitan Archives, CLA/007/FN/02/004: Bridgemasters' Annual Account and Rental, 1484–1509, fol. 96; Christianson, *Archives of Old London Bridge*, 41–42, and plate XVI (detail: reproducing the griffin and bear).

[64] Ibid., 41–42, n. 26, 44, plates XXIX, XXXI.

[65] The same inscription *Normavyle fieri me fecit* appears written with pen flourishing at the foot of a double page of elaborate penwork and cadels ending the accounts for 1492 (Bridge House Accounts, 1484–1509, ff. 119v–20; Christianson, *Archives of Old London Bridge*, 42 and plate XVII). It suggests that the decorative penwork was made for John Normavyle (Clerk of the Bridge Works and sometime bailiff of Southwark), but was not in his hand; see Nigel Ramsay, *The Review of English Studies*, n.s., 41, no. 162 (1990): 236–37, where it is also maintained that the status of clerks of the Bridge Works made it unlikely that they would themselves be scribes who routinely wrote the books and rolls.

[66] Fully described in Kathleen L. Scott, "The Decorated Letters of Two Cotton Manuscripts," *Tributes to Jonathan J. G. Alexander: The Making and Meaning of Illuminated Medieval and Renaissance Manuscripts, Art and Architecture*, ed. Susan L'Engle and Gerald B. Guest (London: Harvey Miller, 2006), 99–110, with figure letters reproduced as figs. 1, 2, 4–6. One of the most noteworthy initials is the letter "I" in the form of a king bearing a scimitar and a scepter (BL, Cotton MS Tiberius B xii, f. 34v); reproduced in Scott, *Later Gothic Manuscripts*, 1: intro., fig. 22.

[67] William J. Connor, "The Register of Robert Stillington, Bishop of Bath and Wells 1466–91," *The Ricardian* 20 (2010): 1–22, figs. 1–16. The similarity between the Beckington drawings (examples at figs. 13–16) and initials in the register is discussed at 18–19.

Stillington's register, dated 1466, incorporates figurative drawing (a bow-man shooting at a peacock) integrated with interlaced strapwork in such a way as to suggest that the scribe and artist may well have been one and the same person; exuberant strapwork and scrollwork initials then feature throughout the register until 1489.[68] Anne Sutton, in discussing the work of a talented scribe employed by the Merchant Staplers of Calais in the 1460s, has drawn parallels with the clerks of the bishops of Bath and Wells. She assigns to the scribe both the writing and the pen decoration of the Merchant Staplers' register of royal grants and compares his work most closely to products of "the scriveners, members of the company of court-hand writers of London, who were the maids of all work to the legal profession, composing and copying legal texts."[69]

Yorkshire, home to the Scropes of Bolton, also had its share of patrons who favored pen drawing. An example of particular interest for our study is the commission by Lady Margaret Clifford for decoration of the so-called Esholt Priory Charter of 1485;[70] this is the royal charter Margaret obtained under letters patent from Richard III permitting her to grant the advowson of a Lincolnshire church to the nuns of Esholt Priory, a small Cistercian house in the West Riding of Yorkshire.[71] Margaret Clifford was a kinswoman by marriage of Lady Elizabeth St John Scrope, second wife of John, fifth Baron Scrope of Bolton (see genealogy chart II, and further below), and the impressive Esholt Charter may well have been known to the Scrope family.[72] The handsome penwork of this royal

---

[68] Ibid., figs. 2, 4, 7, reproduce scrollwork initials (none resembling those of the banderole model alphabets). Scott describes scrollwork letters as overall the most common type of figure letter in English fifteenth-century books ("Decorated Letters of Two Cotton Manuscripts," 104, with examples listed at n. 40).

[69] Sutton, "An Unfinished Celebration," 146–47 (see n. 55, above). See also Prescott, "Administrative Records and Scribal Achievement," 183–86 (see n. 53, above).

[70] Margaret Clifford (d. 1493), widow of a noted Lancastrian, John, ninth Lord Clifford, and wife of Sir Lancelot Threlkeld, was an heiress in her own right with substantial estates in Yorkshire that escaped her first husband's attainder; see Henry Summerson, "Clifford, John, ninth Baron Clifford (1435–1461), soldier and magnate," *ODNB*.

[71] Connor, "The Esholt Priory Charter of 1485," especially figs. 1–21.

[72] In 1486, Margaret's son, Henry, tenth Lord Clifford, married Anne St John (d. 1508) (see Henry Summerson, "Clifford, Henry, tenth Baron Clifford (1454–1523), magnate," *ODNB*). Anne was the daughter of John St John of Bletsoe, brother of Lady Elizabeth Scrope and half brother to King Henry VII's mother, Lady Margaret

charter combines both decorative and figurative drawing: strapwork initials embellish the top line, with heraldic devices, and a scroll left blank for a motto; enclosed within the initial "R" is a shaded drawing of the Virgin and Child; and in the margin, the nuns of Esholt are shown kneeling before a prie-dieu.[73] Though the grant would have been drawn up by chancery scribes, Margaret Clifford as the recipient had responsibility for commissioning the additional decoration. William Connor, in his extensive study, attributes the shaded drawings of the initial "R" to more than one artist. He concludes that Margaret was most likely to have gone outside the chancery for this, choosing among the many limners working in London perhaps in the milieu of the "Caxton Master."[74]

The manuscript known as the Guild Book of the Barber Surgeons of York (BL, Egerton MS 2572), a medical miscellany and ordinances of the Company of Barber Surgeons, is a reminder that accomplished penwork illustration may not be confined to London.[75] Two of the four full-page miniatures (all by the same artist) from the medieval section, dated 1486, have full-length male figures in shaded drawing similar in style to the drawing of SB 89.[76]

Beaufort. The marriage was unhappy and Lady Anne Clifford was taken with her two daughters into the household of Lady Margaret Beaufort (Michael K. Jones and Malcolm G. Underwood, *The King's Mother: Lady Margaret Beaufort, Countess of Richmond and Derby* [Cambridge: Cambridge University Press, 1992], 163–64), one of many of the St John family to have places there. For the Scrope/St John family relationships and connection to Lady Margaret Beaufort, see further below, 132–39, and genealogy chart II. Like the Scropes (see below, 141, n. 124), the Clifford family were consistent members of the fashionable York Corpus Christi Guild; Margaret joined with her first husband (Connor, "The Esholt Priory Charter of 1485," 146–47) and Henry, Lord Clifford, with Anne in 1488 (*ODNB*).

[73] Reproduced in Connor, "The Esholt Priory Charter of 1485," figs. 1–3, and in Alexandra Sinclair, ed., *The Beauchamp Pageant* (Donington: Richard III and Yorkist History Trust in association with Paul Watkins, 2003), plate 6 (detail).

[74] Connor, "The Esholt Priory Charter of 1485," 134–39, 145–46.

[75] Scott, *Later Gothic Manuscripts*, 2: no. 139 (363–64).

[76] On the page containing a volvelle (f. 51), the figures at the four corners, identified by captions in the accompanying scrolls, are, at the top, the patron saints of the Guild, John the Baptist and John the Evangelist, and, at the foot, Saints Cosmos and Damian, patrons of medicine and surgery (reproduced in color in Peter Jones, *Medieval Medicine in Illuminated Manuscripts* [London: BL, 1998], fig. 48). On the verso of the page (f. 51v), a tinted and shaded drawing of the head of Christ surrounded by figures, again with captions on scrolls, shows personifications of the "Four Humours," otherwise known as "The Four Complexions" (Scott, *Later Gothic*

Determining whether pen and ink decoration was likely to be the work of the scribe or that of a separate limner or book illuminator is seldom clear-cut.[77] The copyist of SB 89 never attempts the intricate strapwork or interlace of the most accomplished calligrapher-scribes and only occasionally (in Part I of the manuscript) indulges in modest decoration of top line ascenders (see **Appendix A**). Nevertheless, he clearly shows himself to be a well-trained scribe, writing an attractive, clear hand and with an evident liking for embellishing his work with calligraphic initials. His training—most probably in London, given the "unremarkable London dialect" of the text[78]—may well have involved association with the courts of law or the royal household where both accurate copying and adding decoration to a variety of documents would be regarded as valuable skills. He is likely to have worked in private service, in a household or group of households, and to have been employed in many ways.[79] He is not the compiler of the manuscript, certainly not of Part I. Nor is he familiar with medical language.[80] It was in the capacity of a scribe that he was entrusted with what was always intended to be a handsome book. The shaded scrollwork and shield on the first folio and the oak leaf initial that begins the text would seem to be well within his competence, especially if guided by models or patterns. He may have been copying wholesale from one or more exemplars, the only essential change being that of the arms of Scrope on the shield. The inclusion of the shaded drawing of the crowned head (an image of high quality as far as it can be determined in

---

Manuscripts, 1: fig. 503). Scott notes that representations of the four humors are rare in English illustration but cites, in addition to those in the York Guild Book, the example of the early fifteenth-century illustrations to the *Liber cosmographie* of John de Foxton (Trinity College Cambridge MS R.15. 21), a manuscript that also had an association with York (Scott, *Later Gothic Manuscripts*, 2: no. 31, 114–17, at 115). See **Appendix C**, no. 29, n. 40.

[77] For a summary of recent views, see "Section VI. Scribes ou Artistes?" in Danbury, "Décoration," 105–6.

[78] See section 1 (**Introduction**), n. 1.

[79] It may be noted that an annual account of Henry Percy, fifth Earl of Northumberland, records at least seven clerks with writing duties in the household in addition to the secretary (*The Regulations and Establishments of the Household of Henry Algernon Percy, the Fifth Earl of Northumberland, at His Castles of Wressle and Leconfield, in Yorkshire, Begun Anno Domini, MDXII*, ed. T. Percy [1770; new ed. London, 1905], 316–17).

[80] For example, his mistaken transcript of "garsing" (said to be bad for the eyes) as "gnawyng" (Part I, f. 83; fig. 5).

its damaged state) means that the involvement of a separate artist to provide the decoration cannot be ruled out. On balance, however, it seems
likely that the scribe of SB 89 undertook the penwork himself, entering
each decorated initial first and then writing his text.[81]

The shield of arms, the decoration, and the "pryntyd boke" reference
come in Part I of SB 89, which ends on folio 86v with the words in red
"*ffinis huius libri*." To this, however, the word "Nay" has been added in
another (later?) hand; and Part II does indeed then follow straight on, in
the same hand as Part I and in the middle of a quire (plate 5).[82] The first
folio of this second section is wanting, with only a blank stub remaining (f. [i]). The missing leaf is likely to have included, as well as the first
part of the contents list, another rubric and perhaps more decoration.
Part II need not have been added immediately, but since the same clear,
practiced hand is used throughout, and the format is identical with a
contents list and careful rubrication, there is unlikely to have been any
sizable gap. The evidence that the same hand is responsible for both parts
reinforces a conclusion that the scribe is likely to have been a clerk who
was employed within the household.

Original Ownership of BCM SB 89

A date in the final decade of the fifteenth century or early in the sixteenth means that the arms on the first leaf can be confidently attributed
to the senior branch of the Scrope of Bolton family (genealogy charts
I–III). This senior line was also entitled to quarter the Tiptoft arms by
descent from the elder sister and heraldic coheiress Margaret Tiptoft.[83]
The junior branch of the family, descendants of Stephen Scrope, did not
have the wealth, status, or royal connections to make ownership of such a
book at all probable after the Fastolf generation. In 1465, Stephen Scrope,
then heavily in debt, had conveyed his considerable Yorkshire estates to
the young Richard Scrope (his distant cousin and younger brother of
John, fifth Lord Scrope of Bolton), who had assisted him in his medical

---

[81]   This was clearly his practice when writing the rubrics with calligraphic capitals on folio 78v (see fig. 8 and **Appendix A**).

[82]   SB 89, Part I, f. 86v–Part II f. [i] stub, f. [ii]. See further **Appendix A**.

[83]   *Complete Peerage*, 11:541–43.

researches with William Worcester.[84] Richard managed to retain these estates after the death of Stephen, so that the Yorkshire holdings became completely severed from Stephen's Castle Combe estates in the west country. Stephen's heir, after further financial difficulties, was left with only a modest inheritance from his father's lands. In 1467, in the Earl of Warwick's chapel at Sheriff Hutton Castle, Richard married Eleanor Washbourne, the daughter of Norman Washbourne, a Worcestershire esquire. Although he was a younger son, and had no male heir himself, Richard Scrope's death in 1485 left a formidable array of daughters as his coheiresses. After his widow's second marriage to Sir John Wyndham of Felbrigge in Norfolk, these daughters formed part of an extensive—and bookish—family network in East Anglia (see further below).[85]

In the late fifteenth century, only the eldest son and heir of the senior line would be entitled, on succeeding to the barony, to use the Scrope arms undifferenced by a cadency mark—such as a label, a crescent, or a mullet—introduced into a coat of arms to distinguish different members of a family. Even under ultraviolet light, no such mark can be seen on the armorial shield in SB 89, making it almost certain that these are the arms of the head of the family and holder of the title.

Three generations of the senior line were qualified to use the undifferenced arms in this way during the period in question (see genealogy charts I-III). The first would have been John, <u>fifth</u> Lord Scrope of Bolton, K.G. (d. 1498), eldest of the four sons of Henry, fourth Baron Scrope; he

---

[84] Richard is recorded in William Worcester's medical notebook (BL, Sloane MS 4), in 1465, giving information concerning the Tiptoft and Badlesmere ancestors of the Scropes and land title in Hambledon, Buckinghamshire (f. 50v), and adding a recipe for the stone to two recipes contributed by Stephen Scrope (f. 57v). None of these medical recipes can be associated with SB 89.

[85] The female Scropes as owners of books have received considerable notice since Ian Doyle, in "Books Connected with the Vere Family and Barking Abbey," *Transactions of the Essex Archaeological Society*, 25, part 2 (1958): 222–43, first drew attention to their importance. See, e.g., Carol M. Meale,"'Alle the bokes that I haue of latyn, englisch, and frensch': Laywomen and Their Books in Late Medieval England," *Women and Literature in Britain, 1150–1500*, ed. Meale, (Cambridge: Cambridge University Press, 1993), 128–58; Erler, "Exchange of Books" (see above, n. 32). See also A. S. G. Edwards, "The Contexts of Notre Dame MS 67," *The Text in the Community: Essays on Medieval Works, Manuscripts, Authors, and Readers*, ed. Jill Mann and Maura Nolan (Notre Dame, Indiana: University of Notre Dame Press, 2006), 107–28 (focusing mainly on the Scropes of Masham, original owners of the Foyle manuscript of the *Mirror to Devout People*, now University of Notre Dame, MS 67).

succeeded to the barony in 1459.[86] His arms are to be found on his Garter stall plate in St. George's Chapel, Windsor (plate 4.b).[87] He was succeeded by Henry, <u>sixth</u> Lord Scrope, John's son by his first wife, Joan Fitzhugh (d. 1468), and holder of the title from 1498 to 1506. The sixth lord's eldest son and heir, also Henry, was <u>seventh</u> Lord Scrope of Bolton from 1506 to 1533.[88]

The shield of arms in SB 89 links the ownership or commissioning of the manuscript to one of these three male heads of the household. As has been shown earlier, however, use of the book was directed as much, if not more, toward the women of the household: wives, daughters, mothers, and widows—not just "Aqua vite for my lord," but "As I sent to your ladysheppe." And it was a series of advantageous marriages that brought to the senior branch of the Scropes (described as "peers of the middle rank") intimate contact with the households of several of the wealthiest nobles in the land. It also brought, through John, fifth Lord Scrope's second marriage, a close connection to the Tudor court.

At the time of Henry VII's accession to the throne in 1485, the second wife of John, fifth Lord Scrope, was Elizabeth St John, widow of William, Lord Zouche (d. 1462). Elizabeth was the daughter of Margaret Beauchamp of Bletsoe, duchess of Somerset, by the first of her three husbands, Sir Oliver St John (see genealogy chart II). The marriage of John and Elizabeth is known to have taken place before December 1471.[89] Although John had been a strong supporter of the Yorkist King Edward IV, in 1470 he sided with Richard Neville, Earl of Warwick (the "Kingmaker"), in the rising that briefly restored Henry VI to the throne. This temporary change of allegiance no doubt influenced Henry VI's council in the choice of "our right trusty and welbeloued Elizabeth ladie Scrope" as a safe person to attend Queen Elizabeth Woodville after the queen had sought sanctuary at Westminster Abbey in 1470; it makes the Lady Scrope in question

---

[86]   See P. W. Hammond, "Scrope, John, fifth baron Scrope of Bolton (1437/8–1498)," *ODNB*.

[87]   William H. St John Hope, *The Stall Plates of the Order of the Garter:1348–1485* (Westminster: A. Constable and Co., 1901), plate 70. John was made a knight of the Garter by Edward IV before April 1463.

[88]   *Complete Peerage*, 11:544–47. Joel Rosenthal, "A Case Study of the Scropes of Bolton," *Patriarchy and Families of Privilege in Fifteenth-Century England* (Philadelphia: University of Pennsylvania Press, 1991), 77–90.

[89]   *Complete Peerage*, 11:545. *A Descriptive Catalogue of Ancient Deeds*, ed. H. C. Maxwell Lyte, vol. 4 (London, 1902), no. 6808.

(of at least three Lady Elizabeth Scropes alive at the time) identifiable as John's wife.[90] Elizabeth was subsequently godmother to the infant Edward V born in sanctuary and would have assisted in the care of all the royal children including Elizabeth of York, the future Tudor queen.

More importantly, through the second marriage (ca. 1442) of her mother, Margaret Beauchamp, to John Beaufort, first duke of Somerset, Elizabeth St John was half sister to Margaret Beaufort, the redoubtable mother of King Henry VII. Lady Margaret Beaufort, as her biographers point out, was notoriously fond and protective of her numerous siblings of the half blood and their extended families.[91] The ties between the Scropes and the St Johns, and thus to the household of Lady Margaret Beaufort, were made even stronger by the marriage of John, fifth Lord Scrope's sister Dame Elizabeth Bygod (she retained throughout her three marriages the surname of her first husband) to his wife's brother Oliver St John of Lydiard Tregoze (d. 1497) (see genealogy charts I and II). Oliver St John, the younger of the two sons of Margaret Beauchamp's first marriage, was a member of Lady Margaret Beaufort's riding household.[92]

John, fifth Lord Scrope, may have found his wife's relationship to the king's influential mother of great value in the early years of the Tudor dynasty. He had been well rewarded in the previous reign for a long-standing loyalty to Richard III. In December 1484, he was granted lands in the south west and made constable of Exeter castle for life. As a royal councillor, he was part of a close-knit group of the king's advisers and was related to two of the most influential in Richard's short reign: William

---

[90] *Complete Peerage*, 11:545. Lorraine C. Atwell, "An Indenture between Richard Duke of Gloucester and the Scrope Family of Masham and Upsall," *Speculum* 58 (1983): 1018–25, at 1023, n. 33. The warrant issued in Henry VI's name, dated October 30, 1470, authorized payment of £10 to Lady Elizabeth Scrope for her attendance upon the queen; printed by Cora L. Scofield in "Elizabeth Wydevile in the Sanctuary at Westminster, 1470," *English Historical Review* 24, no. 93 (1909): 90–91. The two other Lady Elizabeth Scropes living at the time were John, fifth Lord Scrope's mother (d. 1504), and his aunt (d. after December 20, 1483), wife of Thomas, fifth Lord Scrope of Masham (see genealogy chart III); there is no evidence that either showed support for the rebellion.

[91] Jones and Underwood, *The King's Mother*, 31–33, 82, 84, 112–14, 165, with genealogical tables 2–4. All later accounts of Lady Margaret's constant care for the St John family rely heavily on this indispensable biography.

[92] Jones and Underwood, *The King's Mother*, 33, 165. The riding household did not remain at a fixed location but would attend Lady Margaret wherever she went.

Catesby, who had acted as administrator of his estates in the 1470s and was his stepson-in-law, married to Margaret, Elizabeth St John's daughter by her first husband (genealogy chart II);[93] and Sir Richard Ratcliffe, who became his sister Agnes's second husband (genealogy chart I).[94] Yet despite his loyal adherence to Richard III, in April 1486 (within a year of the Battle of Bosworth), John was able to join the new king, Henry VII, at York for the Garter banquet and St. George's Day ceremonies.[95] Even after he and his cousin Thomas, sixth Lord Scrope of Masham, had been involved in the Lambert Simnel conspiracy in 1487 and had mounted an unsuccessful attack on York, they escaped attainder. Both suffered only a period of house arrest, in John's case in Windsor Castle.[96] John was pardoned at the beginning of 1488, but remained bound by heavy penalties restricting his movements without the king's license. He was unable to go more than twenty-two miles from London and, even by 1489, not permitted to go north of the river Trent.[97]

Several of the numerous houses associated with Lady Margaret Beaufort were well known to the young families of the intermarried Scropes and St Johns. Maxey Castle, in Northamptonshire, remained a favored residence of Margaret Beauchamp, the Dowager Duchess of Somerset, and passed on her death in 1482 to her daughter Lady Margaret (see genealogy chart II). In London, the great Thameside mansion of Coldharbour came to Lady Margaret Beaufort as a gift from her son after his accession to the throne.[98]

---

[93] Rosemary Horrox, "Catesby, William (b. in or before 1446, d.1485), royal councillor and speaker of the House of Commons," *ODNB*. It was at this time that the Scropes may have had access to the medical texts circulating in the earlier Peniarth manuscript (see 114, n. 18).

[94] Rosemary Horrox, "Ratcliffe, Sir Richard (d. 1485) royal councillor," *ODNB*.

[95] Emma Cavell, ed., *The Heralds' Memoir 1486–1490: Court Ceremony, Royal Progress, and Rebellion* (Donington: Richard III and Yorkist History Trust in association with Shaun Tyas, 2009), 72, 81.

[96] Windsor Castle with St. George's Chapel, home of the Order of the Garter, would have had certain advantages as a place of imprisonment for John as a Garter knight. He may well have remained there after he was pardoned. He was certainly present at the splendid St. George's Day ceremonies held at Windsor Castle in 1488, an occasion when both Lady Margaret Beaufort and the queen, Elizabeth of York, received livery of the Garter (Jones and Underwood, *The King's Mother*, 148).

[97] Anthony J. Pollard, *North-Eastern England during the Wars of the Roses: Lay Society, War and Politics 1450–1500* (Oxford: Clarendon Press, 1990), 383.

[98] C. L. Kingsford, "On Some London Houses of the Early Tudor Period," *Archaeologia* 71 (1921): 17–54, at 43–50; John Schofield, *Medieval London Houses*

In the 1490s, the increasingly grand Collyweston, near Stamford in Northamptonshire, became Margaret Beaufort's principal residence and home to a number of the younger St Johns.[99] Elizabeth St John's granddaughters by her first marriage, Elizabeth and Eleanor Zouche, were among those brought up at Collyweston (see genealogy chart II). In the summer of 1503, Elizabeth Zouche's marriage to Gerald, son and heir of the Earl of Kildare—a political union arranged by Lady Margaret and the king—took place in the Collyweston chapel. The wedding coincided with an occasion for lavish festivities, the royal visit of the king with a large court entourage to say farewell to his elder daughter, Margaret, on her journey north to be queen of Scotland.[100] Another who was given a place at Collyweston was John, fifth Lord Scrope's nephew, the young son of Elizabeth Bygod and Oliver St John. A minor when his father died in 1497, John St John was supported at this vulnerable time by Lady Margaret, who acted to protect his inherited estates. On his marriage in 1498 she presented him with an embroidered hanging said to be by her own hands, worked with gold thread and designed to show the descent of the St John family.[101] In her will Lady Margaret (d. 1509) was to leave him a printed copy of the *Canterbury Tales*.[102]

An inscription beneath memorial brasses in Stoke Rochford church, Lincolnshire, requesting prayers for the souls of Oliver St John (d. 1497) and Dame Elizabeth Bygod his wife (d. 1503) refers to Oliver as "squier sonne unto ye . . . myghtty prynces duchess of Somersete <u>grandame</u> un to our souereyn lorde kynge herre the vij[th]."[103] This reminder that Margaret

---

(New Haven: Yale University Press for the Paul Mellon Centre for Studies in British Art, 1994), 107, 217–18 (no. 170), figs. 24, 38; Vanessa Harding, "The Two Coldharbours of the City of London," *London Topographical Record* 24 (1980): 11–29.

[99] For Margaret's transformation of Collyweston manor into her chief residence, see Michael K. Jones, "Collyweston—an Early Tudor Palace," *England in the Fifteenth Century: Proceedings of the 1986 Harlaxton Symposium*, ed. Daniel Williams (Woodbridge: Boydell Press, 1987), 129–41.

[100] Such was the grandeur of the visit that it appeared among the entries recorded in the calendar margins of the Beaufort-Beauchamp Hours (BL, Royal MS 2 A xviii, f. 31); see below, 136.

[101] Jones and Underwood, *The King's Mother*, 31, 165.

[102] Ibid., 241, 283. Susan Powell, "Lady Margaret Beaufort and Her Books," *The Library*, 6th ser., 20, no. 3 (1998): 197–240, at 202.

[103] Printed in E. T. Smallwood, Arnold Taylor, Charles Barker, and Brian Carne, "Two Margarets: Beauchamp and Beaufort, and the Fortunes of the St John family," *Friends of Lydiard Tregoz*, report no. 29 (1996): 19–34, at 31–32; and in N. Harris

Beauchamp, Dowager Duchess of Somerset—mother to Elizabeth, the wife of John, fifth Lord Scrope, as well as to Oliver—was grandmother to Henry VII, raises the tantalizing question of whether the cure for the wind said to be "Diuysyd for my lady the Kyngis gramother" (SB 89, Part II, f. 12, no. 64) was specifically for her.[104]

Family relationships were not the only connections between the households. The Scropes, themselves notable for the books they owned, would have fitted readily into the circle of family, friends, and members of the household at Collyweston who shared Margaret Beaufort's well-documented interest in both printed and manuscript books.[105] One of the most celebrated of the manuscripts owned by Margaret Beaufort, a book of hours now called the Beaufort-Beauchamp Hours (BL, Royal MS 2 A xviii), came to her from her mother.[106] The complicated structure of this fine illuminated manuscript and the distinctive calendar additions used to record biographical details and family events of significance for Margaret and her son Henry VII have been frequently discussed.[107] Of significance for the present study are the front flyleaves of the book, which contain three medical recipes in English copied in different

---

Nicolas, ed., *The Controversy between Sir Richard Scrope and Sir Robert Grosvenor in the Court of Chivalry, A. D. 1385–1390*, vol. 2 (London, 1832), 80. Elizabeth Bygod held Stoke Rochford in dower after the death of her second husband, Henry Rochford (d. 1470), and continued to live there, less than twenty miles from Collyweston, during her marriage to Oliver St John (see Smallwood et al., "Two Margarets," 21).

[104] Henry VII's paternal grandmother, Catherine of Valois, widow of Henry V, had died much earlier in 1437. For the recipe, see the transcript in **Appendix D**, no. 64, and section 1 (**Introduction**), 95 and plate 8.

[105] See Powell, "Lady Margaret Beaufort and Her Books." For a recent discussion of printed books owned by members of the book-loving Beaufort circle, see Mary Erler, "The Laity," in Gillespie and Powell, *Companion to the Early Printed Book in Britain*, 134–49, at 142–48.

[106] For a full description of the manuscript, see Scott, *Later Gothic Manuscripts*, 2: no. 37; see also McKendrick, *Royal Manuscripts*, no. 25. The complete manuscript is available on the British Library Digitised Manuscripts website (http://www.bl.uk/manuscripts).

[107] More recently, attention has been drawn to the probability that the book remained in the possession of the St John family after Margaret Beaufort's death; see Janet Backhouse "Patronage and Commemoration in the Beaufort Hours," *Tributes to Lucy Freeman Sandler: Studies in Illuminated Manuscripts*, ed. Kathryn A. Smith and Carol H. Krinsky (London: Harvey Miller Publishers, 2007), 331–41.

sixteenth-century hands.[108] One of these, the recipe beginning "Take rosemarie w^t flowres," is written in a hand that closely resembles the anonymous scribe of SB 89, although it cannot be said to be identical (fig. 10). The book of hours also includes a prayer invoking St. Christopher against the plague that is cited in regard to Lady Margaret Beaufort in section 3 of this study (**Epidemic Disease during the Reign of Henry VII (1485–1509)**).[109]

Another manuscript associated with the St John family circle of Lady Margaret Beaufort and of interest for its connection to the Scropes is a copy of the English prose *Gilte Legende*, elegantly written in the late fifteenth century by the London scribe Ricardus Franciscus (BL, Harley MS 4775).[110] Signatures and notes made in a variety of hands by the St Johns and others in the margins and on the end leaf of this manuscript (ff. 263r–v) have been the subject of recent study, primarily for the inclusion of names linking ownership of the volume to the courtier Henry Parker, Lord Morley.[111] Both Morley and his wife Alice St John, daughter of John St John of Bletsoe, held places in Lady Margaret's household.[112] Not previously recorded among the many scribbled names in the *Gilte Legende* volume is the inscription on the end leaf (f. 263): "Your dayghter alys Scrop/ wych ys and schall be yours." This must refer to Alice Scrope (died ca. 1510), wife of John, fifth Lord Scrope's grandson Henry, who succeeded to the title as seventh Lord Scrope on the death of his father in 1506—the third of our three generations of likely claimants

---

[108] "Kolla quyntyta," (f. 1v), "Take rosemarie," and "A Sufferent medson for the meigrem in the hede" (f. 2). The last two recipes are printed by Charity Scott-Stokes, *Women's Books of Hours in Medieval England* (Woodbridge: D. S. Brewer, 2006), 147–48.

[109] BL, Royal MS 2 A xviii, f. 25r–v.

[110] C. Paul Christianson, *A Directory of London Stationers and Book Artisans, 1300–1500* (New York: Bibliographical Society of America, 1990), 107.

[111] James P. Carley, "The Writings of Henry Parker, Lord Morley," *Triumphs of English: Henry Parker, Lord Morley, Translator to the Tudor Court*, ed. Marie Axton and James P. Carley (London: BL, 2000), 27–68, at 39. Julia Boffey and A. S. G. Edwards, "Books connected with Henry Parker, Lord Morley, and his Family," in Axton and Carley, *Triumphs of English*, 69–75, at 70–72. See also Cyril E. Wright, *Fontes Harleiani: A Study of the Sources of the Harleian Collection of Manuscripts Preserved in the Department of Manuscripts in the British Museum* (London: British Museum, 1972), 480.

[112] Jones and Underwood, *The King's Mother*, 114, 241, 280. Alice's aunt, Anne St John, wife of Henry, tenth Lord Clifford, was also in the household (see above n. 72).

to the armorial shield on the first leaf of SB 89 (see genealogy chart III, and further below). Alice's presence in the group is unsurprising; her mother, Elizabeth, Lady Scrope of Upsall and Masham, the daughter of John Neville, Marquis of Montagu, had a room appointed for her at Collyweston and lived there after the death (ca. 1500) of her second husband, Sir Henry Wentworth.[113] The queen, Elizabeth of York, was another among the group of female relatives and high ranking women who had rooms reserved at Collyweston, and Cecily of York, the queen's sister, was a regular visitor.[114] This Beaufort household was a natural forum in which manuscript copies of collections of royal recipes such as "The quenys powder" and "medycyn that the kyng Vsyd euery day" (Part II, nos. 32, 49) might circulate.

---

[113]   Ibid., 163. Malcolm G. Underwood, "The Lady Margaret and Her Cambridge Connections," *The Sixteenth Century Journal* 13 (1982): 67–82, at 77, n. 56, records a chamber reserved at Collyweston for Lady Elizabeth in 1502. In her will, 1514–17 (proved 1521; TNA, PROB/11/20, ff. 145v–147), Lady Elizabeth bequeathed her sister a primer and psalter she had received as a gift from Lady Margaret Beaufort during her lifetime (Jones and Underwood, *The King's Mother*, 163, n. 74). This Lady Elizabeth of Upsall and Masham may also be the "Elyzabeth Scrop" whose name is inscribed on the end leaf of a Sarum Book of Hours made in Bruges (after 1494) for the English market (Cambridge University Library [hereafter CUL], MS Dd. 6. 1, f. 145). The hand does not resemble that of the inscription "Elyzabeth Scrop," possibly a signature, at the foot of BL, Additional Charter 73913 (a covenant dated 1512 concerning the dower of Elizabeth, Lady Scrope of Upsall and Masham), but the entry in the Cambridge manuscript seems unlikely to be autograph since it is in the same hand as the name "[Ma]ry Somer," which is written immediately beneath. Regarding CUL MS Dd. 6. 1, see Paul Binski and Patrick Zutshi, *Western Illuminated Manuscripts: A Catalogue of the Collection in Cambridge University Library* (Cambridge: Cambridge University Press, 2011), no. 386. Prayers by an English scribe in the Cambridge manuscript include, under the rubric "A goode prayer ayenste þe pestilence" (ff. 143r–v), the *Trisagion* in Latin and Greek. This prayer in Latin against the pestilence is also found in Lady Margaret Beaufort's plague manuscript, Fitzwilliam MS 261 (f. 27v). See section 3 (**Epidemic Disease during the Reign of Henry VII (1485–1509)**), 162–63; see also Eamon Duffy, *Marking the Hours: English People and Their Prayers 1240–1570* (New Haven: Yale University Press, 2006), 116 (plate 67), 117; Charity Scott-Stokes, *Women's Books of Hours*, 106, 136. The suggestion by Edwards that the owner of CUL MS Dd. 6. 1 may have been Elizabeth Scrope Beaumont de Vere, Countess of Oxford ("Contexts of Notre Dame MS 67," 116–117 and n. 51[127]), cannot be sustained as after 1494 this Elizabeth would have used her married name of either Viscountess Beaumont or Countess of Oxford (cf. the signatures in BL, Harley MS 1706).

[114]   Jones and Underwood, *The King's Mother*, 161–62.

There were other great houses closely linked to the Scropes. Bolton Castle in Wensleydale, north Yorkshire, with its surrounding estates, was a source of wealth and the main base for the family. The castle, despite its vast, forbidding outward appearance, had been built at the end of the fourteenth century as much for display as for defense.[115] Described by Anthony Emery as a palace-fortress, the interior was remarkable for the extent and comfort of the domestic quarters provided for the lord, his family, and household officers, and for the unusually lavish accommodation included for the many guests.[116] The Neville castle of Middleham was just over six miles away, and Sheriff Hutton near York, another former Neville stronghold, within visiting distance. Both Middleham and Sheriff Hutton reverted to the crown under Henry VII.[117] Sandal and Pontefract with their large distilling operations were a little farther south. (For distillation in Yorkshire, see section 1, n. 18).

In Yorkshire, too, were the castles of Wressle and Leconfield belonging to the Percy family, earls of Northumberland. Large-scale use of distillation of the kind so necessary for the recipes in the Berkeley manuscript features in the well-known Northumberland Household Book (ca. 1512) of Henry Percy, fifth Earl of Northumberland. Particular instructions for regulating this famously opulent household included "to provide yerly for xxx Saks of Charcoill for Stilling of Bottells of Waters for my Lord"; then follows a list of twenty-eight different waters (beginning "Water of roses, Water for the Stone") that the Earl of Northumberland was accustomed

---

[115]   See Andrew King, "Fortress and Fashion Statements: Gentry Castles in Fourteenth-century Northumberland," *Journal of Medieval History* 33 (2007): 392: "[Bolton] . . . was intended as a piece of social theatre, an exercise in keeping up with the Nevilles, rather than as purely military defensive engineering."

[116]   Anthony Emery, *Greater Medieval Houses of England and Wales 1300–1500*, vol. 1 (Cambridge: Cambridge University Press, 1996), 303–12.

[117]   For a decade from 1489, the castles of Middleham and Sheriff Hutton were under the direction of Thomas Howard (d. 1524), Earl of Surrey, afterward Duke of Norfolk, as Henry VII's Lieutenant in the North. During this time, Howard resided mostly at Sheriff Hutton Castle where he was steward and constable. In 1497, in the chapel there, he married, as his second wife, Agnes Tilney, whose authority in the treatment of sweating sickness in her own and other great households is discussed below. See section 3 (**Epidemic Disease during the Reign of Henry VII (1485–1509)**), 175–78 and nn. 68–70, 73.

to have "stilled."[118] Christopher M. Woolgar has estimated from the number of bottles produced that his lordship required over half a gallon of these distilled waters a week.[119] It should be noted here that one of the recipes in Part I of SB 89 (ff. 64r–v) claims "for this medycyne Vsyd the erle of northhumberland for the feuyr in the stomak When that it toke hym And it helpyth yt him Verely well" (see **Appendix C**, no. 27).

The Northumberland household would have been familiar to the Scropes. John, fifth Lord Scrope's son and heir, Henry (the second of our three generations of likely claimants to the armorial shield on the first leaf of SB 89) was married in about 1480 to Lady Elizabeth Percy, sister of the fourth Earl of Northumberland (see genealogy chart III).[120] This Henry, sixth Lord Scrope of Bolton, more than any other holder of the Scrope title, seems to have remained mostly in Yorkshire. All of his seven children were born there, and their marriages were mainly local alliances. He appears to have taken little part in public life and was never summoned to parliament.[121] His father, John, fifth Lord Scrope, in the will he made in 1494, arranged to give all his goods in Bolton castle and his cattle in Yorkshire to Henry, leaving his lands south of the river Trent to his third wife (see below).[122]

Members of the family certainly retained strong loyalties to their northern roots and to the religious houses in the locality. The will of John,

---

[118]   *Regulations and Establishments of the Household*, 341; see above n. 79. A list of spices for a year includes 3 lb. of saffron as one among some twenty expensive spices (ibid., 19).

[119]   Christopher M. Woolgar, *The Senses in Late Medieval England* (New Haven: Yale University Press, 2006), 140.

[120]   *Complete Peerage*, 11:546. In his will, made 1485, Henry Percy, fourth Earl of Northumberland (d. 1489), refers to a fee and life annuity granted to "my brodir-in-lawe Henry Scrope, son and heire apparante to ye lorde Scrop of Bolton"; *Test. Ebor.* 3, Surtees Soc. 45 (London, 1865), 308. The fourth Earl of Northumberland's son, Henry Algernon Percy, fifth Earl of Northumberland, came of age and took livery of his Yorkshire estates in 1498 at the same time as Henry Scrope succeeded to the title of sixth Lord Scrope of Bolton. As one of the wealthiest magnates in the land, and failing ever to attain great office, much of the fifth Earl of Northumberland's energy was then spent in maintaining a household of semi-royal splendor at Wressle and Leconfield.

[121]   Only one parliament, that of 1504 (the last of Henry VII's reign), took place between 1498 and 1506 when Henry was sixth Lord Scrope of Bolton.

[122]   TNA, PROB 11/11, ff. 211–212v; *Test. Ebor.* 4, Surtees Soc. 53 (London, 1869), 94–97.

fifth Baron Scrope, bears witness to this with his bequest of a Bible and a book called *Cronica Cronicarum* (both printed) to St. Agatha's Abbey, Easby, a foundation where his forebears had long been patrons.[123] He left instructions that he should be buried at St. Agatha's in Yorkshire, or at the Blackfriars in Thetford, Norfolk, according to where he died.

Although there is no evidence that the Scropes of Bolton, unlike the Scropes of Masham, kept a town house in York, both families were consistent members of the city's influential guild of Corpus Christi.[124] Founded in 1408 to celebrate the feast of Corpus Christi, the guild increased in popularity after the duke of Gloucester (later Richard III) joined in 1477 with his wife Anne Neville.[125] In the following year, the acquisition by the guild of the hospital of St. Thomas attracted further support. According to Anthony J. Pollard, who made a survey of the membership, the guild's appeal was as much for its social desirability as for reasons of personal piety. Along with city merchants, it included large numbers of high-ranking ecclesiastics, nobles, and wealthy gentry from throughout the north east and beyond, giving it a status of national importance.[126]

Politics, business, and social activities would, however, inevitably have required long periods away in the south.[127] Early in Henry VII's reign,

---

[123] Ibid., 95. Mary C. Erler, "Exchange of Books" (363; also see above n. 32), cites John's bequest to Easby as illustrating a sense of local obligation similar to that shown by his sister Agnes, widow of Sir Richard Ratcliffe, with her gift to Marrick priory in Yorkshire of a fine illuminated English translation of Deguileville's *Pèlerinage de l'Ame*. The gift by Agnes Scrope Ratcliffe to the Benedictine nunnery of Marrick is the second of Erler's "three surviving examples" (362–64, n. 11–24).

[124] John, fifth Lord Scrope, joined with his first wife in 1463; Henry, sixth Lord, and his wife, Elizabeth Percy in 1498 (his aunt, Agnes Ratcliffe, with her son and daughter-in-law by her first marriage were admitted at the same time); and Henry, seventh Lord, and his first wife, Alice Scrope in 1510. See Robert H. Skaife, ed., *The Register of the Guild of Corpus Christi in the City of York*, Surtees Soc. 57 (York, 1872), 63, 148, 170.

[125] Ibid., 101. On the same occasion, Alice Scrope's mother, Lady Elizabeth Scrope of Upsall and Masham (born Elizabeth Neville and a cousin of Queen Anne Neville) was also admitted.

[126] Pollard, *North-Eastern England*, 189–90. See also David Crouch, *Piety, Fraternity and Power: Religious Gilds in Late Medieval York 1399–1547* (York: York Medieval Press, 2000), especially chap. 5, 160–95.

[127] Pollard emphasizes that north eastern England was by no means a poor or remote part of the country in the late fifteenth century, with many, even among the prosperous gentry, "as familiar with London and Westminster as they were with

John, fifth Lord Scrope, as already recounted, was for a time restricted to London and its environs. Wealthy magnates had need of great London town houses.[128] The London house of the Scropes, next to the Bishop of Ely's Palace on the north side of Holborn, was let to the serjeants-at-law (and known as Serjeants' Inn) until John recovered it in 1494.[129] Also available to the family, however, was a large property on the east side of Lime Street, in the parish of St. Andrew Cornhill, known as Tiptoft's Inn, which had come to the Scropes as part of the Tiptoft inheritance.[130] This was sold before 1501 when Richard Knyght, a fishmonger, bequeathed the property—described as formerly belonging to Lord Scrope—to the wardens of the Fishmonger's Company.[131] It seems likely that John Lord Scrope had moved back to the Holborn inn soon after the opportunity arose.

It is clear that by 1492 John had entirely regained favor with the king. In the spring of that year, he saw his grandson, Henry (later seventh Lord Scrope) married to Alice, only daughter and heiress of Thomas, sixth Lord Scrope of Upsall and Masham (d. 1493), thus uniting the two branches of the Scrope family.[132] An entry in the Privy Purse Expenses of Henry VII establishes the date of the marriage, recording on May 20, 1492, a payment of the king at the royal palace of Sheen in Richmond "For offring at Master Scrops mariage . . . 6s–8d" (one gold noble coin).[133] The accounts reveal that the king was at Sheen throughout the month of May,

---

York and Newcastle" (*North-Eastern England*, 397). See also the discussion of the Thornton household book in section 1 (**Introduction**), 100–01, and n. 19.

[128] See Caroline Barron, "Centres of Conspicuous Consumption: The Aristocratic Town House in London 1200–1550," *The London Journal* 20, no. 1 (1995): 1–17.

[129] Charles L. Kingsford, "Historical Notes on Medieval London Houses," *London Topographical Record* 12 (1920): 1–66, at 20–21.

[130] Schofield, *Medieval London Houses*, 198, no. 122.

[131] Reginald R. Sharpe, *Calendar of Wills Proved and Enrolled in the Court of Husting*, vol. 2: 1358–1688 (London, 1890), 607–8; see also Priscilla Metcalfe, *The Halls of the Fishmongers' Company: An Architectural History of a Riverside Site* (London: Phillimore, 1977), 39.

[132] In his 1494 will (see above n. 122), John detailed financial arrangements for the marriage and wardship of Alice (as an heiress, Alice's wardship belonged to the crown); he was committed to four annual payments totaling 400 marks, in addition to 100 marks already paid. If he should die, his son and heir Henry would discharge the debts and enjoy the lands and profits from Alice's inherited estates during the period of her minority.

[133] BL, Add. MS 7099, f. 4; Samuel Bentley, *Excerpta Historica* (London, 1831), 89.

entertained by elaborate jousts and feasting. Both Henry and Alice were then very young, Henry about twelve years old and Alice aged ten, and both may have been present at court while it was at Sheen.[134] Henry's fourteen-year-old cousin, Henry Percy, fifth Earl of Northumberland, was also at court at this time as a royal ward with his own household servants.[135]

In 1492, young Henry's grandfather, John, fifth Lord Scrope, married for the third time (as her third husband) the wealthy Norfolk heiress and patron, Anne Harling. The marriage took place in the chapel of Anne's manor house at East Harling, and afterward the couple lived at least part of the time in East Anglia.[136] Anne, an extensive landowner in both Norfolk and Suffolk, was the only daughter and heiress of Sir Robert Harling and Jane Gonville (herself a Gonville family heiress). She had been a widow for ten years before she married John.[137] Her richly detailed will, with bequests to fifty-eight religious institutions and 133 individuals,[138] has been heavily drawn upon, in particular for evidence of the notable books it contained. The will reflects not only her piety but also her close family ties to the Scropes of Bolton as well as to her numerous East Anglian connections. For example, to Lady Elizabeth Scrope, John fifth Lord Scrope's mother, a widow of almost forty years with her own

---

[134] In May 1495, Alice was said to be thirteen (*Calendar of Inquisitions Post Mortem*, Hen. VII, 1, no. 1047).

[135] The fifth Earl of Northumberland did not enter into his inheritance until his coming of age in 1498. See above 140, n. 120.

[136] The license granted, October 6, 1492, by James Goldwell, Bishop of Norwich, for the marriage to take place in the chapel of the manor, is printed in John Anstis, *The Register of the Most Noble Order of the Garter*, vol. 2 (London, 1724), 225. John's second wife, Elizabeth St John, was still living in 1489 (*Rolls of Parlt.*, vi, 424; *Complete Peerage*, 12:945).

[137] Her first husband was Sir William Chamberlain, K.G., a war veteran some fifteen years her senior, whom she married while a ward of Sir John Fastolf. Her second husband, Sir Robert Wingfield, was controller to the household of Edward IV from 1474 until his death in 1481. She is one of the network of women patrons and book owners first documented by Ian Doyle, "Books Connected with the Vere Family" (see n. 85 above). For a recent study, see David King, "Anne Harling Reconsidered," *Recording Medieval Lives: Proceedings of the 2005 Harlaxton Medieval Symposium*, ed. Julia Boffey and Virginia Davis (Donington: Shaun Tyas, 2009), 204–22.

[138] Calculated by David King (ibid., 206). Anne's will, TNA, PROB/11/11/ff. 212v–14v, is printed in abbreviated form in *Test. Ebor.* 4, Surtees Soc. 53 (London, 1869), 149–54.

dower lands, Anne bequeathed a psalter with an embroidered binding.[139] Other Scrope beneficiaries included her sisters-in-law, Elizabeth Bygod and Agnes Ratcliffe, her brothers-in-law, Ralph and Robert Scrope, and Katherine (Zouche; Robert's wife), as well as the more immediate family, Henry, sixth Lord Scrope, his wife, and children.

It has been claimed that Anne Harling died of the same unspecified "fatal and infectious" sickness that had killed her husband,[140] and the sequence of events strongly suggests this was the case. On August 8, 1498, John, fifth Lord Scrope of Bolton, already ill, added a codicil to the will he had made some four years earlier: "which codicyll though I be not in power to subscribe it w^t myn ease yett I comaunde & will that it be sealed w^t the seale of myn Armys and my privy signett and so annexed to my former testament & last will."[141] He died just nine days later, on August 17. On August 28, Anne also made her final will, "In Witnesse wherof . . . I the seid Anne lady Scrop have put to my seal of Armys and also subscribe it w^t myn owne hande."[142] Three weeks later, she too was dead (d. Sept. 18, 1498). The sickness to which both succumbed within such a short period could have been plague or sweating sickness, but we cannot be sure. Nonetheless, these deaths would certainly have reinforced the Scrope family's preoccupation with highly contagious and potentially fatal disease that is a recurrent concern of many of the recipes in Part II, and some in Part I, of SB 89 (see the

---

[139] Lady Elizabeth Scrope died May 10, 1504 (*Cal. Inquis. Post Mortem*, Hen. VII, iii, nos. 880, 881). Her dower included the manor of Hambledon, in Buckinghamshire, where Lord John's younger brothers, Robert (d. 1500), and his wife Katherine Zouche, and Ralph (d. 1516), Rector of Hambledon and Archdeacon of Northumberland, are buried. A monumental brass in Hambledon church displays kneeling figures of Robert and Katherine with four shields bearing the arms of Scrope quartering Tiptoft differenced with a crescent (William Lack, H. Martin Stuchfield, and Philip Whittemore, eds., *The Monumental Brasses of Buckinghamshire* [London: Monumental Brass Society, 1994], 101, and fig. at 103). The use by Robert of the same cadency mark as his older brother Richard (d. 1485) gives a warning that cadency at this date was by no means a consistently regulated system.

[140] Gail McMurray Gibson, *The Theater of Devotion: East Anglian Drama and Society in the Late Middle Ages* (Chicago: University of Chicago Press, 1989), 96–106, at 97, n. 114, citing W. B. Slegg's unpublished "History of East Harling" (dated 1940), Norfolk Record Office (NRO), MS 10840 36 F 2.

[141] TNA, PROB/11/11/ff. 211–212v. The original will was dated July 3, 1494; proved November 8, 1498.

[142] TNA, PROB/11/11/ff. 212v–214v. Proved November 8, 1498.

discussion in section 3, **Epidemic Disease during the Reign of Henry VII (1485–1509)**).

At the end of the fifteenth century, the Scropes had become part of a great network of close family, landed interests, and social connections in Essex and East Anglia. A central figure in this group was the niece of John, fifth Lord Scrope: Elizabeth Scrope, Countess of Oxford from 1508, the daughter of Richard Scrope and Eleanor Washbourne. Elizabeth's marriages first to Viscount Beaumont and on his death to John de Vere, thirteenth Earl of Oxford (Lord Great Chamberlain and "The Foremost Man of the Kingdom") and her long-term presence in the wealthy de Vere household have been outlined in section 1 (**Introduction**, 105–07). De Vere, the Earl of Oxford, was named by John, fifth Lord Scrope, as a surveyor of his will, and Margaret Neville (d. 1507), first wife of the earl, was among the recipients of a bequest from John's wife Anne.

Because Richard Scrope, Lord John's brother, had no male heir, his daughter Elizabeth and all her eight sisters were heraldic heiresses, each entitled to use their father's arms after his death in 1485. These arms were the quartered arms of Scrope and Tiptoft found in SB 89, but differenced with a small crescent. Elizabeth displayed her pride in these paternal arms on her brass at Wivenhoe in Essex, where she lies buried alongside her first husband (fig. 9).[143] Both sides of her heraldic mantle show the arms of Scrope differenced with a crescent on the bend quartering Tiptoft. Only above her shoulders do we find shields impaled with the arms of each of her husbands. And above those in the arcading are larger shields that repeat her own arms as found on her heraldic mantle. Her personal arms, repeated five times on the brass, overshadow those of her two noble husbands.[144]

The wealth and lavish scale of the household of Elizabeth's husband John de Vere are demonstrated in two surviving household accounts, in his

---

[143]   Jennifer Ward, "Elizabeth Beaumont, Countess of Oxford (d. 1537): Her Life and Connections," *Transactions of the Monumental Brass Society* 17, part 1 (2003): 12.

[144]   A fragment of ecclesiastical embroidery depicting Christ on the Cross, with at the foot a shield displaying the de Vere arms impaling Scrope quartering Tiptoft, is now in the Victoria and Albert Museum (T 138-1909); see Donald King, *Opus Anglicanum: English Medieval Embroidery* (V&A exhibition, 1963), no. 156. The Scrope arms are there differenced with a mullet instead of the crescent that appears on Elizabeth's monumental brass. See also the discussion of shield shape, 114–18 above, and plate 4a.

will and in the extensive inventory of his goods taken on his death in 1513. Already cited is the postmortem inventory listing nine pounds of saffron, a striking demonstration of wealth even if grown on the de Vere estates.[145] Of the two extant accounts, the earlier covers the year 1490–91 and was included in a Howard household book of 1487.[146] The other, an unpublished account for the year 1507 (just after the death of de Vere's first wife), is particularly useful for describing the monthly purchases of spices for the household.[147] It makes clear that, while candles, for example, would be purchased locally at Colchester in Essex, fine wines and expensive spices— including grains of paradise, long pepper, cinnamon, green ginger, cloves, mace, and nutmegs—were bought in London.[148] These household luxuries were then dispatched, frequently by the earl's barge for the first part of the journey, landing at Wivenhoe on the Essex coast at the mouth of the Colne river, and then taken by road if the household was at Castle Hedingham.[149] At the end of each month's record, payments are given for carriage, cranage, and wharfage, and for wine porters at the waterside.

---

[145]   St John Hope, "Last Testament and Inventory," 324 (see section 1 [**Intro-duction**], n. 13). Two recipes in Part II (nos. 56, 58) specify English saffron.

[146]   Account for the year 1490–91, published from Society of Antiquaries of London (SAL) MS 77, ff. 126v–128, in *Household Books of John, Duke of Norfolk and Thomas, Earl of Surrey* [*recte* John, Earl of Oxford], ed. J. Payne Collier (London, 1844), 504–20; Melvin J Tucker, "Household Accounts 1490–1491 of John de Vere, Earl of Oxford," *English Historical Review* 75 (1960): 468–74. Ross gives a description of both this and the Longleat account (*John de Vere*, 216–17). The 1490–91 account concerns mostly expenditures relating to Castle Hedingham and the large, wealthy manor at Lavenham with its extensive deer park. An entry for December 22, 1490 (Collier, *Household Books*, 516), records payment to a servant bringing quails and cheese from Lady Wingfield (Anne Harling, then widow of her second husband, Sir Robert Wingfield [d. 1481]). Regarding the Howard household books, see Anne Crawford, ed., *The Household Books of John Howard, Duke of Norfolk 1462–1471, 1481–1483* (Stroud: Alan Sutton for Richard III and Yorkist History Trust, 1992).

[147]   Longleat House (Wiltshire), Miscellanea xi; household account of purchases and provisions, January 1–December 31, 1507. The accounts for spices and candles are at folios 87–91.

[148]   Caroline Barron observes that, no matter where the lord and his household were actually located, livery cloth and luxury goods will have been purchased in London ("Centres of Conspicuous Consumption," 6). See also H. S. Cobb, ed., *The Overseas Trade of London: Exchequer Customs Accounts, 1480–81* (London: London Record Society, 1990).

[149]   Wivenhoe Hall on the coast was the de Vere manor where Elizabeth and Lord Beaumont mostly resided. John de Vere and all his household (numbering over

The London mansion of the de Veres, known as Le Erber (called "the Arber at London" in the 1490–91 account),[150] was in Dowgate in the parish of St. Mary Botham, conveniently close to the Thames and Dowgate Wharf.[151] Only a few streets away was Lady Margaret Beaufort's great waterside mansion of Coldharbour. A second de Vere inn, further out on the north east side of the city of London, near Bishopsgate, was well placed for the road to Essex and the de Vere estates.[152]

Discussed in section 1, **Introduction**, is the direct connection to the Berkeley household book (the most direct that we have found) revealed by copies of recipes in Part II (nos. 41, 63) on flyleaves of Elizabeth Scrope Beaumont De Vere's volume of devotional texts, BL, Harley MS 1706.[153] The unusual recipe for spiced pomegranate wine (SB 89, Part II, no. 41), in particular, is virtually an exact copy. It is worth noting that it is on the flyleaves of a personal devotional manuscript, as in the Beaufort-Beauchamp Hours, that these recipes occur. In reviewing a number of ways in which Harley 1706 was intended to be read, Andrew Taylor included private reading by Elizabeth alone with her chaplain or within an inner circle of relatives and dependents.[154] That medical recipes should be recorded on flyleaves in the devotional books read in this way demonstrates how an informal exchange of such material, perhaps from a common source, could take place within or between families, with friends, and indeed in the circles of the royal court.

Elizabeth survived John de Vere's death in 1513 as a wealthy and independent widow for twenty-four years. She was named as executor in John's will, an expression of confidence in her practical abilities to control and manage the considerable estates that came to her as dower from each of her two husbands. She continued to play a role at the court of Henry VIII and, as her own will shows, to maintain a large and luxurious household.[155] Although Wivenhoe Hall remained her home, toward

---

a hundred) were also located there for virtually all of 1507. In December of the same year, Viscount Beaumont died at Wivenhoe.

[150]   SAL MS 77, f. 128v. Collier, *Household Books*, 507.

[151]   Schofield, *Medieval London Houses*, no. 67 (179). Ross, *John de Vere*, 216.

[152]   *The British Atlas of Historic Towns. Vol. III, The City of London, from Prehistoric Times to c.1520*, ed. Mary D. Lobel (Oxford: Oxford University Press, 1989), 82.

[153]   See section 1 (**Introduction**), 104–07, nn. 40–42.

[154]   Taylor, "Into His Secret Chamber," 61; see section 1 (**Introduction**), n. 41.

[155]   Named bequests in her will included nine women of her chamber, over forty servants and retainers, as well as a receiver, a comptroller of household, a marshall of

the end of her life she is said to have retired to Polstead, a village in west Suffolk.[156] Part of Elizabeth's dower lands, Polstead was also associated with the Waldegrave family who held the manor and advowson of the church.[157]

The exceptional series of wills for the Scrope family, much studied for patronage and book ownership of the group of women in which Elizabeth Scrope Beaumont de Vere and her sisters played such a central role, illustrates the closeness of the family networks. A notable example is provided by a bequest in Elizabeth's will to her cousin, Margaret Scrope, a nun at Barking Abbey.[158] After the dissolution of the monasteries, this Margaret Scrope gave an English devotional book from Barking to a Mistress Goldwell, identified as the principal gentlewoman of her sister, Lady Elizabeth Scrope Peche, with whom Margaret had gone to live at Lullingstone Castle in Kent.[159] These sisters were two of the four daughters

---

the hall, a gentleman usher, a yeoman usher, an almoner, two named chaplains, and several others; see Ward, "Elizabeth Beaumont," 89.

[156] Diarmaid MacCulloch, *Suffolk and the Tudors: Politics and Religion in an English County* (Oxford: Clarendon Press, 1986), 55, citing TNA, KB 9/534, m.75. The document, dated 1535–36, reports an armed robbery from Lady Elizabeth's house in Polstead. She is likely to have spent only part of her time there as Wivenhoe Hall remained her chief residence. A serious fire cited in her will, probably at Wivenhoe, may have been the cause of her removal to the Polstead house; see Ward, "Elizabeth Beaumont," 8, n. 25.

[157] One rare example of a will recording "bookes of medicyns" may be linked to Elizabeth's household at Polstead. John Fabyan, of St. Clement Danes, London—a brother of Thomas Fabyan, clerk and parson of Polstead in Suffolk—in a will proved on May 21, 1541, in the Commissary Court of London, bequeathed to his cousin and executor Bridget Waldegrave, Lady Marney, "all his drawen bookes, bookes of medicyns, and cronicles that be in Englysshe," leaving his Latin books to his brother, Edward (London Metropolitan Archives, DL/C/B/004/MS09171/011, f. 52v). Bridget Waldegrave (d. 1549), Lady Marney (by her second marriage to John, second Baron Marney of Layer Marney in Essex), was the daughter of Sir William Waldegrave of Bures (d. 1527; see 121, n. 42 above). It is tempting to speculate that John Fabyan (then in the service of the earl of Southampton) might be the John Fabyan, marshall of the household of Elizabeth, Countess of Oxford, who was bequeathed twenty nobles in the Countess's will. See Ward, "Elizabeth Beaumont," 8; Lewer, "Testament and Last Will of Elizabeth," 14; see section 1 (**Introduction**), n. 36.

[158] Lewer, "Testament," 13: she left "to my Cosyn, Dame Margarett Scrope, five pounds in money." See also Doyle, "Books Connected with the Vere Family," 234, 240–41.

[159] This gift, a copy of Nicholas Love's *Mirror of the Life of Christ*, is discussed by Mary Erler "Exchange of Books," 364–67. Also noted (366–67, plates 61–64)

and co-heiresses of Robert Scrope (d. 1500) of Hambledon, Buckingham-
shire, younger brother of John, fifth Lord Scrope (see genealogy chart
I).[160] Elizabeth, Robert's eldest daughter, had married Sir John Peche (d.
1522) of Lullingstone, a prominent figure at the courts of Henry VII and
Henry VIII (see above, 118 and n. 32). Margaret de la Pole, Countess of
Suffolk (d. 1515), Elizabeth de Vere's sister, was also close to her cousin
Lady Elizabeth Peche and is said to have lived at Lullingstone Castle dur-
ing the last years of her life after her husband's execution.[161]

The third generation of the senior line of Scropes of Bolton, Henry,
seventh Lord Scrope, and Alice his first wife, also had their place in this
close family network. In June 1507, when the De Vere household was at
Wivenhoe, the accounts record a payment to two minstrels from the reti-
nue of Lord Scrope.[162] The presence of minstrels suggests the high status
of Henry and Alice's household.[163] It implies too that in 1507 the young

---

are two secular works that appear to have circulated in the Lullingstone household: first, a copy of Lydgate's *Siege of Troy* (Oxford, Bodl. MS Rawl. poet. 144) with
Lady Elizabeth Peche's name in it, and (among other inscriptions) an ill-formed
signature,"Elysabethe Peche," which Erler suggests may be that of Lady Elizabeth's
sister-in-law, a young Elizabeth Peche, later married (ca. 1495) to John Hart; and
second, a "booke of Legenda aurea," perhaps a printed edition, received by Lady
Elizabeth Peche in 1500 as a bequest from a friend. For the first identification of
Lady Elizabeth Scrope Peche's possession of the Lydgate manuscript, Erler is quoting Carol M. Meale, "Laywomen and Their Books," 134, 150, n. 27; see above n. 85.

[160]   For Robert and his wife, Katherine Zouche, see above, 144, n. 139.

[161]   Barbara Harris, *English Aristocratic Women, 1450–1550: Marriage and
Family, Property and Careers* (Oxford: Oxford University Press, 2002), 173, n. 284.
Evidence for this claim is good but circumstantial. Margaret's will requests burial
beside her husband Edmund de la Pole, Earl of Suffolk (executed as a claimant to the
throne in 1513), at the convent of the Minoresses without Aldgate where her daughter was a nun. Nevertheless, bequests in the will name Sir John Peche and Margaret's cousin Lady Elizabeth Scrope Peche, Sir John's wife, before her own sisters and
daughter. Sir John was also named as her executor and further bequests were made
to his sister Elizabeth Peche Harte. TNA, PROB/11/18/ ff. 44v–45.

[162]   Longleat, Misc. xi, f. 119; Ross, *John de Vere*, 217, n. 60. Henry had succeeded
to the title of Lord Scrope of Bolton on the death of his father in 1506, and he also
held the title of Lord Scrope of Upsall and Masham in right of his wife Alice during
her lifetime.

[163]   Already that year, John de Vere had made similar payments for two minstrels from Prince Henry and four from the king; Ross, *John de Vere*, 217. (It may be
noted that, according to the *De conferentibus* text, "noyse of mynstrally or songis"
was considered to be good for the brain; SB 89, Part I, f. 83.)

couple was living in some proximity to the influential Beaumont/De Vere family. As children when they married in 1492, Henry and Alice may well have spent time in the Norfolk household of Anne Harling and her husband, Henry's grandfather, John, fifth Lord Scrope. Anne's bequests in 1498 included, "to my yonge ladye of Vpsale," a glass with silver and gilt and a quantity of luxury household goods and rich apparel.[164] Alice and Henry were certainly in East Anglia in the sixteenth century, living at Fyfield in Essex, a manor that formed part of the jointure of Alice's widowed mother, Lady Elizabeth Neville Scrope of Upsall and Mash-am.[165] Alice's mother, indeed, provides a further connection between the households, as she was herself a niece of John de Vere's first wife, Margaret Neville. The presence of both Alice and her mother among the book-owning circle surrounding Lady Margaret Beaufort has been referred to above.[166] In the late fifteenth or early sixteenth century, the name "Alys Scrope" occurs in a fourteenth-century French prose manuscript of Lancelot romances, which is now Bodleian Library, MS Rawlinson Q.b.6.[167] This "Alys" can almost certainly be identified as Alice, wife to Henry, seventh Lord Scrope of Bolton.[168] It bears further witness to the interests she and her mother shared with the remarkable network of bookish Scrope women in East Anglia at this time.

Henry, seventh Lord Scrope, was present in London at the funeral of Henry VII in May 1509. Both he and Alice took their part in the festivities and ceremonies that accompanied the marriage of Henry VIII and

---

[164]   TNA, PROB/11/11, ff. 212–14. Included were fine sheets, a bedcover of miniver lined in crimson, a black damask gown furred with white and powdered with ermines, and a bonnet of purple velvet (only the first item, the glass, is listed in *Test. Ebor.* 4 [London, 1869], 149–54). The bequest of household bedding may suggest that Alice was, or was about to become, mistress of her own separate establishment.

[165]   In a general pardon roll issued on May 12, 1509, in the first days of Henry VIII's reign, "Lord Scrope of Bolton and Upsall" is referred to as "alias lord Scrope, late of Fyfield Essex . . . and Alice his wife"; *Letters and Papers, Foreign and Domestic, Henry VIII: 1509–1514*, vol. 1, part 1, 2nd ed., ed. J. S. Brewer (London: His Majesty's Stationery Office, 1920), 219 (no. 438). *Complete Peerage*, 11:571.

[166]   See above 138 and n. 113. It may also be noted that, like other members of the Scrope family, Lady Elizabeth Neville Scrope made a bequest (a gilt cup with cover), to Dame Margaret Scrope, nun of Barking.

[167]   Cited by A. S. G. Edwards, "Contexts of Notre Dame MS 67," 124–25, n. 19.

[168]   Alice's paternal aunt, the only other member of the Scrope family called Alice at this date, was married before 1472 to Sir James Strangways (d. 1521) and would have been more likely to use her married name.

Katherine of Aragon on June 11, 1509, and the joint coronation a fortnight later—on midsummer's day, Sunday June 24—at Westminster Abbey. On the eve of the coronation, Henry was made a knight of the Bath, and Alice was among the ladies attending Katherine of Aragon in the great procession marking the occasion.[169] Katherine of Aragon's extended household at the time of the coronation contained a close-knit group of what Neville Williams has termed "a formidable cousinage," among them Elizabeth, Countess of Oxford, and Margaret, Countess of Suffolk, as peeresses and ladies in waiting. Mary Scrope (Mrs. Jerningham) and Jane Scrope (Mrs. Brewse), sisters of Elizabeth and Margaret, and their cousin Elizabeth Scrope, Lady Peche, were also in Katherine's household. [170]

Family relationships may be reflected in the decoration of SB 89. The foliage design at the beginning of SB 89 (f. [i]) contains oak leaves, an oak gall, and at least one lily formed as a fleur-de-lis, all on a single branch. Sprigs of oak leaves have been attributed as a badge to the Scropes of Masham.[171] There is some evidence to suggest use of the fleur-de-lis similarly as a badge by the Scropes of Bolton: John, fifth Lord Scrope, is said to have included the device on a seal of 1465;[172] his grandson, Henry, employed fleurs-de-lis prominently in the architectural decoration of a marble tombstone made for two sons by his second marriage, both of whom died young in 1525.[173] It is possible, therefore, that the drawing (and also the oak leaf initial on folio 1; see plate 2.b) may refer to the alliance of the two branches of the family, namely, through the marriage of Henry, seventh Lord Scrope of Bolton, to Alice Scrope of Upsall and Masham.[174]

---

[169]   *Complete Peerage*, 11:571.

[170]   Neville Williams, *Henry VIII and His Court* (London, Weidenfeld and Nicolson, 1971), 22. Mary Scrope was in the royal household from at least 1506; see *The Great Wardrobe Accompts of Henry VII and Henry VIII*, ed. Maria Hayward, *London Record Society* 47 (2012): 217.

[171]   Michael P. Siddons, *Heraldic Badges in England and Wales*, 4 vols. (Woodbridge: Boydell Press for the Society of Antiquaries of London, 2009), vol.II, part 2: 257. Cited is the seal of Margery, Lady Scrope of Masham, 1417/8; see Roger H. Ellis *Catalogue of Seals in the Public Record Office: Personal Seals*, vol. 2 (London: Her Majesty's Stationery Office, 1981), 95 (no. P2015) and plate 28.

[172]   *Heraldic Visitation of the Northern Counties in 1530 by Thomas Tonge*, ed. W. Hylton Dyer Longstaffe, Surtees Soc. 41 (Durham, 1863), 33.

[173]   Wensley church, co. Yorks; H. B. McCall, *Richmondshire Churches* (London: Elliott Stock, 1910), 174.

[174]   Such a conceit would be familiar from royal alliances. Tudor roses and pomegranates intertwined represented the marriage of Prince Arthur and Katherine

Regrettably, other corroborative evidence for this has not been discovered. Alice died with no surviving children around 1510. At that date, she and Henry are recorded as having joined the Guild of Corpus Christi in York, which suggests that they were by then based at Bolton castle in the north.[175] Henry's second marriage was to Mabel, daughter of Thomas, Lord Dacre of Gilsland.[176] His children by Mabel were born at Bolton, and he was given commissions of peace and array in Yorkshire, implying that the focus of his activities had moved north. Wensley church in Yorkshire was filled with heraldry displaying the Scrope quartering Tiptoft arms, but generally in association with the Dacre arms of his second wife.[177] There is no trace of Alice, who is almost certain to have been buried in London at Blackfriars in the tomb described in her mother's will of 1514.[178]

Conclusion

We may not be able to say with certainty which of the three generations of Lords Scrope of Bolton having a claim to the shield of arms on the first page of SB 89 commissioned and possessed this impressive medical book.

---

of Aragon (e.g., as a royal badge in "Prince Arthur's Book," London, College of Arms MS Vincent 152, p. 84) and were then widely used to show the subsequent marriage of Henry VIII to his brother's widow (see, e.g., the exquisite penwork decoration of roses and pomegranates entwined on the same stem in the King's Bench plea rolls: TNA, KB27/ 992 [1509], 1003, 1004 [1512], and 1009 [1513]: http://aalt.law.uh.edu/). Attribution of SB 89 to the household of Henry, seventh Lord Scrope, and Alice (d. ca. 1510) could mean that, *were* it intended for a particular king, the drawing of a crowned figure alongside the initial letter "h" on the first leaf might represent (although with no attempt at portraiture) either Henry VII or Henry VIII. (A date for the manuscript in the early years of the latter's reign would suggest Lady Margaret Beaufort as the "Kyngis gramother" cited in the rubric for SB89, Part II, no. 64.) Less likely, but possible if drawing and text were a direct copy of, say, a Percy manuscript, is that it could be intended for Henry, fifth Earl of Northumberland, wearing an earl's coronet. Nor could Henry, seventh Lord Scrope, or his father Henry, sixth Lord Scrope, be entirely ruled out, although it seems unlikely that barons would be depicted as crowned.

[175]   Skaife, *Register of the Guild*, 170.

[176]   *Complete Peerage*, 11:547.

[177]   N. Harris Nicolas, *Controversy*, 79–83.

[178]   In her will, Lady Elizabeth Neville Scrope gave instructions for her own burial in Blackfriars, beside her first husband, and commissioned a stone over her grave with images of herself, her first husband and their daughter Alice.

The most likely candidates for ownership may well be Henry, seventh Lord Scrope of Bolton, K.B., who succeeded to the title in 1506, and his first wife, Alice. The shape of the shield imposes a date for the manuscript of not before the closing years of the fifteenth century, and more probably the early years of the sixteenth.

The shield of arms also has significance beyond these crucial considerations of dating and identification. The choice of a waisted Renaissance shield on which to display the arms itself reflects a status the owners had by now achieved, or were aspiring to. It was a new style, a modish import from the Continent, almost exclusive at the beginning to the court and its circle, and for the most part produced by craftsmen employed by the crown.

It is clear who were the wealthy noble families—the Nevilles, the Percies, the Howards, and the de Veres—with whom the Scropes were connected at this period. We can trace the strong ties that these families formed through kinship, political affinities, and landed interests, and as patrons and owners who shared handsomely produced books. We know too of the intimate contact enjoyed by women of the Scrope family with the early Tudor court, and in particular with the household of Lady Margaret Beaufort. It was within this group of royal and noble households that such a grand, decorative, but thoroughly practical and secular medical book with its many royal recipes would be copied or commissioned.

Castles and great houses of the extended Scrope family and their powerful connections—in Yorkshire, East Anglia, and Kent—were all places where there might be need for reference to the medical guidance found in SB 89. But the materials and recipes to be assembled in such a household book were as likely to originate and circulate in London, where the Scropes, like their peers, maintained conspicuously affluent town houses mostly congregated within the one square mile of the City.

The Berkeley Castle manuscript displays the wealth and status of these families of the peerage at the end of the medieval period. It focuses attention upon the activities of a capable, devout, and literate group of Tudor noblewomen in looking after the medical interests of their great households. And it dramatically reveals an understandable preoccupation with pestilence and sudden death.

Genealogy Chart I (GCI)

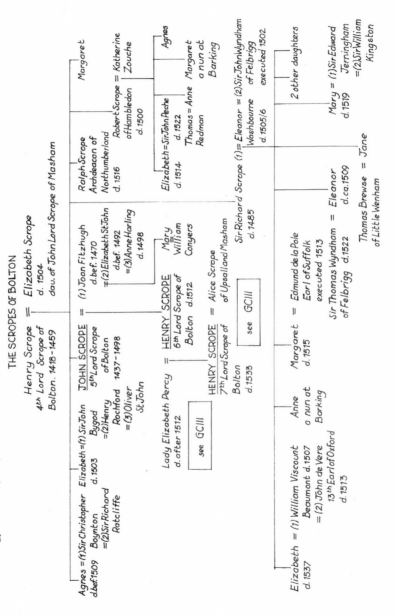

Genealogy Chart II (GCII)

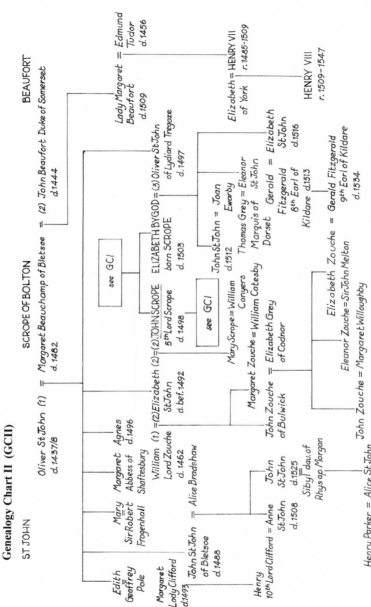

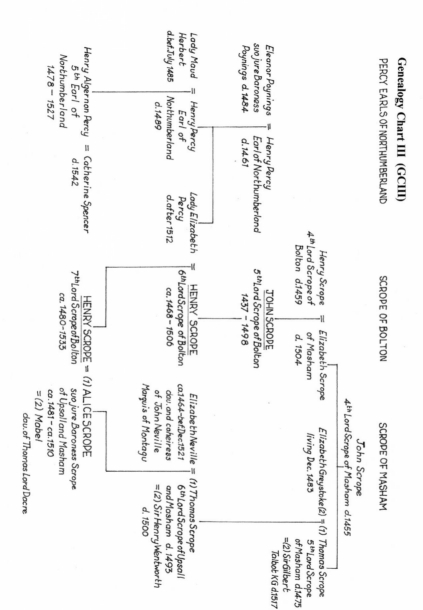

Genealogy Chart III (GCIII)
PERCY EARLS OF NORTHUMBERLAND

SCROPE OF BOLTON

SCROPE OF MASHAM

John Scrope
4ᵗʰ Lord Scrope of Masham d.1455

Eleanor Poynings
suo jure Baroness
Poynings d.1484

= Henry Percy
Earl of Northumberland
d.1461

Henry Scrope
4ᵗʰ Lord Scrope of
Bolton d.1459

= Elizabeth Scrope
of Masham
d.1504

Elizabeth Greystoke (2) = (1) Thomas Scrope
living Dec. 1483   5ᵗʰ Lord Scrope
                         of Masham d.1475
                         = (2) Sir Gilbert
                         Talbot KG d.1517

Lady Maud
Herbert
d.bet.July 1485

= Henry Percy
Earl of
Northumberland
d.1489

JOHN SCROPE
5ᵗʰ Lord Scrope of Bolton
1437 – 1498

Lady Elizabeth
Percy
d.after 1512

= HENRY SCROPE
6ᵗʰ Lord Scrope of Bolton
ca.1468 – 1506

Elizabeth Neville = (1) Thomas Scrope
ca.1464–bef.Dec.1521   6ᵗʰ Lord Scrope of Upsall
dau. and coheiress   and Masham d. 1493
of John Neville   = (2) Sir Henry Wentworth
Marquis of Montagu   d. 1500

Henry Algernon Percy
5ᵗʰ Earl of
Northumberland
1478 – 1527

= Catherine Spencer
d.1542

HENRY SCROPE = (1) ALICE SCROPE
7ᵗʰ Lord Scrope of Bolton   suo jure Baroness Scrope
ca. 1480–1533   of Upsall and Masham
                               ca.1481 – ca.1510
                               = (2) Mabel
                               dau. of Thomas Lord Dacre

3. Epidemic Disease during the Reign of Henry VII (1485–1509)

IT IS NOT surprising that recipes for epidemic disease are prominent in SB 89, for the manuscript appears to have been written in its present form during the reign of Henry VII (1485–1509), a time of widespread infectious illnesses (see table 2). The first *receptarium* in Part I (ff. 58v–77v; **Appendix C**, no. 27) contains a heading for the section, "Remedyse ffor the pestylence And All poyson" (ff. 65v–66v). That section contains six antidotes for poison or venom and four recipes for treatment of—or prophylactic against—the pestilence. Two of the plague cures are brief herbal recipes, for example, "Take femetory that beryth the Sede And gyve it the Syke to drynk with water of dragonis both day and nyght And thou shalt be hole." (f. 66). However, one remedy, "A souerayne medycyn ffor the pestylence" (f. 66), is considerably more complex and requires distillation.[1] It calls for seventeen herbs, bole armoniac, treacle, and one of three herbal waters. Another, a "preservatyve for the pestylence" on folio 66v, requires nine herbs powdered with brimstone and eggshell.[2]

---

[1] Rankin, *Panaceia's Daughters*, cites plague remedies provided by women distillers. For example, Dorothea of Mansfeld distributed a "pestilence electuary" (109).

[2] The ingredients in this "preservative" resemble the recipe "Pro pestilencia" that occurs three times, twice in English and once in Latin, in a contemporary manuscript, St John's College, Cambridge 109 (E.6) as published in John Adams and Stuart Forbes, eds., *The Syon Abbey Herbal: The Last Monastic Herbal in England, c.*

Part I of SB 89 also includes in the section on powders (no. 21, f. 41v) two similar recipes for "Powder imperyall," the second written in red ink (fig. 2). These two recipes are closely related to the abbreviated version of *pulvis imperialis* in the Middle English version of the John of Burgundy/ John of Bordeaux text, "Medicine Against the Pestilence Evil," as edited by Lister M. Matheson.[3]

Part II of SB 89 is of even greater significance in regard to pestilential disease. Seventy-one recipes survive in the second part of the codex, transcribed in **Appendix D**, which may have originally contained eighty-four recipes. Of the seventy-one, at least eleven follow the section rubric, "Here folowith medycyns for the pestylence" (f. 8v), and are remedies for epidemic disease or prophylactics to protect against it (nos. 46–56).[4] The rubrics for two recipes, nos. 48 and 50, suggest that more than one ailment is addressed. Recipe no. 48 will "preserve one from the pestylence And gret Syknes" (f. 9). The rubric for no. 50 is similar: "A preseruacion Agaynst the pestylence And the gret Sykenesse" (f. 9; plate 7). The "Syknes" is apparently an epidemic disease, so it is also possible that the recipe that precedes the section heading for no. 45, "A Conserua Agayn the Syknesse" (f. 8v), is likewise a remedy for a widespread infectious disease. It should also be mentioned that no. 49, also on folio 9, is the only version of this text known to us that contains the words "if A man or A woman be syke of the Syknes" (see table 1). In all these cases, it is possible that "the Syknes" refers to the sweating sickness.

Yet another recipe in Part II, no. 41, on folio 7v, may have also been included as prophylactic against unidentified epidemic illnesses (plate 6).

AD 1517, by Thomas Betson (London: AMCD Publishers, 2015), 226, 256–57, 284–85. The Syon Abbey recipes, however, are for a drink rather than for the powder of SB 89.

    [3] Lister M. Matheson, "John of Burgundy: Treatises on Plague," *Sex, Aging and Death in a Medieval Medical Compendium: Trinity College Cambridge MS R.14.52, Its Texts, Language, and Scribe*, ed. M. Teresa Tavormina (Tempe, Ariz.: Arizona Center for Medieval and Renaissance Studies, 2006), 2:569–606, at 591–92 and n. 35 at pages 600–601. The two recipes in SB 89, Part I, are somewhat longer than the text as edited by Matheson, who points out that this recipe derives from the fuller form of *pulvis imperialis* (also known as *Bethzaer*) for protection against epidemic disease. This fuller version occurs in the author's Latin *De epidemia*, the source for those Middle English plague texts attributed to John.

    [4] The next section rubric, for soporifics, occurs after no. 56 on f. 10. Recipe nos. 46–50 and 56 specify "pestylence" in the rubrics while nos. 51–53 use the term "plage." No. 54 uses the term "infeccoun" and no. 55 "the sayd dyssease."

The rubric, "ffor to make Ipocras of pomegarnettis ffor them that be in An hote cawse," introduces a recipe that has been discussed above in regard to women's medicine. It also occurs in Harley 1706 (the devotional codex of the Countess of Oxford) and in Ashmole 1444. Matheson points out that pomegranates are recommended as protective against the plague in the popular body of treatises attributed to John of Burgundy/Bordeaux.[5]

Of particular interest among the plague recipes in Part II is no. 49, where the rubric includes the information that the remedy "is the same medycyn that the kyng Vsyd euery day which is profytable and hath holpyn lxxj persons the last yere." See table 1 and **Appendix D** for transcription and discussion. Recipe no. 49, the fullest version of the recipe in the manuscripts known to us, and possibly the earliest, will be discussed further subsequently (plate 7).

In addressing epidemics related to SB 89 and Henry VII, we consider here only the early Tudor reaction to these diseases. Modern considerations of nosology, etiology, and symptomology of epidemic disease in that era are not the focus of this study. It is, however, important for an understanding of the texts in the Berkeley Castle manuscript to consider extant records concerning mortality and morbidity along with other writings from that period that address these matters. As is well known, the two frequent and widespread forms of infectious disease during the period 1485–1509 are the plague or pestilence caused by *Yersinia pestis*, and the sweating sickness, often called *Sudor Anglicus*. Although there are large bodies of recent study on these diseases,[6] writings on each

---

[5] Matheson, "John," 584. See also Matheson, "*Médecin sans Frontières*: The European Dissemination of John of Burgundy's Plague Treatise," *ANQ* 18 (2005): 17–28, at 18.

[6] Selected general references on the impact of plague during this period include Carole Rawcliffe, *Urban Bodies: Communal Health in Late Medieval English Towns and Cities* (Woodbridge: Boydell Press, 2013); Paul Slack, *Plague: A Very Short Introduction* (Oxford: Oxford University Press, 2012); and Slack, *The Impact of Plague in Tudor and Stuart England* (London: Routledge and Kegan Paul, 1985). See also W. M. Ormrod and P. G. Lindley, eds., *The Black Death in England* (Stamford: Watkins, 1996). Valuable information is also included in Nicholas Orme and Margaret Webster, *The English Hospital 1070–1570* (New Haven: Yale University Press, 1995). A summary of much preceding historiography on the sweating sickness is included in John L. Flood, "'Safer on the Battlefield than in the City': England, the 'sweating sickness', and the Continent," *Renaissance Studies* 17 (2003): 147–75; however, Flood was unaware that an English-language version of the treatise on the sweating sickness by Thomas Forestier survives in British Library, Additional MS 27,582.

disease rarely refer to the other. Nonetheless, both diseases occurred frequently during the reign of Henry VII—intermittently and perhaps concurrently—and those who lived in the time of these illnesses recorded them and sought such help as was available.

In table 2 we have assembled citations to epidemic disease during this period from eleven documents: chronicles, letter collections, monastic and academic records, miracle accounts, a record from the royal house-hold, and the *Anglica Historia* of Polydore Vergil. While these sources are not comprehensive, and some, such as the miracle accounts, cover less than the entire period, we believe that these records represent the prevalence during this time of infectious diseases associated with high mortality. Where a document specifically records either plague or sweating sickness, we have so indicated.[7]

In considering the twenty-four-year period, 1485 through 1508 (Henry VII died in April 1509), there are only six years, four of which form a cluster in the 1490s, where these accounts do not record illnesses.[8] If we consider three five-year groupings (and one four-year), the largest number of incidents are recorded for the years 1485–89. The remaining five- and four-year groupings each include six or seven records. Although many do not specify the illness, eighteen identify the plague, thirteen the sweating sickness, and in one case "meazullis" accounts for mortality.[9]

While most of these disease identifications represent eyewitness accounts, understanding what was recorded (e.g., plague as opposed to sweat) is complicated by the large and vexed lexicon for epidemic disease during this period.[10] Before 1485, terms used in English to refer to outbreaks of what is often called the "Black Death"—that is, bubonic or

---

[7]   A record of many kinds of epidemics over a longer span of time and using different sources is found in "Appendix: National and Urban Epidemics, 1257–1530," in Rawcliffe, *Urban Bodies*, 360–74.

[8]   These six years are 1492, 1494, 1496, 1497, 1504, and 1506.

[9]   Whether or not this term designates what is now called "measles" is highly problematic because the word could also apply to the varioles of smallpox. See *MED* s.v. masel and *OED* s.v. measles. We are grateful for the comments of Ann Carmichael on the subject.

[10]   See Juhani Norri, *Names of Sicknesses in English, 1400–1550: An Exploration of the Lexical Field* (Helsinki: Suomalainen Tiedeakatemia, 1992), especially s.v. peste, pestilence, and pestilence evel (357); sweating sicknes (376); and *plaga*, which Norri argues can apply equally to the plague or sweating sickness (359). Norri's valuable dictionary draws on many texts not used by the *MED* or *OED*.

pneumonic plague caused by *Yersinia pestis*—included *plague, pestilence, epidemie, pestilential fever, the infection,* and *the great sickness.* In England, however, from 1485, epidemic outbreaks of *the Sweat* or *Sweating Sickness (Sudor Anglicus),* or *English Sweat* were recorded. References to the sweating sickness occurring in contexts that are unambiguous use a variety of English and Latin terms: *venomous fever of pestilence, pestilence, febrem pestilentialem, pestilential,* or simply *this sickness* or *the sickness* or *istas infirmitas, the hot sickness,* as well as *sweat, sweatynge sicknes,* and *sudor.*[11] Later in the mid-sixteenth century such terms as *stoop-gallant* or *the posting swet* are recorded.[12] Subsequent writers also acknowledged the ambiguity of terms for plague and sweat. Andrew Borde in 1542 wrote about "the Pestyferous tyme of the pestilence & swetyng sycknes,"[13] and Paul Slack cites a sermon by Bishop Hall as late as 1626 in which the sweating sickness is described as "one of the kinds of the plague or pestilence."[14]

Recipes addressing epidemic disease in both parts of SB 89 should come as no surprise, given the very high incidence of such diseases in the period when this manuscript was written for a noble household. It is equally unsurprising that no. 49 in Part II (and possibly nos. 51–52) can be associated with Henry VII. See table 1 and plate 7 and the discussion below. Epidemic disease affected both the family and the court of the first Tudor monarch.

A number of historians suggest that the *Yersinia pestis* plague was the cause of death of the monarch's father, Edmund Tudor, three months before Henry was born to his mother, Lady Margaret Beaufort (1443–1509), then thirteen years old, in January 1457.[15] Given her early widowhood and her youth at the birth of her only child, it comes as no surprise

---

[11]   *OED* s.v. sweating-sickness.

[12]   *OED* s.v. stoop-gallant and posting swet. James Carlson and Peter Hammond, "The English Sweating Sickness (1485–1551): A New Perspective on Disease Etiology," *Journal of the History of Medicine* 54 (1999): 23–54 at 41–48, suggest a link to deer ticks encountered in hunting to explain the high mortality in upper-class populations. Both the 1485 epidemic and the 1508 epidemic had a significant impact on the royal court.

[13]   *OED* s.v. pestiferous.

[14]   Slack, *Impact,* 25, n. 12 at 349.

[15]   Michael Jones and Malcolm Underwood, *The King's Mother: Lady Margaret Beaufort, Countess of Richmond and Derby* (Cambridge: Cambridge University Press, 1992), 147.

that Lady Margaret's fear of plague has been well documented, for example, by the provisions in her will for the repair of Melton manor as a plague refuge for Cambridge students.[16] A Book of Hours apparently in her possession contains an image of Saint Christopher and three prayers invoking the saint for protection against the plague.[17]

A particularly important witness is the remarkable thirty-two-folio illuminated manuscript of plague writings commissioned by Lady Margaret sometime after her son's accession to the throne in 1485. This codex, Cambridge, Fitzwilliam MS 261, must be dated from after 1485 because it includes her royal son's heraldic devices: the red dragon, the white hound, and the crowned red rose, along with Lady Margaret's own portcullis and spotted yales.[18] The codex contains the following texts in Latin and English:

ff. 1–9, the plague treatise by Johannes Jacobi attributed to Benedictus Canutus, in Latin (eTK 1502H);

ff. 9v–19 the plague treatise by Johannes Jacobi attributed to Benedictus Canutus, in English (eVK2 2164);[19]

ff. 19–20, *Regimen sanitatis Aristotilis ad Alexandrum magnum*, an excerpt from the *Secreta secretorum* with other health advice, in Latin;

ff. 20–23, John of Burgundy, *Delectissime frater*, in Latin (eTK 431K);[20]

---

[16]   Ibid., 228.

[17]   The Beaufort/Beauchamp Hours, BL Royal MS 2. A.xviii, f. 25r–v. See section 2 (**Date, Decoration, and Ownership of BCM SB 89**), see above 137, n. 109, and Charity Scott-Stokes, *Women's Books of Hours in Medieval England* (Woodbridge: D. S. Brewer, 2006), 125.

[18]   Kathleen Scott, "Manuscripts for Henry VII, His Household and Family," *The Cambridge Illuminations: Yhe Conference Papers*, ed. Stella Panayatova (London: Harvey Miller, 2007), 279–86; Francis Wormald and Phyllis Giles, *A Descriptive Catalogue of the Additional Illuminated Manuscripts in the Fitzwilliam Museum*, vol. 1 (Cambridge: Cambridge University Press, 1982), 194–96; and Kari Anne Rand, *The Index of Middle English Prose, Handlist XVIII: Manuscripts in the Library of Pembroke College, Cambridge, and the Fitzwilliam Museum* (Cambridge: D. S. Brewer, 2006), 51–54.

[19]   Joseph Pickett, "A Translation of the 'Canutus' Plague Tractate," *Popular and Practical Science of Medieval England*, ed. Lister Matheson (East Lansing: Colleagues Press, 1994), 263–82. Pickett's edition is based on the text in BL Sloane MS 404, ff. 282v–93v.

[20]   Matheson, "*Médecin*" describes this text as "a radically new, unattributed version of English origin [that] appeared in epistolary form perhaps before 1407" 21. It survives in at least sixteen manuscripts and an English translation in Sloane MS 76 (eVK2 3614).

ff. 23–26v, John of Burgundy plague text, in English (eVK2 2171);[21]

ff. 26v–27, English plague recipes, possibly from the John of Burgundy tradition;[22]

ff. 27–29, Latin suffrages in time of plague to Saints Sebastian and Anthony, which invoke the tau cross and *Trisagion* and occur elsewhere on a Latin tau-cross plague amulet;[23]

ff. 29–30v, English regimen of health information in time of plague, apparently from the John of Burgundy tradition (eVK2 1310);[24]

ff. 30v–32v, John Lydgate's English verse regimen of health, here called "The most Riche dietarie."[25]

Fitzwilliam MS 261, an illuminated manuscript of texts, prayers, and regimens of health to protect against the plague, surely reveals the deep concerns of its commissioner and owner, Lady Margaret Beaufort, mother of the king. It is perhaps not surprising then that one of the recipes in the Canutus text, on folio 18v of Fitzwilliam 261, resembles very closely the second part of no. 52 in the Berkeley Castle manuscript (Part II, f. 9v; see **Appendix D**). The Fitzwilliam version begins "And that soner a swelling may be made rype take this medicine as foloweth brose the leuys of an elder tree and putte therto ground mustard and make a playster thereof and putt it vpoun the swelling."[26]

---

[21] Matheson, "John," 588–92, edited from Trinity College, Cambridge MS R.14.52.

[22] Kari Anne Rand, "A Previously Unnoticed Fragment of John of Burgundy's Plague Tract and Some Connected Pest Regimens," *Notes and Queries* 53 (2006): 295–97; Rand suggests a possible connection with the preceding John of Burgundy plague tract.

[23] A tau-cross amulet associated with Saint Sebastian that includes the *Trisagion* is found in diagram form in BL, Additional MS 41600, f. 91v; it is discussed in Don C. Skemer, *Binding Words: Textual Amulets in the Middle Ages* (University Park, Pa.: Pennsylvania State University Press, 2006), 180–84. The tau cross is also associated with Saint Anthony and the Knights Hospitallers. See Brian Spencer, *Pilgrim Souvenirs and Secular Badges* (London: Stationery Office, 1998), 176–78.

[24] Rand, "Previously Unnoticed Fragment."

[25] This version of the widely transmitted verse shares a colophon with BL, Harley 2251, f. 5v, and Bodleian Rawlinson MS C.86, f. 62. We are grateful to Jake Walsh Morrissey for this information. See his dissertation, "'Termes of Phisik': Reading between Literary and Medical Discourses in Geoffrey Chaucer's *Canterbury Tales* and John Lydgate's *Dietary*," PhD diss., McGill University, 2011.

[26] Later witnesses to SB 89, Part II, nos. 51 and 52 are discussed in the subsection below titled "Royal Medicine for Epidemic Disease in BCM SB 89."

Polydore Vergil, who was familiar with the royal household and was asked by Henry VII to write the *Anglica Historia*, provides information on the impact of the plague on Henry's circle in 1499–1501.[27] See table 2 for other references to the plague in these years. In 1500, Thomas Rotherham, Archbishop of York, and Cardinal John Morton, the Chancellor and Archbishop of Canterbury, died of the plague, as did four other bishops.[28] This outbreak of the plague at the beginning of the sixteenth century is also posited in Thomas Penn's biography of Henry VII as the cause of the death in 1500 of Edmund, the fifteen-month-old son of the monarch.[29]

Dread of the plague must also have been joined by fear of the sweating sickness. Again, the focus of this study is not on various explanations of *Sudor Anglicus*.[30] What is important here is that there were numerous cases of mortality and morbidity from this disease close to Henry VII. Following the 1485 epidemic, the sweat appears to have remained a chronic problem in the west of England.[31] The death on the Welsh border of the eldest son of Henry VII, Arthur, Prince of Wales, in April 1502 at Ludlow Castle, has frequently been ascribed to the sweating sickness.[32] It has also been surmised that Arthur's bride of a few months, Katherine of Aragon, may have suffered the same disease but survived, a conclusion based on her absence

---

[27]   *The Anglica Historia of Polydore Vergil A.D. 1485–1537*, ed. Denys Hay, Camden Third Series 74 (London: Royal Historical Society, 1950), 118–19. Note that for the reign of Henry VII, Hay utilizes Vatican manuscript Codex Urbino Lat. 498, written 1512–13, which includes material not found in the sixteenth-century printings of this work. Vergil began the *Anglica Historia* in 1512. Book XXIV deals with reign of Henry VII. On the 30,000 who died in London of the *pestilentia* in 1499–1500, see the Vatican MS version in the notes (118–19).

[28]   Christopher Harper-Bill, "Morton, John, d. 1500," *ODNB*. Morton left bequests to Henry VII and to Henry's mother, wife, and daughter.

[29]   Thomas Penn, *Winter King: The Dawn of Tudor England* (London: Allen Lane, 2011), 49.

[30]   For a valuable survey of the range of retrospective diagnoses, see Flood, "'Safer,'" n. 4. He addresses in detail the recent studies that argue for a viral hemorrhagic fever with high mortality, possibly hantavirus or an RNA virus on the order of Crimean-Congo hemorrhagic fever. On the latter, see Carlson and Hammond, "English Sweating Sickness," 23–54.

[31]   Carlson and Hammond, "English Sweating Sickness," 30.

[32]   Penn, *Winter King*, 70–71. See also S. J. Gunn, "Henry VII (1457–1509)," *ODNB*.

at any of the extended funeral rituals following his death.[33]

A number of other sources attest to a preoccupation with *Sudor Anglicus*. A book of hours at Mount Angel Abbey in Oregon, apparently from the Paston family, contains a common Latin prayer invoking Henry VI against the sweating sickness.[34] Henry VII was eager to promote the canonization of this relative and Lancastrian predecessor. See also *Miracles, Henry VI* in table 2. M. R. James published two other manuscript versions of this prayer found in the Paston *horae* and notes that it was also printed by de Worde in books of hours in 1494 and 1505.[35]

The most valuable of the accounts of sweating sickness during the 1485–1509 reign of Henry VII are the sections of the *Anglica Historia* that were not widely known until Denys Hay's edition in 1950 utilized Polydore Vergil's manuscript written 1512–13, now in the Vatican. Vergil's accounts have been cited for his records of plague, and they are also important for his treatment of three epidemics of the sweat: (1) in 1485, "*sudor laetalis*" (6–9); (2) in 1503–6, "*pestilens sudor*" (140–43), a dating for the sweating sickness not often mentioned elsewhere, but one that corresponds to high mortality at Westminster Abbey;[36] and (3) the epidemic of 1508 that began after Henry's daughter Mary was betrothed to Charles of Castille in December 1507. This outbreak continued as the "*sudor ille pernicialis*" that affected Henry's court on his progress the following summer (142–43).

In August 1508, when the king was away from London on that summer progress, many deaths occurred from the sweat. It raged in London, and it seemed to follow Henry's party as he moved from place to place.

---

[33] Ralph Houlbrooke, "Prince Arthur's Funeral," *Arthur Tudor, Prince of Wales: Life, Death and Commemoration*, ed. Steven Gunn and Linda Monckton (Woodbridge: Boydell Press, 2009), 64–76.

[34] Mount Angel Abbey, St. Benedict, Oregon, MS 0027, f. 1: "Rex Henricus . . . Non sudore ne dolore mereamur subito. . . ."

[35] *Henry the Sixth: A Reprint of John Blacman's Memoir* (Cambridge: University Press, 1919), xi–xiv; see 50–51 for a more general English-language prayer inserted on the flyleaf of a 1408 *horae*. The James volume is available through Project Gutenberg. A different prayer invoking the Virgin and Christ, "in praesentia sudore tristi," survives in a manuscript in Keio University Library, ed. William Snell, "A Prayer Against the Sweating Sickness: *Oratio contra infirmitatem sudoris* (Keio Univ. MS 120X. 423. 1" [Keio University] *Academic Papers* 13, no. 73 (1998): 68–76.

[36] Barbara Harvey, *Living and Dying in England, 1100–1540: The Monastic Experience* (Oxford: Clarendon Press, 1993), 122–26. See also table 2.

Three chamber servants of his son Prince Henry died. Three men close to the king—Bishop Richard Fox, Lord Chamberlain; Hugh Denys, head of the privy chamber; and Charles Somerset, lord Herbert, Henry's vice-chamberlain—all fell victim to the disease at that time, but the three survived.[37]

Preoccupation with epidemic disease on the part of Henry VII, whether it be plague or the sweat, is clearly illustrated by the large statues of saints inserted in niches that surround the Henry VII Chapel in Westminster Abbey at the triforium level. This chapel was almost certainly begun during the monarch's life and in accordance with his wishes.[38] It is especially striking that, among the surviving statues, seventeen depict saints invoked in cases of plague and sweat. Four of these saints are, in fact, portrayed by two statues (Armel, Roche, Margaret, and Sebastian), and the last is not only represented twice—but in both cases represented with, in the niches on either side of the martyr, separate statues of the archers who shot him. Others (Anthony, Christopher, George, and Giles) each have single statues. The body of Henry VI was intended to be transferred upon canonization from Windsor to a hierarchal position in the east bay of the chapel.

Texts on Plague and Sweat Associated with Kings

Plague writings addressed to rulers originated with the devastating plagues of the fourteenth century and continued in most European countries. For example, several plague treatises were written by Sigismund Albich (1360–1427), sometime Archbishop of Prague. Albich was chief

---

[37] Penn, *Winter King*, 325–27; Carlson and Hammond, "English Sweating Sickness," 31.

[38] Tim Tatton-Brown and Richard Mortimer, eds., *Westminster Abbey: The Lady Chapel of Henry VII* (Woodbridge: Boydell Press, 2003). In this comprehensive volume, see especially Philip Lindley, "'The singuler mediacions and praiers of al the holie companie of Heven': Sculptural Functions and Forms in Henry VII's Chapel," 259–93, and two studies by Margaret Condon: "God Save the King! Piety, Propaganda and the Perpetual Memorial," 59–97, and "The Last Will of Henry VII: Document and Text," 99–140. See also Christopher Wilson, "The Designer of Henry VII's Chapel, Westminster Abbey," *The Reign of Henry VII*: Symposium Papers, ed. Benjamin Thompson (Stamford: Paul Watkins, 1995), 133–56.

physician to Bohemian King Wenceslaus IV and served at the court of the Holy Roman Emperor Siegmund in Budapest.[39] Matheson also points out that the fullest version of *De epidemia*, originally compiled in 1365 following the 1361–62 plague by the Liège physician called John of Burgundy, was translated into French on the commission of the primary physician to Charles V and copied in 1371 in a luxurious manuscript.[40] Less well known are the six recipes claimed to have been sent to a French king by a pope in BL Lansdowne 380.[41]

Turning to England for plague texts associated with kings, we find the plague treatises attributed to John of Burgundy widely disseminated in England in both Latin and English and subsequently incorporated into many other medical writings.[42] One manuscript of the four-chapter version of *De epidemia* (classified by Matheson as Group B), which survives in eight Latin manuscripts and in forty-plus English-language manuscripts, contains the claim that it was requested by Richard II (r. 1377–99). The text in BL Lansdowne 285 is a sixteenth-century addition to the "great book" of Sir John Paston. It begins, on folio 214, "Here beginnethe a noble tretis made by the ordinance of A great Clark M[agister] John Bordews at the prayer of King Richard & other the Lordis for pestilence." This treatise seems to be associated with the 1390 epidemic.[43] Matheson further points out that the short Latin epistolary treatise attributed to John of Burgundy beginning "Dilectissime frater" contains the date as "inventa est … anno Regis Richardi II sexto"" (1382/83), although that inscription does not establish a secure connection with the king.[44] As noted above, this epistolary text also occurs in Lady Margaret Beaufort's plague manuscript, Fitzwilliam 261.

---

[39] Emil Schultheiss, "Über die Werke des Albicus," *Janus* 49 (1960): 221–34; Schultheiss, "Beitrag zur Pestliteratur des Spätmittelalters," *Centaurus* 7 (1961): 213–19. We are grateful to Lister Matheson for directing us to this information.

[40] Paris, BNF fonds fr. N.a. 4515 (olim 4516), teste Matheson, "*Médecin*," 20.

[41] "Medicine contre lepidemie enuoyee nostre saint pere le pape au Roy de france," ff. 256v–58.

[42] Matheson, "*Médecin*," especially 19–28.

[43] Matheson, "*Médecin*," 22–23. The prologue is eVK2 619K and text, f. 214r–v, are eVK2 7937. Because this text occurs in the post-Paston section of the manuscript, it is not addressed in G. A. Lester, *Sir John Paston's "Grete Boke": A Descriptive Catalogue, with an Introduction, of British Library MS Lansdowne 285* (Cambridge: D. S. Brewer, 1984).

[44] Cambridge University Library MS Ii. I.31, teste Matheson, "*Médecin*," 23.

As elsewhere, the plague recurred several times in fifteenth-century England. In general, however, the Lancastrian and Yorkist eras were not visited with the widespread mortality of fourteenth-century England. In the fifteenth century instead frequent and rather more localized episode occurred.[45] Perhaps lower mortality from epidemic disease accounts for what appears to be less evidence of plague writings for kings in fifteenth-century England before 1485. There is no evidence to support F. J. Furnivall's association of the Huntington flyleaf recipe similar to no. 49 in SB 89, Part II, with Edward IV (eVK2 2101),[46] and still less as described by J. F. D. Shrewsbury as "invented" by Edward IV.[47] Furnivall failed to note that this recipe is a flyleaf addition in a later hand to a manuscript copied from printed books, including one not printed until after July 1482. See the transcription of the Huntington text and correction of Furnivall's misreading in table 1. There is, however, in the Pepys Collection another recipe for the plague that is claimed to have been written for Edward IV in the tenth year of his reign (1471).[48] The only resemblance it bears to no. 49 in the Berkeley Castle manuscript is the final claim that it helped a number of those suffering from the plague.

There is, nonetheless, one important manuscript that deserves attention as illustrating the textual tradition of recipes addressed to members of both Yorkist and Tudor English royal families, BL Harley MS 1628.[49] In his valuable study, Peter Jones points out that Harley 1628 contains a number of recipes added to margins and on formerly blank leaves that are associated with Edward IV (r. 1461–70 and 1471–83) and his brother Richard, Duke of Gloucester and king for two years as Richard III (r. 1483–85).

---

[45]   Slack, *Impact*, 14, 16.

[46]   F. J. Furnivall, "Recipe for Edward IV's Plague Medicine," *Notes and Queries*, 5th ser.. S. 9 (1878): 343.

[47]   J. F. D. Shrewsbury, *A History of Bubonic Plague in the British Isles* (Cambridge: Cambridge University Press, 1970), 146. On the need to use Shrewsbury with caution, see Slack, *Plague*, 130.

[48]   This single recipe, a "Most Sovereign Medicine for the Pestilence," is found in Cambridge, Magdalene College, Pepys MS 1047, ff. 17v-18 (eVK2 4901). A facsimile of the manuscript is in Gerald Hodgett, *Stere htt well: A Book of Medieval Refinements, Recipes and Remedies from Samuel Pepys's Library* (London: Cornmarket Press, 1972).

[49]   Peter Murray Jones, "Witnesses to Medieval Medical Practice in the Harley Collection," *eBLJ* (2008): article 8, 1–13. This study deals with three manuscripts in the Harley collection, 2558, 1735, and 1628. On 1628, see 5–13.

Twelve are specified for Edward IV, if one includes the eight in a group where the royal reference occurs only in the section heading (f. 75v). Another is designated "Preservati Ricardi/preservati regis," and one is for the Duchess of York, the mother of both Yorkist kings.

Many recipes added to Harley MS 1628 are of historical interest, but rarely are we told in the added recipes the ailments being addressed, and many recipes do not specify a patient. Recipes with the imprecise rubric "pro rege" cannot be linked to a specific king, and Henry VII cannot be ruled out. Four added recipes address the plague, but without identifying a patient. There are, among other added recipes, six for *pomum ambre* that likewise do not specify a patient. The most important ingredient in this prophylactic against the plague is the very expensive ambergris (Latin, *ambra*), which is specified in three recipes in SB 89, Part II.[50]

In a study of BCM SB 89, what is most important about Harley 1628 is that a close examination of the codex suggests strongly that the Yorkist recipes discussed by Jones cannot be contemporary. Both Yorkist and Tudor recipes added throughout the volume were supplied after the codex had been assembled, and the scribe of one of the main texts, the *Liber aggregatus* on folios 99–153v, dates the copying of this treatise Anno 1491,[51] that is, to the reign of Henry VII. This later date is confirmed by added recipes for members of Henry's family throughout the codex, and there are some striking similarities between Harley 1628 and BCM SB 89.

Members of the family of Henry VII named in the added recipes in Harley 1628 include three general recipes for Lady Margaret Beaufort, the formidable mother of the king (two on f. 2, one on f. 155). An electuary recipe on folio 32 is identified as being by Lewes Kery, who served as physician to Henry's queen, Elizabeth of York, and to Princess Mary.[52] Like

---

[50] Nos. 37–39. See the introductory discussion to Part II in **Appendix D**, especially for the importance of the study on *pomum ambre* by John Riddle and the mid-sixteenth-century recipes "Pomeamber against the Pestilence" and "A Princelie Pomeamber."

[51] F. 130, originally f. 128. See the very full description by Laura Nuvoloni in the British Library online catalog, in which she draws attention to this date. We argue that is in the hand of the scribe who copied that text, the *Liber aggregatus in medicinis simplicibus* attributed to the Pseudo Serapion (ff. 99–153v). See in eTK three records with the title *Liber aggregationum* and eighteen records for the text beginning "Dixit aggregator."

[52] Kery is likely the doctor who was paid two pounds as "the Queen's physician" from the accounts of Henry VII, and Mary Tudor (1496–1533) is known to have

several recipes in SB 89, this polypharmaceutical recipe calls for pearls, coral, and three precious stones, along with manus Christi, among its many ingredients. It may bear repeating that we have no way to identify the monarch in question in the eight added recipes in Harley 1628 that bear the simple rubric "Pro rege." The Latin rubric could apply to Henry VII.

Other elements in Harley 1628 resemble the Berkeley Castle manuscript. Although it has not been noticed, the Harley codex, like SB 89, contains a copy of the *Antidotarium Nicolai*.[53] The recipe for Diamargariton in the Harley *Antidotarium Nicolai* (folio 38) is identical to that in Part II of SB 89, folio 7 (**Appendix D**, No. 39, although an earlier version in the SB 89 *Antidotarium* in Part I (ff. 46v–47) is much shorter. The distillation possible only in a great house also looms large in both manuscripts, and Harley 1628 includes drawings of distillation equipment on folio 155.

There is yet another important manuscript where we are on secure ground in specifying that the monarch in question is the first Tudor king, and in this case the text unambiguously addresses the sweating sickness. This treatise is an English version of the work by Thomas Forestier on the "venemous fever of pestilence" (also referred to as "februm pestilencialem"), which survives in BL Additional 27, 582 (ff. 70–77). This English text, which contains much Latin and may be dependent on a Latin original, is dedicated to Henry VII. The Latin rubric to the prologue begins, "Illustrissimo ac maximo principi Henrico dei gratia anglie regi & francie & domino hibernie. Thomas fforestier Normandie nacionis facultatis medicine." The *envoi* begins "O noble and meke prince I beseche the of thy noble mageste to spare me though I haue be so bold to wryte to thy

been attended by Lewes Kery (c. 1472–1510). See C. H. Talbot and E. A. Hammond, *The Medical Practitioners in Medieval England: A Biographical Register* (London: Wellcome Historical Medical Library, 1965), s.v. Lewes Kery (204), and Faye Getz, "Archives and Sources: Medical Practitioners in Medieval England," *Social History of Medicine* 13 (1990): 245–83, s.v. Lewes Kery (269).

[53] Harley 1628, Unit 4, ff. 25–98, is apparently an enlarged version of the *Antidotarium Nicolai* as printed in 1471 (reproduced in Dietlinde Goltz, *Mittelalterliche Pharmazie und Medizin* [Stuttgart: Wissenschaftliche Verlagsgesellschaft, 1976]), although it lacks most of the recipes beginning with the letter "A." Approximately ninety-eight of the 142 entries in the 1471 printing occur in this section of the manuscript, often grouped as in the printing, with each group followed by additional recipes in the same category.

hyghnes of this lytell gouernyng . . ." and is followed by the colophon "Editum per Thomam fforestier . . . Notandum est quod ista infirmitas primo tempore regnauit per totium regnum anglie. In anno domini M° cccc lxxxv" (f. 77).[54] The text would have lasting value, as the envoi accurately predicts: "And nobyl prince I se that this forsaid sykenes in tyme to come wyl reyn sore emongist vs. . . ." (f. 77).

BL Additional MS 27,582 is a *Sammelband* containing printed and manuscript texts in English and Latin. In the manuscript text by Forestier, John of Burgundy's *De epidemia* on the plague has been adapted for the sweating sickness that first appeared in England in 1485.[55] Although in the chapters in this treatise on the etiology of *Sudor Anglicus* (*causa supercelesti* and *causa propinqua*), recipes and a regimen of health are largely taken from John of Burgundy, the accounts of sudden death and details of symptoms claim to be descriptions of the sweating sickness. A number of examples of victims who have "dyed sodenly" are cited as eyewitness accounts (ff. 71v–72). Forestier describes the sickness as appearing with "a grete swetyng and stynkyng with reddenesse of the face and of al the body and a contynuan thurst wt a grete hete and hed ache" (f. 72).

The date and origin of this English-language text and its relation to Forestier's Latin and French writings is a matter for discussion elsewhere. But in a number of respects, BL Additional MS 27,582 is relevant to BCM SB 89. Although the recipes in the Forestier text and SB 89 differ, many of the exotic and extremely valuable ingredients are the same, and the layout on the page of the polypharmaceutical recipes in SB 89, Part II, displays the same format as the recipes in the Forestier treatise (see **Appendix D**). Also important is an early sixteenth-century recipe on an inserted sheet in BL Additional MS 27,582 (f. 193) for *pulvis imperatoris*, a plague recipe deriving from John of Burgundy. Two recipes for *pulvis imperialis* in Part I of SB 89 have been discussed above (fig. 2). There are other plague recipes in later sections of Additional 27,582, including those on folios 212v–213. Furthermore, distillation, required in both Part I and Part II of SB 89, is the subject of the John of Rupescissa treatise (ff. 198–213), and the drawing of an alembic on a furnace on folio 213v echoes Harley 1628.

---

[54] For Forestier's printed Latin text, see Thomas le Forestier, *Traité de la Peste* (Rouen, 1490), with introduction, analysis and notes by Gustave Panel (Rouen: Société des Bibliophiles Normands,1909). We hope to discuss elsewhere Forestier's French and Latin writings, as well as the contents and provenance of BL Add. 27,582.

[55] Matheson, "*Médecin*," 26, on the adaptation.

One other treatise on epidemic disease may be associated with Henry VII. The fourteenth-century work by the Montpellier physician Johannes Jacobi and attributed to Benedictus Canutus[56] was translated into English in the fifteenth century and, as has been cited, occurs in Lady Margaret Beaufort's manuscript, Fitzwilliam MS 261, along with the devices of Henry VII. Three slightly varying English versions of this text were printed in London by Machlinia around 1485 or 1486.[57] These books do not obviously address the sweating sickness, but three printings of a pest tract at the time of great mortality from the sweat as well as from the plague may suggest its relevance. George Keiser posits that Henry VII may have been a patron of the Machlinia prints.[58] Although we are not aware of his evidence supporting that inference, we are convinced that the text in in Fitzwilliam 261 is closely related to one of the Machlinia printings.[59]

As was the case with his mother's evident preoccupation with epidemic disease, a concern on the part of Henry VII may have been similarly manifest in prayer.[60] A Book of Hours made for the English market in the mid-fifteenth century contained, among later additions to the codex, an account of the monarch bringing an image from Brittany of Saint Armagillus, who is to be petitioned in cases of agues, fevers, poxes, and "many other infirmytees."[61] It is not surprising that two statues of this saint invoked for fevers, of which the sweat was the most pernicious, are to be found in the Henry VII Chapel in Westminster Abbey.[62]

---

[56] Pickett, "A Translation" (see above, section 3, n. 19), and Matheson, "*Médecin*," 26.

[57] STC 4589–91; ISTC ij00013200, ij00013400, and ij00013600.

[58] George Keiser, "Two Medieval Plague Treatises and Their Afterlife in Early Modern England," *Journal of the History of Medicine* 58 (2003): 292–324, at 318–22.

[59] We intend to discuss this connection elsewhere.

[60] Regarding the prayers in Lady Margaret Beaufort's plague manuscript, Fitzwilliam MS 261, see above, n. 23.

[61] This text was written in English on the originally blank leaf (f. 14v) of Victoria and Albert MS Reid 44 (MSL/1902/1691). The application of a reagent makes it now impossible to read any of the text other than a Latin note on the saint beneath it, but the transcription made prior to the application of the reagent is provided by Rowan Watson, *Western Illuminated Manuscripts: A Catalogue of the Works in the National Art Library from the Eleventh to the Early Twentieth Century* (London: V&A Publishing, 2011), 1: no. 38, p. 226.

[62] On particular interest in this saint by Henry VII, see David Hugh Farmer, *Oxford Dictionary of Saints* (Oxford: Oxford University Press, 1978), 22, s.v. Armel. The survival of pilgrim badges for the cult of Saint Armel/Armagilus/Armagillus has

In addition to extensive evidence linking texts on epidemic disease to Henry VII, two copies of another, more general, medical treatise also testify to the monarch's concerns with matters of health. One of the manuscripts contains his arms, and the other a presentation image. This text, *Le Régime du Corps* by Aldobrandino of Siena, was written in French in 1256 for Beatrix of Savoy. [63] The regimen of health includes general information on the elements and on food, drink, and bathing; discussions of parts of the body; specific advice on drink, meats, fish, vegetables, fruit, herbs, and spices; and a concluding section on physiognomy. In Cambridge University Library MS Ii. V. 11, this text is preceded by the king's arms, impaled with those of his wife, Elizabeth of York, and the manuscript ends with "Roy Henry VII, a qui dieu doint bonne vie et paradis."[64] The other Henrician codex containing this text, British Library Royal MS 19. A. v, is a Netherlandish book written (1494–96) for Jean Chabot (d. 1496), Lord of Emael and Alderman of Liège, as a presentation to Henry VII. The ink and pigment presentation scene on folio 1v represents a presentation to the king, real or symbolic. In the scene, Chabot, wearing his heraldic tabard and the SS collar associated with the Lancastrians, kneels before the enthroned Henry VII to offer the book.[65]

Royal Medicine for Epidemic Disease in BCM SB 89

Royal recipes for epidemic disease in Berkeley Castle Muniments SB 89 occur in Part II. Recipe no. 49 is of particular importance and is discussed in table 1 in relation to five other manuscript and printed witnesses to the

---

been described by Hanneke van Asperin as evidence of a "forgotten cult of medieval England" in "Saint Armel of Brittany: The Identification of Four Badges from London," *Peregrinations* at http://peregrinations.kenyon.edu/vol2-1/. On plague saints represented in the Westminster Abbey Chapel, see above, n. 38.

[63] *Le Régime du Corps de Maitre Aldebrandin de Sienne*, ed. Louis Landouzy and Roger Pépin (Paris: H. Champion, 1911).

[64] *A Catalogue of the Manuscripts Preserved in the Library of the University of Cambridge*, vol. 3 (Cambridge, 1858), 482–83.

[65] Scot McKendrick, John Lowden, and Kathleen Doyle, eds., *Royal Manuscripts: The Genius of Illumination* (London: BL, 2011), 306–7. See also the British Library Catalogue of Illuminated Manuscripts, http://www.bl.uk/catalogues/illuminatedmanuscripts/.

text, from which it differs slightly (plate 7). The SB 89 version is similar to the others in most respects, but in one section of the text, it is fuller than the others. It is the only version of this recipe known to us that supplies the following instructions for administering the medicine: "And if A man or A woman be syke of the Syknes he or she must drynke or supp x tymys of it and a person he or she be not syke then he nede not to drynke of it but onys in the mornyng."

Other recipes relevant to a monarch in SB 89, Part II, are nos. 51–52. Although these recipes contain no reference to a king in SB 89, they are found in later manuscripts and printed books with royal attribution. The two recipes are printed first as discrete texts in T. C., *An Hospitall for the Diseased* (London, 1579), and then again subsequently in that volume where the two recipes are combined and cite Henry VIII and the Lord Mayor.[66]

In Ashmole 1444, a composite manuscript added to over a long period of time and discussed above in connection with recipes in Part I of SB 89, we find SB 89, Part II, nos. 51 and 52 in booklet V, page 332 (from the reign of Elizabeth I), where the rubric reads, "A medisone for the plage w[ch] the Kinges grace sent my lord maior of London." The Ashmole version, like the version in *An Hospitall for the Diseased*, combines what in SB 89 are separate recipes: no. 51, a prophylactic recipe, and no. 52, a remedy for when a patient is already infected with the plague.

Another later witness to nos. 51 and 52, which also combines the two recipes with royal attribution, can be found in an early seventeenth-century record in the London Metropolitan Archives (ca. 1600–1610), where the rubric reads, "a medicine sent from the Kinges maiestie Kinge henry the 8th our soueraigne Lord vnto the maior of the citty of London the 11th daie of August 1543 for remedy against the plague wherewith the citty was sore infected at that tyme to intent that yt should bee notyfied to the commons of the same citty for their preseruation."[67]

---

[66] STC 4303.7, B1 and L1. The volume also contains SB 89, Part II, no. 49, which also appears in the printing of this text in the previous year. See table 1.

[67] London Metropolitan Archives, COL/AC/08/001, f. 85v; the LMA catalog index fails to make clear that the document is a later copy.

The Significance of BCM SB 89

This valuable manuscript sheds light on the world of great households during the reign of Henry VII, and indeed on the roles of women in medical care, in a number of different ways. It provides evidence of the prosperity of such households that allowed them to purchase imported exotic spices, precious metals, and gems for medical use. Similarly, specific instructions in BCM SB 89 on distillation processes suggest the wealth necessary to maintain the furnaces, alembics, and other equipment needed to produce distilled medicines. Preoccupation with remedies for epidemic disease in this manuscript, particularly in Part II, reveals as well a world of constant and justified fear of death or debilitating illness from plague or sweating sickness, especially in the royal household and those households associated with it.

SB 89 is also witness to the women of a great house as providers of medical care. While some of the texts included in the manuscript circulated among physicians, doctors are not the intended users for this codex, not least because the exclusively therapeutic focus of the book omits the texts on diagnosis and prognosis commonly found in the books of professional healers. As many internal references indicate, the women of a great household must have been the intended users of this large compendium of recipes.

A related insight into a great household in the early Tudor era provided by this manuscript is that Scrope women who were associated with the court circulated books and medical information among members of their extended family and affinity. The female heads of household and their relatives supplied medical information and were themselves the managers of health and healing. It is fitting, then, to conclude this part of the study of SB 89 with a letter written by Agnes Howard, married from 1497 to Thomas Howard, Earl of Surrey, made second Duke of Norfolk in 1514. From 1501, her husband was Lord Treasurer, one of the "executive triumvirate" of Henry VII, and executor at the king's death.[68] Agnes, the earl's second wife (ca. 1477–1545), bore him five sons and eight daughters and managed large households at Horsham and Lambeth. She was godmother to Princess Mary and continued to have a presence at court

---

[68]   David M. Head, "Howard, Thomas, second duke of Norfolk (1443–1524)," *ODNB*.

after she was widowed in 1524, being named officially as first lady of the queen's household, after only the king's sister, in 1526.[69]

One or more books like Berkeley Castle SB 89 were likely to have been in Agnes's household when in 1528 she wrote to Cardinal Thomas Wolsey (1470–1530), then still a considerable power in affairs of state, that she had learned of the sweating sickness in his household. Wolsey himself had suffered "several times" from the disease.[70] In this letter, written with a voice of authority, Agnes advises the cardinal on the treatments she used, in terms of both ingredients and instructions for administration, and she suggests a prophylactic *pomum ambre* or pomander. Note that she has administered for *Sudor Anglicus* the remedy "water imperial," associated perhaps, at least in name, with the recipe for "powder impery-all" a plague recipe that appears twice in SB 89, Part I. [71]

Agnes also comments disapprovingly on the disease caused by neglect in the household of her stepson, the third Duke of Norfolk; describes the course that sweating sickness takes; and in a tone of authority, urges avoiding contagion. Of particular importance is her advice to take no food or drink at onset of the sweat and to keep to bed for twenty-four hours, a therapy also found in the Forestier treatise and one that seemed to aid in recovery. This "English cure" became famous throughout Europe as an effective treatment:[72]

> ... My lord, if it would please you, if that you have the sweat, from the which I pray God defend you, for to send me word, I shall send Hogon and William Hastings unto your grace, the which shall keep you as well as is possible, after the temperate fashion. I have the experience daily in my house of all manner of sorts, both good and bad; and, thanked be God, there is none miscarried, neither in my house nor within the parish that I am in. For if they that be in danger perceive themselves very sick, they send for such of my house

---

[69]   Catharine Davies, "Howard, [*née* Tilney], Agnes, duchess of Norfolk (b. in or before 1477, d. 1545)," *ODNB*.

[70]   Sybil M. Jack, "Wolsey, Thomas 1470–1530," *ODNB*.

[71]   See discussion of the two recipes in SB 89, see above n. 3.

[72]   The important study by Flood ("'Safer on the battlefield than in the city'"; see above n. 6) deals at length with sweating sickness on the Continent and the adoption there of the English cure; see especially 15376. For a detailed description of this cure, see John Caius, *A boke, or counseil against the disease commonly called the sweate, or sweatyng sicknesse* (London, 1552), ff. 31v–39. STC 4343.

as hath had it and knoweth the experience, whereby, thanked be God, they do escape: and if they be sick at the heart, I give them treacle and water imperial, the which doth drive it from the heart, and thus have holpen them that have swooned divers times, and that have received the sacraments of the church; and divers doth swell at their stomachs, to whom I give setwell to eat, the which driveth it away from the stomach. And the best remedy that I do know in it is to take little or no sustenance or drink, until sixteen hours be past. And, my lord, such of your servants as have had it, let them not come about your grace of one week after. And thus I do use my servants, and I thank our Lord as yet I have not had it. Vinegar, wormwood, rosewater, and crumbs of brown bread, is very good and comfortable, to put in a linen cloth, to smell unto your nose, so that it touch not your visage. My lord, I hear say that my lord of Norfolk hath had the sweat, and that divers in his house are dead; and, as I think, through default of keeping. . . . My lord, I do not write unto your grace this because I think that your servants cannot keep you; but I hear that other men's servants dare not disobey their masters' commandments in their sickness. Wisdom will not help in this disease; but if they have somebody about them that dare take upon them to order them. My lord, I never saw people so far out of the way in no disease as they be in this; and about twelve or sixteen hours is the greatest danger. There be some that sweateth much, and some that sweateth very little, but burneth very sore: but the greatest surety is in any wise to keep your bed twenty-four hours.[73]

---

[73] Letter of Agnes, Duchess of Norfolk, to Cardinal Thomas Wolsey, 1528, as printed in Mary Anne Everett Wood, *Letters of Royal and Illustrious Ladies of Great Britain* (London, 1846), 2:26–30. Other evidence of treatment for the sweating sickness in Wolsey's and the royal households in 1528 can be found in Bodl. MS Rawlinson A. 393, a "Findern manuscript." Among a number of medical recipes copied by the vicar Sir John Reed are two on folio 71v dated 20 Henry VIII (1529, called the "ye dere yere") for the sweat. The first was "gevyn by doctor chamber Ye kynges fysicioun & send to ye Erle of Shrewysbery Against ye swetyng seiknes," a drink to be taken during complete bed rest. The second is a single recipe for "ye same disess of ye swett devised by my lord kardinall phisicoun." Neither text bears any resemblance to the recipes in SB 89. See William Macray, *Catalogi Codicum Manuscriptorum Bibliothecae Bodleianae Pars Quintae, Fasciculus Primus . . . Ricardi Rawlinson* (Oxford, 1862), cols. 391–93. See also George Keiser, "MS Rawlinson A. 393: Another Findern manuscript," *Transactions of the Cambridge Bibliographical Society* 7 (1977–80): 447,

A book like Berkeley Castle Muniments SB 89 was likely used and valued by Agnes, just as Berkeley Castle Muniments SB 89 was doubtless important in another great early-Tudor household, that of the Scropes of Bolton.

---

n. 6. John Chamber, M.D. (1470?–1549), was a Padua-educated royal physician to both Henry VII and Henry VIII. He served as executor of the will of Lady Margaret Beaufort and was himself extremely wealthy. See C. H. Talbot and E. A. Hammond, *Medical Practitioners*, 131–32.

Table 1. Royal Recipe for Plague in BCM SB 89, Part II, No. 49, with Other Versions

Our transcription of Berkeley Castle Muniments, SB 89, Part II, folio 9 (no. 49) is given below (plate 7). It differs from the other witnesses to this text known to us in that it is the only version that supplies the following instructions for administering the medicine: "And if A man or A woman be syke of the Syknes he or she must drynke or supp x tymys of it and a person he or she be not syke then he nede not to drynke of it but onys in the morning. . . ."

Following the text as found in SB 89, we provide here a transcription of the version that is the most closely related example known to us, a flyleaf addition to San Marino, Huntington Library, MS HM 144, folio 151v. Our transcription of the Huntington text varies slightly from that of F. J. Furnivall in "Recipe for Edward IV's Plague Medicine," *Notes & Queries*, 5th series, 9 (1878), 343. Furnivall's association of the recipe with the Yorkist king has been subsequently repeated, but it is unlikely that the king cited in the Huntington version was Edward IV, who died in April 1483. That manuscript contains copies of several texts from printed books, one of which is the Middle English translation of Ranluph Higden's *Polychronicon*, printed by Caxton sometime after July 1482.[1] The plague recipe was added to a flyleaf of the completed codex. It could possibly refer to Richard III, but the reference is more likely to Henry VII.

The table after these two transcriptions of the recipe lists four other witnesses known to us, with comments on variants. Only one is from a manuscript that makes no connection with a monarch, one cites an unknown king, one from a book printed in 1578 links the recipe to Henry VII, and the last from a late manuscript record associates the recipe with Henry VIII.

---

[1] Lotte Hellinga, *Printing in England in the Fifteenth Century: E. Gordon Duff's Bibliography, with Supplementary Description, Chronologies and a Census of Copies* (London: Bibliographical Society, 2009), 46, no. 172.

Berkeley Castle Muniments, SB 89, Part II, f. 9 (No. 49)

Rubric: ⸿ A medycyn for the pestylence
This is the same medycyn that the kyng
Vsyd euery day which is profytable and hath
holpyn lxxj persons the last yere
Text: ffyrst you must take half a handfull of Rew An handfull of
marygowldis And half An handfull of sorell And A quantyte
of dragons of the croppe or of the Rote And then wasch this
~~water~~ cleane in fayer water and then take A pottell of Rynnyng
water And Seth thes to gyther from A pottell to A quart And
then strayn it throwe A fayer cloth And yf it be bytter putt therto
A quantyte of suger candy And if A man or A woman be syke
of the Syknes he or she must drynke or supp x tymys of it and
a person he or she be not syke then he nede not to drynke of it but
onys in the mornyng And yf he take it or [ere] the purpyllis Apere
ther is no perell ther by the grace of god

San Marino, Huntington Library, MS HM 144, f. 151v

Rubric: Thys ys þe medysyn þt þe kyngis grace vsythe every day
for the raynyng seknys þt now raynthe þe wyche hathe
ben prowyd & be þe grace of god yt hathe olpyn
þys 3ere lxxi personys
Text: he most take a hanfvll of
rewe A hanfvll of marygoldis \halfe/ A hanfvll of fetherfev
A hanfvll of bvrnett A hanfvll of sorell A qvantyte
of dragonys þe crop or þe rovte then take a potell
of rvngnyng water ffyrst wasche them clene
& let them sethe esely tyl yt be a moste cvm from
A potell to a qvarte of leker then take a clene
clothe & strayne ytt & drynke yt & yt be byttyr
pvt therto A lytyll svger of candy & thys may be
dronkyn oft tyme & yf yt be dronkyn before eny
pvrpyl apere By þe grase of god ther schall
be no perell of no dethe

London, British Library Harley MS 218, f. 158v (C16?) Text faded and damaged; preceding alchemical recipes may be in the same hand.	Text begins similarly, citing an **unspecified king**, and indicates that the recipe helped many this year. Ingredients and instructions for preparation are similar to the SB 89 recipe, but instructions for administration are lacking. It may be taken with sugar candy and taken frequently. If taken before a purple appear there is no peril.
London, Lambeth Palace Library, MS 306, f. 132 (Scribe E, C15? C16?)	Text makes no mention of a royal connection. Ingredients and preparation instructions are similar, but there are variants (*river* rather than *running* water; sugar or *licorice* for sweetening). Instructions for administration are limited to "& let the syke persoone drynk hit." The most significant difference is a concluding paragraph with the cure claim that the recipe helped 71 persons in Salisbury, where two of three who drank the recipe recovered, but the third, who refused, died. It concludes that it "was proved in the clooce of Salysburye & also in the towne And hit was proved at Burford in the woold vppoun vi persones And thys medycyne must be yoven betyme the rather the better or the purples apere."
T. C., *An Hospitall for the Diseased* London, 1578 (STC 4303.5) Printed with the same rubric and slight orthographic variations in 1579 (STC 4303.7) and in all later editions.	Rubric [Sig. B2]: "A medicine that was taught **king Henrie the seventh**, by his phisition, against the Pestilence." Ingredients and preparation instructions are quite similar to SB 89, with the variant "Sugar Candie or of other Sugar." There are no instructions for administration other than the conclusion "& if this medicine be used before the purples doe arise, ye shalbe whole by Gods grace."
London, British Library, Sloane MS 4, f. 27 (p. 51) Printed with minor errors by Henry Ellis, *Original Letters, Illustrative of English History*, ser. 1, 2nd ed. (London, 1825), vol. I, p. 287.	Rubric: "A medycyn for yᵉ pestylence of **kyng henry yᵉ viijᵗʰ** þᵉ wyche hath helpyd dyuers persons." Ingredients and instructions for preparation are quite similar to SB 89. There are no instructions for administration other than the conclusion: "And yf yt be takyn be for yᵗ purpullis do a per yt wyll hele yᵉ seke person wyth godis grace."

TABLE 2. SELECTED WITNESSES TO EPIDEMIC DISEASE DURING THE REIGN OF HENRY VII (1485–1509)

This table lists surviving sources that record instances of epidemic disease, or at least exceptional mortality, during the reign of Henry VII. When the witness identifies the cause of death with plague/pestilence (P) or *Sudor Anglicus* (S), we so indicate. Many of these witnesses cite specific dates. Other sources, such as the three London printings of a plague text by Machlinia in the mid-1480s, the "plague manuscript" of Lady Margaret Beaufort (Fitzwilliam MS 261 with armorial devices from her son's reign), and the treatise on the sweat by Thomas Forestier dedicated to Henry VII (BL Add. MS 27,582) are quite important in a more general way but are not addressed here. The following are full references to abbreviated identifications in the table:

Heralds' Memoir

The Heralds' Memoir 1486–1490: Court Ceremony, Royal Progress, and Rebellion. Ed. Emma Cavell. Donington: Richard III and Yorkist History Trust in association with Shaun Tyas, 2009.

Merton Register

Registrum Annalium Collegii Mertonensis 1483–1521. Ed. H. E. Salter. Oxford: Printed for the Oxford historical Society at the Clarendon Press, 1923.

Polydore Vergil

The Anglica Historia of Polydore Vergil A.D. 1485–1537. Ed. Denys Hay. Camden Third Series 74. London: Royal Historical Society, 1950. In 1506, Vergil was asked by Henry VII to compose the *Historia*, and Book XXIV deals with reign of Henry VII. The information used here appears only in

Vatican MS Codex Urbino Lat. 498 (1512–13) as printed in notes in Hay's edition; it does not occur in sixteenth-century printings of the book.

Miracles, Henry VI

Henrici VI Angliae regis miracula postuma. Ed. Paul Grosjean. Brussels: Société des Bollandistes: , 1935.

Paston Letters

Paston Letters and Papers of the Fifteenth Century. Ed. Norman Davis, Richard Beadle, and Colin Richmond. 3 vols. EETS SS 20–22. Oxford: Oxford University Press for EETS, 2004–5.

Plumpton Letters

The Plumpton Letters and Papers. Ed. Joan Kirby. Camden Fifth Series 8. Cambridge: Cambridge University Press for the Royal Historical Society, 1996.

Christ Church Canterbury

John Hatcher. "Mortality in the Fifteenth Century: Some New Evidence." *Economic History Review*, n.s., 39 (1986): 19–38. [Based on obituary book of Benedictine Priory of Christ Church, Canterbury.]

Westminster Abbey

Barbara Harvey. *Living and Dying in England, 1100–1540: The Monastic Experience*. Oxford: Clarendon Press, 1993. [While acknowledging Harvey's caution that high mortality does not necessarily mean plague, we think it worth noting the years of exceptional mortality at Westminster Abbey.]

Syon Abbey Herbal

John Adams and Stuart Forbes, eds. *The Syon Abbey Herbal: The Last Monastic Herbal in England, c. AD 1517, by Thomas Betson.* London: AMCD Publishers, 2015, 2015. [Discussion of mortality records for early summer 1488 (53–54) suggests the sweating sickness.]

Fabyans cronycle

Fabyans cronycle newly printed wyth the cronycle, actes, and dedes done in the tyme of the reygne of the mowste excellent prynce kynge Henry the vii.... London: Printed by Wyllyam Rastell, 1533. [On the death of John Morton, Archbishop of Canterbury, Chancellor, and Cardinal, during the autumn 1500 outbreak of plague, see also Christopher Harper-Bill, "Morton, John (d. 1500)," *ODNB.*]

Crowland Chronicle Continuations

The Crowland Chronicle Continuations, 1459–1486. Ed. and trans. Nicholas Pronay and John Cox. London: Richard III and Yorkist History Trust, 1986. [Latin text with English translation on facing page.]

Source	Dates
Heralds' Memoir	Late March **1486** (P; the King moved to Nottingham, bypassing Newark, because of deaths there [f. 8v, p. 70])
	December 27, **1489** (Queen Elizabeth of York was privately churched after the birth of Princess Margaret because "at that season ther wer the meazellis soo strong, and in especiall amongis the ladies and the gentilwemen, that sum deid of that sikeness, as the ladie Nevill, daughter of William Paston" [f. 63r–v, p. 182])
Merton Register	Autumn **1485** (S)
	late August–September **1486** (P)
	Summer **1487** (P; college dispersed)
	August 20–September 7, **1489** (six deaths)
	April 24–25, **1493** (P; fellows leave)
	May 2, **1501** (P)
	September **1503** (P; portionists leave; eight deaths)
	April **1507** (P; four fellows withdraw, *metu pestis*)
Polydore Vergil	Autumn **1485** (S; detailed description of symptoms and treatment [pp. 6–9])
	1499 (P; more than 30,000 died in London [pp. 118–19 notes])
	1505 (S; *rediit eodem Tempore ille pestilens sudor* [140n])
	1507 (S; *sudor ille pernicialis* [p. 142])
	1508–9 (S; comment that sweat returned near the end of the reign of Henry VII [pp. 88–89])

Miracles, Henry VI (disease identification as listed in miracles)	[88] **1485**, Richard Vyvian (P?; *peste infectus*)
	[128] February 7, **1487**, Alicia Newnett (P; *ex vehementi plaga pestilencie*)
	[5] **1488**, eleven persons in home of Thomas Simon (P; *plaga sevissima* [*sic*] *pestilencie*)
	[145] September 7, **1490**, Anna Swetyng (S; *plaga pestiferi sudoris infecta*)
	[132] July 28, **1491**, Elizabeth Styrman (P; *ex pestilenciali contagio*)
	[146] October 22, **1491**, Margaret Coterell (S; *adeo pestilenciali febre*)
	[147] October 22, **1491**, Johannes Noble (S; *simili plaga percussus*)
	[157] July **1498**, Johanna Reynald (P; *ex vehementi plaga pestilencie mortua fuerat*)
	[154] March 17–30, **1499**, Ricardus Hynstoke (P; *porriginosa peste pustularum percussus*)
	[155] March **1499?** Henry North (P; *ab eadem contagiosa peste*)
Paston Letters (three members of Paston family died of plague in 1479; see II, p. 411, [772]). Note that a Horae at Mount Angel Abbey in Oregon (MS 27) contains on folio 1 a prayer invoking Henry VI against the sweat and a reference to Henry VII. In MS 27, the calendar includes notations to Paston deaths.	[400] between June **1487** and February 1, **1493**, Edmund Paston II to John Paston III (P; because the plage reygnyth at Ormysby), I, p. 641
	[421] ca. **1495**, William Paston IV to John Paston III (S; I am at Ser John Fortescu place be-cause they swet to sor at Cambryg), I, p. 670

Plumpton Letters	[46] November 29, **1486** (P?; also they begyn to dye in London; ther is but few pariches free) [137] September 14, **1499** (P; servant…deceased of the sicknes which hath bene to your disease) [138] **1499** (P; the death seaseth not at Plompton)
Christ Church Canterbury	September–October **1485** (S; nine deaths from sweat [p. 26]) **1487** (P; a lesser plague epidemic [p. 28]) **1501** (P; a lesser plague epidemic [p. 28]; between **1485** and **1507**, plague given as cause of death for eight monks in these two years [p. 30])
Westminster Abbey (high mortality dates reckoned by calendar year rather than accounting year). Note a later event: in "1528 thirteen so-called 'familiares' [servants] of the monastery died on a single day, 4 May, in what was evidently a violent epidemic in the precinct" (pp. 167–68).	Years of crisis with high mortality: **1485** **1491** **1500** **1502** **1503** **1508** (pp. 125–26)
Syon Abbey Herbal (mortality records from *Martyrologium*, pp. 53–54)	May 16–July 4, **1488** (nine deaths of brothers, lay brothers, and sisters)
Fabyans cronycle	October 11, **1485** (S; than beying the swetynge sykenesse of newe begon; two successive mayors, Thomas Hylle and Wyllyam Stokker, died [f. ccxxvii]) September **1500** (P; And thys yere was a great deth in London….And this yere dyed doctor Morton cardynall and chaunceler of Englande in the moneth of October [September? f. ccxxxii])

Crowland Chronicle Continuations	August **1485** (S; *pestem sudatoriam*; cited by Thomas Lord Stanley, Earl of Derby, as the reason he was unable to join Richard III [pp. 178–79])
	October **1485** (S; *lue seu peste sudatoria*; when two mayors and four or five aldermen in London died, as did the Abbot of Crowland, Lambert Fossedyke, less than eighteen hours after onset of sickness [pp. 168–69])

Appendix A. Berkeley Castle Muniments SB 89: Description, Later Use, and Sale

MEDICAL HOUSEHOLD BOOK for the Scrope of Bolton family, ca. 1500

Physical description

Parchment. 278 × 200 mm.

Single line frame, pricked and ruled in ink. Written area: ca. 230 × 145 mm. Mostly thirty-two or thirty-four lines, but some variation in Part II to as few as twenty-eight lines (ff. 11, 13) and twenty-six lines (f. 12v).

111 folios. [xi] + 86 + [i^stub] + [i] + 13.

Part I; ff. [i]–[xi], 1–86v. Part I has eleven unnumbered leaves of contents table plus eighty-six single-column leaves containing what appear to be thirty-two discrete medical texts. Contemporary foliation is supplied on the rectos of the upper margins in red roman numerals (as employed in the table of contents). The first page of the contents table is headed by a lengthy rubric that serves as a prologue. Beside the large scrollwork letter "h" in pen and ink that begins the prologue is a shaded drawing of a crowned head and shoulders of a male figure in plate armor. An oak branch extends beneath bearing an oak gall and acorns (possibly with slight traces of gold or yellow color); stemming from the same branch is an aroid flower shaped like a fleur-de-lis. The initial letter encloses a quatrefoil flower. Centered in the upper margin, also accompanied by scrollwork, is a pen and ink drawing of a shield (cropped at the top) with the arms of Scrope of Bolton (see plates 1 and 2.a). The beginning of the first folio of text (f. 1) has further pen and ink decoration. A five-line initial letter "T" extending into the upper margin is formed by rustic branches ending in an oak leaf, the branches wrapped by two blank scrolls (see plate 2.b). On the last folio (f. 86v), the rubric "ffinis huius libri" is followed by the comment "Nay," indicating that the text continues with Part II. This comment is written in black ink in what may be a later hand (see the last leaf of Part I and the first leaf of Part II, plate 5).

Part II; ff. [i^{stub}]–[ii^v], 1–13v. Part II follows straight on from Part I, in the same hand, and in the middle of a gathering. The unnumbered blank stub of a missing leaf began Part II. It would have supplied the contents table for folios 1–5, possibly with an introductory rubric and further decoration. There remain one unnumbered leaf of a contents table and thirteen leaves of text foliated in red roman numerals. Two folios of text (ff. 14, 15) are lacking at the end. Recipes survive that would have been listed on the missing leaf of the contents table. The remaining leaf of the contents table supplies rubrics for the missing recipes at the end (ff. 14, 15).

Approximately seventy-one of what may have been eighty-four original recipes survive in Part II, a number of them specified for royal or noble families. A significant proportion deal with epidemic disease or the stone. See also section 3 of this study (**Epidemic Disease during the Reign of Henry VII (1485–1509)**), tables 1 and 2, the introduction to **Appendix D**, and the first leaf of Part II (plate 5).

Collation

NB After water damage to the foliation in red roman numerals, another (?) near-contemporary hand has added foliation (likewise in roman numerals) in brown ink in Part I, folios 7–61. We use Arabic numerals for convenience only.

1^8   unnumbered leaves   ff. [i]–[viii]

2^8	ff. [ix]–[xi], 1–5
3^8	ff. 6–13
4^8	ff. 14–21
5^8	ff. 22–29
6^8	ff. 30–37
7^8	ff. 38–45
8^8	ff. 46–53
9^8	ff. 54–61
10^8	ff. 62–69
11^8	ff. 70–77
12^8	ff. 78–85
13^8	ff. 86, unnumbered [i][blank stub], unnumbered [ii], 1–5
14^8	ff. 6–13
[$15^{?8}$] Missing.	ff. 14, 15 of text lacking

Hand

The codex is written throughout in a clear English secretary hand with some Anglicana letter forms. These include a double-bowed "a" in initial position, long "f" and "s" in initial and medial positions and the occasional looped "d" in the abbreviation for *demi*. A distinctive characteristic of this hand is the kidney-shaped short "s" used in the final position with a calligraphic hairline stroke added, not from the top, but

from the midpoint of the letter. The scribe also used the form of letter
"c" described by Malcolm B. Parkes as "consisting of two short strokes
placed at right-angles with a short diagonal stroke placed on the 'back'
of the letter," said by Parkes to be one of the features of French fifteenth-
century documents that "passed into 'Tudor Secretary' in the sixteenth
century."[1] Letter "c" in this new form occurs randomly in both Part I
and Part II (see e.g., Part I, f. [i], plate 2.a, line 6, "Superscrybyd"; Part II,
f. 3, fig. 6, five examples in lines 7 and 8, including "innocent" in line 7
and "chylde" in line 8).

Extensive use was made by the scribe of red rubrication, often with
calligraphic capitals (see Part I, f. 14v, fig. 1, "C" beginning "Capitulum
primum"; Part I, f. 77v, fig. 4, letter "S" passim). See also the elaborate
shell-like "S" that begins "Saturnus" in the first rubric in Part I (f. 78v,
fig. 8), where the second line of the paragraph adjusts to the letter and
demonstrates that here the scribe made the first word of each paragraph
in red ink before beginning the text.[2] Red paragraph marks and informal loops serve as line fillers throughout the codex. Further flourishing
is sparse but appears on occasional ascenders (see "h" of "huius" in the
rubric at the end of Part I, plate 5, and in the top lines of folios 16, 19v,
20r–v, and 68v).

Binding

The manuscript is currently unbound but has been cropped for binding
at the top (losing part of the shield of arms on the front page) and at the
fore edge. That this was done toward the end of Elizabeth I's reign or later
is shown by the cropping that cuts through the word "Elisy[beth]" in a
nearly erased marginal note on folio 77v of Part I (fig. 4): "[?Pd] . . . A^{no}
Regni Elisy[beth]/ 35 [1592–93]."[3]

---

[1]   Malcolm B. Parkes, *English Cursive Book Hands, 1250–1500* (Oxford: Clarendon Press, 1969), xxi, plate 13 (ii).

[2]   We owe this observation to Dr. Kathleen Scott.

[3]   Among other erased notes are partly legible dates, e.g., "8 July," "ante festum
purificationis [2 Feb.]," possibly relating to dates for payments due, or legal jottings
concerning law terms and return days for the court of the Common Bench. We are
grateful to David Smith, Hon. Archivist at Berkeley Castle, for assistance in deci-
phering the erased notes under ultraviolet light.

The stitching on the spine implies the former presence of two different bindings:[4]

(i)   Traces of stitching holes indicate an early binding of the fifteenth–sixteenth century. This first binding was probably sewn on double supports, as would be expected of a book of ca. 1500.

(ii)   The four tanned leather sewing supports do not appear medieval and are likely to relate to a binding of about 1600. This dating fits with the evidence from Part I, folio 77v, indicating that the sizeable cropping at the top and at the fore edge was done after 1592–93 (fig. 4). Traces on the spine show that the boards of a second binding were clearly covered in leather.

It is evident from the convex shape on the inner margin of the final leaf that there is no backing joint to match the concave shape at the beginning of the manuscript. A single gathering (containing the two leaves of text known from the contents table to be wanting [ff. 14, 15] and the rest of a quire of eight) would not be enough to supply such a joint. Consequently, it would appear that the bound volume originally had additional quires that are now missing. Whether these additional quires were sewn with BCM SB 89 from the start, or were added when it was resewn for a later binding, cannot now be known. It is entirely possible that an additional work, perhaps even unrelated, was bound with the SB 89 texts at the time when the manuscript was so severely cropped for the second binding. Sotheby's sale catalog entry (July 29, 1924, lot 157; see below) makes clear that the missing leaves were not present in 1924.

Later Use and Ownership

Marginal annotations in a seventeenth-century (?) hand indicate some attempted classification of the recipes, perhaps by an apothecary (e.g., numbering "A1"–"A29" in Part I, ff. 1v–67; symbols and letters in Part I, ff. 71–86 *passim*, and Part II, ff. 12 and 13; letters "Hi" or "H" in Part I, ff. 59 and 60, and Part II, ff. 12v and 13v).

---

[4]   The following description concerning earlier binding of the manuscript is based upon information kindly supplied by Professor Nicholas Pickwoad from evidence of photographs.

Pen trials with the name "Thomas Griggs" are written twice in the top margin and three times in the left hand margin of Part II, f. 7v (see plate 6). Griggs is a common name in East Anglia and is also found in Kent.[5]

Nothing further is known of the manuscript until its appearance in the Sotheby salerooms in 1924 (Sotheby's sale cat., July 29–30, 1924, lot 157, "The Property of a Lady"), when it was purchased by Randal Berkeley, eighth Earl of Berkeley, FRS.[6] Immediately thereafter, on July 31, 1924, Sotheby's sale of mainly printed books with autograph letters included a section of material relating to a resident of Berkeley, Gloucestershire, Edward Jenner, the pioneer of smallpox vaccination. This section, titled "Jenner Portraits and Relics" (lots 311–40), was also described as the "Property of a Lady." Included were engravings, oil paintings, various items such as "Dr Jenner's cupping case" (lot 322), a large section of books, and a seventeenth-century manuscript commonplace book relating to magic and prodigies (lot 340). It may well have been the Jenner material that attracted the attention of Lord Berkeley and his agent to the salerooms at this date. BCM SB 89 could have been from the same Jenner group but thought more appropriately incorporated into the previous sale, which was primarily devoted to medieval and illuminated manuscripts. Jenner's hand has not been identified in the manuscript.

A sticker, "MS No. 7," on folio [i] refers to numbering in the inventory made after the death of the eighth Earl of Berkeley, January 1942. The date of purchase of the manuscript by the eighth earl, its deposit in the muniments room in 2003, and its renumbering as SB [Select Book] 89, March 1, 2004, are all recorded in a note on the 1924 sale catalog by David Smith at Berkeley Castle.

---

[5] It may be noted that a Thomas Griggs, Apothecary, of Ipswich, Suffolk, was elected as one of twenty-four town burgesses to the borough Assembly of Ipswich on April 14, 1659 (*The East Anglian; or Notes and Queries on Subjects connected with the Counties of Suffolk, Cambridge, Essex and Norfolk*, ed. Samuel Tymms and Charles H. E. White, 6 [1894]: 265). In his will, October 18, 1665, proved October 12, 1666 (TNA, PROB 11/322/78), he is shown to have been a man of property and part owner of two local Ipswich ships. Also recorded in East Anglia is a medical license issued by the Archbishop of Canterbury to another Thomas Griggs, Apothecary, of Norwich, Norfolk, 1685 (Melanie Barber, *Directory of Medical Licences Issued by the Archbishop of Canterbury, 1536–1775*, Lambeth Palace Library, part 1: Vicar General Series Licences, 1576–1775 (TS, Lambeth Palace Library, 1997).

[6] See the entry by John Shorter, "Berkeley, Randal Thomas Mowbray Rawdon, eighth earl of Berkeley (1865–1942)," *ODNB*.

Appendix B. Recipes Occurring in Both Part I and Part II of Berkeley Castle Muniments SB 89

The table below lists recipes that appear in both Part I and Part II of the codex. The first column lists the recipe in Part II that corresponds to a recipe in Part I (column 2); column 3 offers comments on the similarity of the recipes. (See **Appendix D** for a transcription of all surviving recipes in Part II.)

Recipe in Part II	Related Recipe in Part I	Comments
(5) II, f. 1 RUBRIC: The vertu of water of buglose INCIPIT: Water of buglose which is cleapyd wyld borage	I, f. 8 RUBRIC: The vertu of Water of buglose INCIPIT: Water of buglose which is clepyd wyld Borge	Quite similar, but with lexical and orthographic variants; each has phrases not found in the other.
(7) II, f. 1v RUBRIC: A good water for eyn INCIPIT: Take ew-frace vervayn Rew celidony and fynkell	I, f. 1 RUBRIC: A water ffor sore eyne INCIPIT: Take Fenkell Rewe Celidony Ver-vayne...Eufras	Initial similarity of ingredients, but text in Part II is more detailed and includes two processes of distillation not found in Part I.

(8) II, ff. 1v–2 RUBRIC: The Water of melyce otherwyse callyd bawme INCIPIT: Water of bawme is hott and dry when it is drunkyn it he-lythe the marrys of women	I, ff. 8v–10 RUBRIC: The vertu of Water callyd mellise other-wyse clepyd Bawme INCIPIT: Water of Bawme is hote & dry when it is drunkyn & it helyth the martys of women	Initial similarity with lexical and orthographic vari-ants, but text in Part I is lengthier, continuing from middle of folio 9 to middle of folio 10; most of the additional material consists of an extensive list of cure claims, including cure for leprosy and use in aiding concep-tion; the version in Part I ends with an attribution to a "master Relygious of Saynt Bennetis."
(9) II, f. 2r–v RUBRIC: ffor to make water of dam-aske INCIPIT: Take a quart of fyne Rose water	I, f. 1 RUBRIC: ffor to make water of damaske [from contents list] INCIPIT: Take a quarte of ffyne Rose water	Very close simi-larity, with minor lexical and ortho-graphic variants.
(20) II, f. 4 RUBRIC: A nother for the ston INCIPIT: Take gromell and percely and Red nettyll and violet and franken-cence	I, f. 73 RUBRIC: A nother ffor the stonne INCIPIT: Take gromell percly and Red nettyll violet frankencence	Very close simi-larity, with minor lexical and ortho-graphic variants.

Appendix C. Survey of Texts in Part I of Berkeley Castle Muniments SB 89

THE LANGUAGE FOR both Part I and Part II of SB 89 is late Middle English, although rubrics are frequently Latin, here designated by italics. Where Latin occurs in texts, it is noted. The following listing of texts in Part I of SB 89 largely reflects the organization as indicated by section headings in the contents list. These headings indicate subject divisions in the body of the manuscript and frequently, but not always, occur in the text itself. There can, however, be ambiguities in both contents list and text. For example, the section heading written in red in the contents list on folio [i], "ffirst of Vertu of Waters et c," may refer to the larger section on folios 1–10v (eVK2 4855.50) containing sixty-six recipes and cure claims or it may refer only to the initial texts on folios 1–4. The larger unit includes recipes of varying length in several subgroups. Most recipes found on folios 1–10v involve distillation for medical use, and some are known from other manuscripts. Treatises on distilled waters were common in the late Middle Ages in both Latin and vernacular languages.[1] It may be useful, however, to point out similarities between some of the

---

[1] A combined search for "Distillation" and "Waters" in eVK2 and eTK results in sixty-six records for texts on distilled waters in eVK2 and thirty-one in eTK. The latter number is almost certainly too low, because applying standard subject nomenclature to the eTK files based on the Thorndike and Kibre volume files did not involve reading the texts, as was the case in the preparation of eVK2. Not surprisingly, those texts on distillation that are dated or datable are almost always late medieval.

distillation recipes in the first ten leaves of SB 89 and recipes for waters in two other codices: the compendious *Breviarium Bartholomei* (ca. 1387) of John Mirfield[2] and the Syon Abbey medical manuscript contemporary with SB 89.[3] (See **Appendix B** for five recipes occurring in both Part I and Part II of SB 89.)

    1.   Ff. 1–4, *Rubric*: "ffor to make water of damaske";[4] *Incipit*: "Take a quarte of ffyne Rose water And A pynt of water of whyght Rosys And A pynt of Water of eglantyne flowrs."[5]   plate 3

> Twenty-four recipes, some lengthy, most involving distillation, often of alcohol (sometimes designated *Water of lyffe* [Aqua vitae] and *Aqua ardens*). Five recipes on folios 2r–v and two on folios 3 and 3v are entirely or mostly in Latin. Four of the recipes in this section are similar to ones in the Syon Abbey manuscript: *Aqua mellis* (f. 2v) and *Lac virginis, aqua aromatica*, and *aqua preciosa* (all on f. 3v).[6]

> The first recipe is typical of the first group in its emphasis on the details of distillation, including instructions such as the proper sealing of the joint between alembic spout and glass receptory. The third recipe, "ffor to make water of lyffe" (ff. 1r–v), contains extensive instructions for fractional distillation and includes conventional claims for the curative and preservative qualities of high-proof alcohol as found in treatises

---

    [2] BL, Harley MS 3. See Faye Getz, "Mirfield, John (d. 1407)," *ODNB*. On the constituent parts of the *Breviarium Bartholomei*, see N. M., "Mirfeld John (fl. 1393)," in the 1894 *DNB* (accessible in the *ODNB*).

    [3] St. John's College, Cambridge MS 109 (E.6), *The Syon Abbey Herbal AD 1517: The Last Monastic Herbal in England c. AD 1517, by Thomas Betson*, ed. John Adams and Stuart Forbes (London: AMCD Publishers, 2015).

    [4] Because the rubric at the top of folio 1 is nearly unreadable as a result of water damage, the rubric given here is from the contents list on folio [i]. *Damask* in reference to roses is not cited in the *MED*, but the *OED* gives *damask water* s.v. *damask* f. with a 1306 Latin citation, followed by a 1519 citation. The *OED* entry for *damask rose* is d. (originally *Rosa gallica* var. *damascena*) with the earliest citation being Vicary's *Anatomy*, ca. 1540. According to Vivian Nutton's *ODNB* entry "Linacre, Thomas (c. 1460–1524)," "Hakluyt in 1582 made the plausible, though far from proven, claim that he [Linacre] had introduced the damask rose into England" (*Oxforddnb.com*).

    [5] This recipe is also found in Part II of the codex, f. 2r–v. See also **Appendix B**.

    [6] See *Syon Abbey Herbal*, 265, 267, and 268.

on distillation.[7] In this third recipe, the distillate is compared to "bawme," and this recipe may be related to the lengthy text later in Part I on folios 8v–10 (no. 4), part of which is repeated in Part II (no. 8).[8] "The vertu of Water callyd mellise otherwyse clepyd Bawme" provides elaborate cure claims, preservative claims, and information on administration.

2.   Ff. 4–5v, *Rubric*: "Here begynnyth doctor gylys of good waters"; *Incipit* (to short prologue following the rubric and preceding the recipes): "Here begynnyth doctor gylis the bok of Vertus & of Waters that be made in desert be the which All Sykenes are curyd that are curable."

Fourteen recipes. The first recipe, for *Aqua pharorum*, begins "Take pyȝyall & garlophiliet & clotys." The SB 89 version and the version in National Library of Wales Peniarth MS 369B, folios 36–38[9]—dated post-1485—and at least one other text found in SB 89 are related, but Peniarth and SB 89 are not part of the textual tradition called "The waters of Seynt Gyle," also referred to as "The Alchemical Waters of Saint Giles" in the edition published by W. L. Braekman. Braekman was unaware of the different textual tradition represented by SB 89 and Peniarth MS 369B.[10] Following *Aqua pharorum* are nine numbered recipes: *Aqua prima*; *Aqua secunda*; *Aqua tercia*;

---

[7]   For a representative distillation treatise, see the text from BL Royal 17.A.iii, ed. Linda Ehrsam Voigts in "The Master of the King's Stillatories," *The Lancastrian Court*, ed. Jenny Stratford (Donington: Shaun Tyas, 2003), 233–52, at 251.

[8]   See **Appendix B** on the relationship between the texts on melyce/melisse or balm in Parts I and II.

[9]   eVK2 2207 and 5849; on this and other texts in Peniarth MS 369B related to SB 89, see William Marx, *The Index of Middle English Prose, Handlist XIV: Manuscripts in the National Library of Wales (Llyfrgell Genedlaethol Cymru), Aberystwyth* (Cambridge: D. S. Brewer, 1999), 46. The dating of the Peniarth manuscript is discussed above in section 2 of this study (**Date, Decoration, and Original Ownership of BCM SB 89**). We are grateful to Daniel Huws for sharing with us his notes on the codex and to Maredudd Ap Huw of the National Library of Wales for making available to us digital images of the Peniarth codex, which is too damaged to be consulted. The digital images are unfortunately unreadable in many instances.

[10]   The recipes in SB 89 begin on folio 4 with "*Aqua pharorum*," followed by nine numbered recipes and four unnumbered recipes (*Aqua pro oculis, Aqua pro lapide, Aqua de pimenta,* and *Aqua vitae*; ff. 5–5v), before double capitula signs introduce

Aqua quarta this is callyd water of Swalows; *Aqua quinta* that
is callyd *lacida*; *Aqua sexta* this is *aqua conservancia* calyd;
Aqua septima this is callyd *aqua epulencia*; *Aqua octaua* this
is callyd water of Sauge; *Aqua nona*. Appended then are four
additional recipes on folios 5r–v: *Aqua pro oculis, Incipit*: Take
whyght wyne As moche As thou wilt & streberys; *Aqua pro
lapide, Incipit*: Take phylopendula earthnut; *Aqua de pimento,
Incipit*: Take ginger canell galingale; and *To make aqua vite,
Incipit*: Take the Rotys of percely Isope. The last two recipes
are not found in the Peniarth version, which ends with *Aqua
pro lapide*.[11]

3. Ff. 5v–8v, *Rubric*: "The Vertu of Water of Rosys"; *Incipit*: "If Water
of Rosys be dronkyn with Suger it swagyth all heatis & feuers that
be Shakyng."
    Nineteen additional waters. We take this as a separate group-
    ing, both because it is introduced with two capitula marks
    and because most of the recipes from this point are unified
    by rubrics with the formula "water of _____" that designates
    plants: rosys, centory, endyve, avence, langueydbeff, bawme,
    turmentyll, fenkell, buglose, myllefoile. There are also recipes
    interspersed for ailments or other purposes. In some instanc-
    es, the rubric designates the disorder to be cured (f. 6, "*pro
    lapide*" and "for the stone"; f. 7, "for the canker"; f. 7v, "for the
    syght of man or woman"; f. 8, "*pro collica*"). In other instances,
    the rubrics are vague, as in the cases of "*aqua pro pluralibus
    infirmitatibus . . . aqua perfectissima*" (ff. 6v–7). On folio 7v,

---

the next grouping. The version edited by Braekman consists of nine numbered recipes and one additional recipe that combines the nine preceding waters.

"The Wateres of seynt Gyle" called "The Alchemical Waters of Saint Giles," in
Braekman, *Studies on Alchemy, Diet, Medecine [sic] and Prognostication in Middle
English* (Brussels: Omirel, URSAL, 1988 for 1986) is found on 7–41. Braekman's base
text is BL Harley 2381, ff. 56v–60 (eVK2 5543), and he supplies variant readings from
two manuscripts closely related to each other: BL Sloane 706, ff. 128v–132 (eVK2
7885) and Cambridge, Trinity College R.14.32, ff. 96–99 (in eVK2 5548). In the latter
two manuscripts, distillation recipes precede and follow the Saint Giles text. Braekman also supplies the Latin version from BL Sloane 3149, ff. 29–30 and 45–46.

[11] It should be noted that the *Aqua pro lapide* recipe, which concludes this text
in Peniarth, but not in SB 89, is repeated in SB 89, Part I, on folio 6.

"perysshyng water" is a chemical recipe not apparently therapeutic, but one that dissolves "stocke and stone." It is followed
by "water of rayne" and "a water to wryte in steel," a chemical-
metallurgical recipe (f. 7v).

The recipe for Aqua [vitae] perfectissima on folio 6v contains a similar set of cure claims as in the *Breviarium Bartholomei*, although the Mirfield version is longer.[12]

4. Ff. 8v–10, *Rubric*: "The vertu of Water callyd mellise otherwise
    clepyd Bawme"; *Incipit*: "Water of Bawme is hote & dry. "
    This text was discussed above in connection with the third
    recipe in the initial group of distillation texts on folios 1r–v,
    "ffor to make water of lyffe" (where distillation fractions are
    called bawme). The first half of this text also occurs in Part
    II of SB 89, no. 8 (see **Appendix B**). This "virtue" text is not
    strictly speaking a recipe, but rather is a long discussion of
    cure claims, some gynecological, when balm is mixed or dis-
    tilled with other ingredients. This text ends on folio 10 with an
    authority citation to "the ryght reuerent & worshypfull master
    Relygious of Saynt Bennetis an excelent & an expert person in
    the science off medycyn." The resemblance of this short trea-
    tise to "Aqua qua dicitur mater balsami" in Mirfield, with its
    even longer list of cure claims, may be significant.[13] Both wit-
    nesses deserve investigation in relation to other short treatises
    on "artificial balsam or balm."[14]

5. Ff. 10–10v, *Rubric*: "The Vertu of dyuerse waters of erbys"; *Incipit*:
    Who So drynkyth water of dragans it sleith wormys within mans
    body."
    This section should not be confused with the virtues of plants
    above, or with the *Circa instans* text beginning on folio 22. This
    text consists of brief notices of the curative claims of waters
    of dragans, turmentill, beton, egremony, avence, langdebeefe,

---

[12] BL, Harley MS 3, ff. 266vb–267b.
[13] BL, Harley 3, ff. 264a–b.
[14] A text, "Balm Artificial and the Virtues Thereof," occurs in Cambridge, CUL
Kk.6.33, III, ff. 75v–77 (eVK2 5662). A sixteenth-century text designated "The Virtue
and Operation of this Balsam" occurs in London, Wellcome Library 559, ff. 53v–54
(eVK2 2427). Further study of these texts is a desideratum.

borage, bawme (recipe at top of folio 10v is obscured by water damage and not in the contents list), hony sokyllys, and
wormewoode. The comparatively lengthy concluding section on water of wormwood (Artemisia) cites Galen and Di-
oscorides and ends with a gynecological cure claim.

6. Ff. 10v–14 (eVK2 6160.75), *Rubric*: "Here ffolowith of oyntmentis" (section heading also in contents list, f. [i]); *Rubric*: "A Souerayne oyntment for the vanyte in the hed"; *Incipit*: "Take the Iuce
of walworte Salt hony And wax & stere them well to gyther And
boyle them."

Nineteen recipes for ointments, some lengthy, and several with
discursive rubrics. "A souerayne oyntment for the vanyte in
the hed" begins the section, followed by "A good oyntment . . .
for all maner of cold Achys," "*Vnguentum fustulum,*" "*Vnguen-
tum mamillum,*" "*Vnguentum fustum et nigrum,*" "*Vnguen-
tum quod valet serpingnosis et elefanciosus,*" "*Vnguentum album,*" "*Vnguentum salsum,*" "*Vnguentum ad omnies timores,*"
"*Vnguentum dialtum* & dewte," "*Vnguentum angelicum*" that
was "cast vnto a recluse in Almayne by An Angell," "*Vnguentum laxativum,*" "*Vnguentum popiliun,*" "*Vnguentum quod
Agrippa rex Judeorum,*" "*Vnguentum mariaton,*" "*Vnguentum
Ranum*[?]," "*Vnguentum Alabastri* nardy most precious for the
Romanys of Jerusalem . . . Soone it helpyd mary magdelyn
and Martha the Syster of lazar this oyntment vsyd all ther ly-
vys tyme," "*Vnguentum colorum,*" and "*Vnguentum genestii.*"
These ointments with a rubric beginning "*Vnguentum*" apparently derive from a full version of the widely popular compendium of compound recipes attributed to Nicholas of Salerno,
Antidotarium Nicolai, a shorter version of which occurs later
in Part I (see no. 25, ff. 43v–58). Only six of these Unguentum
recipes in this section of Part I (no. 6) correspond to those
in the Middle English version edited by Maria José Carrillo
Linares.[15]

---

[15] For an accessible study of the *Antidotarium Nicolai* with the facsimile of
the 1471 incunable, see Dietlinde Goltz, *Mittelalterliche Pharmazie und Medizin
Dargestellt an Geschichte und Inhalt des Antidotarium Nicolai* (Stuttgart: Wissenschaftliche Verlagsgesellschaft, 1976). For an edition of the Middle English version

7. Ff. 14r–v Written entirely in red (no rubric): fig. 1
"A Surgyon workyng craftely Shall bere with hym V.
maner of oyntmentis that is to Say basylicon that is
[f. 14v] ffor m[ateryng *Vn*]*guentum Apostolorum* for clensyng
or mundy
fying [mundifying]And Also *Vnguentum Aureum* for make
flesch & *Vnguentum*
album to knyttyng And *dialtum* for to make Swete that sore
that is on cleane [*sic*]

While these ointments also derive from the *Antidotarium
Nicolai,* the five here form a discrete text that occurs in Latin
and vernacular versions of the Surgery of Guy de Chauliac
which was printed as late as 1579.[16] Unusually this brief text is

---

in Glasgow University Library, Ferguson MS 147, see María José Carrillo Linares,
"Edición de una version en Inglés medio del *Antidotarium Nicholai.*" PhD Thesis,
Universidad de Sevilla, Facultad de Filología,1997. See also Carrillo Linares, "Middle
English *Antidotarium Nicholai*: Evidence for Linguistic Distribution and Dissemi-
nation in the Vernacular," *International Journal of English Studies* 5 (2005): 71–92.

[16] We are grateful to Michael McVaugh for pointing out to us that this short
text can be found in his edition of the Latin academic surgery of Guy de Chauliac:
*Ex quibus apparet quod curyrgicus artificialiter operans debet secum portare quinque
unguenta, scilicet basilicon ad maturandum, unguentum apostolorum ad mundifi-
candum, unguentum aureum ad incarnandum, unguentum album ad consolidan-
dum, dyalteam ad dulcorandum.* See Guidonis de Caulhiaco (Guy de Chauliac),
Inventarium sive chirurgia Magna, vol. I: Text (Leiden: E. J. Brill, 1997), 4. The text
also appears in the two Middle English translations of the surgery edited from different manuscripts: Paris, BNF fonds anglais 25 by Margaret S. Ogden, *The Cyrur-
gie of Guy de Chauliac.* EETS OS 265 (London: Oxford University Press, 1971); and
New York Academy of Medicine MS 12 by Björn Wallner in a series with various
titles including "Chirurgia Magna" by the University of Lund, with several publishers from 1964 to 1989. The text in the Ogden edition reads, "Of þe whiche it semeþ
þat a cirurgien wirchynge craftily schulde bere wiþ hym fyue oynementes: þat is to
wite, *basilicon* to maturynge, *vngentum apostolorum* to clensynge and mundefieng,
vnguentum aureum for to make flesche, *vnguentum album* to knyttynge, and *dial-
team* to make swete." On Guy de Chauliac, see McVaugh, "Who Was Gilbert the
Englishman?" *The Study of Medieval Manuscripts of England: Festschrift in Honor of
Richard W. Pfaff,* ed. George Hardin Brown and Linda Ehrsam Voigts (Tempe, Ariz.:
Arizona Center for Medieval and Renaissance Studies, 2010), 295–324. A popular-
ized text for surgeons based on Guy de Chauliac, called *Gvydos Qvestions, newly
corrected,* printed in London by Thomas East in 1579, contains the following: "Question. How many and what oyntments commonly ought the Chyrurgion to beare with
him. Aunswere. Fiue: that is to say an Oyntment Basilycon for to rype, Apostolorum

also given in its entirety (with some variation) in the contents list as well as in the body of Part I, allowing reconstruction of the water-damaged text on folio 14v.[17]

8.   Ff. 14v–22v (eVK2 2637.25), *Rubric*: "Capitulum Primum"; *Incipit*: "And yf the brayne panne be hurt the skynne must be cut iii cornerwyse Sumdell largerly that All the wound may be Sene"   fig. 1

An unidentified treatise on the conservative treatment of wounds organized in sixteen chapters.[18]

Although it is one of the longer discrete texts in Part I, it neither bears a title nor is given a section listing in the contents list. This treatise addresses wounds, arrow extraction, and the reduction of fractures and dislocations. The text includes charms and recipes and advises phlebotomy. It concludes with seven chapters of recipes that represent a change of focus. Chapter 9 (f. 19) consists of a brief introduction to the following chapters of recipes: "Dere fryndys though I haue travelyd [travailed] here in my wrytyng for to shew you Some dele partyculer cunnyng of surgery it [*sic*] Shall I tell you more cunnyng and experte & in generall thyngis as powders intreatis And oyntmentis, drynkis of erbys inward charmys purgacouns clysters and suppesytoris that will not fayle in ther workyng wt the grace of god" (f. 19).

Expensive and uncommon ingredients such as mummy[19]

---

to cleanse, Aureum to encrease flesh: And the white oyntment for to drie & binde, and de Althea for to souple" (Facsimile of STC 12469 [Amsterdam, 1968]).

[17] F. [iir]: V maner of oyntmentis A sorgion owght euer to bere wyth hym that is to Say Vnguentum basylicum for materyng Vnguentum apostolorum ffor clensyng or mundifying Vnguentum aureum for to encrease fflesche Vnguentum Album for knyttyng & Vnguentum dialtum for to make Swete the Sore that is not cleane[.]

[18] While not immediately relevant to this text, a range of studies on the subject can be found in *Wounds in the Middle Ages*, ed. Anne Kirkham and Cordelia Warr (Farham: Ashgate Publishing, 2014).

[19] *Mumia* or *mummy* was an expensive black and foul-smelling medical substance believed to derive from embalmed corpses. See Paul Freedman, *Out of the East: Spices and the Medieval Imagination* (New Haven: Yale University Press, 2008), 13–15 (his translation is from a French version of the *Circa instans*; the SB 89 version of this text does not include mummy); see *MED*, s.v. mummie, and *OED*, s.v. mummy, n. 1. Mummy has attracted a good deal of popular interest, for example,

and bdellium[20] are called for in these recipes. The treatise as a whole shares with the recipes in Part II a number of characteristics: fractional distillation, polypharmacy, many imported spices, chemical ingredients, and loaf sugar. Unlike Part II, however, it rarely calls for precious metals or stones.

As in the case of the preceding five ointments, which are also found in the surgery of Guy de Chauliac, the wounds text uses some terminology of academic surgeries (*velamina, dura mater*),[21] but unlike academic surgeries, it urges a cautious approach.[22] Medieval surgery treatises can be grouped as either translations of what are called "academic" or "rational surgeries," on one hand, or as less theoretical and more practical, on the other, as in the case of the writings of John Arderne and

---

as addressed by Richard Sugg, *Mummies, Cannibals and Vampires: The History of Corpse Medicine from the Renaissance to the Victorians* (London: Routledge, 2011). Sugg's emphasis on *mummy* as wound treatment is relevant here.

[20] *Bdellium*, a fragrant gum resin from a tree of the genus Commiphora, occurs in English recipes from the late fourteenth century and is also found in the *Circa instans*. See *MED* and *OED*, s.v. *bedellium, bdellium*.

[21] We are grateful to Michael McVaugh and Peter Jones for their observations that this text does not seem to derive from an academic surgery. Peter Jones notes that it "does fit well with the idea that there is a form of non-scholastic surgical writing that nevertheless relies for 'doctrina' on the rational surgeries" (letter of August 28, 2013). See Michael McVaugh, *The Rational Surgery of the Middle Ages*, Micrologus' Library 15 (Florence: SISMEL, Edizioni del Galluzzo, 2006). A considerable number of these rational surgeries were translated into Middle English. They include those of Guy de Chauliac, cited above in n. **16**; Lanfranc, ed. Annika Asplund, *A Middle English Version of Lanfranc's "Chirurgia Parva": The Surgical Part*, Stockholm Theses in English 2 (Stockholm: Stockholm University, 1970); Henri de Mondeville and an anonymous London surgeon of 1394, both ed. Richard Grothé, "Le ms. Wellcome 564: deux traités de chirurgie en môyen-anglais," PhD Thesis, Université de Montréal, 1982; and Theodoric of Cervia, unpublished, in Cambridge Magdalene, Pepys MS 1661, 35–211 (eVK2 6641 and 6642), and BL Sloane 389, ff. 2–26v (partial) (eVK2 3849, 6642, 8215).

[22] The practitioner in SB 89 is advised to avoid the treatment of perilous wounds, especially in cases of arrow extraction:
> An therfor in suche perleous woundis and placys of the body it is good to be well avysyd or you medle therwith for no thing . . . for it is better to say you canne not then other men to say that you do not well and therfor I passe ouer soche perlows woundys. . . . (I, f. 15v).

John Bradmore.[23] The wounds text in SB 89 is closer to the latter classification, which can be applied equally to Latin and Middle English writings.[24]

9. Ff. 22v–23v, *Rubric*: "Here folowythe the Vertu of diuerse erbys" (section heading also given in contents list, f. [ii verso]); (eVK2 6100.75), *Rubric*: "Rosa marine"; *Incipit*: "Take the flowers of Rosemary And put them fast in A lynyn clothe and Sethe it in water tyll halfe be wastyd."

Four short sections on rosemary, betony (eVK2 1260.50), fennel seed (in Latin), and plantago minor (ff. 23–23v), precede the compendium that follows. The first two brief texts also circulate independently. There are twenty-three records in eVK2

---

[23] Middle English surgery texts from late medieval England that cannot be called "rational surgeries" although they utilize some university traditions include the writings of John Arderne, which survive in both Middle English and Latin; see D'Arcy Power, ed., *Treatises of Fistula in Ano, Haemorrhoids and Clysters by John Arderne*. EETS OS 139 (London, 1910; rpt. London: Oxford University Press for EETS, 1968); and Power, "The Lesser Writings of John Arderne." XVIIth International Congress of Medicine, History of Medicine Section XXIII, August 7, 1913 (London, 1914): 107–33. Another surgery treatise surviving in both Latin and English, which differs from the academic tradition, is the *Philomena* by John Bradmore; excerpts of the Middle English version in BL Harley 1736 (eVK2 1409 and 6214) were edited by R. Theodore Beck, *The Cutting Edge: Early History of the Surgeons of London* (London: Lund Humphries, 1974), but there wrongly attributed to Thomas Morsted (see S. J. Lang, "John Bradmore and His Book *Philomena*," *Social History of Medicine* 5 [1992]: 121–30; Lang, "The 'Philomena' of John Bradmore and Its Middle English Derivative: A Perspective on Surgery in Late Medieval England." PhD Thesis, St. Andrews University, 1998; and Hector Cole and Tig Lang, "The Treating of Prince Henry's Arrow Wound, 1403," *The Journal of the Society of Archer-Antiquaries* [2003]: 93–101). The wounds text in SB 89 more closely resembles these writings of Arderne and Bradmore than the treatment of wounds in rational surgeries.

[24] On such Latin texts, see three studies by Peter Murray Jones: "Medical Libraries and Medical Latin 1400–1700," *Medical Latin from the Late Middle Ages to the Eighteenth Century*, ed. Wouter Bracke and Herwig Deumens (Brussels: Koninklijke Academie voor Geneeskunde van Belgie, 2000), 115–35; "Language and Register in English Medieval Surgery," *Language in Medieval Britain: Networks and Exchanges*, ed. Mary Carruthers (Donington: Shaun Tyas, 2015), 74–89; and "Medicine," *Medieval Latin: An Introduction and Bibliographical Guide*, ed. F. A. C. Mantello and A. G. Rigg (Washington, D.C.: Catholic University of America Press, 1996), 416–21. Also in the same volume is the relevant study by Richard Sharpe, "Latin in Everyday Life," 315–41.

on the virtue or virtues of rosemary. These rosemary texts have been extensively studied by George R. Keiser.[25] The second short text (*Rubric*: "The Vertu of betony"; *Incipit*: "Betony etyn and drunkyn is good to breke the ston") derives from Antonius musa, *De herba vettonica*.[26] There are twenty-five records in eVK2 on the virtue or virtues of betony. The short Latin section on the virtues of fennel seed (*Rubric*: "Semen de feniculo"; *Incipit*: "Semen ffeniculi tot habeth virtutes fugat demones pellat febres") is written in red ink.[27] The fourth of these brief sections addressed the description and virtue of the narrow-leaved plantain (*Rubric*: "plantago minor"; *Incipit*: "Plantago minor is an erbe that haue levys lyke plantayn but they be lenger and mor nerver and it is clepyd ribwort").[28]

10. Ff. 23v–29v, *Rubric*: "Here begynnyth A nother matter that is Vsyd"; *Incipit*: "I shall wryte to you other thyngis that you must worke with And the same thyngis must go in your medycynis And day [*sic*] And fyrst begynne with Aristologia."

This text on fifty-one herbal simples, largely in alphabetical order, appears to derive from the twelfth-century *Circa instans* attributed to Matheus Platearius.[29] The Middle English versions of this treatise present a vexed and complicated

---

[25] George R. Keiser, "A Middle English Rosemary Treatise in Verse and Prose," *ANQ* 18 (2005): 7–17, and Keiser, "Rosemary: Not Just for Remembrance," *Health and Healing from the Medieval Garden*, ed. Peter Dendle and Alain Touwaide (Woodbridge, UK: Boydell and Brewer, 2008), 180–204. See also John Harvey, "Mediaeval Plantsmanship in England: The Culture of Rosemary," *Garden History* 1 (1972): 14–21.

[26] Antonius Musa, *Epistola missa Caesari Augusto de herba vetonica*. This short text, often attached to the *Herbarium Apulei*, was widely transmitted from the early Middle Ages. See eTK 112C, 183A, 609H, 915B, 1007A.

[27] The following records in eTK on *semen feniculi* may be relevant: 12B, 75K, 100G.

[28] eVK2 nos. 1514, 4021, 5824, and 7191 may be relevant to this short text.

[29] See edition by Hans Wölfel, *Das Arzneidrogenbuch "Circa instans" in einer Fassung des XIII. Jahrhunderts aus der Universitätsbibliothek Erlangen* (Berlin, 1939). The text in this Latin edition begins with *aloe*, and *aristilogia* is the nineteenth entry. There are forty-four records for *Circa instans* in eTK. The text takes its title from the incipit "Circa instans negotium de simplicibus medicinis nostrum."

tradition.[30] In the case of this text, the equivalent passages of the Peniarth MS 369B (ff. 34–35v, difficult to read because of damage) are similar to SB 89 but not identical (this National Library of Wales codex is cited several sections in this study; see above n. 9). It is important to point out that Peniarth does not separate out the *Circa instans* sections dealing with the medical virtues of plants from those on other sorts of *materia medica* as does SB 89. This separation of sections of *Circa instans* in SB 89, Part I, makes it probable that it is a codex written later than the related Peniarth MS 369B, where *Circa instans* appears to be a unified text.

11. Ff. 29v–30v (eVK2 918.25), *Rubric*: "The Vertu off certayne gummys with other thyngis" (section heading also in contents list, f. [iii verso]); *Rubric*: "Armonyak" *Incipit*: "Armonyak is a gumme hote & dry and it distroith all hardnes."

This section on twenty gums also appears, like no. 10, to derive from the *Circa instans*. The series of excerpts from that compendium is interrupted by the following synonymy.

12. Ff. 30v–33, *Rubric*: "Here begynnyth the namys of erbys that ar drawyn in latyn And in inglysch tong" (section heading also

---

[30]   See edition and several studies by María Edurne Garrido Anes: "De simplici medicina (Circa instans) en ingles medio: vernacularizacion del tratado salernitano de Mateo Plateario," PhD Thesis, Universidad de Huelva (Spain), 2005, and *A Middle English Version of the Circa Instans according to CUL Ee.1.13, ff. 1r–91v*, Middle English Texts (Heidelberg), forthcoming. See also her "Addenda al Listado de Manuscritos del 'Circa Instans' Preservados en Bibliotecas Británicas," *Cronos* 8 (2005–6): 139–46; "Geographical and Dialectal Distribution of Platearius' 'Liber de Simplici Medicina' in England," *International Journal of English Studies* 5 (2005): 93–114; "Manuscript Relations through Form and Content in the Middle English 'Circa Instans,'" *Revista del la Sociedad Española de Lengua y Literature Inglesa Medieval* 13 (2005–6): 199–224; "Transmisión, vernacularización y usos del *Liber de Simplici Medicina*: Las versiones del *Circa Instans* en inglés medio," *Medicina e Historia* 2 (2004): 1–15.

We are grateful for correspondence from Garrido Anes, especially her comments that this and subsequent sections from the *Circa Instans* in SB 89, along with the *Circa Instans* material in Peniarth MS 369B, appear to be anomalous. She has suggested in electronic correspondence that there may be a distant relationship between the SB 89 and Peniarth MS 369B versions, on the one hand, and Sloane MSS 404 and 770, on the other.

given in contents list, with some variation from text rubric, f. [iii verso]); *Incipit*: "*Absyntheum*—Anglice wormewode."

Two-column alphabetical synonymy citing 162 Latin names in the left column with English equivalents in the right column. Use of the tabular format is facilitated by the use of black ink for Latin lemmata and red for English, but the coloring is reversed as a readers' aid in cases of the first entry for each new letter of the alphabet. Eye-skip occurs on folio 33 where the scribe has repeated the first two English equivalents from the T lemmata in the V listings.

A valuable discussion of plant synonymies and the manuscripts in which they occur is to be found in Tony Hunt's *Plant Names of Medieval England*.[31]

13. Ff. 33–33v (eVK2 8250.75), *Rubric*: "Here will we tell you of all grecis And in what maner they Shall be gaderyd (section heading also given in contents list, f. [iii verso]); *Incipit*: "Thus you must gader All maner of fattnes of grece of bestys and fowlys onto medycyns"; *Incipit*: "ffyrst and foremost tak Away the skyne And the Ryme."

This short section ends with a *Rubric*: "All grecys in ther kynd are hote and moyst and all thes that I shall Shew you are good to your medycyns"; *Incipit*: "That is for the first grese sanders grese capons grece."

The brief section on greases following the Synonymy uses the same formulaic wording of the *Circa instans*. Following greases is an herbal recipe with no rubric and the following *Incipit*: "Take bayes of A lawrell tre A quarterne of a pownd ye Rotys off okeferne."

14. Ff. 33v–34v (eVK2 6092.25), *Rubric*: "The makyng of All maner of oylys of All maner of erbys" (section heading also given in

---

[31] Tony Hunt, *Plant Names of Medieval England* (Cambridge: D. S. Brewer, 1989); see the sections "Synonymies" and "The Plant Names in the *Synonyma Herbarum*," xliii–li, along with Hunt's discussion of sixty-four manuscripts dating from 1280 to 1500, xxv–xxxvi. On the need for further study of such texts, see David Moreno Olalla, "A Plea for Middle English Botanical *Synonyma*," *Probable Truth: Editing Medieval Texts from Britain in the Twenty-First Century*, ed. Vincent Gillespie and Anne Hudson (Turnhout: Brepols, 2013), 387–404, especially "A Preliminary Handlist," 401–4.

contents list on folio [iii verso]); *Rubric*: "Oyle of camemyll"; *Incipit*: "Take the flowers of camemyll And All to stampe them with oyle olyff."

The second recipe in this group (*Rubric*: "Oleum Rosatum that is to say oyle of Rosys"; *Incipit*: "Thus it is made in v ℔ [pound] of comyn oyle of olyff well clensyd") comes from the *Antidotarium Nicolai* and is also found in the English version edited by Garrido Linares. This section appears to mark a return to excerpts from the *Antidotarium Nicolai*, a text often transmitted with *Circa instans*.

The third recipe, "Olium Mandragoratum," and the fourth, "Olium frigidissimum Viride," are followed by an anomalous recipe on folio 34r–v requiring distillation: (eVK2 6018.75), *Rubric*: "ffor to make A candell to burne in water without tarter"; *Incipit*: "Take sulfur Vyfe An vnce oyle tarter an vnce Alum de plumbum."

15. F. 34v, *Rubric*: "Here begynnyth the workyng of all maner of oylys made of flowers erbys levys or ffrutys"; *Incipit*: "ffyrst tak olyle olyff as moch as thou wylt."

    This general description is followed by another recipe for *Oleum Rosatum*, which differs from the recipe with the same rubric on folio 33v.

16. F. 34v, *Rubric*: "Here begynnyth_the makyng of al maner of Syropp yt is made of flowers erbys & Rotys"; *Incipit*: Iff thou wilt mak a Syropp of flowers."

    This single recipe concludes with instructions to write the names of the ingredients in the syrup on the "Jene [Genoa] pott."

17. Ff. 34v–35, *Rubric*: "Here folowith of emplaysters" (section heading also given in contents list, f. [iv verso]); *Rubric*: "A good emplayster for the fester"; *Incipit*: "Take waybrede tansay & nose blede and the whyte oke."

    Compare this recipe to eVK2 1760 from Sloane 3153, f. 41v.

18. Ff. 35–38 (eVK2 5599.25), *Rubric*: "Here Begynnyth the emplaysters that are full good Vnto maledyse of bochys & bylys And Warrys [*sic*]" (section heading not in contents list). *Rubric*:

"Emplastrum Appostolicum [*sic*] that is to Say a hard confeccoun"; *Incipit*: Tak lytarge vij vnce new yellow wax colophony."
A section on seventeen plasters again apparently from the *Antidotarium Nicolai* tradition. The first four plasters here are the only plasters included in the English version edited by Garrido Linares (95–98), and the first three correspond to nos. 43, 45, and 46 in Goltz. This section includes two recipes with the common designation *Gratia dei*.

19. F. 38 (eTK2 5933.25), *Rubric*: "The making of bawme riall with other Salvys (section heading also given in contents list, f. [iv verso]); *Rubric*: Bawme Riall"; *Incipit*: "Take sawge ryall a Ꝉi bawme a Pownd butter."
Five salves.

20. Ff. 38v–41v (eVK2 5244.75), *Rubric*: "Intret *Intractum Viridum* that is to say A grene trete" (section heading also given in contents list, f. [iv verso]); *Incipit*: "Take comfory waybred howndystong crowfote."
Twelve entretes, a term used for salves or plasters. The last recipe (ff. 40v–41), another for *Gratia dei,* is long and complex. Here the usual Latin title is given in the vernacular, "the grace of god."

21. Ff. 41v–42 (eVK2 6276.75), *Rubric*: "A powder for All maner of Sykenes in manis body" (section heading also given in contents list, f. [iv verso]); *Incipit*: "Take the Sede of Smalach bays the rote off Annys the Rote of turmentyll."   fig. 2
Four powders, the second and third of which, on folio 41v, are for Powder Imperial. These two recipes are almost identical, but the second iteration is written in red (eVK2 6276.75). These two recipes are similar to, albeit slightly longer than, the abbreviated version of *pulvis imperialis* found in the John of Burgundy/John of Bordeaux Middle English text, "Medicine Against the Pestilence Evil" as edited by Lister M. Matheson,[32] who points out that this recipe derives from the

---

[32] See the edition by Lister M. Matheson, "John of Burgundy: Treatises on Plague," *Sex, Aging and Death in a Medieval Medical Compendium: Trinity College*

longer form of *pulvis imperialis* (also known as *Bethzaer*) for
protection against epidemic disease. The longer version occurs in the author's Latin *De epidemia*, the source for the
Middle English plague texts attributed to him.[33]

22. Ff. 42–42v (eVK2 5958.50), *Rubric*: "A purgacyoun" (section
heading also given with variants in contents list, f. [iv verso]); *Incipit*: "Take vii penywayte of catepuce and let the syke ete them."
Six purgatives.

23. Ff. 42v–43 (also eVK2 5958.50), *Rubric*: "Here folowyth laxa-
tive purgacoun" (section heading also given in contents list, f. [iv
verso]); *Rubric*: "A Medecyn to make a man laxatyve & to make
a man to speke [*sic*]"; *Incipit*: "Take lawryell and make powder
therof And drynke it fastyng."
Four laxatives.

24. F. 43 (eVK2 674.75), *Rubric*: "The maner of Wrytyng of bylllis of
Receytes" (section heading also given in contents list, f. [iv ver-
so]); *Incipit*: "A pownd is wrytyn thus ℔."
A traditional table of weights and measures providing apothecary symbols from pound to scruple. Such information is
often embedded in *receptaria*. A version of this short table
has been edited from BL, Sloane MS 3171, folios 1v–2 (eVK2
7529).[34] As is the case with the table in SB 89, a similar listing of weights and measures in Sloane 4 in Latin also immediately precedes the *Antidotarium Nicolai*: "De ponderibus
secundum Nicholaum in Antedodario [*sic*] suo qui sit Incipit Ego Nicholaus rogatus."[35]   fig. 3

Cambridge MS R.14.52, Its Texts, Language, and Scribe, ed, M. Teresa Tavormina
(Tempe, Ariz.: Arizona Center for Medieval and Renaissance Studies, 2006), 2:569–
606, at 591–92.

[33] Ibid., 2:600–601, n. 35, and p. 569. There are many eTK entries for the writings of John of Burgundy/Bordeaux, but for *De epidemia*, see 1290H and 1290I.

[34] Voigts, "The Character of the *Carecter*: Ambiguous Sigils in Scientific and
Medical Texts," *Latin and Vernacular: Studies in Late-Medieval Texts and Manu-
scripts*. Proceedings of the 1987 York Manuscripts Conference. ed. A. J. Minnis
(Cambridge: D. S. Brewer, 1989), 91–109.

[35] BL, Sloane MS 4, f. 20. This version of the *Antidotarium* in Sloane 4 begins
with *Athanesia* rather than the traditional *Aurea Alexandrina* in SB 89.

25. Ff. 43v–58 (eVK2 2499.75), Prologue (no rubric): "I nycolas haue
    Iprovyd of Sume men in practyse of medycyns stodyyng to them
    that folowith and that I Shuld teche" (section heading given in
    contents list, f. [iv verso]: "I Nichi et cetera The confeccons of
    Vsyall medicyns be letter"); (eVK2 1208), *Incipit* (ff. 43v–44):
    "Aurea Alexandria it is cleapyd So of ali aurea of gowld Alexan-
    dria"; second *Incipit* (f. 44): "Take Asary the which is lyke yvery
    carpobalsamy henbane Sede of ich ii."

    Note that the incipit usually begins "Aurea Alexandrina"; see
    seventeen records in eVK2.

    This version of *Antidotarium Nicolai* follows previous unat-
    tributed short excerpts from that text in SB 89, Part I (e.g.,
    nos. 17, 18). Here, however, we have ninety-eight recipes in
    alphabetical order. They follow the traditional prologue to this
    well-known compendium of compound recipes attributed to
    Nicholas of Salerno. It should be noted that the rubrics for
    this work in SB 89 given in the contents list vary from those
    found in the body of the text. The Middle English version of
    this compendium as edited from Glasgow University Library,
    Ferguson 147, by Maria José Carrillo Linares, contains ca. 118
    recipes, many of them identical with these in the SB 89 ver-
    sion.[36] As observed above, the *Antidotarium Nicolai* on com-
    pound medicines complemented and was often transmitted
    with the *Circa instans* on simples.[37]

    This coherent version of the text is important to under-
    standing the entirety of SB 89 in several respects. First, it
    contains a number of recipes relevant to the recipes in Part II
    of SB 89. For example, it includes a recipe made with pearls,
    Diamargariton (f. 46v), and calls for juice of pomegranates
    (f. 54v). Furthermore, the recipes selected for this version of
    the *Antidotarium Nicolai* are particularly relevant to a house-
    hold book for use by women. *Atanasta* (ff. 44v–45), calling
    for red coral and pomegranate rind, is for "the flyx of blode

---

[36] See above, n. 15, for edition and study of a Middle English version of the
Antidotarium Nicolai by Carrillo Linares.

[37] Freedman, 64-69. See above, n. 19. There are thirty-three records in eTK for
the *Antidotarium Nicolai* (and commentaries) and fourteen Middle English records
for this text in eVK2 (prologues and texts numbered separately).

of women." *Antytotum/Antitotum Imagogum* (f. 45) purges
uterine problems and brings out a dead fetus. *Confectio ver* (f.
46v) is a fumigation for the womb, "makythe ye matryx Redy
to conceyve verely," and is described as "good for the matryx."
Pigra galien pigran & bytter gallian (ff. 54v–55) in a bath "helpyth moche to consayvyng [conceiving]." *Trifera magna* (f.
57v) is prescribed "agayn yll of the matryx of coldnes" and
"provokyth also menstruys."

26. F. 58v, *Rubric*: "To claryfy hony"; *Incipit*: "Take a galon of hony
and A pottel of water"; *Rubric*: "ffor to mak suger plate bothe red
and whyte"; *Incipit*: "Take suger the fayrest thou mayst get and
melt it with water."
Two recipes of the sort found in Part II of SB 89.

27. Ff. 58v–77v (eVK2 6253.75), *Rubric*: "ffor the hed ache" (section
heading given in contents list: "Remdyse for the hede"); *Incipit*:
"Take the Rote of wormewode and ach and waybred percely."
The first of two *receptaria* (A), this one in traditional *a capite
ad calcem* [head to heel] order, containing ca. 205 recipes and
an embedded text, cited below as no. 28.
The following divisions of this *receptarium* are given in
section headings in the contents list: "Remedyse for eyne" f.
[vi verso]; "Remedyse for ylle herynge" f. [vi verso]; "Remedyse for the tethe" f. [vi verso]; "Remedyse ffor the stomake
And the hart" f. [vii]; "Remedyse for dropsye" f. [vii]; "ffor
Seknes in the mouthe" f. [vii]; "Remedyse for the pestylence
And all poyson" f. [vii verso]; "Remedyse for the cowghe" f.
[vii verso]; "Remedyse for the brest" f. vii [verso]; "ffor the
ffeuer" f. vii [verso]; "Remedyse for them that lacke appetyte
to meate or desyer to moche drynke" f. [viii]; "ffor all maner
of Woundys A remedy" f. [viii]; "Remedyse Agaynst diuerse
Akyng And Swellyngis" f. [viii]; "Remedyse for the palsy" f.
[viii verso]; "Remedise for vermyn cropyn in to manis body" f.
[viii verso]; "Remedyse ffor bytyng of Venemus bestys" f. [viii
verso]; "Remedyse ffor the morfewe" f. [ix]; "Remedyse for the
Jandys" f. [ix]; "Remedyse ffor the stone" f. [ix]; "Remedyse to
drawe out Iron or thorne of A body" f. [ix]; "ffor brynnyng or
scaldyng" f. [ix]; "ffor the gowte And Siatica" f. [ix]; "To make

here to growe & to do Away here" f. [ix]; "ffor Spyttyng blode"
f. [ix verso]; "ffor maledyse in the fface off man or woman"
f. [ix verso]; "Remedyse for the kanker" f. [ix verso]; "To do
Away wertis f. [ix verso]; "ffor the fflyx And the blody mene-
son" f. [ix verso]; "Remedyse for costyfnes" f. [ix verso]; "ffor
women that lacke mylke" f. [ix verso].

Of particular interest in this household book is the recipe
associated with a Northern noble family on folio 64r–v (*Rubric*: "ffor the feuer in the stomake a medycyn provyd"; *Incipit*:
"Take lyuerwort A good handfull and washe it cleane and
then hake yt small"). The recipe concludes, "for this medycyne
Vsyd the erle of northhumberland for the feuyr in the stomak
When that it toke hym And it helpyth yt him Verely well ffor /
ffor [*sic*] it hath bene provyd many dyuerse tymys on dyuerse
persons both men And Also of wymen."

On folio 77r–v of this compendium are four recipes for
problems with lactation.

28. F. 69r–v (eVK2 6364.75), embedded in *receptarium* A; *Rubric*:
"ffor to make a drynk that men callyth dwale that is to make a
man for to sł [*sic*] slepe whyle the Surgyons cutt him" (the rubric
as given in the contents list reads, "To make a drynke to cause A
man to Slepe when he ys cutt," f. [viii]); *Incipit*: "Take iii Sponfull
of the gall of A barowe Swyne and for An woman of a ȝelte & iii
Sponfull of the Juce of hemlokis."
   This Middle English anesthesia recipe, called "Dwale," survives in many manuscripts.[38] It was edited from Cambridge
   University Library, Dd.6.29, folio 79–79v by Voigts and Hudson.[39]

29. Ff. 77v–79 (eVK2 4433.25), *Rubric*: "The knowlege of the iiij
complecouns the xxxij days perlous The xij Sygnes And the Vij
planettis" (section heading also given in contents list, f. [x]);

---

[38]   See the sixty-seven records in eVK2 for manuscript witnesses of this text.

[39]   Voigts and Robert P. Hudson. "'A drynke that men callen dwale to make
a man to slepe whyle men kerven him': A Surgical Anesthetic from Late Medieval
England," *Health, Disease and Healing in Medieval Culture*, ed. Sheila Campbell,
Bert Hall, and David Klausner (New York: St. Martin's, 1992), 34–56._

Rubric: "The knowlege of the iiij compleciouns *Signa sangui-nei* hote and moyst"; *Incipit*: "A Sangwyn man oor Woman is large in hart louyng And mery."   fig. 4

A summary treatment of (a) the physical and behavioral characteristics determined by the four humors, (b) the signs of the zodiac in terms of solar astrology, and (c) the physical and behavioral characteristics determined by the planets with the times of planetary transit in the zodiac. The section cited in the rubric on thirty-two perilous days is wanting. Each of the three parts of this text circulates independently. Opening section (a) on physiognomy as determined by dominance of humors is a common prose version of the Latin poem beginning "*Sanguineus*."[40] Section (b) on the signs of the zodiac in relation to the sun also circulates independently (see eVK2 1055), but it is less common than a version on the signs in relation to the moon. Section (c) on personalities and actions determined by planetary influence, often called "*Planetenkinder*," circulates widely as an independent text.[41]   fig. 8

30. F. 79r–v (eVK2 5202.75), *Rubric*: "Here folowith certayne conclusyouns"; (section heading also given in contents list, f. [x]); *Rubric*: "A good conclusyon for to take conys"; *Incipit*: "Take campher Arsafetida comyn And spemacete of iche a penyworth."

Five recipes for hunting, magic, and taking birds.

---

[40] See the thirty-two records in eVK2 for manuscript witnesses of this text. The widely distributed Latin poem is cited under several numbers in Hans Walther, *Initia carminum ac versuum medii aevi posterioris Latinorum* (Göttingen: Vandenhoeck & Ruprecht, 1959). See nos. 10126, 10131, 13474, 17265, 17266. Figures representing the four humors are illustrated in two English medical and scientific manuscripts: the Guild Book of the Barber Surgeons of York, BL, Egerton 2572, f. 51v (contemporary with SB 89); and Trinity College Cambridge MS R.15.21, ff. 12v–15v (early fifteenth century). See Kathleen L. Scott, *Later Gothic Manuscripts 1390–1490* (London: H. Miller, 1996), on the Guild Book illustrations (vol. 1, fig. 503, and vol. 2, no. 139; pp. 363–64), and on the Trinity College manuscript illustrations to the *Liber cosmographiae* of John de Foxton (vol. 1, figs. 134–37, and vol. 2, no. 31; pp. 114–17).

[41] See two groups of such texts in eVK2: nos. 4459–63 and 4471–75. Trinity College Cambridge MS R.15.21, cited above, also contains illustrations of the *Planetenkinder* with the John de Foxton treatise. See Scott, *Later Gothic Manuscripts*, vol. 1, plate 8 (Luna), and vol. 2, no. 31 (pp. 114–17).

31. Ff. 79v–86v (eVK2 5399.75), *Rubric*: "Here folowe Remedies ffor dyuerse disseasys And maledyes in man or in woman" (section heading also given in contents list, f. [x]); *Rubric*: "To make a boyle to brek And to Rott anon"; *Incipit*: "Take galbanum And cleanse it at the fyer and make therof a playster."
   This second *receptarium* (B) contains approximately seventy-five recipes, more randomly organized than is the case with *receptarium* A, and unlike in A, the categories of recipes in B are not given in the contents list. *Receptarium* B includes an embedded text, no. 32] with scribal interruption inserting recipes from the main *receptarium*.

32. Ff. 82v–83, 84v (eVK2 7251), *Rubric*: "This diatory folowyng was sent to dame Isabell quene of ynglond by the kyng of ffraunce her brother And who So will take hede therof shall nede non other fysyck" (Rubrics in contents list: "A diatori Wherby A man may be preseruyd / With out Another Syege"; "Thyngis good for the eyn & thyngis yll for the eyne"; "Thyngis good ffor the hart for the throte And for the stomake," f. [x] verso); *Rubric*: "This is good for the braynys"; *Incipit*: "To smele the Saver of must And the Saver of camemell To drynke wyne mesurably." A scribal interruption occurs where eleven unrelated recipes (part of the larger *receptarium*) have been inserted in the opening 83v–84r, before the text concludes on folio 84v with things ill for the heart, good for the stomach, and evil for the stomach.   Fig. 5
   A common text, here called the dietary of Queen Isabella, more widely known in Latin and English as *De conferentibus et nocentibus* and attributed to Arnald of Villanova.[42] It lists things deemed good for various body parts, beginning with the brain. The version here differs from that edited by W. L. Braekman.[43] Of particular interest for dating the manuscript is the reading on folio 83 regarding things evil for the eyes: "to

---

[42] See the nine records in eVK2 for Middle English manuscript witnesses to this text, and thirty-nine records for the Latin version in eTK. BL Harley 2390 contains both Latin and English versions (ff. 51v–56 and ff. 109–10v). The version in Wellcome Library (MS 408, ff. 13v–14v) displays some similarities to SB 89.

[43] Braekman, *Studies on Alchemy, Diet, Medecine* [*sic*] *and Prognostication*, 43–82 (text edited from BL, MS Sloane 100). See above, n. 10.

study moche on whyte bokis And namely pryntyd boke" (fig. 5.). We have not found this reading in the numerous English and Latin manuscripts and early printed books we have consulted. It suggests that this manuscript was written after the introduction of printing to England in 1476 and/or after there was significant import of printed books from the Continent.[44]

---

[44] See the discussion on dating above in section 2 (**Date, Decoration, and Original Ownership of BCM SB 89**).

Appendix D. Transcription of Part II of Berkeley Castle Muniments SB 89

PART II: INCOMPLETE. See **Appendix A** for the physical description of the manuscript. Part II apparently contained ca. eighty-four recipes, but a description of the original contents is complicated, both by the fact that the contents list does not always correspond to the texts (rubrics often differ significantly) and by the fact that three leaves of Part II are missing: one at the beginning and two at the end (plate 5). The first missing leaf may have contained an introductory rubric. It certainly listed the texts now found on folios 1–5. We have arbitrarily assigned nos. 1–33 to those recipes.[1] The surviving second leaf of Part II (f. [ii]) lists recipes on folios 5v–15. We have assigned nos. 34–71 to those discrete texts, although nos. 37–40 and 62 are not identified in the contents list. The contents list (II, f. [ii verso]) provides section headings and rubrics for the thirteen recipes missing on folios 14–15. Five recipes in Part II (nos. 5, 7, 8, 9, 20) also occur in Part I, sometimes with significant variation. See **Appendix B** for a table of recipes occurring in both parts.

The recipes in Part II specify uses both medical (electuaries, waters, powders, plasters, aqua vitae, subfumigation) and culinary, with a high

---

[1] The first recipe cited on the surviving contents leaf, "A pouder that seruyth ffor charequyncis" (no. 33), occurs on folio 5v following the rubric at the bottom of folio 5.

proportion for epidemic disease and for stone.[2] Some recipes are specified for members of royal or noble families: no. 14, for my lord (f. 3; fig. 6);
no. 32, the queen's powder (f. 5); no. 44, as I sent to your ladyship (f. 8v);
no. 49, medicine that the king used every day (f. 9; plate 7); and no. 64,
devised for my lady the king's grandmother (f. 12v; plate 8).

It should also be noted that recipe nos. 37–40, not cited in the contents list, differ from most of those in the rest of Part II and may have
been interpolated at some point. In particular, nos. 37–39 vary from the
others in a number of significant respects: they are predominantly Latin
rather than English; they provide measurements for ingredients; they
utilize a high percentage of exotics; and they have a different appearance
on the page. Ingredients are listed in columns and do not resemble the
narrative household book format of the rest of SB 89. Rather, they are presented in the manner of medical compendia by or for university-trained
physicians, for example, in the main texts of Harley 1628 and the Forestier treatise on the sweat in Additional MS 27,582. Such tabular recipes
in both codices use symbols rather than words for weights and measures,
as do recipes 37-39 in SB 89, Part II.[3] These symbols are defined in the in
the traditional table of weights and measures in Part I (see **Appendix C**,
no. 24, f. 43).

Recipes nos. 37–40 bear a striking resemblance to Latin plague recipes
cited by the speaker called "Medicus" in William Bullein's 1564 *A Dialogue against the Feuer Pestilence*.[4] That character in the dialogue advises
in time of plague to "be not without Manus Christi to eate often tymes"
(50). Recipe no. 40 in Part II of SB 89 provides instructions for the preparation of manus Christi. Another significant connection between the two
texts can be seen in the mixed Latin and English polypharmacy recipes in Part II of SB 89, nos. 37–39. All three call for *ambre* or ambergris
together with *musti/musci* or musk, and all three display Latin inflected
forms for the other ingredients. Bullein's English-language recipe with

---

[2] On epidemic disease, see section 3 (**Epidemic Disease during the Reign of
Henry VII (1485–1509)**) and tables 1 and 2. On the stone, see Harold Ellis, *A History
of Bladder Stone* (Oxford: Blackwell Scientific, 1969).

[3] For an example of this format and the use of apothecary's symbols, see figure 7.

[4] William Bullein, *A Dialogue against the Feuer Pestilence*, ed. Mark W. Bullen
and A. H. Bullen from the edition of 1578, collated with editions of 1564 and 1573,
EETS ES 52 (London, 1888). The recipes, some in English, most in Latin, advocated
by the Medicus are found on 46–55.

the rubric "Pomeamber against the Pestilence" calls for amber [ambergris] and musk (49). Bullein's Latin recipe titled "A Princelie Pomeamber" also includes "ambrae, musci" (54). The *Middle English Dictionary* cites ambergris as the first definition of *aumbre*.

These three SB 89 recipes and Bullein's also resemble one another in that they call for other rare and expensive exotica such as lignum aloes, sandalwood, and cloves (gariofilum), among others. What is most significant, however, is that all likewise specify the ingredient *ambra* or ambergris. In his landmark study surveying considerable numbers of *Pestschriften* both in Latin and in German, John Riddle makes clear that *ambra* (ambergris) was the most desired ingredient in the appropriately named *pomum ambrae*, the aromatic medicine believed to protect against the plague.[5] *Ambra* was usually accompanied by other aromatic imports such as musk, lignum aloes, cloves (gariofilum,) and sandalwood. Riddle emphasizes that ambergris was not a common ingredient because of its scarcity and expense, and he cites three recipes where it is specifically prescribed for royalty and two where it was recommended for the pope. The cost of ambergris made it inaccessible for most people.

The transcription of Part II that follows is diplomatic, with some exceptions. Manuscript lineation is observed, but numbers have been assigned to the recipes to aid in reference. Rubrics that appear in red and numbers are given in boldface. Scribal orthography, which varies considerably, has been retained, as has scribal capitalization. The scribe's division or joining of syllables in a word has likewise been retained, as have his strike-throughs for cancellations. The only scribal punctuation in the manuscript is the stroke used at times between syntactic units; it is retained. A significant characteristic of this scribe is his use of capitalization, both to begin lines and as a form of punctuation. Although he is not consistent throughout, his dominant pattern is to use capital letters to emphasize words and often to indicate the beginning of syntactic units. He also uses capital letters with articles and conjunctions as the equivalent of *item* to introduce new ingredients in recipes, especially where there might otherwise be confusion. The scribe usually differentiates between the minims for *u/v* and *n* by supplying a macron over the nasal.

---

[5] John Riddle, "Pomum ambrae: Amber and Ambergris in Plague Remedies," *Sudhoffs Archiv für Geschichte der Medizin und der Naturwissenschaften* 48 (1964): 111–22.

We have, however, silently expanded common contractions and abbreviations. In the case of the yogh (ȝ and capital Ȝ), z has been supplied when it is required, as for the word *lozenge*, but we have retained yogh where its use is ambiguous. Rubrics, almost always in red, are so designated both for groups of recipes and for individual recipes. Measurements given in apothecaries' symbols are expanded in curly brackets { }. Where the scribe's spelling varies so much as to make identification difficult, we have glossed the word in square brackets [ ]. In most cases, the gloss simply gives the familiar vernacular name, in many instances for a plant occurring in the "Index of Vernacular Names" in Tony Hunt, *Plant Names of Medieval England*.[6] In other instances, the gloss refers to a Latin name in Hunt, in Willem F. Daems, *Nomina simplicium medicinarum ex synonymariis medii aevi collecta*,[7] to Middle English terms in Juhani Norri, *Names of Body Parts in English, 1400–1550*,[8] or lemmata in the *Middle English Dictionary* (*MED*) or the *Oxford English Dictionary* (*OED*). In a few instances, plant names that occur in Part I with variant orthography are identified where they occur in Part II as (S) "Synonomy," (*AN*) *Antidotarium Nicolai*, or (*CI*) *Circa instans*.

[f. [i] missing; stub only]	plate 5, showing end of SB Part I and beginning of SB Part II	
[f. [ii] recto contents list for folios 5–11]		
A pouder that seruyth ffor charequyncis (33)	**folio**	**v**
A powder to be inbastyd within A cappe (34)	**folio**	**v**
ffor cold dysseasys in the hed (34) [idem]	**folio**	**v**
A powder to vse in your Sawcis (35)	**folio**	**v**
[section rubric] **Here folowith electuarys**		
and Syroppis	**folio**	**vj**
and conserue and Ipocras	**folio**	**vij**
A specyall electuary to conserue on in helth (36)	**folio**	**vij**

---

[6]   Tony Hunt, "Index of Vernacular Names," *Plant Names of Medieval England* (Cambridge: D. S. Brewer, 1989), 269–316.

[7]   Willem F. Daems, *Nomina simplicium medicinarum ex synonymariis medii aevi collecta* (Leiden: E. J. Brill,1993).

[8]   Juhani Norri, *Names of Body Parts in English, 1400–1550* (Helsinki: Finish Academy of Science and Letters, 1998).

[n.b., the text contains Latin recipes for Aromaticoun Rosarum (no. 37), Dia galange (no. 38), and Dia margariton (no. 39), ff. 6–7v, and an English recipe for manus Christi, lacking rubric (no. 40), f. 7v, none of which are cited in this contents list; as discussed above, these recipes may be an interpolation.]

[f. 1 recipe texts begin]

(1) f. 1 [rubric] ¶ **ffor to make aqua vite ffor flewme** [eVK2 5541.75]
               ¶ **in the brest and for ympostyms** [apostemes]
ffyrst take ysope a greate handfull more penyryall A handfull stabious ij
handfull pympernell iij handfull

(2) f. 1 [rubric] ⸿ **A nother souerayne compowndyng of aqua**
        ⸿ **Vite agayne malencoly**
Take borage langdebeffe of iche ij handfull hartis tong xv leuys
germaunder [CI, quercula maior=germander] iij handfull

(3) f. 1 [rubric] ⸿ **A nother for the lyuer**
Take endyve thouthystyll [S, Labrum=thowfystyll; *MED*, soue-thistel]
    egremony of ich iij handfull borage and
langdebyffe of iche ane handfull Saynt Johns worte ij handfull

(4) f. 1 [rubric] ⸿ **A nother for the wynd**
Take halfe a pownd of fenell Sede half a pownd off Annes
Sede langdebyff iiij handfull endyue and hartystonge off
iche ij handfull

(5) f. 1 [rubric] ⸿ **The vertu of water of buglose** [S, bluglose=oxtung]
Water of buglose which is cleapyd wyld borage it hath the same
vertu that borage of the garden hathe Water of this erbe made of the
fflowers alone is best or ellis it may be made of the erbe withe rotys
fflowers and leuys This water is good for them that vsyth not to be
lett blode for it makyth and purgyth the blode from all maner of cold
humours and of all maner badd corupt blood and makyth good blode and
the blood that is to hote it colyth it and that / that is to cold it warmyth
it he multyplyeth the sperme and amendyth it / it coumfortyth the
hart and purgyth yll humours malencolyk and the brayne whiche
ys infecte be bad humours malencolyk it helpyth grettly to cure them
that are folys and frentyk which oftyn tymes Ar So sore infect
Rynnyng About let them drynke of this water iij or iiij tymys
ffastyng and it shall helpe the fransy

(6) f. 1 [rubric] ⸿ **The vertu of the water of valeryaun**
Take this erbys and the Rotys and make therof water stylyde ffor hem
[f. 1v] That drynkyth of this water ix days ffastyng it largyth and purgyth
the bryst of all flewme it largyth the vayne of the hart It coumfor
tyth the stomake it avoydyth the hart of all Sykenesse it is good
ffor stoppyng of the leuer and the longys and the Raynys it largyth
marvelously a manis nature and gyvith grett will to medyll with
women when a man vse it oftyn At euyn and at morowe and at

euyn when he goith to bed all his nature shalbe warmyd And also
Augmentyd grettly And he that vse it oftyn thowgh he be ryght
dry he shall come Agayn to his nature and also it makyth a man
well to make water

(7) f. 1v [rubric] ❡ A good water for eyn

Take ewfrace [euphrasy] vervayn Rew celidony and fynkell [fennel] of
    iche a quantyte
and hacke them small with ij handfull of flowers of Rosys and
yf you haue no Rosys sprynkyll them with water of Rosys & a cupfull
of whyte wyne and let them stand all a nyght & in the morowe
styll them As water of Rosys This water warysthyth the eyn of
Rednesse and of terys and yf you will make this water more strong
styll it onys Agayn and put it in A fayer glasse and After that sett it
in the sonne be the space of eyght days and afterward wasch well
your eyn ther with

(8) ff. 1v–2 [rubric] ❡ The Water of melyce [melissa] otherwyse callyd bawme

Water of bawme is hott and dry when it is drunkyn it helythe the
marrys [matrix] of women it hath such A vertu As margerome whiche is
    also
good for all cold sykenesse of the mother of women it helpyth them
gretly to conceyve it is good for all maner gowte of the Joyntis And
potacy [podagra] it helyth woundys and ded flesch and makyth good
    flesche it is
Ryght good for the cold gowte and fester but [sic] noli me tangere [facial
    skin disease] it is good
ffor all venemus bytyngis if it be layd theron with oyle of Rosys
or when so euer stonys or erbys be layd in the fyer and temperid with
the sayd water it Receyvith of them and yf wyne be apeyeryd in ye
towne it makyth it to come Agayne to hys fyrst nature in halfe a
[f. 2] pype of wyne put a cuppfull of this water it makyth a man remem
bereratyue and thynk on thyngis that he hath done both on thyngis that
    be
past and on thyngis that be present Item who so euer haue his stomak
    char
gyd or Replete with cold let hym tak ij sponfull of this water and drynk
it fastyng and the payne shall aswage also he that is Sory or heuy or

malencolious of hart or of corage tak of thys water and drynke it
with wyne and he shall be joyfull and mery and out of hys malenco
ly Item this water vsyd oftyn At morow conseruyth and kepyth a person
in helth and in good colour and quyck and his face shall be mery &
Joyous and kepe the herys for waxyng whyght Item who So hath ye
palsy or trymlyng of members As handys or feet take euery day of this
water Asmoche as may go in A lytyll nutt shell and put it in a goblet of
wyne And drynk it and it shall waryschen hym in Short tyme also
yf a man haue hys tong apeyeryd [appeared] not naturally but by
    aduenture
Take a lytyll lynyn cloth and dypp it in this water and wasch your
tong therwith and you shall speke as he dyd Afore Item if a man be
disseasyd with the grett Syknesse that is callyd the fallyn evill be
the which some men fallyth sodenly take of thys water and a
lytyll tryacle and temper them to gyther and gyve it hym to drynk
And it shall profytt him moche and make hym hole from fallyng Also
yf a man haue not his mouth well brethyd let him vse oftyn of
this water and it shall amend hym Item he that waschyth hys
mouthe in thys water it shall profytt hym moche a gayne all
payne of the tethe Item yf thou wilt long without corupcoun kepe
fflesche or fysche wett them in this water and they shall not apeyer
nor corupt but be well kept Item this water is good for the ston
And the gravell and it breakyth the ston in to Small kyrnellis As
Sond and make it to go out with the water

(9) ff. 2r–v [rubric] ❡ **ffor to make water of damaske** [recipe also begins
Part I, f. 1]
Take a quart of fyne Rose water and a pynt of water of whyte Rosis
and a pynt of water of eglentyn flowers and a pynt of mauiuysse [*MED*,
    malvesie; *OED*, malmsey]
[f. 2v] And put them all to gyther in a lymbecke that you styll in Rosys
    then take
iiij or v handfull of lauendre flowers And As many handfull pure Rosys
fforcyd [added; *MED*, farsen] as you do conserua And then take An vnce
    of campher and ij vncys
of the powder of erchose [euphrasy] and An vnce of Annes ij vncis of
    clowis & ij vncis
of macys and ij vncis of ffyne canell And bett all thes to gyther in a mortar

whan All your wateris be put to gyther in your lymbecke then take parte off
your powders and cast them into the water then cast the flowers of Rosis
    And
of lauender in the water euer a handfull of the on And An handfull of the
other and the powders betwyx the flowrys whan All your waters floweris
And powders be in bynd fast your lymbeck with a fayer cloth take a glasse
And put in it muske Asmoche As it plase you let the Spout of your lym
beck be put in your glasse and stopp it ffast with wax and kepe A ffyer
    vnder
the lymbecke of on heate both nyght And day

(10) f. 2v [rubric] ❡ **The makyng of A water**
Take quart of fayer water And Sett it on the fyer in A fayer vessell And
when it Sethe take it of and So sethyng put in this powder folowynge
As long As the water do Ryse so long put in the Sayd powder and when
    the
Sayd water is cold wasche the pacyent therwith

(11) f. 2v [rubric] ❡ **This is the powder**
Take grene coporose A quart and Roche Alom ij quartis and boyle
    them in
A panne And stere them to gyther tyll they be consumyd and then bett ye
Same in A fayer morter And make therof A powder

(12) f. 2v [rubric] ❡ **The meanys to make water**
            ❡ **ffor to Alay your wyne with**
Take fyrst A pottell of Rynnyng water then take vi levys off endyve
And yf they be yonge take the more And Asmany of bluglose and for lak
of buglose take langdebyffe then take halfe a dosyn levis of southystyll
And and [sic] handfull of synkfyld [cinquefoil] Than take Asmoch suger
    As turnythe
the water to A lytyll swettnes and boyle all them to gyther tyll
yt Semyth to be turnyd to a lytyll greannesse And than put it in
A fayer cloth and lat it Rynne throwghe lyke Ipocras And So lett
[f. 3] yt be cold And Alay your wyne withall

(13) f. 3 [rubric] ❡ **A specyall water for the eyne** fig. 6
Take Red fforell [sorrel?] red Rosys Rew eufrace vervayn turmentyll
   betony en
dyve oculus crysti chyckmete [S, apia maior=chykynmete] pympernell
   Selidon [celidony] fiolage [*MED*, filago] pione the leuys
of grene marche egremony woodbynd flowers of ich A handfull and
bruse them A lytyll to gyther then on day lay them in whyte wyne the
Second day in a man chydis [childs] vryn an innocent the iij^de day in wo
mans mylke of A man chylde the iiij day in cleane claryfyed hony and
So put them to be styllyd in A lymbek And kepe well this water ffor
it is stronly profytable for oldmen and yong men that shall work for ther
Syght sotely this water helpyth to do Away darknes And dymnes and
wateryng of eyne And for the feblenesse of Syght in to the ende of lyff
it kepyth th[e] syght As some tyme to drynk it with wyne And some tyme
to wasch thyn eyn with A fether therwith And if ther be A webb take
the gall of a cooke [cock] And medle ther with

(14) f. 3 [rubric] ❡ **Aqua vite for my lord** fig. 6
Take Sawge Isope horchound Rose mary of ich A handfull ij vncis of
lycorys styk brusyd A good Rote of elena campana Infuce all these to
gyther be the Space of xij owers in iij galonis of wyne or of Ale and
After that styll them to gyther in A styllatory

(15) f. 3 [rubric] ❡ **ffor the debylite of th[e] memory** fig. 6
Take the erbe of Rose mary with the flowers oculus christi buglose bake
them in A loffe in the ouyn & So put of the sayd loffe So bakyn in
to clarett wyne And drynke of that wyne fastyng and vse that same
dyuerse tymys and the more the better

(16) f. 3 [rubric] ¶ **To breke the ston hastely** fig. 6
Take Alysaunder loueache and Smallache and water cressys of
euery lyke moch and boyle them in A galoun And halfe of water
And put therto lycorous or sugar and drynke therof At morne and
At euyn hote iij days And So shall the stone breke

(17) ff. 3r–v ❡ **That the ston shall neuer growe agayn** [eVK2 4978.50]
[f. 3v] Take an vnce of gromell and on vnce offe Sedys of saxuifrag

halfe an vnce of phylopendula [filipendula] An [sic] a quarter of An vnce
off
meubre [MED, marble] wayte and a quarter of an vnce of whyte corall
and
Red [AN, corall whyte and red] in powder and Alway in thyrde day do A
sponfull in thy
potage of thys powder and neuer shall the stone come Agayn
in the bledder and this provid master Robert of grostede the good
bysshope of lyncoln

(18) f. 3v [rubric] ¶ A water agayne debilyte off
the stomake & indigestioun And
Ventosytees and opilacouns [oppilations] off your
Sydys And Splene And cold
Dysseassys off the brayne
Take of betany Rosemary sawge wormewoode myntis hartis tong
The ouer partys of tyme of iche of thes on handfull of borage
of buglose of myllysse [melissa] of iche on handfull and a {1/2} dry all
thes erbys all out of the Sonne and then A lytyll brvse them
And ley them infusyd in a galoun of good Red wynne by the
Spase of ij days and ij nyghtis with annes Sedys And cara
way sedys and fenkell Sedys brusyd of iche ij vncis &
then with an easy fyer dystyll out of A lymbeck A water after
An Aqua Vite and thys water Reserue in A hote glasse close
or sylver pott And hang ther in A sylke bag of Synamun
brosyd ij vncis of galyngale of lyngnum Aloes of nuttmugis
of zedwary of iche one grote wayte and after A good infusyon
you shall take the Spycys out and in the myddis of your dyner
drynke off the water on sponfull with wyne or ber

f. 3v [section rubric] ¶ Her folowith medycyns for the ston
(19) f. 3v [rubric] ffor mother colyk or wynd in the body
Take bays comyn clowis and macys safferoun Alysaunder sede &
graynis [of paradise] and grynd all these in A peper quern and take stale ale
And hete it ouer the fyer and flete [skim; MED, fleten] of the Ryall [foam;
MED, rial] and do in the
powder and medle them to gyther And drynke it As hote As
[f. 4] thy blode iij or iiij tymys And it will helpe the

(20) f. 4 [rubric] ❡ **A nother for the ston**
Take gromell and percely and Red nettyll and violet and frankencence
an kyrnell of cherystonys And stampe them to gyther And temper
them to gyther with stale Ale and drynke it

(21) f. 4 [rubric] ❡ **A nother ffor the Same**
Take euerferne that growith on the oke and take the Rote in apryll
And wasche it well and poyne [prick; see *OED*, poin] it And take ij cupfull
    of Ale that
ys stale and a cupful ~~of dewys~~ of hony and vse it

(22) f. 4 [rubric] ❡ **To breke the stone**
Take a cock that is a ӡere old and opyn hym and thou shallt fynd
in hys mawe small stonys take and breke them in A brasyn morter
And the powder therof ꝶ temper yt with wyne and drynke it and
yt will helpe the

(23) f. 4 [rubric] ❡ **ffor the ston A Solempe medycyn**
Take iij penywayt of black fflynt A peny wayt of aumber a peny
wayte of Jett A penywayte of Red corall iij peny wayght off
gromell ij penywayte of alum glasse ij peny wayght of other
glasse iij penywayt of gray marbyll iij peny wayght of chery
stonis kyrnellis ij peny wayte of bays a peny wayte of glois [Glaucia? Hunt,
    glaucium] ij
peny wayght of graynys [of paradise] ij peny wayte of powder of gynger A
peny wayte of powder of canell ij peny wayte of powder off
lycorews A peny wayte of annes A peny wayte of fenell Sede
ij peny wayte of Alebaster and grynd all thes to powder and
Drynke it with lycour And Vse it ix days At euyn And At morn
but At onys A sponefull

(24) ff. 4 r–v [rubric] ❡ **A powder for the ston**
Take tyme Sede Rosemary Sede percely sede the medell wall off
the walnut gromell Sede Saxifrage Sede the curnellys of
the bery that growith vpon and eglantyne and the almonde yt
growith within the Asche kaye [ash-key] all thes must be dryed in thys
ffourme put them in A dysch and Sett them in An ouyn when ye

[f. 4v] brede is out drawyn tyll they be dry and then bett them to powder
   and of
eche of thes take lyke quantyte and As you will haue moche or lytyll
made so in proporcoun euery thyng And when this powder is made
   Receyve
it with your drynke or withe your potage ffastyng luke warme And
it will helpe you

(25) f. 4v [rubric] ⸿ A playster for the ston

Take A good handfull of fetherfoy [feverfew; S, febrifuga=ffedyrfoy] A
   handful of Sawge A good
quantyte of dowes [doves] grece and doung bruse All thes to gyther And
ffry them in swett butter and put them in A lynyn bag And lay it vpon
the Same Syde wher you fele your payne As hote As you may wel
Suffre it betwen your hokyll bonys [hip bone; Norri, hucklebone] and
   your small Rybbys but in no
wyse lay it not to your bake

(26) f. 4v [rubric] ⸿ A souerayne powder for the colyck & the ston

Take percely sede a quarter of an vnce gromell Sede a quarter of An
vnce brome sede so moch annes Sede So moche plantayn sede As
moche of fyne Suger iiij vncis All thes Sedys do be betyn in powder
and to be sarsyd [sifted; MED, sarcen] throwe a fyne Sarce [strainer;
   MED, sarce] and Suger to be betyn with
All and then take of the powder to the mountenaunce of a gret hasyll
nutt and lett the man And the woman Vse to drynke it mornyng And
euynyng iij tymys in A weke with warme wyne or bere wyne is best
And when the pacient felyth the sore payne come than drynk it with
warme malvessay At ony tyme when it comythe And be the grace
of gode he shall haue Remedy

(27) f. 4v [rubric] ⸿ ffor the colyk

Take a tost with browne brede that it may be throwly tostyd then
Take A lytyll malvessay and cast ther vpon and vpon that cast
lauender flowers and then sprynkyll more malvessay yerupon And
Sett it in A fayer dysch tyll it be threwe hote and put it into A
lynyn cloth and So lay it to your bely

(28) ff. 4v–5 [rubric] ❡ **ffor the ston**
Take the Sede of smallache of percely of loueache of fenell of
Saxuifrage the Rotis of philopendula [Hunt, filipendula] and the kyrnell
of che
rystonys of euer iche lyke moche and make a powder of them
[f. 5] And drynk in A mornyng A Sponefull in new wyne Sumwhat
hote And At euyn asmoche

(29) f. 5 [rubric] ❡ **ffor the ston**
Take coddys of beanys with the leuys and stalkis then take dryed
cherystonis with the kyrnell and bett them all into powder and styll
them in saynys [? *MED*, seini, place of bloodletting] And when your
     water gader corupcoun cleanse your
Water And kepe it So As long As is your pleasure And drynke it
mornyng And euynyng

(30) f. 5 [rubric] ❡ **A Souerayne powder for the ston**
Take percely sede Alysaunder Sede gromell Sede the kyrnell within
Ashe keyis the kyrnell within eglantyne buryes the leuys off
parspere [samphire; *MED*, per-spere] dryed the pyth with in the walnut
     dryed of ich of thes
take ij vncis of saxifrage sede of the bone of hartys horne And
of [illegible] kyrnellis within the bays of iche of these iij take an vnce and
So make vp your powder

(31) f. 5 [rubric] ❡ **A Synguler dredge for wynde in
     Any place in A manis or womans body** [sweet medicine; *MED*,
     dragge]
Take comyn Infusyd halfe An vnce caroway fenell Sede anys
Sede of iche on an vnce cynamun gynger galyngale long peper
graynis [of paradise] of iche on halfe an vnce macys nuttmugis clowys blak
peper of iche ij {dram} piony cleansyd coliandre calamy Aromatycy [*AN*,
     calamus aromaticus] ij
{dram} and iiij vncis of good lycorows sheryd and powderyd vse
this dradge At All tymys necessary

(32) f. 5 [rubric] ❡ **The quenys powder** [eVK2 5411.25]
Take gynger Synamun A galyngale an vnce Annes camy [camomile] And

ffenell Sedys of iche half An vnce long peper graynis [of paradise]
macis And nuttmugis of ich ij {dram} Sedwale a {dram} and powder
all these sottely and put ther ij ij [sic] pownd of whyte Suger
And Vse this powder After your meate And before At your
pleasure it may be takyn At All tymys it coumfortythe
mervelously the stomak And carmynatyth [disperses; *MED*, carminaten]
    wynd And
causyth good dygestion

(33) ff. 5r–v [rubric] ❡ **A powder tha** [sic] **seruythe for charquyncis**
    [*MED*, char de quince]
[f. 5v] Take cynamon An vnce And halffe / An vnce of gynger A quarter
of an vnce or halfe an vnce galyngale halfe An vnce clowys
macys nuttmugis of eche A quarter of An Vnce Spyknard lygnum
Aloes cardamun of iche of they A {dram} wayte that is v [illegible] in gowd
peper halfe an Vnce bett All these to gyther And sarce [strain] them And
put them into the Receyte befor Thes be the vertuys of thys electuary
it makyth good digestyoun in the stomake takyn ffastyng After
dyner or supper and puttyth away All fumosytes And wyndys
ffrom the hart and it stoppyth vomettis All fluxis And it is good
Agayn Ilica pastio [iliaca passio] which is a dissease betwyx the stomak
    and the [sic]
which is in the small bowell

(34) f. 5v [rubric] ❡ **A powder to be inbastyd with**
    A lytle thyne cotton And in A
    cappe the outward part callet [*OED*, calotte]
    and the inwarde sarcynet [fine silk; *MED*, sarsenet] **agaynst**
    colde disseasys of the hed [eVK25673.25]
Take of clowys of cubebys of Rosys the leuys and stycados [houseleek;
    Hunt, sticados] off
camemyll flowers of marieron [Hunt, marieron] of macys nuttmugis
    Rosemary
fflowers of Sandrake [S, sanguis draconis=sangdragon] of bay beryes
    excortycate and A lytle tor
rysyde [?] of storax calamynt of lignum Aloes of A iche the wayte
of on grotte powder these same sumwhat grossly And vsse them
As is befor wrytyn

(35) ff. 5v–6 [rubric] ¶ **A powder to Vse in your Sawcis**
And specially with fysche agaynst
coldnes of the stomake and Also
opulacouncis [oppilation] **in the lyft Syde**
Take of pure Synamun the wayte of ij grotis of coryander sede
preparyd the wayte of one grotte of fyne gynger lignum Aloes
galyngale Annes Sedys fenell Sedys ffenell Sedys [dittography] clowys
zedoary of iche ij peny Wayte of nuttmugis calamus Aromaticus
myntis hartis tong leuys the graynis of jeneper of the bark of
[f. 6] the Rotis of caperis of the barke of quyke beme of ich on peny wayght
of long peper of whyte peper of Rownd peper of iche the wayte of An ~~ob~~
    [*obolus*, halfpenny]
of fine gynger an vnce make a fyne powder

(36) f. 6r–v [section rubric missing; contents list: here folowith electuarys
and Syroppis and conserue and Ipocras]
[rubric] ¶ **A speciall electuary to conserue one in helth**
To defend from the palsy and to provoke
slepe it may not be takyn in iij monythes
At the lest After the confeccoun

Take Rubarbe	)	
olibanum	)	
Castory	) Off iche an vnce	
nuttmugis	)	
Nucys Indie [coconut;		
Hunt, nux Indica]	)	
Clowys	)	
Bay levys		)
Spiknard		)
Dill Sedys		)
Smallach sedys		) of iche {1/2} an vnce
Safferon		)
Basell Sedys		)
Alysander sedys		)
Annes sedys		)
ffenell Sedys		)
Neppe	)	
Calamynt	)	

Oryganum   ) of iche {1/2} An vnce
Isope   )
Rewe Sedys   )
Henbane Sedys   )
Whyte popy sedys   )
camphyr   ) of iche a drame
muske   )

Take a quart of Whyght wyne of Angoy And on pottell of cleane
[f. 6v] Claryfyed hony and make your Syrope wherewith your sayd
powder must be medelyd And oftyn tymes stere it

(37) f. 6v [new recipe, Latin; rubric is not red, paraph is lacking; not noted
in contents list]
[rubric] Aromaticoun Rosarum this coumforthe
         the stomake and Rebatythe [reduces] the heate
         of the lyuer & is a precyous thyng
Recipe rosarum   {dram} xv
Lignum Aloes   ) ana {dram} iij
Sandali citri   )
Lyquirece   {dram} viij
Cinamon elect   {dram} v
Macys galoffolarum   ana {dram} ij 1/2
Gum arabicis dragagante
      [S, dragance=serpentaria]   ana {dram} ij   {scruple} ij
Cardamorum   ) ana {dram} j
galunge   )
Spicys   {dram} ij
Musti   {scruple} ij
Ambre [ambergris; *MED, aumbre,* n.1]   {scruple} ij
Misci et fiat pulvus

(38) ff. 6v–7 [new recipe, Latin; rubric is not red, paraph is lacking; not
noted in contents list]
[rubric] Dia galange is for the wound
         in the stomake And for good digestioun
Recipe Cinamon   )
Galange   )
ʒenʒibris   )

spyce   )
Zeduary   ) ana {dram} {1/2}
Liquirece   )
storacis calamint [*AN*, storax
    calamint]   )
Rosis violarum   )
garyoffolorum   )
blata bazancis   [Blata bazancis, drug]
    of Byzantium; *AN*, Blacre
    bayzansye]   )
[f. 7] Rasure eboris [ivory]   {dram} iij
Mergaritarum   ) ana {dram} ij
Oss de corde cervi   )
Musti   ) ana {dram} j
Ambre   )
Lignum Aloes   {dram} iij
oniunis   ) Ana {dram} j
Sandalorum   )
Mysci et fiat pulvus

(39) ff. 7r–v [new recipe, Latin; rubric is not red, paraph is lacking; not noted in contents list]
[rubric] Dia Margareton

Recipe garyoffis   )
cinamoun   )
Spycys   )
galange   )
Lignum Aloes   ) ana {dram} iij
Trosisti [? troschiscus] de Aroden)
liquirece   )
trosysti [troche]   )
deaby [?]   )
Ciperi   [Daems, ciperus]   )
Spica   )
Aelicis   [CI, Alita holiok; Daems, alica])
nucis ing [? coconut; Hunt, Nux Indica])
Aliptunus[?]cate [? *AN*, Alipenius; Hunt,

Aleptafilus]   ) ana {dram} j
Macis Zeduary   )
Rubarbe   )
storacis   )
calamynt   )
Muste   )
Ambre   ) ana scruple} ij {1/2}
Cordamoun [AN, cardomoum]
    Leuistice [S, leuisticum=loueache]   )
Sem basyliconis [basil; AN, Semen basyliconys]   )
[f. 7v]   plate 6
ʒenʒyberys   )
Margaryt [pearls]   ) ana {dram} j
Oss de corde cerui   )
Rasure eborys   [shavings of ivory]   )
Blutyzancis [Blata bazancis, drug of
Byzantium; AN,
    Blacre bayzansye]   )
Camphore gre   [AN, camfore]   ) xi [measurement illegible]
Misci fiat pillus

(40) f. 7v [new recipe for lozenges and manus Christi, lacking paraph and
    rubric; not noted in contents list]   plate 6
Item you must take to euery iiij vncis of suger ij {demi} {dram} of powder And
So make your lozengis of manus crysti or What so euer you will with
Suger and Remember the perfeccoun of the suger ffor you must Sethe
your suger hyer for lozengis than you do for manus crysti And yf you
Will make manus {Christi} ye must When you haue Soode [p.part. of
    seethe] your suger As
Sone As you take it of the fyer put you[r] gowld in And so stere it
A good whyle and put your powder what So it be And when it
begynnyth to be cold then cast it vpoun your stonis well coueryd with
starch And when it is cold take it of your stonis

(41) f. 7v [rubric] ⸿ ffor to make Ipocras of pomegarnettis
    ffor them that be in An hote cawse   plate 6
Take the wyne of A good pomegarnet And medle it with asmoch
water of Rosys and put therto A good quantyte of manus {Christi} with

A few macIs And A lytyll galyngale grossly broke then put therto
Asmoch clarett wyne As you haue of wyne of pomegarnettis And of
Rose water and let them stand to gyther iij owers Afterward lett it rynne
throwe A Ipocras bagg

(42) ff. 7v–8 [rubric] ¶ **A Syrroppe ffor waykenes**
     o[f] the brayne   plate 6
Take an handfull of Rosemary A handfull of Sawge And An hand
ffull of margerom And A handfull of ysope And An handfull betayn
of the woode And the Rotis of piony And the sedys of the same piony
[f. 8] And take all the Sayd erbys and put them to gyther cleane
waschen in a pottell of fayre water And lett them seth to gyder
Vnto the on halfe be Sodyn Away and then take out the same erbys
cleane and put to the sayd water halfe A pynt or sumwhat lesse
of hony and claryfy it And let it Seth All to gyther And A dram
wayte of stycados [houseleek; Hunt, sticados] Knytt in a fayr lynyn clothe
     And let it Seth
in the Same tyll it haue A way the swettnes of the Same
hony And then take out the same stycados and put therto a quarter
of an vnce of gynger and A quarter of An vnce of Synamoun
And iij good nuttmugis well brosyd not all to powder And putt
them in the Same lycour And lett them sethe well to gyther A
good Whyle And then strayne it throwe A fayr lynyn clothe &
So Vse it to drynke euyn And morn blode warme

(43) ff. 8r-v [rubric] ¶ **ffor to make conserua citoniorum that is to**
     Say of quincis or diacitoricoun [*AN*, Diasitoniton] **whiche is**
     A lectuary to cast in bokis [jar; *MED*, box n.2] **And is callyd**
     charquyncis [char de quince] **and Also you make it in lozengis**
Take quincis As many As will please you quarter them pare them
and cut out cleane the corys boyle them tender and put them in
A baskett or colender to let the water Rynne clene from them
And to iiij pownd therof Take v pownd And A half of suger or
of claryfyed hony And [as] you will but they must fyrst be brayed
Small in A morter And straynyd As you know to parte the sto
nys And graynys from them / then put your suger made in powder
therto And boyle them vpon the fyer without flame And euer
stere it well A Bouie [above?] tyll you Se it gadyr well vpon the

styck ende So that you shall haue moche labour to stere yt
Then it is Well Also you may take A lytyll therof And lay it
Vpon a dyschys botom And let it cole and after be styff And
Sumwhat hard take it of the fyer and put this powder folowying
[f. 8v] Therin And stere them well to gyther and cast it into your bokys
Whylys it is soft and hote and if you will make it in lozengis
Anoynt your ston With Rose water And then cast it vpon And
bet it with a sklyse [spatula; *MED*, sclice] thynne and So cutt it in lozengis

(44) f. 8v [rubric] ⸿ **To make conserua of quikbeme**
Take v handfull of quykbeme [*OED*, rowan, service tree] beryes And on
      handfull of hartis
tong and half An handfull of the medle barke of An yong
Asche And A pottell of fayer Rynnyng water And Sett it on the
ffyer vnto the water be consumyd and let it be steryd that it bryn
not to the panne and After that strayn it And put to the lycour
ij {pound} and A half of Suger and So seth it to gyther And late it
be steryd well for fere of brynnyng And when it is as hye soden
As I sent to your ladysheppe And sumewhat hyer.

(45) f. 8v [rubric] ⸿ **A Conserua Agayn the Syknesse**
Take the quantyte of A small nut ij or iij tymys fastyng in
the weke howe be it / it ys very bytter wherfor it wold be the more
Redelier Receyvid down more ouer wormewood Juce myx withall &
Restyd in A close pott And drynk it ij tymys in the weke Suffre
no putryffacoun in the body Also endyve or dragon water with ij
Sponfull of vineger Asmoche And {1/2} A sponfull of good tryacle
Well myxed to gyther and drynke it in the begynnyng of the
Sykenesse kepyng them waytyng puttyng out the coruppcoun

f. 8v [section rubric] ⸿ **Here folowith medycyns for the pestylence**
(46) f. 8v [rubric] **A Souerayne medycyn for the pestylence** [eVK2 5315.75]
Take euery day fastyng iij levys of Rewe & on fyg or ij or iij or
iiij nuttis And Vse this in tyme of the plage

(47) ff. 8v–9 [rubric] ⸿ **A medycyn to putt fourth the pestylence**   plate 7
Take tryacle of Jene Sedwary fyne betyn brymston very fyne
[f. 9] And lyke quantyte temper them to gyther with tryacle

(48) f. 9 [rubric] ⸿ **A medycyn to preserve one from the**
pestylence And gret Syknes plate 7
Take tryacle of Jene Also Sedwary fyne betyn temper them to gyther
to preserue you ete of it euery second day or iij^de day And drynke Also
And Also walke Also be the space of half an ower

(49) f. 9 [see table 1] plate 7
[rubric] ⸿ **A medycyn for the pestylence**
This is the same medycyn that the kyng
Vsyd euery day which is profytable and hath
holpyn lxxj persons the last yere [eVK2 8253.50]
ffyrst you must take half a handfull of Rew An handfull of
marygowldis And half An handfull of sorell And A quantyte
of dragons of the croppe or of the Rote And then wasch this
~~water~~ cleane in fayer water and then take A pottell of Rynnyng
water And Seth thes to gyther from A pottell to A quart And
then strayn it throwe A fayer cloth And yf it be bytter putt therto
A quantyte of suger candy And if A man or A woman be syke
of the Syknes he or she must drynke or supp x tymys of it and
a person he or she be not syke then he nede not to drynke of it but
onys in the mornyng And yf he take it or [ere] the purpyllis Apere
ther is no perell ther by the grace of god

(50) f. 9 [rubric] ⸿ **A preseruacion Agaynst the pestylence**
And the gret Sykenesse plate 7
Take an vnce of sedwall A quarter of An vnce of bole armonyak
ij handfull of wormewood dryed and myngle All thes powders
to gyther And put them in A pott of new Ale of ij galon And
Set A new yest vpon it And lett it worke xxiiij^te owers And
drynke therof dayly fastyng the quantyte off iij or iiij spone
full And it shall preserve the

(51) ff. 9–9v [rubric] ⸿ **A drynke for the plage** plate 7
[f. 9v] Take an handfull of Sawge vertu A handfull of Sawge &
of erbe grace [rue; *OED*, herb-grace] And A handfull of elder leuvys And
      A handfull
brymble levis And A handfull of marygould flowers And
stampe them to gyther and strayn them throwgh A fayer

cloth with A quart of whyght wyne And then take A quan
tyte of fyne powder of gynger And A sponfull therof euery
day And After the fyrst sponfull you may contynue xxiiij days
And After the ix day shalbe swer [sure] for All the hole yere by ye
grace of god

(52) f. 9v [rubric] ❡ **ffor hym that is infect with the plage**
       before he hathe the drynke before sayd
Take A sponnefull of water of stabious And A sponnfull
of water of beten A good quantyte of fyne tryacle and myxe
them all to gyther and do them drynk it And it will cause
the venym to goo out And if it fortune the Sore to Apere
Then take brymbell leuys And ellder levis And musterd sede
and stamp them to gyther And make A playster of them And lay
it to the sore And it will cause the venym to come out or [ere] long
tyme be godys grace

(53) f. 9v [rubric] ❡ **A preseruatyve for the plage**
Take and egg of [*sic*] Rost it Rere / and than put therto A lytyll
tryacle of Jeane and onwrowght sulfur or ellis bole Armonyak
And ete it fastyng next your hart and it will preserve you
be the grace of god

(54) ff. 9v–10 [rubric] ❡ **This is A medycyne for the Infeccoun**
Take maywede [*OED*, mayweed; S, amerciosus=maythe] wormwood Rew
       Sauge gowldys [*OED*, gold n.2; *CI*, solsequium=goldes] Sume plan
tayn and bruse them And strayne them And put in a goode quan
tyte of tryacle And put therto stale Ale make powder of centory
And Asmoch fyne powder of brymston and put therto a good quan
[f. 10] tyte of it And gyve A lytyll to the patient and As oftyn tymis
As he may well broke it
Also it is good to lett them blode and Also not to let them slepe
xij owers After in no wyse

(55) f. 10 [rubric] ❡ **A nother good medycyn for the sayd dyssease**
ffyrst take marygowdys vineger and treacle And make A drynk
of them gyve ij it vnto the pacient ij or iij sponefull and
be goddis grace he shalbe hole

(56) f. 10 [rubric] ❡ **A gaynst the pestylence** [unclear if this corresponds to contents list]

Take Aloes well wasched

Myrre	an vnce
Mastyke	and vnce and {1/2}
Ynglysche safferon	2 peny wayte
nuttmugis	) of ich
Garyof that is clois [cloves]	) A pennyworth
Sinamoun	an vnce and {1/2}
Suger vi vncis [*sic*]	vj vncis

And myxte All thes to gyther with Syroppis of endyue & feme/tory\

f. 10 [section rubric] ❡ **Here folowith medycyns to make a
man or A woman to slepe**

(57) f. 10 [rubric] ❡**To make A man or a woman to slepe**
Take an handfull of wormewood and bray it and kepe the Juce
therof Then take iij or iiij eggis and put the whyghtis in a dysch
And bray it with a spone and take the fome therof and medle
it withe the Juce of the wormewoode to gyther take then A quan
tyte of newe made butter And melt it with ~~of~~ out the heate of any
ffyer and put them All to gyther and all to myxte them well &
lay it on a fayer clothe and make a playster therof and lay it
Aboute the tempullis of his hed and that shall cause hym to slepe

(58) ff. 10v–11 [rubric] ❡ **To make A man or A woman to slepe**

Take Rubarbe	)	
Olibanum	)	
Castory	) of iche	
Nuttmugis	) an vnce	
micis Indie [? coconut; Hunt, nux Indica]	)	
Alowes	)	
Bay levys	)	
Spiknard	)	
Annes Sedys	)	
Smallache sedys	)	
basell Sedys	) Off iche	
Alexander sedys	) {1/2} an vnce	
dyll Sedys	)	

ffenell sedys	)	
ynglysch safferoun	)	
Neppe	)	
Calamint	)	
Oryganum	) Off eche	
Isope	) on dram	
The sedys	)	
of Rewe	)	
popy sedes	)	
Hennebane	)	
Sedes	) On halfe vnce	
Campher	) of iche	
Muske	)	

[f. 11] Then take on quart of whyght wyne of Angy [Anjou] And A pottell of
claryfyed hony and make A syrroppe And the sayd ingrediens
Sotelly powderyd put to the same Syroppe and myxte them
to geder well in the maner of an Electuary inopyat And vse it
ffyrst And last After iij monythys At the erlyest yff it stond
vi monythys or [ere] it be occupyed it is the better

(59) f. 11 [rubric] ⸿ To cause A man or A woman [*to sleep*, according to
contents list]
Take yong elderburys Rede Rose flowers an handfull of iche
v croppis of camemell bruse them And A lytle powder of comyn
Sume vinegre And Sume letuce Juce vij Sponfull frye
thes with Vinegre And strewe theron powder of fenkell Sede
And make A fyllet [headband; *MED*, filet] playster and lay it to his
     tempullis and forehed
but lytyll warme and Just [correct; *MED*, just(e)]

f. 11 [section rubric] ⸿ **Here ffolowithe A specyall bakyng of oryngys**
(60) ff. 11–11v [rubric] ⸿ To bake oryngis [eVK2 4885.25]
Take A sharpe knyffe And ouer pare your oryngys Rownd about
So that you do but pare Away only the thyn Red pyll than
gyve euery orynge iiij gasshes and put them in A fayer panne
with A lytyll water or ellis in a lytyll chapher And pott And
when they haue So Sodyn A good whyle chaunge them into a
newe Sethyng water and So serue them v Sundry tymys

At the lest measuryng the lengh euery tyme betwyn the sethyng
And chaungyng of your waters As your oryngys do wax soft
And when you shall put them in the last water take out All the
corys At the forsayd gasshes and put in that water amongs
A good dele of hony the Same to be measuryd After the quantyte
of the water And Also After the number of the oryngis and lett
them Seth So to gyther A praty [little; *OED*, praty b.] Whyle and After
    put them
[f. 11v] In your coffyns And fyll euery coffyn full of Suger and So bake
    them
It is to be consyderyd that the oftyn chaungyng of Waters takyth A
Way the bytternesse of the oryngys And yf your waters that you chaun
ge them into be not Always sethyng hote yt shall be then moche the
Lenger or [ere] your oryngys be Redy
And yf you will do more cost Vpon your oryngys you may conserue them
In the water with Suger And not with hony And So it is best And
Also yf you lyft to hard your coffyns fyrst in the oven you may put Rose
    water
or water of damaske with your Suger in to the coffyns And So bake
them or ellis you may At A lytyll hoole to be made At A lytyll hole [sic
    dittography] in
the toppe of the coffynis put in such water when they be bakyd And powre
out the other lycour that was in the coffynis
[l. margin: *theryac* in later hand]

(61) f. 11v [rubric] ❡ **Yf you will make cownfettis** [*OED*, comfit]
ffyrst you make seth your Suger to a lowe perfeccoun And then take your
Sedys or what you will make counfettis of And dry it vpon your fyer
in your panne that you will cast your counfettis in And when they are
dry then take a Ladyll And fyll it with your suger that you Soode be
ffore And lett A nother powre it vpon your Sedys and So cast your
Sedys euer when he doth put Suger And so when he hath put All the suger
out of the ladell then cast them vpon the fyer tyll they be hard &
put a nother ladylfull of Suger Agayn And So Do tyll you[r] sedys
be well and then put then [sic] in a fayr coffyn well paperred

(62) ff. 11v–12 [rubric] ❡ **ffomigacoun**   fig. 7
Recipe lapdani [*AN*, lapdanum])

storacis	)		
Calamynt	) Ana {dram} {1/2}		
Olibani	)		
Cinamoun	)		
[f. 12] Lygnum Aloes	) Ana {dram} ij		fig. 7
Garyoffeles	)		
Masticis	) Ana {ounce} {1/2}		
Calobre [AN, clobre]	)		
Lauendulie		) Ana {dram} ij	
Rosys maryn		)	
Musti dragagant	) {dram} {1/2}		
Dragagant	)		

Item put Rose water And So lett your dragagant Satell [*OED*, settle] After
you haue powderyd your other thyngis And So medle them to gyther
And then make your fomigacoun As you haue Sene them And So lett
them dry And So put in the fyer And so lyght them And it will put
A way yll savours

(63) f. 12 [rubric] ❡ **To make oreniette**   fig. 7
Take the pyllys of oryngis And lay them in water ix days or x and
chaunge them euery day with fresche water then boyle them in water tyll
they be tender then put them in A wycken baskett to lett the lycour rynn
ffrom them And let them stand So A day and A nyght then take hony
or syroppe made of course hony And lett them lye therin vi or sevyn
Days to the Syroppe or hony be ryght thynne for in that tyme it will
drawe out And Suke out well the water then lett the Syrroppe Rynne
ffrom the pylys And boyle your hony or Syrrop on the fyer Agayn
tyll A droppe therof stand perfyttly on your nayle Agayne without
Rynnyng And that is the perfeccoun of euery Syroppe in the sethyng
And when the Syropp is cold put your pylys of Oryngis Agayn ther
in And neuer When the Syrroppe is hote for that wold make the[m] towgh
And hard And thus you must chaunge your Syrroppe iij or iiij tymis
And then put it to a fynne Syrroppe and so you may kepe it iiij or v ꝟere

(64) ff. 12–12v [rubric] ❡ **brackett with Ale and SpycIs**   fig. 7
[f. 12v Upper margin: pen testing; Manus Christi in later hand]   plate 8
[f. 12v] [second rubric] ❡ **Diuysyd for my lady the Kyngis gramother**
[eVK2 5611.75]

Take macys clowys of eche ij grotte wayte ffyne galingale iij grote
wayte graynnys [of paradise] iiij grote wayte long peper iij grote wayte
gynger iiij grote wayte nuttmugis Asmoch spyknard ij grotte wayte
barberys iiij grote wayte comynis sede caroway Sede Annes Sede
of ich A grote wayte Sedwale ij grote wayte bruse All grosly put
All in ij baggis be euyn porcioun And put the halfe in on pott han
gyng in the same bag by A threde to the medyll of the pott con
taynyng v or vj galouns of good Ale with A pynt of fyne hony
well claryfyed from his feces and medle the hony and the Ale in
perfytly to gyther and then put in your spycis As Aboue sayd and lett
it so Rest At the lest iiij or v days And drynke of it fastyng & Also
before your supper A good drawght Will coumfort your stomake And
breke the wyndynes of the same And After this make your other pott
     with
the tother halfe of spycis yf you please to make this drynke A lytle lax
easly put to halfe A pott an vnce of fyne turbytt clensyd within And with
out And so I trust it shalbe A good drynke to your pleasure

(65) f. 12v [rubric] ¶ To make manus cristi in A fluxe [eVK2 5676.25]

plate 8

Take of fyne Red corall the wayte of vj pennys of good cynamon
The wayte of on grote of perle the wayte of ij {dram} powder these ech
on be them Selfe As sotelly As canne be And take of the levys off
gowld i {dram} of whyte suger on quart dyssolve the gynger with Rose
     water
wherin you haue Infusyd be the space of A day of Red saunders And of
Lapides emathytes [hematite; *MED*, ematites] of iche grossly powderyd ij
     peny wayght And
then the water straynyd dyssolue your suger And cast your manus
     {Christi} /be craft\

(66) ff. 12v–13 [rubric] ¶ To make A good gely [eVK2 4735.50]   plate 8

[f. 13]

Take a knokyll of vele And A lyrypece [tail? *OED*, Liripipe] of beffe Seth
     them in
Whyte wyne to gyther tyll they be very tender then take up ye
fflesche And make the broth cleane without falt And take tronsell [*OED*,
     turnsole]

And lay it in A pynt of vineger And lett it lye the space of An owr
And more then wryng it out cleane into the vineger and put All
to gyther in to the brothe Than tak Synamoun A grett quantyte
And gynger leffe And A praty quantyte of graynis [of paradise] And Also
    A
lytyll clowys And macis And A praty porcyon of safferoun And A
grete dele of suger then put in the whyght of vi eggis then sett it
vpon the fyer All to gyther And lat it boyle A lytyll than take it of
And lat it stond A whyle then put it in your bag And when it is
Rynne moche you may hete it Agayne

(67) f. 13 [rubric] ¶ To make salet oyle of walnuttis
Take walnuttis throwe drye the elder the better for yf they be grene they
Will gyve mylke And non oyle crack them And stampe the kyrnellis
Small that you can not perceyve by the pomys [pulp; *MED*, pomis] what
    it is then put
them in A canvas bagg And pl [*sic*] presse them hard And so you shall
haue oyle but you must fyrst weate your bagg and wryng it very
hard or ellis Take A brasse pott full of water and sett it on the fyre
And let it sethe then take your nuttis when they be stampyd As
it is Aboue Wrytyn And put them into A pott of peuter or of sylver
And put it into the pott of sethyng water And couer it close that
no water Rynne In And lett it seth tyll the nuttis be throwe
warme And then put them in your bag And presse them

(68) ff. 13r–v: [rubric] ¶ To make oyle of quyncis
Take All the hole quyncis withe the paryngis An coueryngis that
they be lytyll And half Rype and bett them Small of what
quantyte you will And take Asmoche of the Juce of quyncis and
[f. 13v] put therto oyle olyff in A suffycent quantyte As you make oyle
of Rosys And Sett All to gyther in A glass xv days in the
hote sonne then boyle them in A fayer vessell with water iiij owrs
And then strayne it then put to the Same oyle So moch quyncis
brosyd and Juce An So Sett it in the Sonne Agayn other
xv days And After that boyle it in water iiij owers And then stra
yne it And thus Renewe it iij or iiij tymys At the last ster
yt Reserve it to your vse And yf you make it in wynter boyle it
many dyuerse days in water iiij or v owers and So with

labour it may be made perfytt this tyme of the ʒere but ye quincis must be of the grenest that you can gett

[f. 13v] [section rubric] ❡ **Here folowith medycynis for the hed**
  Ache and the mygrym
(69) f. 13v [rubric] ❡ **ffor the hed Ache**
Take the Juce of Celedony And Vinegre And mengle to gyther And made hote wherin put A spunge or A lynyn clothe And lay it to the forhed and it quenchyth the grett heate And preserue yt that it comyth no more

(70) f. 13v [rubric] ❡ **A nother for the Same**
Take pympernell And Powunde yt and put thereto may butter And ffry them on A soft fyer And strayne it And kepe it And Anoint the forehed and tempullis

(71) f. 13v [rubric] ❡ **ffor the mygryme hed ach or**
  Any other payne in the hed
Take a slyse of fresch beff iij fyngers brode So that it Rechith ffrom the on ere to the othyr ouer the forehed cast powder of [illegible] theron And with your hand patt it on And bynd it fast unto ye forehed in on nyght this shall helpe

[Part II ends here; the rubrics for texts on the missing leaves, f. 14 (and f. 15?), survive in the contents list (Part II, f. ii verso; see above). The thirteen missing recipes there listed included additional headache remedies, purgatives, medicines for diarrhea, and recipes for jaundice and morphea.]

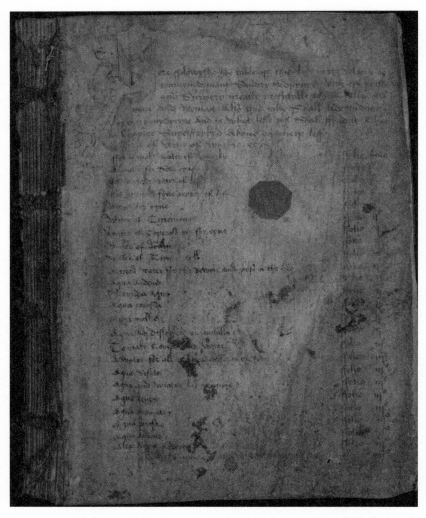

Plate 1. Berkeley Castle Muniments, Select Book 89, Part I, , f. [i], first leaf, containing arms, scrollwork letter "h," prologue, and beginning of contents list for Part I.

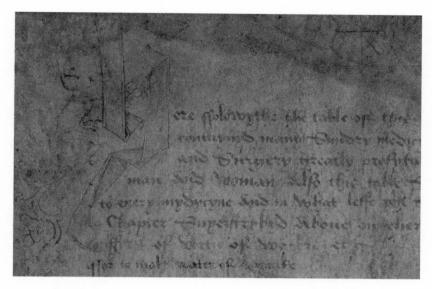

PLATE 2.A. Berkeley Castle Muniments, Select Book 89, Part I, f. [i], detail of scrollwork letter "h," arms, and prologue.

PLATE 2.B. Berkeley Castle Muniments, Select Book 89, Part I, f. 1, detail of oak leaf initial letter "T."

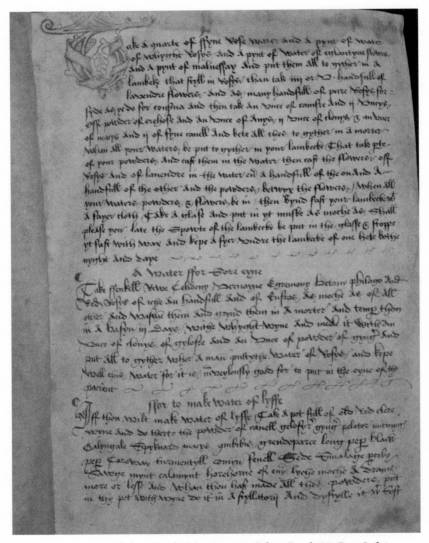

PLATE 3. Berkeley Castle Muniments, Select Book 89, Part I, f. 1,
recipes for three distilled waters: "of damaske," "ffor Sore eyne,"
"of lyffe" (beginning).

PLATE 4.A. Shield of arms of John de Vere, thirteenth Earl of Oxford, impaling the arms (Scrope, *azure a bend or*, quartering Tiptoft, *argent a saltire engrailed gules*), of his second wife, Lady Elizabeth Scrope, Countess of Oxford (d. 1537). Oxford, Bodleian Library, MS Ashmole 1504, f. 48v.

PLATE 4.B. Garter stall plate of John, fifth Lord Scrope of Bolton, from William H. St John Hope, *The Stall Plates of the Order of the Garter: 1348-1485* (London, 1901), plate 70

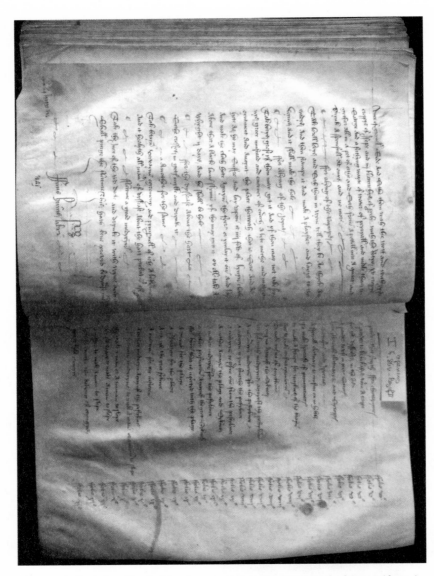

PLATE 5. Berkeley Castle Muniments, Select Book 89, end of Part I (f. 86v), beginning of Part II, showing stub and first surviving leaf (f. [ii]) of Part II.

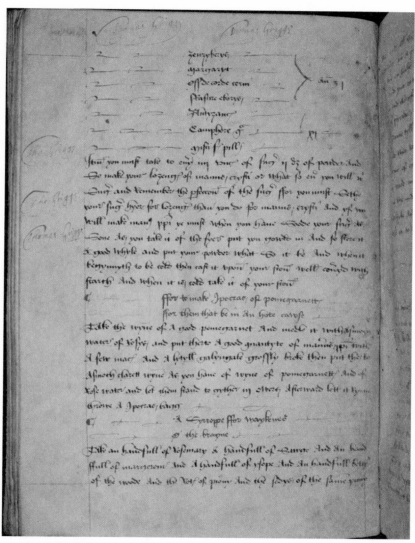

Plate 6. Berkeley Castle Muniments, Select Book 89, Part II, f. 7v, recipes: (no. 39) Dia Margareton (end), showing tabular format and apothecary symbols; (no. 40) manus crysti (without rubric); (no. 41) Ipocras of pomegarnettis; and (no. 42) Syrroppe ffor waykenes o[f] the brayne (beginning); "Thomas Griggs" (later hand) noted in margins.

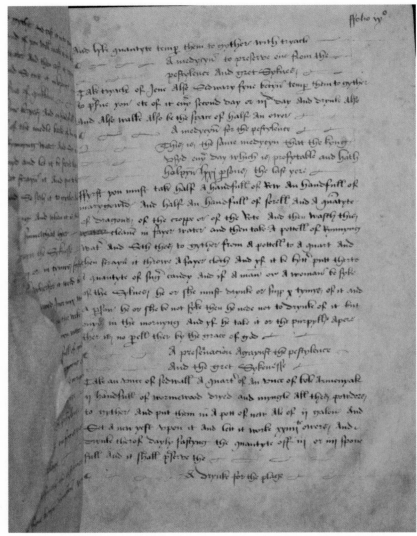

Plate 7. Berkeley Castle Muniments, Select Book 89, Part II, f. 9, recipes: (no. 47) to putt fourth the pestylence (end), (no. 48) to preserve one from the pestylence And gret Syknes, (no. 49) A medycyn for the pestylence . . . that the kyng Vsyd . . . , (no. 50) A preseruacion Agaynst the pestylence And the gret Sykenesse, and (no. 51) A drynke for the plage (rubric only).

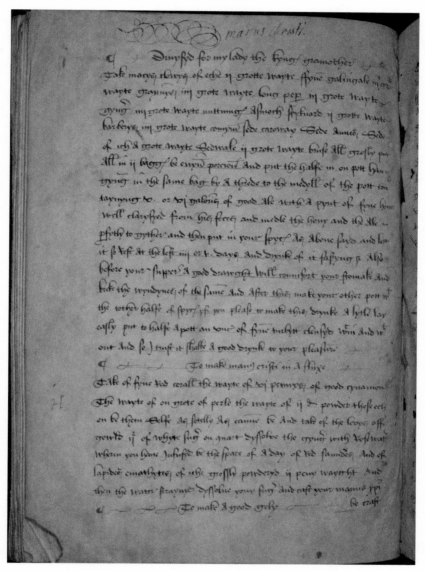

PLATE 8. Berkeley Castle Muniments, Select Book 89, Part II, f. 12v, recipes: (no. 64) Diuysyd for my lady the Kyngis gramother, (no. 65) To make manus cristi in A fluxe, and (no. 66) To make A good gely (rubric only); "manus christi" (in upper margin; later hand); see also fig. 7 for the first of two rubrics for no. 64.

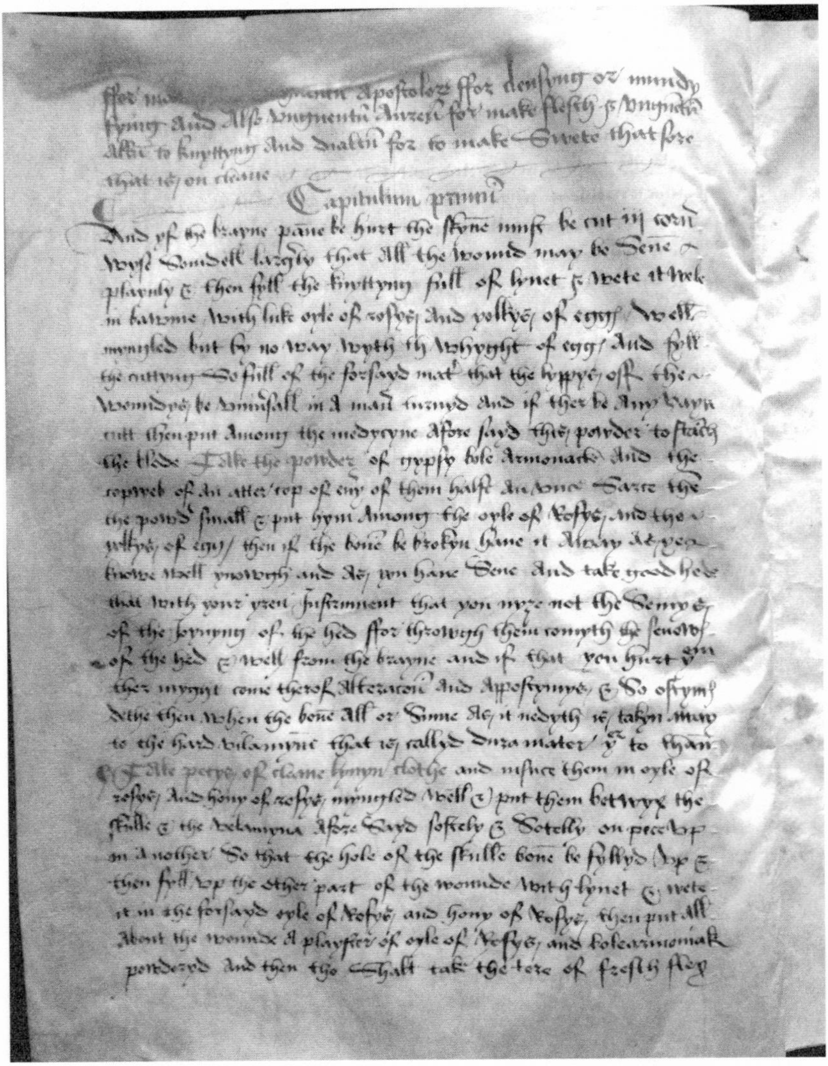

Fig. 1. Berkeley Castle Muniments, Select Book 89, Part I, f. 14v, five ointments text (conclusion, in red) and beginning of wounds text.

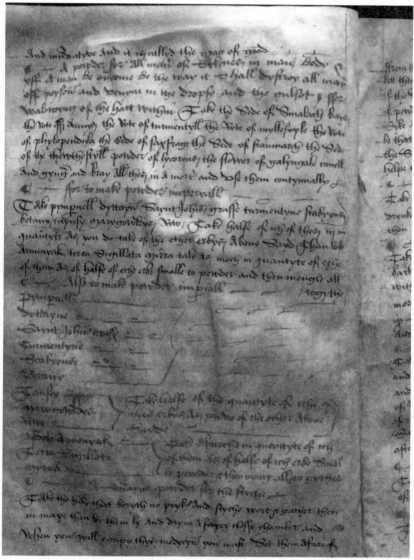

FIG. 2. Berkeley Castle Muniments, Select Book 89, Part I, f. 41v, recipes: "gratia dei" (last line), "powder for all maner of Sykenes," "powder imperyall" (two copies, the second in red), "souerayne powder for the styche" (beginning).

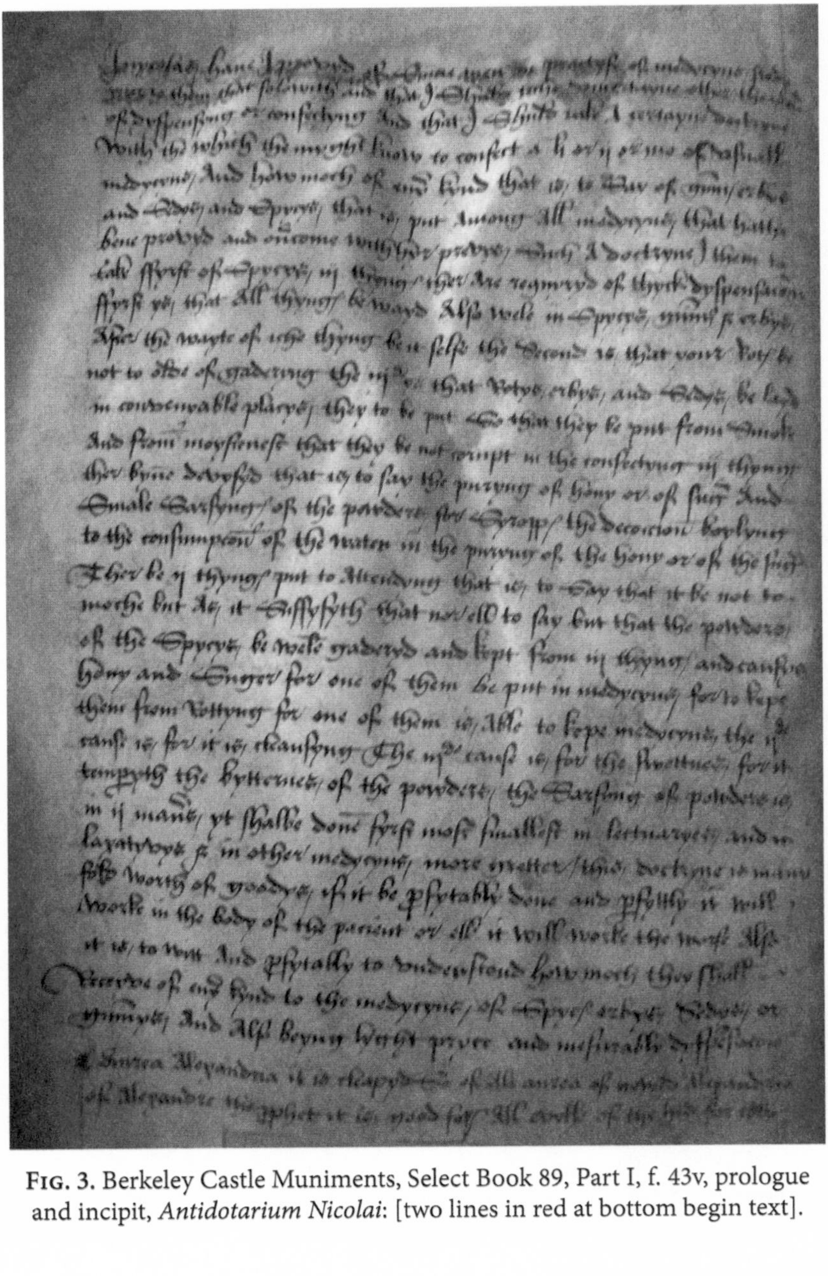

FIG. 3. Berkeley Castle Muniments, Select Book 89, Part I, f. 43v, prologue and incipit, *Antidotarium Nicolai*: [two lines in red at bottom begin text].

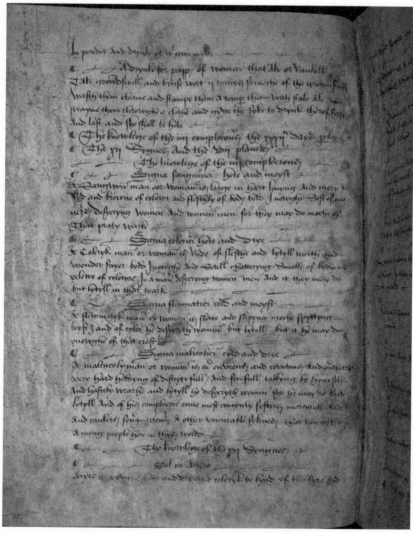

Fig. 4. Berkeley Castle Muniments, Select Book 89, Part I, f. 77v, last two recipes in *receptarium* A, "ffor lack of mylk to an nurce" (end) and "A drynke for pappis of women"; text beginning with complexions based on humoral dominance and addressing humours, signs of zodiac, and planets; scraped legal jottings, temp. Elizabeth I, in left margin.

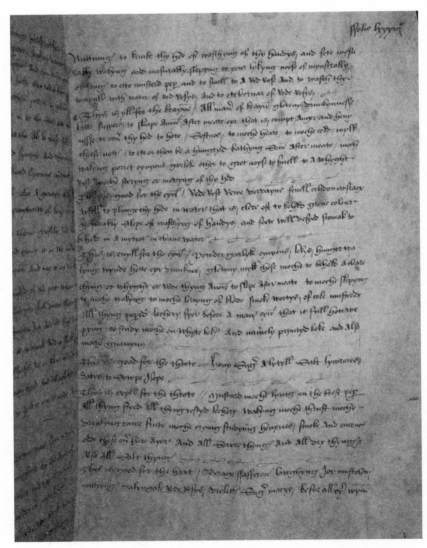

Fig. 5. Berkeley Castle Muniments, Select Book 89, Part I, f. 83, *De conferentibus* including sections "good for the eyne" and "euyll for the eyne."

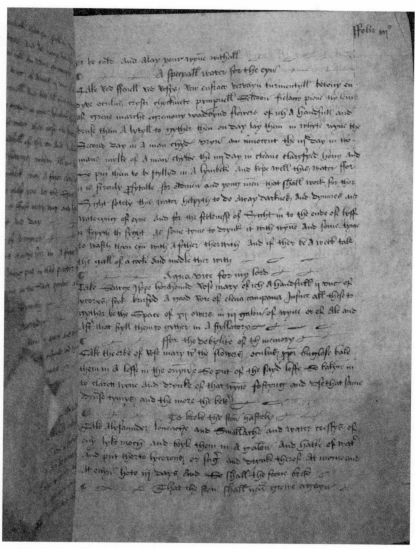

Fig. 6. Berkeley Castle Muniments, Select Book 89, Part II, f. 3, recipes: (no.12) water ffor to Alay your wyne with (end), (no. 13) A specyall water for the eyne, (no. 14) Aqua vite for my lord, (no. 15) ffor the debylite of th[e] memory, (no. 16) To breke the ston hastely, and (no. 17) That the ston shall neuer growe agayn (rubric only).

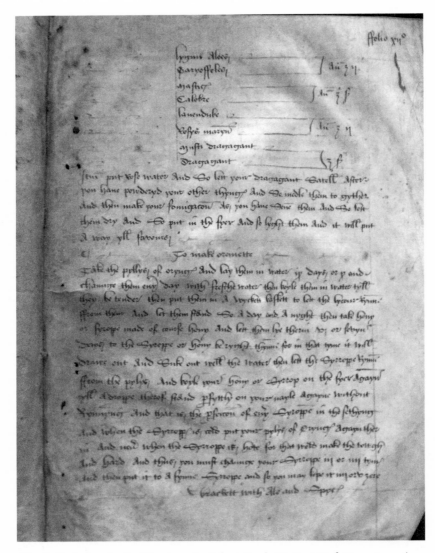

Fig. 7. Berkeley Castle Muniments, Select Book 89, Part II, f. 12, recipes: (no. 62) ffomigacoun (end), showing tabular format and apothecary symbols; (no. 63) To make oreniette; and (no. 64) brackett with Ale and Spycis (rubric only; see also plate 8 for second rubric and recipe text on f. 12v).

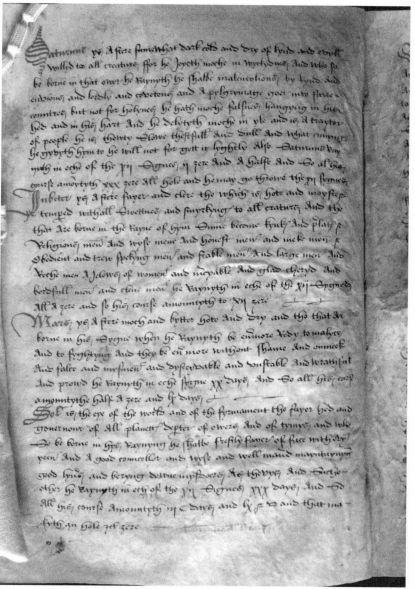

Fig. 8. Berkeley Castle Muniments, Select Book 89, Part I, f. 78v, Planetenkinder for "Saturnus," "Jubiter," "Mars," and "Sol" (showing scribal decorative red initials).

Fig. 9. Monumental Brass of Lady Elizabeth Scrope (d. 1537), widow of John de Vere, thirteenth Earl of Oxford, in Wivenhoe Church, Essex.

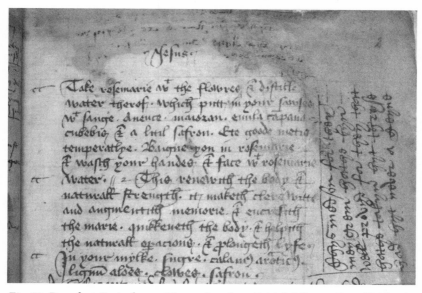

Fig. 10. Beaufort-Beauchamp Hours. London, British Library, Royal MS 2 A. xviii, f. 2 (flyleaf), detail of medical recipe in script similar to Berkeley Castle Muniments, Select Book 89.

Fig. 11. London, British Library, Arundel MS 130, f. 1, shield of arms of Henry Algernon Percy, fifth Earl of Northumberland, at the beginning of a Breviary, after 1489.

"It's good to talk: conversations between gods, men and beasts in Early Modern English versions of Lucian's 'Dialogues'"[*]

Paul Hartle
St Catharine's College, University of Cambridge

THE "very *Proteus* of Wit"; thus Ferrand Spence, in the "Epistle Dedi-catory" to his five-volume complete translation of Lucian, published in 1684–1685.[1] While the phrase may sound merely conventional, in Lucian's case it has a peculiar appropriateness, because, pre-eminently among classical writers, the Greek satirist, so popular in the long Renais-sance, so almost unread since, is—to adapt Falstaff's account of Mistress Quickly—"neither fish nor flesh; a man knows not where to have [him]."[2] Janus-faced, Lucian provokes a combination of admiration and revulsion from the moment when his works first enter the marketplace of print (in Latin translation) in about 1470; between 1496 and 1550, the original

---

[*] Note: As the result of a series of miscommunications between AMS and the editors of SMRH, the images that were meant to be printed with Paul Hartle's article were left out of the pages of SMRH, Third Series, Volume 11. We are thus reprinting the article as a courtesy.

[1] *Lucian's Works, Translated from the Greek . . . by Ferrand Spence*, 5 Vols. (1684–85), Vol. 1, sig. C3ᵛ.

[2] *1 Henry 4*, 3.iii.127–28 (eds. S. Wells and G. Taylor, William Shakespeare, *The Complete Works*, (Oxford, 1988), 472).

Studies in Medieval and Renaissance History, 3rd Series, Vol. 12 (2016)

Greek text was printed more than sixty times, while the number of Latin versions exceeded two hundred by the same date:[3] Lucian was hot. For the humanists of the early sixteenth century, his witty and elegant prose offered a welcome model for young scholars: carefully expurgated selections were on the syllabus of the grammar schools of Winchester, Canterbury, Westminster, Eton, and St. Paul's,[4] but while Thomas Linacre (who taught Greek to Thomas More) encouraged students of the language to "read a little Lucian every day,"[5] in his *A New Catechism* (c.1560) Thomas Becon advised his exclusion from the curriculum as "wicked and ungodly."[6] In *The Boke Named the Governour* (1531), Sir Thomas Elyot (the probable translator of the first English version of the Dialogue *Cynicus*),[7] aimed to strike a balance:

> The next lesson wolde be some quicke and mery dialogues, elect out of Luciane, whiche be without ribawdry, or to moche skorning, for either of them is exactly to be eschewed, specially for a noble man, the one anoyeng the soule, the other his estimation concerning his gravitie . . . thus moche dare I say, that it were better that a childe shuld never rede any parte of Luciane than all Luciane.[8]

The problem was simple: not only did Lucian scoff directly at Christianity itself, but his scabrous mockery of both pagan religions and moral philosophy might be seen to offend against all sense of religious or ethical value. In Dryden's words (borrowed without acknowledgement from one of Lucian's editors, Gilbert Cousin),[9] "he doubted of every thing; weigh'd all Opinions, and adher'd to none of them; only us'd them, as

---

[3] See Christopher Robinson, *Lucian and His Influence in Europe* (Chapel Hill, 1979); C. R. Thompson, *The Translations of Lucian by Erasmus and St. Thomas More* (Ithaca, 1940), 3.

[4] Brenda M. Hosington, "'Compluria Opuscula Longe Festivissima': Translations of Lucian in Renaissance England," in Dirk Sacre and Jan Papy, eds. *Syntagmatia: Essays on Neo-Latin Literature in Honour of Monique Mund-Dopchie and Gilbert Tournoy* (Leuven, 2009), 187–205, at 194.

[5] Douglas Duncan, *Ben Jonson and the Lucianic Tradition* (Cambridge, 1979), 26.

[6] Duncan, *Ben Jonson and the Lucianic Tradition*, 82.

[7] See C. R. Thompson, ed., *Works of St. Thomas More* (New Haven, 1963–), vol. 3 Part 1 (1974), 140–41.

[8] Foster Watson, ed., *The Governour* (London, 1907), 36.

[9] See Duncan, *Ben Jonson and the Lucianic Tradition*, 50.

they serv'd his occasion for the present Dialogue; and perhaps rejected them in the next."[10] Whilst one admirer might write of him, "deos . . . et ridet et lacerat,"[11] that too readily transmuted into "[Deum] et ridet et lacerat." That particular admirer was Erasmus, and it is in him and his friend Thomas More that Lucian found his greatest humanist advocates. Each translated several dialogues, working in tandem, and their Latin versions were among the most often reprinted of their works in their lifetimes. For More, dedicating his *Cynicus* (and it was More's Latin that Elyot rendered English) to Thomas Ruthall, Henry VII's Royal Secretary, Lucian ranks among the foremost of those "qui Horatianum praeceptum impleuerit, uoluptatemque cum utilitate coniunxerit."[12] In *Utopia*, Hythloday assures us, the natives are "delyted wyth Lucianes mery conceytes and jestes."[13]

For Erasmus and More, Lucian offered a model of a space for independent thinking that might be opened by the form of dialogue, together with a brilliance in the deployment of irony which Dryden (no mean exponent himself) later acknowledged: "[N]o Man is so great a Master of Irony, as our Author: That Figure is not only a keen, but a shining Weapon in his Hand; it glitters in the Eyes of those it kills, his own God's his greatest Enemies, are not butchered by him, but fairly slain: they must acknowledge the Heroe in the stroke."[14] Lucian's influence on *Utopia* and *The Praise of Folly* is profound, not in local detail alone, but in the protean quality of those works, which dare to trifle with both secular and sacred authority in challenges whose humor disarms censure. In the ecclesiastical and monarchical context of the time, such challenges were dangerous—"circa Regna tonat," as Wyatt wrote, quoting Seneca's *Phaedra*—thunder surrounds the throne.[15]

Later sixteenth- and early seventeenth-century writers manifest the same divided response as their predecessors, although (as Gabriel Harvey

---

[10] *The Works of Lucian, translated from the Greek, by several eminent hands* (1711), 4 Vols., "The Life of Lucian," 1:26.

[11] Thompson, *The Translations of Lucian*, 21. Thompson gives the fullest account available of the two humanists' engagement with Lucian.

[12] More, *Works*, 3, 1:2.

[13] John O'Hagan, ed., and Raphe Robinson, trans., (1551), *Utopia* (London, 1910), 82.

[14] "The Life of Lucien," 42–43.

[15] The refrain of 'Who lyst his welthe and eas Retayne', in Kenneth Muir and Patricia Thomson, eds., *Collected Poems of Sir Thomas Wyatt* (Liverpool, 1969), 187–88.

commented in 1580), "*Lucian* [is] never so much" "studyed, as [he was] wonte"[16]—perhaps being placed on the first *Index Librorum Prohibitorum* in 1559 might have discouraged some.[17] Thomas Nashe finds him "admirably blest in the abundant giftes of art and nature [and yet an] abhominable Atheiste;"[18] In 1621 Richard Brathwaite casts "*Lucian* a professed enemy to Christ" as addressee of his "Third Satyre. Of Atheisme," condemning "thy lascivious works" in a tone more of sorrow than anger, since "*Ingenious* Lucian" is "*in all Morall knowledge excellent.*"[19] Even the fiercely virtuous Samuel Sheppard, whose "*Lucians memoriall*" consigns Lucian to a Hades where "fishes worrie / Thy Ravens Soule" while "all the deathlesse Dieties [sic] / Laugh at thy dolor," in another epigram acknowledges "thy wilie hand" and "applaud[s] thy wit."[20]

---

[16]   Duncan, *Ben Jonson and the Lucianic Tradition*, 84. Stern records Harvey's copy of Lucian, in the four-volume edition (Basle, 1563) by Gilbert Cousin [Gilbertus Cognatus], books which Harvey was to forfeit to Edmund Spenser, should Harvey fail to read several comical works in English (including Skelton) lent to him by the poet, on condition that he completed reading them over the last twelve days of 1578 (Virginia F. Stern, *Gabriel Harvey: A Study of His Life, Marginalia, and Library* [Oxford, 1979], 226, 228). Harvey was nonetheless keen to use Lucian's atheism as a stick with which to beat his own pamphleteering enemies, Robert Greene and Thomas Nashe. Greene he castigates as "a derider of all religions: a contemner of God, and man: a desperate Lucianist: an abhominable Aretinist: an Arch-Athiest [sic]:" (G. B. Harrison, ed., *Foure Letters and certeine Sonnets* [London, 1922], 40); Harvey's term "Lucianist" had been in use from 1573 (John Bridges, *The supremacie of Christian princes*, 354) and was still current in 1655 (Alexander Ross, *Pansebeia, or, A view of all religions in the world*, 234). Nashe's writings "sauour wholty of the same Lucianicall breath" (*Pierces Supererogation* (1593),135–36); this second adjective (which may be Harvey's coinage) is also found in Robert Parsons, *A manifestation of the great folly and bad spirit of certayne in England* (1602), 92. The notorious charge of atheism levelled against Marlowe is also expressed in terms of Harvey's glancing identification with the Greek writer: "Though *Greene* were a Iulian, and *Marlow* a Lucian: yet I would be loth, *He* [Nashe] should be an Aretin" (*A New Letter of Notable Contents* [1593], sig. Dʳ).

[17]   Hosington, "Compluria Opuscula Longe Festivissima," 188. Harvey himself characterized Lucian in 1592 as one of "that whole venemous and viperous brood, of old & new Raylers" (*Foure Letters*, 15).

[18]   R. B. McKerrow, ed., revised by F. P. Wilson, *The Works of Thomas Nashe* (Oxford, 1966), 5 vols., 1:285.

[19]   *Natures Embassie* (Boston, Lincs., 1877), 86, 93, 87.

[20]   Samuel Sheppard, *Epigrams theological, philosophical, and romantick* (1651), "The Third Book: Epig. 23" (52); "The Fourth Book: Epig. 5," "*On* Lucians *true History*," 72.

However, these are for the most part passing remarks. What I want to focus on now is the major task of bringing Lucian to an English readership.[21] This was work barely begun until the second quarter of the seventeenth century saw the posthumously published selections penned by Francis Hickes (eight dialogues and the *True Historie*),[22] and by Thomas Heywood (fifteen dialogues).[23] Only *Timon, or the Man-hater* is common to both writers. Heywood, a veritable factory of Early Modern literary production, concentrates on the *Dialogues of the Gods* (nine, including *The Judgment of Paris*) and is careful to exclude scatology and too much bawdry, while affixing a moralistic "Argument" to each; the two dialogues dealing with Jupiter's abduction of Ganymede, teasingly erotic in Lucian, are decisively labelled *"Joves Masculine love this Fable reprehends"* and *"Base sordid lust in man [this Fable] reprehends."*[24] Like many before him, Heywood regrets that Lucian's atheism damns his talent, offering this elegy in *The Hierarchie of the Blessed Angells* in 1635:

> Yet for the love I to his learning owe,
> This funerall Farewell I on him bestow.
> Unhappy *Lucian*, what sad passionate Verse
> Shall I bestow upon the marble stone
> That covers thee? How shall I deck thy Herse?[25]

Francis Hickes was brought up as an arras-maker, and the family held supervisory office to maintain the royal tapestries. But he appears to have spent his later years in *"a countrie retirement,"* translating Thucydides and Herodian in addition to Lucian out of *"a true love[r] of Schollers,*

---

[21] See Hosington, "Compluria Opuscula Longe Festivissima," 193–99. For more general surveys of Lucian's influence in Britain, see Gilbert Highet, *The Classical Tradition* (Oxford, 1949), esp. 123–24, 304–5; J. A. K. Thomson, *The Classical Background of English Literature* (London, 1948), 129–30, 139–41, and *Classical Influences on English Prose* (London, 1956), 193–206, 273–74); Peter France, ed., *The Oxford Guide to Literature in English Translation* (Oxford, 2000), 390.

[22] *Certaine Select Dialogues of Lucian: Together with his True Historie, Translated from the Greeke into English* (Oxford, 1634).

[23] *Pleasant Dialogues and Dramma's, Selected out of Lucian, Erasmus, Textor, Ovid, &c* (1637).

[24] Heywood, *Pleasant Dialogues*, 96, 101.

[25] *The Hierarchie of the Blessed Angells* (1635), 1:506–10 (14).

and Learning," albeit "*indeed no profest scholler*" himself.[26] In his prefatory "Life," Hickes proclaims his aim that Lucian be "in some sort vindicated from certaine grosse Aspersions, heretofore cast upon him" (sig. B[r]); while he cannot deny Lucian's blasphemy, "*that his whole workes so much admired and approv'd of by the most learned in all ages, both for wit and language should be therefore utterly banisht from the world, and condemn'd to a perpetuall obscurity, or those parts of him denied the light in which there is no such impietie found, but on the contrary, many rules and documents both of vertue and good learning . . . seemes unto mee a most unjust, and partiall censure*" (sig. [B3][r/v]). Therefore, he concludes, "*it is no such impious thing, as some of the rigid censurers of these times would persuade us, to make a good use even of the worst Writers, yea and that if occasion serve, in matter of divinity*" (sig. [B3][v]). Improbably, Lucian the skeptic steps into the pulpit.

Hickes's versions were reissued in 1663 and 1664 accompanying Jasper Mayne's more substantial and complementary *Part of Lucian Made English*, translations actually completed, according to Mayne whose word there is no cause to doubt, a quarter of a century earlier at Christ Church Oxford, forming a composite volume which can for the first time claim to be an English Lucian, the dignity of which is attested both by its publication at Oxford, bearing the University's arms on its title page, and by William Faithorne's serene bust of the satirist, who gazes directly at the reader, presented without embarrassment as "*sharpe* Lucian *who reform'd y[e] Times.*"[27] Mayne dedicated his work to the duke of Newcastle, a royalist peer whose sufferings for the Stuarts were recognized at the Restoration, but even in the looser moral climate of the time, his long and careful "Epistle Dedicatory" bears witness to his sense of the risk incurred in publishing his Lucian, now that he is no longer an Oxford student but archdeacon of Chichester and chaplain to Charles II:

> *For if I be thus censured for turning a few pieces of him into* English
> *. . . your* Excellency *knowes, I was no* Divine, *but a* young Student *of*

---

[26]   See *ODNB*; [Thomas] Hickes, "To the Honest and Judicious Reader," sig. A3[r].

[27]   *Part of Lucian made English from the Originall. In the Yeare 1638* (Oxford, 1663), Plate facing title page. Faithorne's bust became the model for the plate in the two editions of Cotton's *Burlesque upon Burlesque* of 1675 and 1686/7 (see below); the 1675 version is plate 1 in this article.

Fig. 2. From Ferrand Spence, *Lucian's Works*, Translated from
the Greek (1684-5), Volume 1.
Private Collection of Paul Hartle.

Fig. 3. From Ferrand Spence, *Lucian's Works*, Translated from
the Greek (1684-5), Volume 2.
Private Collection of Paul Hartle.

Fig. 4. From Ferrand Spence, *Lucian's Works*, Translated from
the Greek (1684-5), Volume 3.
Private Collection of Paul Hartle.

Fig. 1. Bust of Lucian, a later version of the engraving by William Faithorne
for Jasper Mayne's *Part of Lucian Made English* (1663), here reproduced from
a copy of Charles Cotton's *Burlesque upon Burlesque* (1675).
Private Collection of Paul Hartle.

> *this Colledge, when these* Sheets *past through my* Pen. . . . *How am I to be* accused ., .? . . . *[H]e* Wrote . . . Obscœne . . . *and* Meretricious Dilaogues [sic], *not fit for the* Eyes *or* Eares *of a* Chaste, *or* Christian Reader. These . . . *I have left with their* owne Curtaine *drawne before them* [i.e. untranslated], *and have not held a* Candle *to the* mysterious *doings of a* Stewes (sig. [A7]ᵛ).

Arguing, with even more hyperbole than Hickes, that we may *"owe our* Christianity, *where the* true God *hath succeeded such a* multitude *of false,* . . . *to his* facetious wit" (sig. [A6]ʳ), Mayne positions himself and his Lucian not only in opposition to the critical "Vineger *men, at whose* Births *sure* Saturne *raign'd, and convey'd his* leaden Influence *into their* Morosity *and* Manners" (sig. [A5]ᵛ), but specifically to the manners and language of the now abolished English Republic:

> *[A]* canting Generation *of men, whose* Rhetorick *was as* rude, & mechanick *as their persons, [did]* defile *the English Tongue with their* Republick *words, which are most* immusicall *to the* Eare, and scarce significant *to a* Monarchicall *understanding. Words which are the meer* Excrements *of Language; which proceeded from the late* Body politick *of this* Vncivilized Nation, *and were not allowed their legitimate* concoxion, *but broke forth into the World with* Brutishness, *and* Rebellion. Coyned, & *minted by those* Seditious, Rump Grammarians, *who did put their own* impressions *to the Kings* Silver, *and so committed* Treason *against their* Prince, *and their own* rude stamp *and* sense *to their* Goth *and* Vandall *words; and so committed* Treason *against His* good people (sig. A4ʳ).

For Mayne, good language (including good translated language) is authenticated, like the national coinage, only by the king's head, and it needs to be a king whose head is still on his shoulders; without this guarantee, words are not only inelegantly unmusical, but "scarce significant," signs without referents.

Mayne's work is succeeded a decade later by Charles Cotton's *Burlesque upon Burlesque: OR, THE Scoffer Scoft. Being some of LUCIANS DIALOGUES Newly put into ENGLISH FUSTIAN* (1675), a burlesque version of the "Dialogues of the Gods," trading on Cotton's commercially successful travesty of Virgil, *Scarronides* (1664–65), but based not on the original but on Nicolas Perrot's very popular French version of Lucian's works;[28] these knockabout comic transvestings of Lucian have an energetic Bakhtinian physicality about them, but proved less popular than *Scarronides*,[29] although an anonymous but acknowledged imitation, *The Scoffer Scoft. The Second Part*, appeared in 1684, printed for Edward Goldin and Charles Corbet, initially in the form of travesties of individual Dialogues *"Publish'd every* Tuesday *and* Friday" in January and February.[30]

Two declared "compleat" Lucians round out the century: Ferrand Spence's five-volume *Lucian's Works, Translated from the Greek* (1684–85) and John Dryden's edited collaborative four-volume *The Works of Lucian, Translated from the Greek, by several Eminent Hands*, which, although not printed until 1711, was begun, according to the publisher, "*before and in the Year* 1696, *and* [completed] *in the subsequent Years*" (sig. [A3ʳ]). Spence's version has been much overlooked, partly because its piecemeal printing leads to an extremely messy bibliographic status, and it is far from a common book.[31] The two copies in institutional Cambridge, in St. John's College and the University Library, are both defective, while my own three assorted bound-up tomes, although between them containing all but a single leaf of the five volumes issued, are severally mispaginated and misbound.

Spence was unlucky. The publication of his version coincided with the death of Charles II and the far from straightforward or fortunate succession of his hapless brother James. His publisher piously hoped to

---

[28]   *Lucien. De la Traduction de N. Perrot Sᴿ D'Ablancourt,* first published at Paris in 1654, with further editions in 1655, 1659 (Leiden), 1674 and 1683 (Amsterdam).

[29]   Only one further edition was issued in Cotton's lifetime (in 1686/7), in contrast with the six editions of the collected *Scarronides* (1666, 1667, 1670, 1672, 1678, 1682).

[30]   In the same year, printed for William Bateman, appeared *Lucians Dialogues (Not) from the Greek: Done Into English Burlesque,* in two Parts issued together. With the exception of the two title pages, the sheets of this volume are identical with those of *The Scoffer Scoffed, The Second Part,* except that the 'Epistle to the Reader' is sewn in not at the beginning but before 'The Second Part', preceding the Dialogue between Menippus and Cerberus rather than that between Mercury and the Sun. It is impossible to ascertain priority between the two issues.

[31]   Hosington, for example, observing ("Compluria Opuscula Longe Festivissima," 203–4) that "the *Dialogues of the Courtesans* . . . never saw the light of day before the 1711 translation," has missed Spence's version in Volume 5:293–335.

have no reason to doubt of my satisfaction in the business, especially,
when I consider, how kindly Lucian has been entertain'd in all Ages
and Countreys in the very Disguises of his Translatours, and that the
greater and better part of him, was never yet turn'd into our Mother
Tongue, and how this present time is more than ordinary prone to
and fond of Satyr, his Company will certainly be sought after by all
sorts of Persons. . . . I am so publick a spirited person [sic], that I am
willing to communicate him to the Age (sig. [x2]^v).

But Spence's racy prose had perhaps missed its historical moment, and the
"Epistle Dedicatory" to his friend Brian Turner comments sharply on the
contemporary hypocrisy of "the *Grand Reformers* of our Age, who whilst
in *Publick* they Exclaim against the *Lewdness of the Times*, yet at the same
Instant are Contriving to *Act* and *Improve* in *Private* all the *Enormities* of
the Ancients" (sigs. A4^v–[A5]^r). Spence has, he acknowledges, rehabited
Lucian in the fashions of the day, fitted him "to be entertain'd in any
Civil Company" (sig. [A5]^v); "he is (as it were) born again, and *Baptiz'd*
into our *Language*, that he may be able to pass *Safely* and *Handsomly* in a
Christian Commonwealth" (sig. [A5]^r).

Like Mayne before him, Spence is a conservative royalist, and by the
mid-1680s we can probably call him a Tory, since one of the prefatory
eulogies to Volume 3 pauses to lambast "*the* Whiggs *unequall'd Crimes.*"[32]
Spence's own "Epistle Dedicatory" launches a savage attack upon "Our
Preaching *Fanatical* Gang [who] think because they are *Familiar* with
God *Almighty* in their *prayers*, they may top upon him too in their
Actions, Especially on Princes, his *Vicegerents*" (sig. B3$^{r/v}$); this "Gang"
turns out to be the Earl of Shaftesbury and the nonconformist ministers Richard Baxter and Stephen Lobb (sigs. B4^v–[B6]^v), leaders of Whig
thought. Dryden too will later use his preface as an opportunity to attack
"*Calvinists* or *Quakers*," whom he sees as heirs to Lucian's earliest detractors, "the first *Christians*, with their cropt Hair, their whining Voices,
melancholy Faces, mournful Discourses, [and] nasty Habits" (20), sharing the same "*want of Charity, . . . presumption of meddling with God's*
Government, and . . . Spirit of Calumny" (14), quite unlike the admirably
robust "*Roman Catholicks*, or *Church of* England-Men" (20).

---

[32] D. M., "To his Worthy Friend Mr. *FERRAND SPENCE*, On His Excellent
Translation of Lucian," sig. [A6]^r.

Given their similar affiliations, one might have expected that Dryden would have treated Spence with some courtesy, but publishing rivalry proved the stronger motive, and Dryden's "Life of Lucian" viciously impugns Spence's abilities in both Greek and English:

> *Lucian*, that is the sincere Example of *Attique* Eloquence . . . is only a mass of *Solecism*, and mere Vulgarisms in Mr. *Spence*. I do not think it worth my while, to rake into the filth of so scandalous a Version; nor had I vouchsaf'd so much as to take notice of it, had it not been so gross an Affront to the Memory of *Lucian*, and so great a scandal to our Nation . . . he makes him speak in the Stile and Language of a *Jack-Pudding*, not a Master of Eloquence . . . for the fine Raillery, and *Attique* Salt of *Lucian*, we find the gross Expressions of *Billings-Gate*, or *More-Fields* and *Bartholomew* Fair (53–61).

Snobbish and commercially motivated as this transparently is, Dryden is right to claim that Spence's Lucian speaks in the voice of a contemporary Londoner. In this ventriloquial act, Spence is building upon foundations laid by his predecessors; Heywood's Mercury complains about having to clerk not only for the Gods' "Consistorie," but also "at the Bar" of Pluto's "generall Sessions," ecclesiastical and legal assemblies of seventeenth-century England (115); Hickes dresses one pompous Pooh-Bah in a "ruffe" and "purple cassock" (99), while his Jupiter has become so unintimidating that even a "knight of the post" (151)—a professional perjurer—contemns him; in Jasper Mayne's world, meanwhile, Bacchus "is the Leader of a Morris [dance]," and the Colossus of Rhodes is so amply-buttocked as to "take up the whole wooll-sacke" (274), traditional parliamentary seat of the English Lord Chancellor.

But Spence goes well beyond these occasional allusions, immersing his Lucian into the same world of seventeenth-century idiom and social context as that of his several burlesquers; figures are variously and colourfully berated as "Buffle-Head" (1:113), "swinging Bully-Rock" (3:221) and "but a Taper'd Scull'd Gallant, . . . an Effeminate Doodle" (1:177). In a brilliant exchange between Bacchus and Apollo, the former advises the latter to beware of that "strange Belswagger" Priapus:

> *Bacchus.* Nay, and thou'rt a good plumpt, bonny *Sawny* too: Wherefore if he comes near you, have a care he does not fall to Gambetting.

> *Apollo.* To Gambetting! Faith, I would not advise him to rummage
> in my Quarters; for notwithstanding my white Wigg, I carry a Bow
> and Arrows, and as I look out very sharp, he will find it a hard mat-
> ter, to surprize my Back-Door. (1:102)

A "sawny" is a fool, first recorded in *OED* in 1699, while "gambetting"
seems likeliest to be from chess "gambit," the opening play (*OED* from
1656 as a noun only)—this is the latest 'street'.

While Spence's comedy probably owes something to Wycherley's
famous 'China Scene'—"Wife, he is coming into you the back way." "Let
him come, and welcome, which way he will"[33]—the influence of Cotton's
burlesque version of Lucian's Dialogue (76-85) is also evident:

> *Apol.* Well! well! but he were best take heed
> How he attaques my *Maiden-head.*
> His mighty *Trap-stick* cannot scare-us;
> For we have good Yew-bow, and Arrows,
> As well as a white Wig to tempt him,
> And if he draw, he will repent him.
> Besides, I'me so set round with light,
> And am withal so quick of sight,
> That much I do not need to fear,
> To be surprized in my Rear.[34]

One can see why Dryden may have felt that Spence fell short of "that
Nice and *Delicate Raillery*" which he claimed to embody in his English
version (Vol. 1, C3ᵛ). But what Spence grasped as essential was that sat-
ire find its mark, and that refinement and decorum were not the way to
attain it. As 'J.P.' wrote in his pointedly entitled '*To Mr.* Spence *on his
Accurate Translation of* Lucian', prefacing Volume 4, "For Satyr must be
still allow'd / To speak the Language of the Vice corrected: / The Crime
would else be not the Crime detected: / And thus our Ladies all despise /
The Mirror that resemblance falsifies." In the dying decadence of Charles

---

[33] *The Country-Wife* (1675), 4.i.533–35 (M. Summers, ed., *The Complete Works*
[Soho, 1924], 4 Vols., 2:62).
[34] "Dialogue. *Apollo* and *Bacchus*," 76–85 (*Burlesque upon Burlesque* [1675],
183).

II's "Obscæne Rout/Of English Whores" (Vol. 4, [A7]^v), there was no place for the mealy-mouthed. In the diarist Evelyn's powerful evocation:

> I am never to forget the unexpressable luxury, & prophanesse, gaming, & all dissolution, and as it were total forgetfullnesse of God (it being Sunday Evening) which this day sennight, I was witnesse of; the King, sitting & toying with his Concubines Portsmouth, Cleaveland, & Mazarine: &c: A french boy singing love songs, in that glorious Gallery, . . . a sceane of uttmost vanity; and surely as they thought would never have an End: six days after was all in the dust.[35]

Lucian had always offered a model for political and social iconoclasm, in his attacks on both earthly and heavenly hierarchies, on the vanities of wealth and of desire, in his relentless emphasis on death's democracy. Even his admirers saw the dangers in this, while his detractors swiftly moved to align him with the Renaissance bugbear, Machiavelli; the early seventeenth-century Divine Thomas Adams proclaimed that "*Sinnes* text is from Hels *Scriptum est*: taken out of the Devils *Spell*; either *Lucian* his old *Testament*, or *Machiavell* his new."[36] In his *Religio Medici*, Thomas Browne picks up Adams's idea and runs with it a little further: "I confess every Countrey hath its *Machiavell*, every Age its *Lucian*, whereof common heads must not heare, nor more advanced judgements too rashly venture on: 'tis the Rhetorick of Satan, and may pervert a loose or prejudicate beleefe."[37] Less soberly, Nathaniel Lee in his tragedy of *Cæsar Borgia* (1680) has Machiavel breathlessly celebrate the triply and generationally incestuous Borgias, "Such a triumvirate of Lawless Lovers, / Such Rivals as out-do even *Lucian*'s Gods!"[38] In the world of Early Modern England, Lucian's spokesman Menippus could be used to expose the ills of a whole social hierarchy: ". . . in the Courts of their Kings, adulteries, murthers, treacheries, rapines, perjuries, feares, and false-heartednesse towards their friends . . . what should I tell you of other men, of whom some were breakers up of houses, some wranglers in law-suits, some

---

[35] Ed. E. S. De Beer, *The Diary* (Oxford, 1955), 6 Vols., 4:413–14.

[36] "The Fatall Banket" (*Workes* [1629], 167).

[37] Geoffrey Keynes, ed., *The Works of Sir Thomas Browne* (London, 1928), 4 Vols.,1:31.

[38] 1.i.277–78 (7).

usurers, some exactors" (Hickes, 19). In the context of its first printing (in 1634), Hickes's more detailed account of the life of rulers (in the zoomorphic voice of Lucian's Cockerel) would read uncomfortably like an account of the "Personal Rule" of Charles I:[39]

> What should I rehearse unto you . . . their feares, griefes, and suspicions; the hatred and conspiracies of those that are nearest to them, their short and unsound sleepes; their fearefull dreames, their variable thoughts, and ever evill hopes, their troubles and vexations, their collections of money [1634 was the year of Ship Money], and judgment of controversies [the Court of Star Chamber was the principal instrument of the Personal Rule from 1629], their militarie affaires, and warlike expeditions, their edicts and proclamations, their leagues and treaties [Charles's military and diplomatic failures from 1625-1630 in the Thirty Years War], their reckonings and accounts, which suffer them not once to enjoy a quiet dreame, but they are compel'd alone to have an eye in all things, & a thousand businesses to trouble them (Hickes, 65).

It is then unsurprising that the cobbler Micyllus lists among the benefits of Hades, "no calling for debts, no paying of subsidies" (Hickes, 81).

Remarkably, one case of the impact of Hickes's Lucian on a reader at the dawn of the English Republic survives, in the figure of William Walwyn, renowned as a leading Leveller thinker and writer.[40] In John Price's *Walwins Wiles* (1649), the following story is told of Walwyn and a companion (9):

> Having once upon a Fast day (as his usual manner was both upon those, and the Lords days) gone from place to place, hearing here a

---

[39] See Kevin Sharpe, *The Personal Rule of Charles I* (New Haven, 1992).

[40] See Nigel Smith, "The Charge of Atheism and the Language of Radical Speculation, 1640–1660", in Michael Hunter and David Wootton, eds., *Atheism from the Reformation to the Enlightenment* (Oxford, 1992), 131–58. For other work on influences (including Lucian's) on what might (cautiously) be described as atheism in the period, see George T. Buckley, *Atheism in the English Renaissance* (Chicago, 1932), 5–8; Michael Hunter, "The Problem of 'Atheism' in Early Modern England," *Transactions of the Royal Historical Society*, 5th ser., (1985), 135–57, at 144; M. J. Buckley, *At the Origins of Modern Atheism* (New Haven, 1987), 46.

little, and there a little what the Ministers said, making it the subject
matter of his prophane scorning and jeering, came at last to his own
house with one of his supposed Fast disciples, (though even at that
time his heart did rise against *Walwins* wickedness, but having got
within him, he did resolve, though with much reluctance of spirit, to
fathom the deep devout hypocrisie of this man for a through detec-
tion of him,) being at home, he fetcht out that prophane scurrilous
Lucians Dialogue, come (said he) let us go read that which hath
something in it, *Here is more wit in this* (saith he) *then in all the Bible.*

This very circumstantial attack drew a defensive salvo from Humphrey Brooke (*The Charity of Church-Men* [1649], 334–35):

'Tis true, that *Lucian* was taken off a shelf either by me, or Mr *Walwyn*, I can't say which, and that we read one of his Dialogues, which
was the Tyrant, or Megapenthes; and afterwards commended it as
very usefull in the time he lived; when by setting forth the foul-
nesse and deformity of Tyrannie in a third person, he informed the
people of the wickednesse of such under whom they lived: but that
any comparison was made between that and the Bible, is as false
as in it self ridiculous . . . Besides, Mr *Walwyn* prefer'd *Lucian* (as
the Pamphlet saies) for wit, before the Bible: 'Tis well known, that
Mr *Walwyn* hath the lowest esteem of wit that may be, counting
it the lightest, volatile and superficiall part of a man; whence his
observation is, that commonly those that have most wit, have most
wickednesse. . . . What ground is there for the least supposall that
he should for that prefer *Lucian* before the Bible?

Brooke's barely convincing casuistry carries less weight than Walwyn's
direct denial of the allegation in *Walwins Wiles*, in his own *Walwyns Just
Defence* (1649):

So in short time, we came to my house, where we went on dis-
coursing, from one thing to another, and amongst other things, of
the wisdom of the heathen, how wise and able they were in those
things, unto which their knowledge did extend; and what pains
they took to make men wise, vertuous, and good common-wealths
men . . . with which kinde of discourse, he was very much affected,

though it did not appear he had been accustomed to the reading of humane authors; which for twenty yeers before I had been, but I used them alwayes in their due place . . . and truly, I do not see I have cause to repent me of taking liberty in this kinde, having never in my life, I blesse God; made an ill use thereof, amongst which *Lucian* for his good ends, in dis[c]overing the vanity of things in worldly esteem, I like very well, whereof I can read only such as are translated into *English;* such a wise Jesuite I am, that withall [sic] my skill, I cannot construe three lines of any *Latin* author, nor do understand any, except such common proverbs, as are more familiar in *Latine* then in *English,* which sometimes I use not to dignifie my selfe, but because of the pertinency of them in some occasions . . . I am certain most of the university men in England, and most of the liberaries are not without all *Lucians* works, some whereof, as I am informed, are much more offencive to Christianity then these in *English.*

And why then I might not without blemish read one of his dialogues to this, Mr. *Richard Price,* I cannot yet perceive? as I take it we read that which is called his tyrant; a discourse, though possibly not in all things justifiable, yet such as he might have made a better use of, being so pointed against ambition, pride and coveteousnesse as he might have been the better for it whilst he lived . . . I was far from any such thought of impious blasphemy, as to say, here is more wit in this (meaning *Lucian)* then in all the bible: all our discourse was before my wife and children, and my friend, and a maid servant . . . *I* dare appeale to them all if ever they heard me value, any, or all the Books, or Sermons either, in the world Comparable to the Bible . . . (9–10)

Since Walwyn confesses that he could read in English alone, the only version of Lucian's dialogue he could have known was Francis Hickes's 'The Infernall Ferrie, or, the Tyrant,'[41] and as Nigel Smith observes, Walwyn's use of translations "thus justif[ies] the perennial fear of the privileged that the vulgar should not be permitted to have ideas that they might use to a subversive end . . . [ideas] which were introduced into a radical religious context where they were largely unknown and could be employed in a radically critical way."[42]

---

[41]   Hickes, *Certaine Select Dialogues,* 71–88.
[42]   Smith, "Atheism and the Language of Radical Speculation," 147.

Jasper Mayne's loyalist attack on the language of early republican-
ism has already been cited; more dazzling is Alexander Brome's 1661 version of *Cynicus*, where the ragged Philosopher denounces the wealthy for
their lack of social responsibility:

> . . . poor Men,
> . . . your fellow Creatures, [who] have been
> Made of the self same matter, and inspir'd
> With the same soul, and form, and have acquir'd
> The same perfections too, and by their birth,
> Have as good interest in what's here on Earth,
> As the Great'st He[43]

That last instantly recognizable phrase is from Colonel Rainsbor-
ough's famous plea for universal suffrage in the *Putney Debates* of the
Army in 1647: "For really I think that the poorest he that is in England
hath a life to live, as the greatest he; and therefore truly, sir, I think it's
clear, that every man that is to live under a government ought first by his
own consent to put himself under that government."[44]

By the later seventeenth century, the two sides of British politics, as we
have already seen from the language of Whigs and Tories in Spence, have
metamorphosed into a new sense of "party," and Spence evenhandedly
deplores on the one hand a Jupiter in an "outragious Passion, . . . [fear-
ing] he had lost a great deal of Prerogative [a royal power hotly debated
in Charles II's reign]" (1:53) and on the other "those great Parliaments
. . . [where] one takes delight in undoing what another does" (3:187).
Struggling to order their affairs, the Olympian Gods engage in a flurry
of bureaucratic activity: ". . . it seems good to the Council, and present
Assembly, to convene a Parliament against the next Winter-solstice . .
. to Elect a Committee . . . [to] exercise their Commission . . ." (Spence,
4:128). Aficionados of both British and American politics will estimate
the likelihood of effective governmental action.

Translating the same passage as Hickes on the woes of monarchs, Spence
goes further, to develop a brilliant argument on the theatricality of power:

---

[43] "*An Essay of the Contempt of Greatnesse, being a Dialogue of* Lucian *made
English*," 296–302 (R. R. Dubinski, ed., *Poems* [Toronto, 1982], 2 Vols., 1:329).

[44] A. S. P. Woodhouse, ed., *Puritanism and Liberty* (London, 1938), 53.

Add hereto the Spight of a Mistress [remember Evelyn's "Portsmouth, Cleaveland, & Mazarine &c"], . . . The Jealousy of a Favourite, that has been rais'd too high: The fear of a Sedition of the People, or of the conspiracy of Grandees [the Exclusion Crisis 1678-1681]; the fatal Example of Princes de-/thron'd, Assassinated [Charles I] . . . and other Tragical Histories, which Ring and Eccho upon the Theatres. . . . they are only *Comedians*, who under a Royal Cloak hide the Soul of a Skip-Jack, & shew the smalness of their Foot in the greatness of their Buskin (3:227–28).

In the same year, the anonymous author of *The Scoffer Scoffed. The Second Part* has Menippus accuse Trophonius of having "like a true Dissenter, strove / To break th' Allegiance, sworn to *Jove*" (5), whereas Achilles praises Antilochus as an "honest Tory" (9). For this writer, "Monsieur *Mors* [Death] . . . Was always known, to be a Leveller [the once-dominant Republican political faction]" (8), and in Hades (15–16):

Here's no Ambition, no great places,
No haughty looks, nor bold Menaces.
No striving to be Rich, or great
But all's Hail-fellow here, well met.
'Tis like a Pop'lar-state,[45] for here
No one must huff or domineer;
Where ev'ry Cobler is as free
And of as high Nobility,
As any man dare shew his face,
Or live, in such a Govern'd place. . . .

It is particularly telling that even translators who can be loosely described as conservative and sometimes even as passionate monarchists nonetheless expose through Lucian a powerful vision of "the World turn'd topsy turvy" (*The Scoffer Scoffed. The Second Part*, 1). What is more, instead of simply deploying this familiar image as a satirical strategy to argue for the reestablishment of conventional norms and hierarchies, they respond to its deeper, darker fears of a world without order, without government terrestrial or celestial, a world without guidance. In

---

45 Democracy (*OED* dating from 1546).

Lucian's merciless analysis, the models of excellence bestowed by culture are mere fables: "neither was *Ajax* so mighty, nor *Helen* so faire as [the *Iliad*] would have them to be," the Cockerel tells his human interlocutor Micyllus, since, due to the universality of Pythagorean metempsychosis, "[Homer] in the time of those warres, . . . was a camell in *Bactria*" (Hickes, [5]8). Heywood, whose *Troia Britanica* of 1609 had rendered the Trojan war in heroic *ottava rima*, a quarter-century later gives us Menippus's gloating encomium:

> O thou ingenious *Homer*, see how bare,
> How groveling and how dejected lie,
> How low the heads of thy great Rapsodie:
> Ignoble and obscure they now are all,
> Ashes and dust, trifles in value small (134)

Homer is now "a meer Dunderhead" (Spence, 3:214), and Lucian, according to Samuel Sheppard, "*Homers Momus*":[46] Momus the son of Night, "*[t]he carping god.*"[47]

In *Icaromenippus*, "like *Homers Jupiter*," Menippus looks down upon the Earth, "and fixing mine eyes more stedfastly on it, the whole life of man was made apparent to mee, not by Nations and Cities, but all particular sort of persons, Marriners, Souldiers, plough-men, Lawyers, Women, Beasts, and whatsoever feedeth upon the face of the Earth" (Hickes, 16). In that deliberately archaic final clause the echo of the 1611 Bible resonates, but—unlike God—Menippus does *not* see that it is good, and the hierarchy of the social orders is deliberately jumbled—ploughmen above lawyers (although we might all sympathise with that)—"I thought I might compare the life of man to nothing so well, as to a long shew or pageant, in which fortune was the setter out, . . . and fitted every person with sundry and different habites . . . but when the time comes that the triumph must have an end, then every man unclothes himselfe, and puts off his proportion together with his bodie . . . when the play is ended, every man must be disrob'd of his gorgeous garments, lay aside his vizard, step out of his buskins, and walke aloofe of[f] like a forlorne fellow . . . (Hickes, 39–40).

---

[46] "The Socratick Session," 236, in *Epigrams* (1651), 198.
[47] Francis Gouldman, *A Copious Dictionary* (1664), sig. 4K^v.

Three of the four engraved plates in Spence's translation display the reach of Lucian's radicalism: a satyr unceremoniously heaves Jupiter from his Olympian throne (plate 2); another tumbles a king from his triumphal chariot (plate 3) while a third offers a mask to the eulogist who awaits him—and who no doubt will turn the disaster into good journalistic copy (in *Timon*, Lucian adumbrates the spin doctor's dark art);[48] while in the third plate (plate 4), although the ostensible focus is the bestial head of the unmasked struggling figure in the lawyer's gown, his discarded headgear lies beside a laurel wreath. The satirist undoes his own profession as well as all others. Because "he doubted of every thing," Lucian blurs the distinction between divine, human and animal kingdoms; the form of dialogue, "that great and pow'rful art," as Mulgrave calls it,[49] "the best and surest *Vehicle*, to Convey and Insinuate [his Design] into Men's Minds" (Spence, Vol. 1, sig. C3ᵛ), allows his gods, men and beasts to debate on a levelled footing (and it is characteristic of his wit that, in "The Double Accusation," Dialogue herself takes Lucian to task for misusing her "grave and serious" nature, "speaking only of God and of Principles" (Spence, 3:271). Occupying the same spaces, there is no room for deference to species.

Lucian's espousal of metempsychosis as literary trope creates a metamorphic world surpassing Ovid's, in which a cockerel (who was once Pythagoras himself) can chatter away to both gods and men, shape-shifting not only between human and animal forms (Hickes, 55), but across genders too (60). And the disparate orders of being are subjected to the same sharp-eyed assessment; Jupiter's revenge on Prometheus "is unworthy, I say not of a God, or of the King of Gods, but of a meer private Gentleman" (Spence, 1:51); "Mortall men deal much discreetlier in the like cases" (Mayne, 27). The unstable body of Greek myth enables Lucian to question not only the nature but the quality of the divine, especially in "The Councell of the Gods," summoned by Jupiter (with Momus as secretary) to define the essence of "any perfect God" in a context where heaven is invaded by "forraigners . . . who are not themselves content of men to be made Gods," but also wish to deify "their followers and servants"

---

[48]   A. M. Harmon and M. D. MacLeod, eds. and trans., *Lucian* (Cambridge, Mass., 1913–67), 8 Vols., 2:382–85; for Hickes's version, see 172–74.

[49]   John Sheffield, "An Essay on Poetry (1682)," 212 (*Miscellanea* [Halifax, 1933], 48).

(Mayne, 238). As Momus complains, "wee have need of mysteries, *Jupiter*, by which wee may know Gods to be Gods, and Dogs to be Dogs" (242); not so easy, though, when: ". . . the *Memphites* have an Oxe for their God; the *Pelusiots* an Onion; some a Storke, or Crockodile; others a Dogge, or Catt, or Ape. . . . Some adore an earthen cup, others a dish. Are not these Gods to be laught at . . .?" (Mayne, 289).

In the absence of a stable order ("Take but degree away, untune that string . . ."),[50] atheism becomes a logical stance; as Jupiter acknowledges, "it stands upon the edge of a rasour whether we shall hereafter be wor-shipt, and receive sacrifice, or be utterly neglected, and held in contempt . . . when [men] see such an unequall disposition of thinges, they may dis-pute whether there bee such thinges as Gods" (Mayne, 270, 278). Trapped in a predestiny anticipating Calvin, "wee men do nothing voluntarily, but as wee are moved by an inevitable necessity" (Mayne, 310). Whereas for More and Erasmus, Lucian's atheism did not seriously threaten their own Christian Humanism, in the later seventeenth-century, Lucian's chal-lenge to any kind of belief was more potent; in Bacon's shrewd analysis, Lucian was the more dangerous because he might be characterised as a "Contemplative *Atheist*":[51]

> *Merchant.* What are Men?
> *Heraclitus.* Mortall Gods.
> *Merchant.* What are Gods?
> *Heraclitus.* Immortall men. (Mayne, 186)

> *Micyllus.* But let's now proceed to Brute Animals, what think ye of their Condition?
> *Cock.* . . . I'le only say, it's more Calm and Sedate than ours, because its confin'd within the bounds of Nature; and is not disturb'd by so many Evils, and so many Crimes. (Spence, 3:228)

Inferior to the beasts, then—one is reminded of Rochester's shame, ending his visit to 'Tunbridge Wells', when he "us'd the insolence to

---

[50]   *Troilus and Cressida*, 1.iii.109 (Shakespeare, *The Complete Works*, 721).
[51]   See Michael Kiernan, ed., *The Essayes or Counsels* (Oxford, 1985), 'Of Athe-isme', 52.

mount my horse,"[52]—driven by inescapable necessity in a godless universe, where even if there is something after death, it is indeed to be dreaded:

> When you are faln to Dust and Ashes;
> And Threed-bare Vicar going first,
> Cries here's the hole, and in you must.
> And tell the Smock-fac't *Megibus*,
> And the Wrestler *Damoxenus*,
> That here strong Back, nor able Thighs,
> Nor curled Hair, nor sparkling Eyes,
> Nor all the Charms adorn'd by Art,
> In this place signifie a Fart.[53]

In that indecorous emission resounds the collapse of the unchallenged social, political, ecclesiastical, and cultural authority of tradition—*all* laurels in the dust—and the birth of the Royal Society. Job done, Lucian: job done.

---

[52] 'Tunbridge Wells', 185 (Harold Love, ed., *The Works of John Wilmot Earl of Rochester* [Oxford, 1999], 54).

[53] *The Scoffer Scoft. Part Two,* 8.

INDEX

A

Aragon, Katherine of, 115, 151
Arthur, Prince, 115

B

Bachrach, Bernard S., 1–65
Barcelona, siege of, 40–41
Beaufort, Margaret, 116
Beaufort-Beauchamp Hours, 136–37
Beaumont, Joan, 70, 71
Beaumont, John (John Bodrugan), 70, 72, 78–79, 80, 84, 85, 86
Beaumont, William, of Shirwell, 70, 71, 84
Beckinston, Thomas, 126
Bede, Venerable, 59
Berkeley Castle Muniments
  Select Book, 87–269
  significance of, 175–78
  Part I, medical therapy, 94
  Part II, epidemic illnesses and the Stone, 95
Black Death, terms for, 160–61
Bodrugan of Gorran, Sir Henry, 69, 70, 71, 72, 83
Bonville, William, Lord, 70
Brackman, W. L., 201, 219
Braithwaite, Richard, 274

Broke, Robert, 99
Brooke, Humphrey, 288–89
Brunner, Heinrich, 33, 34
Bullein, William, 222–23

C

Campbell, Thomas, 115
Capitularies of Charlemagne, 20–26
Carloman the Elder, 29
Carpenter, Christine, 67
Caxton, John, 113
Charlemagne, Emperor of the West, 1–65
  bureaucracy, 60–61
  cost of military service, 42–56
  large armies, 40–42
  liberi homines, 5–26 et passim;
  wealth of, 57–60, 63
  magistratus (general staff), 2
  military expeditionary organization, 1–65
Charles II, 282
Charles Martel, 1, 33
Christianson, C. Paul, 125
Clifford, Margaret, 128
Connor, William, 128
Cosmos and Damian, Saints, 128n76
Cotton, Charles, 281
Courtenay, Thomas, Earl of Devon, 70

Submission Guidelines

For current submission guidelines and calls for papers, please visit the *Studies in Medieval and Renaissance History* website at http://acmrs.org/publications/journals/smrh/submissionguidelines.